BODILY CHARM

The Abraham Lincoln Lecture Series
This series aims to reflect the principles
that Abraham Lincoln championed:
education, justice, tolerance,
and union.

Bodily Charm
LIVING OPERA

Linda Hutcheon &

UNIVERSITY OF NEBRASKA PRESS : LINCOLN AND LONDON

Michael Hutcheon

The lectures on which this book is based
were sponsored by the University of Nebraska
Press, the College of Arts and Sciences,
and the Departments of English and Music at
the University of Nebraska–Lincoln.
Acknowledgments for the use of previously
published material appear on page xii.

Library of Congress Cataloging-in-Publication Data
Hutcheon, Linda, 1947–
Bodily charm : living opera / Linda Hutcheon
and Michael Hutcheon.
p. cm. – (Abraham Lincoln lecture series)
Includes bibliographical references and index.
ISBN 0-8032-2385-4 (cl: alkaline paper)
1. Body image in opera. I. Title: Living opera.
II. Hutcheon, Michael, 1945– III. Title.
IV. Series. ML1700.H85 2000
782.1–dc21   00-028654

For all those who have *lived* opera with us and for us

Contents

Illustrations

Acknowledgments

As always, there are many people to thank for their encouragement, criticism, and scholarly assistance.

Over the years of working on this book, we have been fortunate to work with two gifted and indefatigable teams of research assistants: we are deeply indebted to the dedication, the amazing research "noses," and the constant inspiration of, first, Russell Kilbourn, Helmut Reichenbächer, Erika Reiman, and Jill Scott (all now graduated) and, then, Michael Doherty, Sarah Henstra, and Scott Rayter.

Many friends and colleagues read our work at various stages and gave us constructive advice, bibliographic suggestions, learned corrections, and devastating critiques. While each will know into which category he or she falls, we are grateful for all their responses: Suzanne Akbari, Gary Bortolotti, Ted Chamberlin, Caryl Clark, Juanita Djelal, Marina Gilman, Sander Gilman, Grace Kehler, Herbert Lindenberger, Tim McCracken, Heta Pyrhönen, Janice Simon, Brian Stock. (This list does not include all our friends, family, and acquaintances who had to put up with our many questions and, no doubt, boring obsessions about operatic bodies, but we would like to thank them all as well.) A number of institutions have invited us to speak specifically on this material, and so to both the organizers and the audiences whose critical and supportive voices helped us rewrite and rethink the various chapters go our thanks: the Canadian Opera Company, the University of Saskatchewan "Body Projects" conference, the organizers of two panels at the annual convention of the Modern Language Association (1997 and 1998), the University of Georgia Department of English, the 1999 LEXIS conference, and the

University of Victoria Department of English. But it is chiefly to the Department of English, the School of Music, the College of Arts and Sciences, and the Press at the University of Nebraska for their hosting of the Lincoln Lectures that our thanks must go. We are grateful for the Press's support of our first book together, *Opera: Desire, Disease, Death*, but this second vote of confidence was perhaps even more deeply appreciated. A special thanks to Mary M. Hill for her fine copyediting.

We would like to acknowledge that a small section of what eventually became chapter 2 was published in the Modern Language Association's *Profession 98* (New York: MLA, 1998), 11–22, and some of the ideas eventually used in the postlude appeared first in *Forum Italicum* 33.1 (spring 1999): 73–94 in a tribute to our friend and mentor, the late Gian-Paolo Biasin.

It is important that we note that, without the generous funding assistance of the Social Sciences and Humanities Research Council of Canada, this project would quite literally not have been possible. As with our last book, we owe much once again to its support of interdisciplinary collaborative research.

A final note: the errors and infelicities of this book are all ours; the insights, such as they are, are the fruit of collaborative work – not only between the two of us, but between us and all our research assistants, not to mention all the scholars whose work we gratefully cite in notes.

Before We Begin...

An Introductory Note on the Operatic Body in Context

I hear what beats in the body,
what beats the body, or better:
I hear this body that beats.
– Roland Barthes, listening to Schumann's *Kreisleriana*

Bodily Charm: Living Opera is a book about the physical dimensions of the art form – singers' bodies, spectators' bodies, but also dramatized representations of bodies. It is about live opera and the experience of living opera, both on the stage and in the audience. Because of this, its focus will be on the musical, the textual, the dramatic, and the narrative ways in which the corporeal is put on stage and thus given meaning for the audience. Written by a physician and a literary theorist, it brings together different perspectives on what these "operatic bodies" mean, as well as what they experience. As such, it is by definition interdisciplinary, but one of the disciplines involved has been unavoidably obsessed with the bodily realities of life, while the other, until recently, had managed to ignore these quite handily. Today, however, most people working in the humanities and social sciences have had to come to terms with the corporeal, thanks to a major shift in thinking about the body. The exuberantly embodied dramatic art form called opera offers what Peter Brooks has described as "stories on the body, and the body in story."[1] Not surprisingly, then, opera studies too have been influenced by the recent fascination with the body as the source of both meaning and meaning-making. What medicine takes as a given has finally been noticed by other disciplines.

Indeed, for the last few decades, we have been witnessing what could be called a massive collaborative enterprise to write a new cultural history of the body. Yet a moment's reflection will suggest that the interest in the corporeal is nothing new in Western culture. As the medically trained literary theorist Jean Starobinski points out, the awareness of bodily reality came with Adam and Eve: "They knew that they were naked." From then on, "it has been impossible to ignore the body."[2] Yet in some fields of study we have – or at least we have tried to do so. The recent rise of what has been labeled generically as "body criticism" is one attempt to right the balance and to reconsider the body in all its interrelated dimensions: physical, biological, and sexual as well as social and cultural. Some of this rethinking has been culturally oriented, arguing that bodies are constructs of language and society, products of ideology; other versions have been more materially based, studying the physical and biological dimensions, usually of pleasure, pain, or sensation in general. We would like to review some of this work briefly in this preface in order to give readers a sense of the context in which this study is written.

The 1980s saw an explosion of celebrations of the body from feminist and gay and lesbian (and, later, queer) perspectives, as the cultural theory mirrored the more general changes in social attitudes and in awareness about issues of gender and sexuality.[3] The 1990s supplemented this with explorations of the darker side, that is, trauma, illness, pain, and death.[4] All scholarly disciplines appear to have been influenced by this new interest in physicality: literature, visual art, music, dance, philosophy, psychology, history of medicine, anthropology, political science, religion, biological science, sociology. While few of these new studies seemed fully aware of the others, to the point that they were "completely incommensurate – and often mutually incomprehensible," as Caroline Bynum has noted, entire new fields, such as cultural studies, probably owe much to this fascination with the bodily.[5] The media too have joined the debates, in part because, in these years, the body became big news: think of the scandal of Mapplethorpe's photography or all those feature stories on eating disorders. In Terry Eagleton's memorable terms, "from Bakhtin to the Body Shop, Lyotard to leotards, the body has become one of the most recurrent preoccupations of postmodern thought. Mangled members, tormented torsos, bodies emblasoned [*sic*] or incarcerated, disciplined or desirous: the bookshops are strewn with such phenomena, and it is worth asking ourselves why."[6]

By way of reply, the work of Michel Foucault, especially his multivolumed *History of Sexuality*, has certainly been an important influence on these discussions. In the first volume, he argues that the seventeenth century marked the rise of a new view of the human body in Western culture: the body was no longer merely something to be restricted but something to be excited.[7] As we shall see, it is not accidental that this same century marks the birth and rise of opera. What has been most influential about Foucault's work across various fields of study is his assertion that the body is not (and never has been) a simple and unproblematic entity; it is not a given or a universal. Instead, he argues, it is given meaning by culture; it is, in this sense, "constructed" and certainly defined and organized by the way societies talk about it and deal with it. We need only look at some of the many articles in the three volumes of *Fragments for a History of the Human Body* to get a sense of the breadth and depth of Foucault's impact, as these various studies trace the history of how the human body has been "constructed" and represented in diverse ways by different cultures at different historical moments.[8]

Body criticism has often demanded interdisciplinary work, some of it collaborative, in recognition of the complexity of the phenomenon being considered. But sometimes single scholars have undertaken cross-disciplinary examinations of complex corporeal matters.[9] Even when scholars working within specific individual disciplines focus on the body, they usually find themselves compelled to draw upon other areas of study. Louis Marin writes a political-theological treatise on the body as consumer and consumed.[10] An art historian investigates body images in the various visual arts in order to show what corporeal representations tell us about race, gender, and sexuality; in short, we are shown how the aesthetic body shapes and is shaped by political and cultural identity crises.[11] A literary critic who has looked at verbal representations of body language builds upon communication theory and psychology; another theorizes "corporeal semantics," arguing that linguistic meaning has ultimately much to do with the body.[12] Biblical scholars examine how religious, political, and cultural issues around gender and ethnicity become literally embodied in biblical discourse.[13] If we are going to rethink the body, it has even been argued, we will need to rethink many of the central tenets of the humanities and social sciences, for the history of the body and of the meanings given to it is fundamental to our understanding of the world.[14] The tools and techniques by which we can undertake such a task are indeed still being developed, as Elizabeth Grosz notes,[15] and part of the reason for the time and effort required is the complexity of the variety of tools and techniques being brought to bear on the question.

This is as true in the study of opera as anywhere else. For that reason, in *Bodily Charm* we will also draw on that variety of interdisciplinary tools in our attempt to study real and represented bodies on the operatic stage. As such, even though not written by musicologists, this study situates itself within recent new directions in musicology. There has been some resistance in traditional positivist and formalist circles to discussions of meaning in music (even "texted" music like opera). This resistance is based in part on the tacit assumption that "music and language lie on different sides of an epistemological divide," as Lawrence Kramer puts it, and that music is the superior of the two.[16] This view has changed somewhat, in part because of the provocative work of people from outside as well as inside the discipline – work such as *Opera, or the Undoing of*

Women by the French feminist philosopher Catherine Clément, with its interest in the meaning of the body, specifically the gendered body in opera. Feminist musicologists like Susan McClary and Ruth Solie followed with ground-breaking work that set the stage for these new directions. Carolyn Abbate brought the resources of narratology and literary theory to the study of music, with productive and refreshing results.[17] Suddenly, conferences and volumes abounded on bodily issues in opera; suddenly, opera – as the art form that includes so many others (music, poetry, drama, visual art) – found itself the subject of work by nonmusicologists. And one of the main areas of interest turned out to be the body – both the real and the staged body.

Witness Susan Leonardi and Rebecca Pope, two literary critics who introduce their book *The Diva's Mouth: Body, Voice, Prima Donna Politics* (1996) with these words: "This is very much a book about bodies. A book about body parts. Fragile throats, open mouths, powerful lungs, swollen epiglottises, larynxes on the edge, pierced ears, notes from the chest, notes from the head, heaving breasts, bared breasts, bound breasts, snipped testicles, clipped frenums. It's a book about muscles, hair, fat, blood, sweat, and secretions."[18] Schenkerian analysts of musical form would no doubt disapprove, but even within musicology, feminist work on the gendered body of the performers, creators, and characters of opera opened the field up to new discussions of gender and sexuality. Studies of Western classical music, like those of other forms of high art, had for some time tried to transcend the body in a concern with "nobler domains of imagination and even metaphysics."[19] But it is harder to deny the body or repudiate the erotic in opera, with its recurring stories of love and death. McClary has argued that musicology's interest in the magisterial formal order of music as "autonomous and invulnerable" in fact betrayed a fear, specifically a fear of the body and therefore a fear of women.[20] The linking of the female with the bodily can be seen in both absences induced by fear and in strange presences: Theodor Adorno once claimed that a woman's singing voice did not record well because it demands the "physical appearance of the body that carries it."[21] Feminist criticism like McClary's has worked to expose how the "constructions of *feminine* sensuality and suffering . . . are exhibited – for the pleasure of the patriarchal gaze and ear."[22] It has also shown how, "like the body from which it emanates, the female voice is construed as both a signifier of sexual otherness and a source of sexual power, an object at once of desire and fear."[23] For that reason, the "glorious moment" of which Clément writes – the "sung death" – becomes represented woman's operatic fate.[24]

More recently, with provocative collections such as *Queering the Pitch: The New Gay and Lesbian Musicology* (1994), even more attention has been paid to those elements sometimes repressed in academic work on the experience of music: "our emotional attachments to music, our needs met by music, our accommodations to society through music, our voices, our bodies."[25] Elizabeth Wood, for instance, has coined the term "Sapphonics" to describe "a range of erotic and emotional relationships among women who sing and women who listen."[26] In *Opera in the Flesh*, Sam Abel constructs a very physically based gay model of operatic response as sexual arousal, while Wayne Koestenbaum's *The Queen's Throat* theorizes identification with opera's excess.[27]

It is probably safe to say that the body is no longer totally ignored, but the need for its restoration in opera has rarely been made the sole focus of attention. This book is written in the spirit of the critical recovery and rediscovery of bodies as sites of meaning – the bodies both represented and performing on stage. Unlike other studies, this one also concerns itself with the perceiving bodies of the audience. Less personal and revelatory as autobiography than some of the recent books along these lines (such as those of Koestenbaum or Abel), *Bodily Charm: Living Opera* nonetheless is very much about our living with opera: it is the result of our engagements with our separate areas of study and, of course, with each other. Though we draw on the work of musicologists and are ourselves musically trained, we are not experts in the field. As scholar-amateurs, we write not only for music specialists but also for general readers who, like us, love opera. Therefore, like our long bibliography of reference works cited, our endnotes can either be ignored by those so inclined (for they are never crucial to the argument) or they can be consulted at leisure by the curious or the expert.

BODILY CHARM

Restoring Opera's Bodies

The time: antiquity. The place: Greece, the foot of Mount Olympus. The operatic action: Apollo decides to take on human bodily form and come to earth on the day of the spring festival of the "young Dionysus," the god of life, fertility, and, of course, wine. Utterly insensitive to the inappropriateness of an Olympian god of the sun interrupting these earthly (as well as earthy) Dionysian festivities, Apollo disguises himself as a common herdsman in order to win the affection of the lovely Daphne. But he has a rival: a flute-playing disciple of Dionysus, in fact. Out of jealousy, Apollo kills his rival and then must beg the forgiveness of Dionysus.

This is the story of Richard Strauss and Joseph Gregor's opera *Daphne* (1939), and it is striking in its rare bringing together of two deities whose realms are sometimes considered as polar opposites: the god of music, Apollo, and Dionysus, the god of intoxication and burgeoning fecundity who infuses the bodies of his worshipers with a "driving mysterious force" ("triebend geheime Kraft"). (See figures 1 and 2.)

For centuries now, one way to talk about the human body in relation to opera has been to invoke the Dionysian, usually in opposition to the Apollonian. As two of the gods who presided over the development of the arts, Dionysus and Apollo came to stand very early on for two very different artistic realms: on the one hand, the seductive darkness of imaginative energy and physicality; on the other, the bright light of aesthetic control and rationality.[1] In 1872, in *Die Geburt der Tragödie aus dem Geiste der Musik* (*The Birth of Tragedy from the Spirit of Music*), Friedrich Nietzsche gave his

1

own idiosyncratic spin to this pairing of apparent opposites in the context of both Greek drama and Wagnerian opera, but even before Nietzsche, the two gods were frequently invoked, either explicitly or implicitly, in debates about the nature of opera.

✒ Opera's Apollonian and Dionysian Impulses

The origins of musical drama are found in the late-sixteenth-century Italian attempts to revive the power of Greek tragedy by uniting music and words in a new art form. But it seems that the idea of what constituted Greek drama held by the group of Florentine noblemen known as the Camerata was highly conditioned by its dominant Neoplatonic philosophy and aesthetics and thus by its view of the physical body. As we shall examine in more detail in the next chapter, this meant that the physical was not of particular importance: it functioned instead as the outward sign of inner spiritual worth. The corporeal body, in brief, concealed the important essence beneath. This implicit Neoplatonic denigration of the carnal was reinforced later in European culture by such influential figures as Johann Wolfgang von Goethe (1749–1832) and, before him, Johann Joachim Winckelmann (1717–68), whose important reflections on ancient art offered a strangely decorporealized, ideal image of Greece in terms of the serene, restrained order and austere, formal grandeur of its sculpture.[2] Against this "Apollonian" conception of Greece, dramatists like Hugo von Hofmannsthal and philosophers like Nietzsche erected their "Dionysian" alternatives. Yet it was out of the aesthetic cooperation – not opposition – of these two divine powers that the rebirth of Greek tragedy in Wagnerian music drama would come, argued Nietzsche in *The Birth of Tragedy*. Apollonian aesthetic control and form wed to Dionysian energy and corporeality would yield great modern art. Those are not quite Nietzsche's exact terms, of course. While drawing on some of the German philosopher's concepts where historically necessary, our more explicitly body-oriented examination of opera's Dionysian and Apollonian impulses

2

will not be totally faithful to his particular philosophical frame of reference.[3] He was not the first and certainly not the last to invoke the two deities, though he was one of the most influential.[4] Since the time of Nietzsche's often extravagant pronouncements, opera critics have linked Dionysus to such things as the "massive emotional scale" of opera as well as to the "passionate audience engagement" it creates. Others have invoked the opposition that Apollo and Dionysus appear to incarnate without expressly naming the gods. For instance, Susan McClary talks about the paradox of Western music since 1600 in terms of "its compulsion for theoretical control and yet its craving for strategies that violate and exceed that control."[5] In short, the Apollonian and Dionysian have been in negotiation since the beginnings of the operatic genre. To see this at work and to observe how the early Neoplatonic attempts to transcend the body were countered with Dionysian reassertions of the physical, let us look at a few more of the operatic representations of the two gods who came to symbolize what we will argue to be the complementary yet warring impulses at the heart of this musical dramatic art form.

In an attempt at stage verisimilitude (or perhaps as a sign of the new form's self-consciousness), many of the earliest operas were on the theme of Orpheus, who is by profession a singer of great power.[6] But it is equally significant that Orpheus is also the son of Apollo and the lover of the deceased Eurydice. In the version of the story told in the 1607 opera *Orfeo* (by Claudio Monteverdi and Alessandro Striggio), Apollo himself appears at the end of the work, descending from the sky as the god of the sun. He journeys to earth because he disapproves greatly of what he sees as his son's excessive lamenting over the loss of his mortal lover: Orpheus has renounced all women, declaring himself incapable of loving anyone but the dead Eurydice. Chastising him for giving in to both scorn and pain, Apollo tells him it is unworthy of him to become enslaved to emotion ("servir al proprio affetto"). This is the god of reason and intellect, and as such he was particularly attractive in symbolic terms to Neoplatonic writers attempting to represent the transcendence of the physical.

3

It is also significant here that the Apollonian stands for the specifically "manly" world of clarity and control.[7] Apollo tells his son that he has enjoyed his fortune in love too much and therefore now suffers and weeps too much. These mortal pleasures and pains are by definition transitory and thus not important, he explains. ("Ancor non sai / Come nulla quaggiù diletta e dura?") The immortal god rejects the excessive, the contingent, and the transient joys and pains of human life, offering his son eternal life in the heavens in exchange. Were he to accept this offer, however, Orpheus would have to give up all hope of ever again seeing Eurydice as a flesh-and-blood person; he would only see her beautiful face in the stars and the sun, reflected in the glory of the gods. Only if the mortal and the bodily are left behind, Apollo implies, can peace and pleasure and also true virtue be found ("virtù verace / Degno premio di se, diletto e pace"). Agreeing to this, Orpheus ascends to the heavens: the body is not needed in this disembodied realm.[8] Since this ideal transcending of the physical cannot be attained by mere mortals, the shepherds and shepherdesses on stage are left to dance a *moresca* to celebrate Orpheus's ascension – and to ease the merely mortal audience back into the real world of the undeniable body.[9]

In early-seventeenth-century opera, gods and goddesses routinely appeared on stage like this, as indeed they had in Greek tragedy. By the twentieth century, however, such appearances had become considerably less common – except, intriguingly, for Dionysus or, as he is sometimes called, Bacchus. This may be a sign of the impact of *The Birth of Tragedy*, published toward the end of the previous century, with its assertion of the power of the Dionysian in opera. But it might also be the marker of an historical reaction against what many see as a progressive public (if not private) repudiation of the body in the nineteenth century in the West: we need only think of all the asexual or antisexual associations with the word "Victorian," for instance, to get the flavor of this disavowal of the corporeal that historians have linked to the rise of the bourgeoisie.[10] And, as in earlier centuries, if Apollo represented the rational, the civilized, and the ordered, then Dionysus stood for the suspect contrary: passion, instinct, and the life of the senses (wine, music, dance, sexuality).

This opposition can be seen clearly in the twentieth-century operatic version of Euripides' classical Greek drama *The Bacchae*. Written by W. H. Auden and Chester Kallman and composed by Hans Werner Henze, *The Bassarids* (1963) presents Dionysus on stage, as in the original play, but here the Apollonian values are represented by Pentheus, the king of Thebes, who dares to deny and defy the godhead of Dionysus. Standing for law, the intellect, the repudiation of the body (for he renounces both women and wine), Pentheus is doomed to defeat. He has denied a part of himself, the dark side represented by Dionysus: the animal, the physical, the emotional side. As E. R. Dodds has written, "those who repress the demand [for Dionysiac experience] in themselves or refuse its satisfaction to others transform it by their act into a power of disintegration and destruction, a blind natural force that sweeps away the innocent with the guilty." In defeat, it is the neglected body of Pentheus that is torn apart by his own mother; fittingly, only his head remains.[11]

The power of the Stranger from the East, as Dionysus is known here, is evident in the reaction of the opera's opening chorus. Presented at first as very orderly citizens, they hear the god's call and respond at once – viscerally. Their music changes dramatically as they suddenly turn into Bassarids (or Bacchae):

> Dance, O Boeotia,
> Clap hands, O Thebes,
> Run, run, run to welcome
> The god Dionysus.

Associated with ecstatic dance, with the frenzied music of the flute and Phrygian drums (not the safe Apollonian cithara and lyre that Plato would allow into his ideal republic), and with the cry of the Bassarids ("Ayayalya"), the Stranger is a creature of the body and of the abyss: "The dark blood best in darkness glows to woo /

The darkness to itself." In the opera, if not the play, the release of inhibitions associated with wine, Dionysus's gift to all humankind, leads not only to pleasure but to pain and destruction: the violent and the bestial are released as well.

Taken for an "oriental conjurer" from Lydia in the original Greek play, Dionysus is described by Euripides as effeminate:

> . . . a magician with golden hair
> Flowing in scented ringlets, his face flushed with wine,
> His eyes lit with the charm of Aphrodite; and he
> Entices young girls with his Bacchic mysteries.

In Auden and Kallman's modern context, the Stranger's sexuality becomes more ambiguous: Pentheus calls him "Perfumed. Aloof. Effeminate. Sly." The stage directions describe him in terms that recall a more modern, even gay aesthetic: he "looks like a rather affected adolescent, his affectation that of Byronic languor. . . . He has elaborately waved long hair. A half-smile constantly seems to come and go over his whole expression." Pentheus says to him: "You are beautiful. No doubt you . . . dance . . . with much success." And, for his final appearance on stage, he is "dressed up to the nines in Beau Brummel fashion: elaborate cravate, monocle, lorgnette, etc., whistling and twirling his thyrsus like a cane." This is not the conventional "manly" world of *Orfeo*'s Apollo but the more sexually ambivalent – and seductive – world of Dionysus.[12]

In both the play and the opera, Dionysus is described as the giver of a great boon to humankind: wine. Tiresias expounds at length on its virtues: it offers joy, soothes regret, and banishes grief. It also clearly plays an important role in the communal celebration of the Dionysian rites. But the Apollonian Pentheus can only see it as a sign of excess, a threat to control, and an incitement to violence and sexual transgression.[13] But the related linking of Dionysus specifically with the forbidden and the sexual is evident in another stage appearance of the god, this time in Richard Strauss and Hugo von Hofmannsthal's *Ariadne auf Naxos* (1916).[14] In the *opera seria* plot of this decidedly mixed-genre opera, the disconsolate Ariadne, abandoned on the island of Naxos by Theseus, awaits Hermes, the messenger of death. However, the young and beautiful god Bacchus arrives instead, fresh from his sexual adventures with Circe. Finally persuaded to accept love instead of death, Ariadne is carried off to the realm of Bacchus, who has been filled with godlike desire ("göttlicher Lust") for her. The more earthy and bodily realities of the high-flown language and music are underlined by the *commedia dell'arte* characters: Zerbinetta happily claims that every new lover is like a god to her also ("Als ein Gott kam jeder gegangen") and that each time she too is transfigured and transported, just like Ariadne.

The god of transformation, renewal, change – and therefore of both life and death, creation and destruction – is the contradictory Dionysus.[15] In almost every way, then, he represents the opposite of what Apollo came to stand for. Born in Thebes of Zeus and the mortal Semele (details of importance to the background of *The Bassarids*), Dionysus is associated with carnal passion, emotion, and the animal body of humankind, not godlike reason, intellect, or mind.[16] He represents chaos, energy, excess, and intoxication, rather than Apollonian order, form, and control. His rites are communal, social, shared; he is the instigator of group emotions.[17] If Apollo is the distanced god of the individual as well as of civilization, social order, and abstract law, Dionysus is the very physically present god of public sacrifice, disorder, destruction, but also of regeneration – and thus of suffering as well as pleasure.[18] Yet, as Dodds explains, in the Archaic Period (800–480 BCE), both gods had their complementary social roles:

> each ministered in his own way to the anxieties characteristic of a guilt-culture. Apollo promised security: "Understand your station as man; do as the Father tells you; and you will be safe to-morrow." Dionysus offered freedom: "Forget the difference, and you will find the identity; join the θίασος [troupe] and you will be happy to-day." He was essentially a god of joy . . . [a]nd his joys were accessible to all, including even slaves, as well as those freemen who were shut

7

out from the old gentile cults. Apollo moved only in the best society, from the days when he was Hector's patron to the days when he canonised aristocratic athletes; but Dionysus was at all periods . . . a god of the people.[19]

As the god of both the sensuous and the internal life, Dionysus is associated with the feminine and, specifically, through the women Bacchae or bacchantes who are his followers, with "the life mystery of blood and the powers of earth."[20] No Olympian sky god like Apollo, symbolizing the abstract mind, Dionysus is decidedly the earthy god of the body.[21] In other words, we do not have to wait until René Descartes' *cogito ergo sum* or the Age of Reason to find the infamous division between the mind and the body in Western culture: in addition to this strong ritualistic and mythic representation, the same division is present in other aspects of Greek culture, most obviously in Plato's description of the body as the tomb of the soul.[22] And despite Christ's incarnation, the mind/body split also appears in general Christian teachings about the body as the source of sin, as it does in Saint Augustine's specific worries about the body as the threat to attempts at mental and moral control.[23] Arguably, the same division lives on in the mentalism of psychoanalysis, where all these earlier articulations are implicitly revived in the idea that the psyche commands the base flesh. In short, in the West, the mind has come to stand for all that is Apollonian; the body, for all that is Dionysian.[24]

These general associations are central to opera's development as an art form through the centuries, but so too is the more specific association, made by Nietzsche in his early writings, of Apollo not as the god of music but instead as the god of the plastic arts and epic poetry. It is Dionysus (also known as Bromios, the Thunderer) who is said by Nietzsche to be the god of music and dance as well as the patron of tragedy.[25] It is thus he who accepts the dissonance of the destructive and the ugly that forms the core of tragic stories.[26] But it is the job of Apollo, with his "veil of beauty," to cover over

8

the "eternal and original artistic power" of Dionysus in order to make these stories bearable.[27] Apollonian moderation and beauty are contrasted with Dionysian excess, the "art that, in its intoxication, spoke the truth." It is music, not poetry alone, that Nietzsche claims can transport people, bring them to ecstasy.[28] *The Birth of Tragedy* was dedicated to and written in dialogue with Richard Wagner, to whom Nietzsche looked for the operatic regeneration of musical tragic drama. And it was to Dionysus that he turned for the symbolic language in which to describe the desired shift from the Apollonian values he saw dominating opera (and life) in the nineteenth century.[29] That his language should become excessive and extravagant is therefore consistent: "Yes, my friends, believe with me in Dionysian life and the rebirth of tragedy. . . . [P]ut on wreaths of ivy, put the thyrsus into your hand, and do not be surprised when tigers and panthers lie down, fawning at your feet. Only dare to be tragic men; for you are to be redeemed. You shall accompany the Dionysian pageant from India to Greece. Prepare yourselves for hard strife, but believe in the miracles of your god."[30] It was Wagner who was to lead the Dionysian revels, at least at this early stage of Nietzsche's thinking. He would awaken the slumbering German spirit, dreaming its primordial Dionysian myth.[31]

Central to all of Nietzsche's complex argumentation about the Dionysian is the earlier Greek association of the god with humanity's animal-like body, in contrast to its Apollonian godlike reason. But once he had reasserted the importance of the physical aspects, Nietzsche went on to argue for the integration of the two impulses. Just as the two gods had come to share the festival year at the oracle at Delphi, so their symbolic forces would come together for Nietzsche in making possible the renewal of opera.[32] The physical and the spiritual, the body and the mind, the music and the text would unite, as they had done in ancient Greece to give birth to drama; the theatrical paradox Herbert Blau later described as "blooded thought" would bring together opera's sensuous rationality and rational sensuousness.[33]

9

The need to reassert a silenced Dionysian dimension, however, is also evident in Nietzsche's reminder of the communal and social nature of the theatrical event: he argued that, as the devotees sing and dance, they lose their individuality; so too does the audience of opera and drama.[34] But as a complex multisensory and performed art form, opera also requires the individual artistry, the control, and the discipline that are symbolized by Apollo. Once again, the two complementary forces must be balanced. In fact, what Nietzsche later came to label Dionysian was a fusion of the two impulses. But no matter what he called it, what this combination always implicitly meant for him, in both the early and late writings, was an acceptance of the bodily. In characteristically extravagant prose, Nietzsche later asserted in *Thus Spoke Zarathustra* (written between 1882 and 1884): "I want to speak to the despisers of the body. I would not have them learn and teach differently, but merely say farewell to their own bodies – and thus become silent."[35]

✥ Technology and the Disembodied Voice

"Despisers of the body" may perhaps be too strong a term to use for those today who prefer listening to opera on audio recordings rather than being in an audience at a live performance. But the advent of powerful new audio technologies has distanced audiences and therefore has made the disembodiment and subsequent fetishizing of the operatic voice a particularly modern issue: removing the uncontrolled, chaotic, contingent Dionysian world of human bodily performance, the Apollonian audio recording can control and perfect. It is not coincidental that it was specifically the theater of Dionysus below the Athenian Acropolis that was the site of the performances of those great Greek tragedies: composers of opera too have always been concerned not only with the music but with the theatrical realization of their work on the stage.[36] The Dionysian body of opera is the performed and performing body; it is the living, embodied voice.

In earlier centuries, opera as an art form was experienced by audiences in the context of other live performing arts: ballet, theater (both spoken and musical), concerts. By the twenty-first century, those live performances are still part of our context, but what have had an even stronger impact are the more technologically mediated forms of art: film, television, and audio and video recordings. Paradoxically, new technologies have made opera both more available and more distant. They have eliminated the direct contact and communication between human bodies that characterize unmediated performances "in which performers and audience members occupy the same space at the same time."[37] These changes have also led to different audience expectations and demands regarding relevance, accessibility, and even realism. As well, of course, they have allowed opera to reinvent itself in this new technological age. Productions such as film director Atom Egoyan's 1997 *Salome* for the Canadian Opera Company brought the resources of the cinema to the opera stage. Operas themselves have changed as well. Composer Libby Larson is writing an opera based on H. G. Wells's novel *The Invisible Man* and is doing it, fittingly, for radio – the theater of the mind – using both a regular orchestra and technological musical sounds. Philip Glass uses Jean Cocteau's film screenplay as the libretto for his opera *Orphée*, and he actually screens a silenced version of Cocteau's film *La Belle et la bête* in his own opera of the same name. Using media-mythologized, real-life characters of our own time, American operas have been written about Jackie Onassis, Marilyn Monroe, Harvey Milk, Richard Nixon, and many others.[38] On a more radical scale, Tod Machover's *Brain Opera* took place both in a physical and a virtual environment and involved its audiences – present and on-line – in untraditional and decidedly active ways. Clearly, not all technological change has worked to distance us.[39]

From the point of view of the live opera audience, some of the new technologies have enhanced our bodily as well as our intellectual involvement in actual performances. Surtitles are perhaps the most obvious example, for they have made operatic texts accessible and, arguably, have forced (or enabled) directors to work more closely with the libretto. Even if the audience may be temporarily distracted from the stage business by the act of reading, our increased knowledge of what is actually being sung about (and thus our better understanding of the story) makes our experience of the opera a more active and engaged process. But as audiences, we also increasingly live today in the "posthuman" age of cyberspace in which, some argue, the actual body all but disappears and the virtual persona or mask is all. The temptation is to declare the real Dionysian body and its markers (of gender, race, age, class) irrelevant to the times.[40] In its own way, this book is a plea not to do so.

There is no doubt that certain forms of audio technology, especially, have worked to distance audience bodies from stage bodies. In fact, over the last century, we have witnessed the progressive disembodiment of voice, thanks to the telephone, radio, phonograph, film, television, (audio and video) tape recorder, CD technology, and, most recently, electronic media.[41] This erasing of the actual body is not without its complexities. In television and film, for instance, the body loses its brute corporeality; nevertheless, the close-up can allow the camera to give an illusion of intimate contact unavailable in a live theatrical experience. Of course, film, especially on a large screen, can provide impressive spectacle through special effects, on-location shooting, and other technological resources that live performed opera in a theater cannot hope to offer. But the impact of that spectacle on the audience's physical experience of it is different from a live performance. While that impact may be profound, the source is always distanced and under someone else's visual and aural control: the director directs our eyes and ears. It is, in this sense, a less immediate experience, also because of our knowledge that a film is utterly Apollonian: that is, controlled, complete, "perfected" (at least to the producer's or director's liking). During a normal screening, it cannot be changed, and the audience can have no impact upon it;[42] there is none of the excitement and insecurity that go with both the accidental and the sublime possibilities of live performance.

Television or video recordings of live opera retain some of this visceral appeal of the present, the unique, and the unrepeatable, but they are not usually experienced in a communal setting. In addition, once again there is always a director editing, selecting what and how we see. As Tom Sutcliffe puts it: "In the live experience eye and mind take in and respond to everything, creating a far profounder, more intriguing happening in the realm of the imagination. The live audience edits for itself, discovers its own emotional, metaphorical and philosophical overlaps and connections."[43] It is not simply that opera is a "spectacle of excess," as David Levin argues, though it does indeed pack "a peculiarly hyperbolized and highly stylized punch": it is also the case that live opera, unlike film or television, is experienced *corporeally* by audiences in a technologically unmediated way, even if we are sitting in the back row of the theater.[44] We have also become part of a collective, responding body, so to speak, and chapter 4 will explore just what this entails.

Writing soon after the invention of the gramophone in the 1920s, Theodor Adorno noted that the new technology had altered "the dimensions of the live musical event, transforming everything – in a manner similar to radio – into chamber music, i.e. music for domestic environments."[45] Not only was music domesticated in scale and social function, but the relationship between the actual performers and the audience of opera was changed utterly.[46] The invention of the operatic long-playing record, argued Adorno, allowed for "the optimal presentation of music."[47] And he is correct: it is music alone and not embodied drama that can be optimally presented on audio recordings. As he later confirmed, opera for him is "only drama and only action to the extent that it is drama and action through music. . . . One ought to do without optical stimuli."[48] Before him, Arthur Schopenhauer had also argued that the visual stage business of opera was distracting: it took away from the "sacred, mysterious, intimate language of music."[49]

Adorno felt that listening to the music of an opera was comparable to reading, to immersion in a literary text. Yet an opera is

13

fundamentally different from a novel or a poem: it is intended as a social and public form of art as well as a dramatic one, involving warm bodies immediately present.[50] As such, the expectations of those perceiving it should be very different. While Adorno admitted that recordings reify the live event and lose the immediacy of performance, he personally preferred the technologically mediated experience, which allowed him to replay the piece at leisure "in quite-authentic form." This is a listener "desirous of auditioning and studying" – but only the music, not the staged drama or what he called the "ritual of performance."[51] Recordings are not only, as Adorno noted, infinitely replayable, but they are ultimately perfectable in a way that the raw, live performance can never be; they can be "flattened out *into perfection*," as Roland Barthes put it.[52] Retaking, editing, splicing, and other increasingly sophisticated electronic means of altering voice production ensure that what we hear on a recording is as perfect as the performer or producer wishes it to be. One of the most famous examples, of course, is Glenn Gould's definitive move from the concert stage to the recording studio in his desire for such control and perfection. Sometimes, however, it is not the artist who is in control but the technical expert. The famous recording producer Walter Legge tells the story of taping Maria Callas in *Tosca* in the early 1950s and how he used, in the process, miles of tape that needed editing. The opera's conductor, Victor De Sabata, declined to assist, announcing: "My work is finished. We are both artists. I give you this casket of uncut jewels and leave it entirely to you to make a crown worthy of Puccini and my work."[53]

Audience demands, in turn, adapt to this new Apollonian perfectibility. With our ears accustomed to the technologically perfected voice, our expectations for actual live performances are raised beyond the humanly possible. Disappointment can result from comparing what we are used to hearing on recordings with what we actually hear in performance. Yet operatic recording history is full of instances of aural creations that never actually existed naturally: in the 1950s, in a recording of *Tristan und Isolde* conducted by Wilhelm Furtwängler, high Cs sung by Elisabeth Schwarzkopf were interpolated into Kirsten Flagstad's rendition when the famous soprano could no longer hit the notes.[54] Or, to offer another example, in order to give modern ears a sense of what the singing voice of a *castrato* might have sounded like, Gérard Corbiau's 1995 film *Farinelli* used electronic technology to blend together the voices of a soprano and a countertenor. But such Apollonian transcending of the actual body and its physical limitations can never be part of the reality of live performed opera. Many live contemporary musical works – from Laurie Anderson's performances to operatic avant-garde productions – do use electronic technology, of course. But *Farinelli's* technological creation of a humanly nonexistent sound is arguably an attempt more to transcend than to extend the real body, in all its human limitations. Grace Kehler describes the voice constructed "out of the embodied voices of Ewa Mallas-Godlewska and Derek Lee Ragin" as "pure myth." She continues: "The lax throat of the actor – Stefano Dionisi – convinces us that 'Farinelli' does not really sing, while the soundtrack envelops us with the seductive sound of the untraceable and unnaturally produced voice – the eerily unreal voice which can appear to coincide with fantasies of perfection."[55]

It is not hard to see how a technological disembodiment could make possible a fetishizing of voice, separated from the body of the singer. Wayne Koestenbaum argues that the contrast between "the sound's power and the invisibility of its source" is crucially important to the act of listening to recordings.[56] Perhaps this is true, but the experience of live opera is very different – in physical terms – from what he describes: real and very visible bodies emit those sounds. And, as we shall argue in this book, opera stories themselves are always reminding us of the physical as they put the represented but very corporeal human form front and center on stage.[57] Both the real and the represented bodies of opera are the subject matter of this book in an attempt to counter the disembodiment of what is, after all, not only an Apollonian but also a Dionysian art form.

As we shall explore in more detail in chapter 4, the audience of live opera experiences the Dionysian both in their own bodies and because they partake in a public communal event. *Pace* Camille Paglia, it is not just Italian opera (or even rock and roll) that can be in touch with Dionysian physicality. It may well be the case that the figure of Dionysus is a kind of litmus test for every era's obsessions, for certainly much modern opera has turned to the Dionysian theme to explore the corporeal dimensions of life and art. As a symbolic force, Dionysus does indeed consolidate tendencies and effects that go beyond specific geographical, cultural, and historical contexts.[58] However, he certainly comes into his own in the twentieth century on the operatic stage in powerful works that never allow their audiences to ignore the Dionysian body.

✣ *Elektra* and the Deadly Dancing Body

One of these works appeared in 1909, when Richard Strauss and Hugo von Hofmannsthal collaborated to bring to the stage an operatic version of the playwright's modern adaptation of a Sophocles tragedy. *Elektra* tells the story of the culmination of the curse of the House of Atreus, the bloody tale of Electra and her matricidal avenging of the murder of her father, Agamemnon. But Hofmannsthal made a crucial addition to the plot of the ancient Greek story: at the end, his Elektra is made to dance with macabre and Dionysian joy and then fall not only silent but dead on stage. No one sings about her death, though the triumphant music arguably comments on and guides the interpretation of the viewing audience. If we were only listening to the opera on an audio recording and not reading the libretto, we would miss the point of the ending, for we would not necessarily even realize that Elektra had died. There are many such staged and literally embodied – but *unsung* – moments in opera that are lost without either reading the text or viewing a staged performance (or video), but this one is particularly striking, for it comes at the end of an opera that is obsessed from beginning to end with the body, as perhaps only a twentieth-century opera could be.

In adapting a Greek play for their *Elektra*, Strauss and Hofmannsthal were implicitly engaging not only the origins of opera in the Florentine Camerata's respect for Attic tragedy but also Nietzsche's and Wagner's shared sense of the power of both Greek drama and mythic subjects. Even closer to home for the opera's creators, though, and in these same years, Sigmund Freud was exploring myth (especially the Oedipus story) as a way of understanding both the human psyche and its pathology. As Jill Scott has shown, the particular story of Electra had proved and would continue to prove attractive to writers: the multigenerational blood feud of the House of Atreus was first described by Homer and then staged by Aeschylus, Sophocles, and Euripides. It would later inspire French neoclassical dramatists like Racine and many modern playwrights as well, from Hauptmann to Giraudoux, from Sartre to O'Neill.[59] In his play and then, later, in his opera libretto, Hofmannsthal refocused the tale through the lenses of his time: this Elektra becomes a woman obsessed, one who has sacrificed all, including her normal life and sexual development, to avenge her father's murder.[60] Hofmannsthal was writing in open opposition to that "bloodless sublimity and calm dignity" of the Greece of the German neoclassical tradition.[61] Stressing blood, violence, sexuality, and, especially, the physical body, from the opening scene onward this *Elektra* was intended to be dark and claustrophobic. Indeed, it was evidently this demonic, ecstatic – in short, Dionysian – image of sixth-century Greece that attracted Strauss to the play as a potential opera.[62]

The Elektra we witness on the operatic stage is very corporeally real. Her physicality is stressed from the very first scene to that final ecstatic dance of death. She is consistently presented in animal images, as if to emphasize her bodily excessiveness. She is, in one critic's felicitous terms, vengeance become flesh ("Fleisch gewordene Rache").[63] And Strauss's music underlines and contributes to both the physicality and the excess: it has been called a music of "split hairs, screaming nerves, nightmare hallucinations, visceral obsessions of blood and shame" rendered with all the "physical immediacy of a nettle-sting or a mosquito at your ear."[64] Ironically, however, the very physical Elektra is, at the start of the opera, an absent body. She is described before being seen, but the maidservants do speak of her in the most physical of terms.[65] Yet the animal imagery used, the physicality of her reported actions, the sexual obsession of her reported words, and the tales of verbal as well as physical abuse do not really prepare us for the dignified and moving Elektra who enters in scene 2, lamenting her father's death. She returns to the physical and emotional site of this trauma, compulsively repeating her grief and her desire for revenge. Her ritual recapitulation of Agamemnon's slaughter offers every gory detail; the bodily reality of the murder is still very much with her, as she tells of the dragged body, the staring eyes:

> Sie schlugen dich im Bade tot, dein Blut rann über deine Augen,
> und das Bad dampfte von deinem Blut. Da nahm er dich,
> der Feige, bei den Schultern, zerrte dich hinaus aus dem Gemach,
> den Kopf voraus, die Beine schleifend hinterher; dein Auge,
> das starre, offne, sah herein ins Haus.

> [They struck you dead in your bath, your blood ran over your eyes,
> and the bath steamed with your blood. Then he took you,
> the coward, by the shoulders, dragging you out of the chamber,
> your head in front, your legs trailing behind; your eyes,
> which were staring, open, looked back into the house.]

It is as if she cannot stop herself from almost physically reliving this scene of bodily horror.

In this opening monologue, she dwells obsessively on the sexual relationship between her mother and the usurping Aegisth. Not only is Elektra described in bodily terms, she is made to think in such terms as well. But so too is her sister, whose desire for a normal married life is also expressed in very physical and sexual terms: she wants to have children before her body "wilts" ("Kinder will ich haben, bevor mein Leib verwelkt"). The woman's destiny

("Weiberschicksal") she desires is very physical, but unlike that imagined by the death-obsessed Elektra, it is associated with the other aspect of Dionysian energy, the forces of life.

The powerful scene in which Elektra confronts her mother is another in which the body is the center of attention, and the music contributes greatly to the horror and power of the encounter.[66] Strauss used Wagner tubas in the orchestration of this scene with Klytämnestra to give what has been called "a kind of hormone-charged alto-tenor throb, suggestive of her sexuality, her guilty bed redolent with memories and nightmares, her diseases of body and mind."[67] Klytämnestra is indeed portrayed as diseased: the stage directions emphasize her sallow, bloated face, her sick, pale body that breathes heavily. She even calls herself a living corpse ("lebendiges Leibe") whose power and strength are now paralyzed. Fixated on her decaying body, Klytämnestra is prey to nightmares and to her sinister confidantes' negative comments about her body: they stress her swollen eyes, her sick liver; they even suggest that demons are sucking her blood. She decides to bare her soul to Elektra, who, she says, speaks like a doctor ("redet wie ein Arzt"), and thus allow the figurative breeze of revelation to cool her soul, like sick men cooling their boils and suppurating sores ("ihre Beulen und all ihr Eiterndes").[68] To disturbingly creepy music, Klytämnestra tells Elektra about her dreams and the "something" ("Etwas") terrifying her to the point that her body has become a putrid living carcass ("lebend, wie ein faules Aas"). Her daughter's sadistic and vivid imagining (and then recounting) of her mother's future murder is presented in equally physical terms, from the chase through the palace to the blow of the fatal ax.

Almost every scene of the opera is similarly oriented around the body. There is, for example, what amounts to a seduction scene between Elektra and her sister as she tries to persuade Chrysothemis to help her kill their mother. But most strikingly, Elektra's obsession with the sexual and the bodily is evident in the recognition scene, when her brother Orest finally appears. Elektra recounts to the stranger whom she has not yet recognized that this is a palace where people eat and drink and sleep, while she is treated worse than an animal of the woods ("das Tier des Waldes"). Orest's response – to music as aurally uncomplicated as is his personality and his role as Elektra's weapon of revenge – is a reaction to the deprivations of time and hardship on the body of this as yet unknown woman. He asks if they have let her starve or have beaten her: her eyes are terrible, he says; her cheeks, hollow and sunken. Here Hofmannsthal is ironically inverting the conventions of the classical recognition scene: according to Aristotle's theory, this moment should come about through seeing some mark on the body of the new arrival, in this case, Orest: "It is the body marked in a significant moment of the person's past history that enables recognition."[69] And, indeed, in the Greek plays by both Aeschylus and Euripides, it is a lock of Orestes' hair that makes the recognition possible. In the opera, instead, it is Elektra who is *not* recognized by her brother because of the marks of pain and abuse on her body. When she does tell him who she is, she describes herself as the corpse of his sister ("der Leichnam deiner Schwester") and turns away, ashamed of her physical decline. This is a body marked in visible and negative ways, a Greek body presented in ways antithetical to the much admired and idealized representations of Greek bodies in classical sculpture.[70]

Elektra fondly recalls her own earlier beauty in very sensual and sexual terms, singing of her naked body viewed in the moonlight and of her fine hair. All this, she claims, she has given up, including the sweet shudderings ("süssen Schauder") of love; all has been offered up as a sacrifice to her dead father, whose jealous spirit sent her hollow-eyed hatred as a bridegroom ("den hohläugigen Hass als Bräutigam"). Her young sensual innocence and her sexual awakening have been contaminated by the memory of Agamemnon's murder: "Wenn ich an meinem Leib mich freute, drangen seine Seufzer, drang nicht sein Stöhnen an mein Bette?" [When I rejoiced in my body, did not his sighs and his groans press as far as my bed?]. Now, she tells Orest, her body is only good for curses and despair.

It perhaps is not surprising that in 1912, three years after the opera's premiere, Carl Jung would posit the Electra complex to counter Freud's Oedipus complex.

Of all the opera's many corporeally oriented scenes, it is nevertheless that ecstatic, Dionysian dance to the death that is the most memorable. (See figure 3.) It has been prepared for by Elektra's opening monologue in which she tells her father's spirit that, after his murder is avenged, his children will dance together around his grave ("dein Blut, dein Sohn Orest und deine Töchter, wir drei . . . tanzen wir, dein Blut, rings um dein Grab"). As Elektra describes this dance, she will lift her knees high over the bodies of the slaughtered Klytämnestra and Aegisth ("über Leichen hin werd' ich das Knie hochheben Schritt für Schritt"). These kingly victory dances ("königliche Siegestänze") are not, however, what we see at the end at all. In ancient Greece there were two very different kinds of dances. One was a solo individual one, such as the wild, ecstatic dance of the Dionysian-inspired maenads or bacchantes, in which the entire body was used in orgiastic movements. But there were also communal ones such as Elektra describes here: round dances in which people held hands and moved in unison.[71]

It is this round dance ("Reigen") that Elektra knows everyone is waiting for her to lead after the murders ("ich weiss doch, dass sie alle warten, / weil ich den Reigen führen muss"). However, she finds that she physically cannot dance with the others. Yet at her description of herself and Orest as being godlike "accomplishers" ("Wir sind bei den Göttern, wir Vollbringenden"), she is transformed and leaps up, announcing that she had been a blackened corpse ("ein schwarzer Leichnam") among the living but is now the fire of life burning up the darkness. She feels that to look upon her white face must mean either a preparation to die or death itself, a death from "Lust" (in German, a word that means joyous desire or its satisfaction). Elektra then does dance, but alone, paradoxically, like a maenad, with her head thrown back and knees up: it is a Dionysian dance intended both to celebrate and to transcend the present world of the flesh.[72]

21

Hers is silent dancing, in the sense that she does not sing as she dances. The orchestra takes over when words become inadequate or unnecessary; at least, this is the case if we are watching a production and not simply listening to a recording. As we shall see in our later discussion of *Salome*, the opera Strauss wrote just before this one, the dancing body takes on its full meaning only for the eyes, even though the music offers the ears at least a mimetic analogue or commentary. Hofmannsthal, as we have seen, added something to this dance, making it into a dance of death, a *danse macabre* or *Totentanz*.[73] Unlike the traditional visual representations of this theme, this time it is not the figure of Death that dances but the living woman who is about to die. And when she does expire, no one comments on it, though the music offers an interpretation of what has occurred.[74]

Without seeing the body do its deadly Dionysian dance, someone simply listening to the music misses a crucial part of the ending – and thus the meaning – of the opera. Such are the corporeal limits of audio technology. What no one who knows the libretto in particular can miss, however, is *Elektra*'s obsession with the bodily. This work about matricide, obsession, revenge, and physical degradation was received, predictably, with shock and dismay at the time – as often since then.[75] This is a twentieth-century work in which the psyche is made flesh, and, arguably, it could not have been created (or at least staged) earlier: its Dionysian physicality and sexuality would have made it grossly inappropriate in some ways for the operatic stage, despite the rise of the more realistic operas of *verismo* in the nineteenth century. There is none of *The Bassarids'* Dionysian ritualistic dismemberment here, but Elektra's excessive dance is one done *in extremis*, at once celebrating and escaping "the tormenting bondage of our life in the body."[76]

✎ The Body as "Sign" in Opera

Our focus in this book is both on real bodies – the physiology involved in the experiences of both performers and audiences –

and on represented bodies like those in *Elektra*. Real bodies are relatively straightforward: as we shall explore in Act 2, they exist on stage and in the audience, and it is they who experience opera as *theater*, that is, as live performance and not texted drama. The focus of Act 1, however, is on represented bodies, that is, bodies presented as "signs" whose multiple meanings are generated in both the dramatic texts (musical and verbal) and contexts (social and cultural) and then interpreted by audiences.[77] Specific theatrical productions are obviously enactments of these represented bodies, offering one particular director's interpretation of the texts through one particular *mise-en-scène*. Act 1 of this book, however, is a study of the textually and contextually provoked meanings given to the operatic body in the dramatic texts, that is, in the language of the libretto (what characters sing about bodies), in the dramatic action of the narrative (which includes stage directions as well as characters' descriptions of that action), and in the texted music written to go with those particular words and dramatic situations of the libretto. By the "contexts" of production and reception we mean those of both the operas and their source texts: social, cultural, literary, theatrical, musical, and, given our focus on the human body, medical. What the body might "mean" or "signify" in these various texts and contexts has not until relatively recently been of much interest to musicology proper, but it is clearly a rich area for interdisciplinary study, as we have shown in our prefatory note.

The represented body is not the flesh-and-blood, real body of the singer on stage: "In representation the body appears not as itself, but as a sign. It cannot but represent both itself and a range of metaphorical meanings, which the artist cannot fully control, but only seeks to limit by the use of context, framing and style."[78] The interpretation of the audience, as limited by and thus implied in the dramatic texts, is important to any study of the represented body. Just as Wolfgang Iser described an "implied reader" in every literary work (a reader implied by the work's textual strategies), so, too, we would argue, there is an "implied audience" for every opera.[79] The words, the actions of the narrative, the music, the stage directions all imply what an audience is supposed to infer, that is, supposed to see and hear and thus to interpret. Of course, actual individual audience members will bring different expectations and knowledge to their experience of an opera, but their interpretive moves will to some extent be limited by what the texts and contexts of the work allow, by what is made available to the implied audience.

This is not to say that the responses and interpretations of real audiences will not be part of this examination of the operatic body as sign. After all, in true Dionysian fashion, opera is not only a dramatic, performed art, but it is also a public and social one. The audience is where the social and the cultural meet, where meanings are negotiated – during performances, in the intermissions, and after the show. During breaks we always hear some people talk only of voices as if they were disembodied ("I just closed my eyes and listened!"), but others talk about what they saw as well as heard, about the *mise-en-scène*, the singing actors, and their embodiment of the operatic story. They talk about how difficult it must be for the performers in director Robert Wilson's recent Metropolitan Opera production of *Lohengrin* or his Salzburg Festival version of *Pelléas et Mélisande* to sing while wearing such heavy costumes and holding stiff and unnatural postures. Or they marvel at how the Rhinedaughters in Harry Kupfer's production of *Das Rheingold* at Bayreuth (1988–92) could manage to sing and, at the same time, perform the tumbling acrobatics demanded of them. Audiences notice these Dionysian bodies; audiences interpret bodies as signs. Since we too have been part of those very real audiences, we will inevitably bring that experience to bear on our readings of opera's bodies in various performances we have seen. But our major focus in Act 1 will be on the dramatic texts and their representations of the operatic body.

Everyone possesses a biological organism we call the body, and we all accept its presence, even if we may not always appreciate its appearance or functioning. In the second part of this book, we will deal with the physiological realities of both singing opera and experiencing it in a live audience. But the body is clearly also "our visible expression in the world and in culture" and so projects social and cultural meanings about us.[80] Our past, too, is, in a sense, "sedimented" in our bodies.[81] In literally embodied art forms such as opera, the body is given meanings, both literal and metaphorical: "meaning and truth are made carnal."[82] But do bodies today "mean" the same thing and in the same way as bodies did when Wagner or Verdi were writing their operas?[83] Do they mean the same to North Americans as to Europeans? After all, medicine regards the body utterly differently today than it did before the nineteenth century, when the biomedical model (of which Michel Foucault wrote in *The Birth of the Clinic*) changed for good its idea of the body and how it functioned. No longer the meeting place of universal forces of nature and the cosmos, the body became the isolated site of disease entities, made vulnerable and visible in new ways by the technologically assisted medicalized gaze.[84] Legal and juridical regulations of the body have similarly changed over time. In social terms, certain once-accepted aspects of bodily existence have progressively become embarrassing and shameful; bodily fluids are perhaps only the most obvious.[85] Clearly, different cultures at different moments in history are going to have radically different interpretations of the meanings of the human body.[86] So, too, with individuals. Nevertheless, it is still possible to talk about the meanings of the operatic body, in part because operas themselves limit, control, and in very real ways direct the range of possible interpretations for the implied audience.

In Dionysian theatrical forms of art, the acts that are made visible on stage are "acts that we attribute over and over again to bodies" and not to some disembodied notion of an imagined literary character.[87] Theatrical performance assumes warm, material bodies – existing in space and time – with visible markers of, for instance, gender, race, and age. But as we have seen, those bodies are never "natural"; they are always cultural and historical: "No body ever simply appears on stage. Bodies are, rather, made to appear in performance, rendered visible as the encoded tissues interwoven by systems of ideological representation that mediate the anxieties and interests at play in specific historical moments. On stage, even the naked body represents not natural material, but the matter of history."[88] That body may speak, but in true Dionysian fashion it also moves: gesture, mime, and dance all become modes of "corporeal expressivity" that add layers of meaning and ultimately overdetermine the interpretation of that body, multiplying meanings and making them resonate through other physical senses besides the ear.[89] In this way, the body on stage is in a technologically unmediated relationship to the bodies in the audience, linked both emotionally and intellectually through the verbal and the gestural.

In opera all of this still holds, but we must add not only the power of music but the consideration that its stories are so often openly concerned with the body. Opera has always been a body-obsessed art, even in ages when society at large has preferred to ignore the physical. We need only think of the central role of the rotund, excessive body of the protagonist of Verdi and Boito's *Falstaff* (1893): even the insults hurled at him by those "merry wives of Windsor" are corporeal insults. On the operatic stage, bodies eat and, even more often, they drink; they make love and they fight. In Adorno's words, "opera is in its element wherever it gives itself over breathlessly to passion."[90] Of course, it cannot do so "breathlessly" and remain opera: the Dionysian physicality of that passion, both as represented and as enacted, must not be ignored. Even when bodies on stage sleep, they sometimes manage to move and sing, as in the sleepwalking scenes in *Macbeth* or *La Sonnambula*. If they cannot sleep, as Azucena cannot toward the end of *Il Trovatore*, they sing of that bodily torment.

Operatic bodies, of course, are not always what they appear to be: the cross-dressed mezzo-sopranos in their trouser roles, like the sometimes cross-dressed *castrati* before them, can confuse the eye, if not the ear. Voice ranges and types are never completely fixed

26

biologically: there are high male voices (not only the *castrati*, but sopranists and countertenors like David Daniels today), just as there are deep female voices (contraltos like Ewa Podleś). Nevertheless, in opera, the body is very much both "the protagonist of stories and the scene of stories,"[91] and librettists and composers are always very conscious of this as they attempt to direct in advance the implied audience's responses to what they will see and hear on stage. As Sander Gilman has shown, opera's creators are usually aware of the cultural implications of their representations, just as they know that the responses of their implied and real audiences are also culturally determined. To pick a contentious example, Marc Weiner has argued that Wagner's representations of the body actually incarnate his anti-Semitic theories: "Beliefs concerning the body provide a nexus linking the composer's personal agenda and the response granted his works by his nineteenth-century audience, for by using bodily imagery, Wagner was able to evoke specific associations linked to the body in his culture and to grant his ideas a degree of persuasive credibility to a nineteenth-century audience that can only be imaginatively reconstructed today."[92]

In opera the libretto's actual words are clearly as important as the music, especially today with the use of surtitles. The story they tell is enacted and embodied on stage, even as the music provides additional meaning and impact through its connotative and expressive powers.[93] The singer must be an actor, acting with the body as well as the voice. The act of singing may use the body "exorbitantly," as Koestenbaum argues, but so too does acting.[94] And the careers of the famous singing actors of opera like Maria Callas and, before her, Pauline Viardot are witness to the impact of this use of the body.[95] With the acting and singing body we have moved from the represented body to the actual physiological body. That "exorbitant" use of the human voice embodied in the flesh of the performer is experienced physically by audiences. Sitting silent and relatively motionless, as modern theatrical convention demands, the audience is nonetheless actively interpreting, responding (intellectually, emotionally, and even physically), and even communicating with the performers. This complex response is felt by bodies as well as apprehended by minds; it is simultaneously Dionysian and Apollonian, in the extended senses in which we have been using these terms. While some claim that the music not only reinforces but in the end overwhelms the verbal message of opera, the response of audiences' bodies – as we weep or laugh, for instance – is manifestly a reaction to both the meaning of the words and power of the music. In opera, words and music are equally embodied.[96] Working together, they layer and overdetermine the meaning of the represented operatic body on stage, even as they influence and sometimes overwhelm the bodies of the audience members. The fact is that we can be moved by both sound and sense and by both the aural and the visible as we experience them physically in a live opera performance. That we can thus give multiple and complex meanings to the bodies represented on stage clearly reflects a complicated process of engaging both the Dionysian and Apollonian impulses, a process that is one of the central subjects of this book.

As many have argued, the Western aesthetic tradition may indeed be oriented around what can be seen by the eye. But, as we noted above, for many the experiencing of opera, on the contrary, has become audiocentric and thus disembodied, thanks to certain forms of audio technology. As an art of performance, though, opera not only is itself multisensorial, but it engages plural sensory fields in its perceivers.[97] Nevertheless, there is a striking lack of vocabulary to talk about the plural bodily engagement of the actively interpreting audience. Even the word "audience" – like the words "listener" and "auditor" – involves etymologically only one sense, that of hearing. Other terms such as "spectator," "viewer," and "observer" involve only that of sight. There would appear to exist no special term for the actively apprehending Apollonian/Dionysian perceiver of opera with mind and all senses alert. Opera is indeed primarily seen and heard. But it is also felt, and not only figuratively or in emotional terms. The sense of touch can surely intervene in the operatic experience: if we sit near the front, we can be rained upon by singers' saliva; the seats can be hard or otherwise uncomfortable. Smells from the stage or from the perfumes and bodies of fellow audience members can impinge on our senses. Today, about all we will taste during a performance is likely a preventive cough candy, though in earlier times eating and drinking during a performance were not uncommon.

There are still other ways in which our perceiving operatic bodies make us take notice of them. We might well feel the need to urinate as much as the desire to laugh or cry; we might get caught up in the communal emotion shared with those around us or luxuriate in the private pleasures of our hearts racing or the hair on the back of our necks standing on end. However we experience live opera, we perceive it through multiple sensory channels, even though the visual and aural dominate. Whenever we use the term "audience" in this book, then, we would like readers to supplement the obvious aural associations of the word with the visual and for that matter with the other senses as well. (While the roots of the word "perceiver" do indeed suggest notions of becoming aware through the senses, the term itself is perhaps too awkward and unfamiliar for constant use; yet we would like readers to translate mentally "audience" into "perceivers," in this sense of the word.)

The responses of audiences and performers are not only Dionysian, of course; they are also rational, aesthetic, Apollonian. And both sets of players have a dual physical or perceptual presence: they can see and be seen, hear and be heard.[98] As we shall see in the coming chapters, the operatic bodies of represented characters often enact these dualities: the pleasure of looking – especially at beautiful women's bodies – that has been argued to be so central to theater and cinema is the theme of operatic plots from *Don Giovanni* to *Salome*, but the related pleasure – and power – of being gazed upon is also important.[99] Bodies, in short, are operatic in many possible ways, but in the end, the Dionysian and Apollonian are intricately interwoven to make those bodies into complex "signs."

29

✖ *Death in Venice*: Balancing the Dionysian and Apollonian

Benjamin Britten and Myfanwy Piper's 1973 opera *Death in Venice* exemplifies the delicate balancing of these opposing but complementary impulses: *thematically,* it succeeds in presenting the story of the Apollonian writer, Gustav von Aschenbach, and his total fall into the Dionysian abyss through his physical love for the beautiful boy Tadzio; but at the same time the opera itself *formally* enacts the balance of the two forces that the protagonist fatally fails to achieve. Both Greek gods are themselves literally made part of this story, though, ironically, both are present only as disembodied voices. (Some productions, such as Peter Hall's 1990 Glyndebourne version available on video, ignore this irony and choose instead to present the gods in the flesh on stage.) Apollo and Dionysus, however, allegorically play out the opposing forces within Aschenbach himself: mind and body, aesthetic control and physical passion. While sensitive to Philip Brett's criticism that this kind of allegorized reading has proved a convenient way to neutralize the homoerotic dimensions of the story, we would argue instead that, as in *The Bassarids*, the presence of Dionysus in an opera is a sign of the powerful presence of the body and that the eroticized body certainly need not be heterosexual in either Greek tragedy or modern opera.[100]

Piper's libretto is based on Thomas Mann's novella *Der Tod in Venedig* (1911), in which the balancing of these opposing Apollonian and Dionysian impulses within the protagonist is established from the start as central to Aschenbach's very essence as an artist.[101] He is the son of a bourgeois father and a bohemian mother: "The union of dry, conscientious officialdom and ardent, obscure impulse, produced an artist." Yet in full knowledge of the aesthetic need for both dimensions, what Aschenbach the artist has produced are works that thematically enact the progressive victory of the Apollonian: in one, "the pallid languors of the flesh [are] contrasted with the fiery ardours of the spirit within," and in another there is an "impassioned discourse on the theme of Mind and Art," carried on with "ordered force" and "antithetical eloquence." We are told that there is an explicit renunciation of "sympathy with the abyss," thanks to a "miracle of regained detachment."[102] Aschenbach's style is described as austere, simple, symmetrical: in a word, Apollonian. So, too, is his life. Not as arrogant in his rejection of the Dionysian as is Pentheus in *The Bacchae* or *The Bassarids*, the German Aschenbach is, in fact, tempted by the lure of the sensual Italy of Venice.[103] In the opera we watch and listen to the observing, restrained, rational artist as he recounts to us how "the mind beats on," but also how self-discipline has perhaps led to the loss of passion in his life.

The quasi-*parlando* dry recitative with accompanying piano is the perfect aural analogue for the inhibited, formal personality of the man we witness on stage. But the drums we hear when the writer contemplates a change, such as a voyage to Venice, are signals of something lurking, ready to disturb this calm Apollonian surface. As Donald Mitchell has argued, the percussion in the opera comes to represent "everything that is strange, an encompassing symbol of all the diverse kinds of strangeness that disrupt the ordered, super-civilized rational world of Aschenbach."[104] Thus, in accord with mythic associations as well, the drums also stand for the Dionysian, the sexual, the dark appetites that Aschenbach has repressed. The problem is not that his passion for the beautiful Polish youth Tadzio releases the Dionysian, though it does; the problem is in his initial resistance and then in his subsequent failure to control his surrender to this new physical dimension of life. As Dodds explains about the early Greek Dionysian ritual, "To resist Dionysus is to repress the elemental in one's own nature; the punishment is the sudden complete collapse of the inward dykes when the elemental breaks through perforce and civilisation vanishes."[105] This is why Aschenbach experiences his passion as degradation, as a fall: after such strong resistance, the Dionysian alone is felt as disintegrative, as Euripides and Nietzsche both knew. Just as the Apollonian alone, in its civilized rigidity, can be destructive, so, too, after repression, the Dionysian alone can lead to the release of dark impulses.

Aschenbach originally comes to beautiful Venice in search of renewal, regeneration, and aesthetic inspiration. What he finds is an increasingly plague-ridden city. Nevertheless, he believes he has found his inspiration in the beauty of Tadzio, and, as the next chapter will explore, the language in which he voices this discovery is Plato's. This Neoplatonic and Apollonian context allows Aschenbach to fool himself for a time into believing that, for him, the boy's physical body and its beauty are but means to the spiritual and the aesthetic. (See figure 4.) Through the Hellenizing eyes of the artist, we watch Tadzio and his friends play sports on the beach: Greek notions of physical beauty are here expressed in the controlled forms of athletic achievement, fittingly referred to in the libretto as the Games of Apollo.[106] But this scene does not represent some "pinnacle of idealism" from which Aschenbach falls when he realizes, at the end of it, that he loves the boy. On the contrary, watching the pentathlon does not undermine his idealism or his self-control; instead, the very act of watching (his act, but also ours) is already colored from the start by Aschenbach's rationalizing, idealizing, Hellenizing attempts to delude himself about the physicality of his attraction to Tadzio.[107] However, the fact that the boys' games are *danced* underlines the Dionysian element at the heart of the scene and, "as the ballet progresses, the text and dance become progressively less controlled and remote and more explicitly sexual" – with the javelin throwing and wrestling.[108] Precisely when Aschenbach resolves to translate feeling into thought, to celebrate "Eros . . . in the word," that is, when he tries consciously to assert the aesthetic value of sublimation, the music gives him away. The passage begins in a thematically appropriate manner by expanding on Apollo's music, but it is founded on Tadzio's harmony and ends with a reworking of his Dionysian theme on the tuned percussion.[109] And the constant sound of the tom-toms that accompany all the games acts as a danger signal, aurally reminding us of the sublimated Dionysian presence.[110]

The scene immediately before this had closed with Aschenbach's renewed decision to stay in Venice, a decision made mostly because he sees Tadzio playing on the beach: "So be it. Here will I stay, here dedicate my days to the sun, and Apollo himself." And so he does, yet his Apollonian and Platonic ruminations during the games are revealed as the self-delusory, rationalizing projections they really are when Aschenbach then tries to blame the sun for the "absurd" "frenzy" he feels as he utters, "I – love you." But it is not the Apollonian sun that is to blame; it is the Dionysian abyss that he must now face. This abyss is within himself, and it is allegorically enacted through a dream. The librettist had read *The Bacchae* while preparing the text and had come to feel strongly that the two godly forces had to fight it out dramatically in dialogue.[111] Britten's bold music enacts both their dialogue and their struggle in terms of its tonal polarities (the Dionysus-associated key of E and Apollo-linked F), as John Evans has shown.[112] But it is in the night (not in the sun) and in dream (not in rationalizing wakefulness) that "the full Dionysian power of music" is finally unleashed.[113]

Aschenbach's dreaming self tries at first to cling to his Apollonian idealization of Tadzio and his beauty, just as his waking self had tried to retain his aestheticized vision of Venice, despite the increasingly obvious presence of cholera in the city. The unearthly countertenor voice of Apollo tells him to "love beauty, reason, form." But his is no match for the voice of the "stranger god," the more earthy baritone of Dionysus, which urges him not to "turn away from life."[114] The tame invocation of Apollonian "laws" cannot withstand Dionysian appeals to the excesses of "nature" in its darker, even sacrificial forms. The "reeling dance" and the drums and ecstatic cries ("Aa-oo! Aa-oo!") of the followers of Dionysus finally drive Apollo away. The aural violence of this struggle has often been remarked, and it is not rare to find accounts of the "abrupt shortening and acceleration" or the violent "discharge" of the music with its "brutal ostinato."[115] The triumphant Dionysus urges the visceral lifting of repression:

Taste it, taste the sacrifice.
Join the worshippers,

embrace, laugh, cry,
to honour the god.

At this point, "Tadzio's music bursts in, hideously bloated and interspersed with grotesque quotations of the plague motive, to envelop the dreamer in the orgy."[116] Those telling drums erupt "in *fortissimo* rhythmic abandon"[117] as Aschenbach surrenders to the Dionysian and the bodily as totally as he had earlier held himself to Apollonian rational restraint: he awakens to find himself crying "Aa-oo!" in his sleep. He describes what he is experiencing in terms of a "fall" and a "taste of knowledge," recalling not only Eden's forbidden fruit but the sensuality of the taste of the sacrifice that Dionysus had offered. Not once but twice he articulates his surrender, first to Dionysus – "Let the gods do what they will with me" – and, in the next scene as he watches the boys on the beach, implicitly to Tadzio – "Do what you will with me!" As Mann had put it, the dream "left the whole cultural structure of a lifetime trampled on, ravaged, and destroyed."[118]

The dream may well liberate Aschenbach to accept his physical desires and give up his former passionless aestheticizing, but the text continues to make clear that this is not a totally positive move: having gone from one extreme to the other, the once austere bourgeois now allows the Hotel Barber to tint his hair and rouge his cheeks, becoming in this way the very image of the "Elderly Fop" who had so disgusted him earlier on the trip to Venice. Musically, too, Aschenbach can no longer fully sustain the " 'detached' musical idiom" of the earlier interior monologues, as he "loses self-possession and surrenders to fate."[119] It is for this reason that Aschenbach must die in the end. The message of the story is not a total condemnation of the physical; rather, this is a narrative about the fatal consequences of a lack of balance, that is, of either a passive surrender to the destructive Dionysian or, before that, an equally passive acceptance of what is presented here as the Apollonian death in life.[120] It is the necessary balance that is missing here: to ignore the body and the emotions caused by physical attraction is as deadly as giving in to them utterly.

In the novella and the opera alike, the protagonist cannot both experience bodily passion and control his response; he cannot balance the Dionysian and the Apollonian.[121] But both Thomas Mann and Benjamin Britten could, as many have pointed out. Both had autobiographical connections to the story of the man who fell in love with a beautiful boy, but both offered clear evidence in their work that Dionysian passion can inspire the balanced artist.[122] The narrative Mann wrote and Piper adapted is a parable of the artist's struggle to create by keeping in balance the forces of Apollo and Dionysus, but the music Britten wrote for the parable also enacts that balance. It is certainly not Wagnerian (despite the fact of Wagner's death in Venice) or even Mahlerian (though the composer died while Mann was writing his novella); instead, it is limpid music that allows yet another balance – that of words and music – to be retained throughout.[123]

Though the story may end in disintegration, the works of art do not. Peter Evans argues that the orchestral postlude after Aschenbach's collapse "washes away the corruption that has festered throughout this second act, recalling the idea of beauty celebrated in the Hymn to Apollo, counterpointed by Tadzio's alluringly bright music."[124] But Apollo is really recalled here only to right the balance upset by the Dionysian surrender. W. H. Auden had written to Britten in 1942 that "Goodness and [Beauty] are the results of a perfect balance between Order and Chaos, Bohemianism and Bourgeois Convention."[125] Over thirty years later, Britten would enact that perfect Dionysian/Apollonian balance in creating a work whose memorable qualities are, fittingly if paradoxically, "intensity and restraint."[126]

Here we return to a point made earlier in this chapter: Aschenbach's death, like Elektra's, is not actually narrated. In no way could someone only listening to *Death in Venice* on an audio recording achieve full understanding of the opera's meaning: we cannot *hear*

Aschenbach's body slump in its chair or Tadzio walk into the sea and beckon to him. For that, we need to be able to read the stage directions if not actually see the action on stage. The music, as we have noted, comments on the events, but it cannot totally substitute for them. As the chapters to follow will explore, we frequently need to see as well as hear the operatic body.

Represented Bodies

The true meanings of words are bodily meanings, carnal knowledge.
– Norman O. Brown

The next two chapters will focus both on the balance of the Dionysian and the Apollonian in opera and on the symbolic struggle between them as we study how operatic plots persist in telling the story of the Dionysian body, however much Apollonian artistic convention may attempt its repression. We will see that the represented body in opera always has a sex and indeed is sexualized, as feminist and queer criticism has indeed taught. It also has a race: the seductive body of the Judean Salome takes control of the stage in powerful ways, as we shall witness. The staged body is usually given an age and, sometimes, a specific state of health: Amfortas's wound in Wagner's *Parsifal* or Violetta's consumption in *La Traviata* are central to the operas' meanings.[1]

In chapter 1 we investigate in more detail how opera's origins in the Neoplatonism of Renaissance Italy have conditioned its conventions for portraying the corporeal: for much longer than we might expect, the beautiful body was seen as an externalization of the good soul, just as the unbeautiful body was considered a sure sign of moral deformation. Later European neoclassicism continued this classical tradition by establishing what Barbara Stafford refers to as artistic "zones of purified emptiness."[2] With the nineteenth century came both a medical fascination with the physically "monstrous" (in the study of teratology) and a Romantic literary interest in the grotesque body of the deformed.³ Through adaptations of the novels and plays of Victor Hugo, this interest was translated into operatic terms as the stage became the site of the rethinking of the Platonic and Apollonian heritage through the reassertion of the Dionysian body. Beauty and its lack, of course, are qualities visible on stage: because of this, the audience becomes implicated, through the act of looking, in the behavior of characters: we too stare in fascination or with curiosity; we sexualize or desexualize; we empower or disempower. Unlike real life, operas do not usually allow us to avert our eyes: normally we stare at the staged deformed bodies of Rigoletto or of Tonio in *Pagliacci.* Likely less uncomfortable than we would be in life, we participate in the characters' act of giving meaning to the physical bodies we too observe.

This is never more evident than in the opera obsessed with staring, Richard Strauss's adaptation of Oscar Wilde's *Salome.* And as in *Elektra,* the opera that immediately succeeded it, *Salome* offers us another example of the vocally silent dance, but this time it lasts for an extended period of time. As we have seen, in ancient Greece a certain kind of dance was explicitly Dionysian and, because of the bacchantes, associated with women. And we know that Nietzsche's reiteration of this connection had a striking impact on the development of a theory of Dionysian modern dance through choreographers like Rudolf Laban and female dancers like Mary Wigman and Isadora Duncan.⁴ Chapter 2 will examine the relation between the dancing woman's body and the role of the audience who, like Herod, cannot but stare at Salome during her famous Dance of the Seven Veils. Whether our gaze disempowers the dancer or, on the contrary, grants her a deadly power is one of the questions this chapter addresses.

In terms of the representations of the body in opera, the traditional dichotomy usually articulated in operatic criticism, the one between the words and the music, is less relevant than the newer dichotomy between the embodied and the disembodied voice brought about, in part, by modern technology. All the operas examined in these two chapters teach that the Dionysian body is not to be denied its due. Represented bodies are always given meaning by audiences, and those meanings will reflect or challenge the dominant cultural norms at the time of the experienced performance, for they will engage in complex ways the belief systems and values of real audience members. But the dramatic texts (the libretto and score) are also composed to provoke an implied audience to interpret and respond in certain ways. If, as Peter Conrad argues in *A Song of Love and Death*, operatic plots all seem to revolve around precisely love and death, then activities like embracing and kissing or fighting and expiring are the corporeal staples of traditional dramatic action. In these chapters, however, we want to look at a group of less obvious (but just as culturally revealing) Dionysian embodied stage actions: the performing of beauty (and its absence) and dancing. Both are potentially socially disruptive, hence their attractiveness as operatic plot devices and their significance as cultural signs.

The Body Beautiful

In Jacques Offenbach's opera *Les Contes d'Hoffmann* (1881), the poet Hoffmann offers a song to the students gathered in Dionysiac celebration at Luther's tavern in Nürnberg. He tells of the court of Eisenach, where a strange little man named Kleinzach attracts the comic attention of all for his stunted legs, his hump ("une bosse en guise d'estomac"), his odd feet. But when Hoffmann begins to describe the features of Kleinzach's face, his voice suddenly changes, and he dreamily sings:

> Ah! sa figure était charmante! Je la vois,
> belle comme le jour où, courant après elle,
> je quittai comme un fou la maison paternelle.
>
> [Ah! the face was charming! I see it,
> beautiful as the day when, running after her,
> I left like a madman my paternal home.]

The oddly shaped man of the song has suddenly metamorphosed into his opposite in terms of both sex and appearance: a beautiful woman, with long coils of dark hair, an elegant neck, blue eyes, and a voice "vibrante et douce" that wins Hoffmann's heart. Not surprisingly, his companions comment on this bizarre shift of topic, asking him if he is still painting a verbal picture of Kleinzach. Coming to his senses, Hoffmann never names this beautiful woman but simply asserts that ugly Kleinzach is worth more – deformed though he may be – than that monster of a beautiful woman.[1]

Derived from the historical E. T. A. Hoffmann's story entitled "Klein Zaches, genannt Zinnober," the operatic Hoffmann's song presents in miniature two of the major themes of nineteenth- and twentieth-century European representations of the body on the opera stage: on the one hand, the mutual implication of beauty and ugliness, and on the other, the question of the consistency of the internal self with external appearance. Despite the fact that the appearance of most of humanity falls between the dichotomies of beauty and its absence, drama – including opera – seems to have been attracted to staging such extremes, perhaps because of the obvious effectiveness of the resulting tensions and conflicts. Like the mythic figures of Venus and Medusa, the very concepts of beauty and its opposite are testaments to the power of the visual in Western culture. But opera clearly involves the aural as well. Musical beauty as consonance came to be defined not only in its own positive terms but by its contrary, dissonance. That definitions of musical beauty are relative is obvious: every age's avant-garde composer, be it Monteverdi or Schoenberg, has created sounds ugly or dissonant to an ear accustomed to dominant musical conventions. Opera composers in particular have had additional problems, trying to reconcile aural beauty and the "smoothness of vocal production with the achievement of dramatic power."[2]

As Herbert Lindenberger has argued, opera as drama openly deals in extremes – aesthetic, moral, political. Apollo and Dionysus are clearly its contrasting reigning deities. On the stage, characters are sometimes differentiated in relatively unsubtle ways: conventionally a soprano's voice is associated with moral goodness; a lower-pitched voice often signals an evil character.[3] Think of Desdemona as opposed to Iago in Verdi's *Otello*. Another equally traditional association with goodness, however, is beauty: Desdemona's beauty adds to her vulnerability but also to her ethical stature. This linking of interior moral worth and exterior physical beauty has a long history, as we shall see shortly, and indeed it would appear to be an accepted truism in much opera. Its power can also be seen whenever, as in Hoffmann's song, a discrepancy is found to exist between inside and outside. As we shall see later, and as Mary Douglas has shown, such ambiguities are disturbing to us, since humans seem to require clear categorizations.[4] Opera offers many examples of these kinds of ambiguity, in part because its music often has the power to reveal to the audience the internal reality that the staged body's appearance belies. Such disturbing and dramatic cases, however, only serve to underline the power of the convention even as they deconstruct it.

✎ Platonic Beauty

The correlation of the beautiful and the good has multiple cultural origins, but Plato stands historically as its most influential articulator in the West. When, in the *Symposium*, Socrates recounts Diotima's teaching that "ugliness is at odds with the divine, while beauty is in perfect harmony," he means beauty of soul as well as beauty of body and takes for granted the connection of both to moral superiority. In the *Republic* Socrates asks: "when there is a coincidence of a beautiful disposition in the soul and corresponding and harmonious beauties of the same type in the bodily form – is not this the fairest spectacle for one who is capable of its contemplation?"[5] The physically beautiful is a means to true, ideal beauty and therefore virtue. When Riccardo Zandonai and Tito Ricordi (with the aid of D'Annunzio) created their opera *Francesca da Rimini* (1914), they were able to draw on this longstanding tradition in setting up the contrast between the rival male characters. Francesca is presented as being in love with the man known in the opera as "Paolo il Bello" (the handsome), who is described as tall and slim, with royal carriage and white teeth. But unfortunately, she is wed to his brother, whose full name is "Giovanni lo Sciancato" (the lame). This rough man, said to have the eyes of a furious demon, is provided by his creators with a harsh voice and even harsher words. He is matched in physical and moral terms by his younger brother, the cruel and violent Malatestino, who has lost an eye in battle. The entire household feels oppressed by "lo zoppo e l'orbo" [the lame man and the blind one]. After the enraged Giovanni, at Malatestino's urging, kills his wife and her lover, Paolo, the stage directions guide the audience's eyes to his disability: he leans over in silence, bends one knee with great difficulty, and breaks his bloody sword on it. The complicated moral position – given the adultery involved – is nonetheless that the good and the beautiful have here been destroyed by the evil and the ugly. Platonic consonance of inside and outside prevails against considerable odds, perhaps in part because this is a twentieth-century opera.

Yet the notion that beautiful people are somehow inherently good and that ugly people are evil is not one that is given any conscious credence today, for we now tend to accept that beauty is autonomous and distinct from morality or even intelligence. But this is a more modern notion of beauty and one more different than we might expect from that which dominated operatic representations in the nineteenth and even into the twentieth century, as we have just seen. It has been argued that what is considered beautiful has not in itself changed significantly over the centuries, but the value placed upon it has.[6] If this is true, then it is important that we keep that (continuing) older tradition in mind if we are to understand the meaning of the representations of beautiful bodies – and their opposites – on the operatic stage. But it is also true that this modern notion of the autonomy of beauty from moral worth has not extended to the ugly or disabled body to quite the same degree. And this failure too needs to be kept in mind and, indeed, confronted in this chapter, as in our daily lives.

Clearly the Platonic tradition privileges the visual or the visible: unlike wisdom or justice, beauty as an ideal can be apprehended directly through physical phenomena. As Socrates explains in Plato's *Phaedrus*, beauty is manifest to sight, "the keenest mode of perception vouchsafed us through the body."[7] For this reason, in a study such as ours that investigates representations of the staged body in opera, the sense of sight is also inevitably privileged over the others: in other words, while there are, for example, comic characters who stutter (and tragic ones too, like Billy Budd in Benjamin Britten and

E. M. Forster's opera of that name) and others who are without sight (Tiresias in Stravinsky's *Oedipus Rex* or La Cieca in *La Gioconda*), we will concentrate in this chapter on those outward characteristics of the unbeautiful as well as the beautiful body that are described in the libretto and sometimes actually made visible on stage. It is these narratively significant corporeal clues that influence strongly the responses of the listening and watching audience members, for they too have come under the influence of that long Platonic tradition.

As an art form, opera itself came into being at a time when what has been called the "long arm of Neoplatonism" dominated Renaissance Italy. The Florentine Camerata was imbued with these philosophical ideas as articulated by Marsilio Ficino and rendered poetic by writers like Poliziano. One appeal of the Orpheus story to many of the early operatic composers (Peri, Caccini, Monteverdi) was that the protagonist seemed a kind of proto-Platonist by anticipation.[8] It would not be until the nineteenth century that the continuing power of the Platonic concept of the beautiful would be challenged in opera by the Romantic notion of the grotesque. Until then (but even thereafter, as we shall see), Neoplatonic thought had an immense impact on the operatic imagination through its repeated correlation of the beautiful and the good.

This impact was in part made possible by the power of the Neoplatonic model of beauty, one specifically defined in terms of its formal – Apollonian – attributes. The relation of beauty to proportion is a commonplace of Greek philosophy. In the *Timaeus*, Plato explains how the world was created as order out of disorder: "all measures and harmonies" are granted to things in relation to themselves and to each other. The beauty of the human body (and thus the goodness of the soul) depends upon actual mathematical form (triangles, in fact). In Plato's terms, "Everything that is good is fair, and the fair is not without proportion, and the animal which is to be fair must have due proportion. . . . [T]here is no proportion or disproportion more productive of health and disease, and virtue and vice, than that between soul and body themselves. . . . [T]he due

45

proportion of mind and body is the fairest and loveliest of all sights to him who has the seeing eye."[9] The aesthetics of proportion also dominates medieval conceptions of beauty, beginning with musical theories, but this all comes to be overlaid with more explicitly Neoplatonic moral values in the Renaissance.[10] The proportionately perfect human body takes on symbolic aesthetic and moral value at this time, beyond even Vitruvius's earlier architectural statement that the symmetry needed in designing temples was that of the proportions of a well-shaped human body. Albertus Magnus, in his *De Pulchro et Bono*, links the beautiful not only to the good but specifically to a "resplendence of form": "corporeal beauty requires a due proportion of its members."[11]

In Latin antiquity, the word used by Virgil or Ovid for beautiful was as likely to be "formosa" (form-full) as the more common "pulcher."[12] In the Vulgate Bible, the Bride in the Song of Songs tells us: "Nigra sum sed formosa" (I.4). While the Bridegroom calls her "pulchra," she describes herself as "form-full." When Neoplatonic thought dominated, as in the twelfth century, "formosa" was used often. Rooted in pre-Socratic notions of congruence and proportion, this almost mathematical concept of beauty and its absence can be traced from Cicero's idea that in the body "a certain symmetrical shape of the limbs" constituted beauty. It continues in Aquinas's later belief that beauty was what the senses delight in through "rightly proportioned things" and that ugliness is what is not structured in this way.[13] We can see the same concept even in the scientific discourses of the eighteenth century. As Nicolas Andry writes in his *Orthopaedia: Or, the Art of Correcting and Preventing Deformities in Children* (1742): "There is such a nice Exactness in the Proportions of the human Body, that upon this the whole Science of Mechanicks is founded."[14]

We have deliberately switched to a scientific discourse here for a reason. The question is: Can we attribute the persistence of the Platonic notion of beauty *as form* simply to the power of cultural tradition to assert universals? Or is something else going on here?

Current work on patterns of human mating suggests that biological forces may also be at work. Feminist theory has forcefully argued that beauty is a relative and culturally constructed concept, a "beauty myth," as Naomi Wolf put it, and not universal and changeless.[15] There is little argument that the social meanings attached to certain aspects of beauty (such as weight) are culture- and time-specific: plumpness is valued in places where (and at times when) food is scarce, thinness where and when it is plentiful. But there is also considerable evidence that humans exhibit body-related, species-typical desires in mating that are "highly patterned and universal."[16] These patterns exist, biologists argue, because they are strategic and advantageous in evolutionary terms. As Nancy Etcoff summarizes in her recent book, *Survival of the Prettiest: The Science of Beauty*, physical clues to a woman's health and youth are found attractive and thus valued in sexual selection as signs of her fertility and reproductive value. Among these clues is "low fluctuating asymmetry" or, more simply, regularity of facial features and other bodily parts; in this way, Platonic symmetry and proportion become visible indicators of hormone status as well as definers of sexual attractiveness and beauty.[17]

Whatever the reason – biological, aesthetic, metaphysical – for the persistence of these form-full ideals, we are left with the (Apollonian) fact that beauty and form have been inseparable in the Western imagination for many centuries. Because of this inseparability for Plato and those who followed, the beauty of the body is a reflection of an ideal beauty and thus the expression of the good. And as Umberto Eco has pointed out, by the medieval period moral values had been firmly provided with this aesthetic foundation.[18] The Christianizing of this linkage by Saint Augustine and others merely reinforced its conceptual and imaginative impact. However, the implicit heterosexualizing of the Platonic notion of beauty that took place in the Roman and then medieval worlds should not allow us to forget the fact that the beautiful body of which Socrates spoke was always the young male body, as it was in the Renaissance revival of those myths of Adonis, Hyacinth, Narcissus, and especially Ganymede.[19] It is this homoerotic Neoplatonic context that was brought to the stage in an opera to which we now return: *Death in Venice.*

❧ Love and Beauty in *Death in Venice*

As we have already seen in the last chapter, in both literary and operatic versions of the story, the aging Gustav von Aschenbach is presented as the austere artist of form who is overwhelmed by the sheer corporeal beauty of the boy Tadzio.[20] The only language in which he can express his response is Platonic. While Mann's text offers, through its allusions to other literary and philosophical works, a sense of the ambiguities and confusions in Aschenbach's mind, the opera libretto necessarily simplifies and thereby ends up strengthening the Platonic elements, emphasizing the moral issues that are tangled up with the aesthetic ones.[21] When Aschenbach – the artist who has built his work on "simplicity, beauty, form" – sees the "beautiful young creature" in a Venice hotel, he describes him as the "soul of Greece" and as a "[m]ortal child with more than mortal grace." (See figure 4.) Just as Socrates is totally taken with the physical beauty of Phaedrus but sees it as a manifestation of ideal and universal beauty (and, therefore, of the good), so Aschenbach marvels, in Platonic terms, about Tadzio: "How does such beauty come about? What mysterious harmony between the individual and the universal law produces such perfection of form? Would the child be less good, less valuable as a human being if he were less beautiful?" The addition of this last sentence, absent from the novella, suggests that the moral issues associated with beauty and love are never far from Piper's and Britten's minds.[22] While the first act of the opera shows Aschenbach's devotion to the Platonic notion that physical beauty should merely be a bridge to the appreciation of an ideal beauty and that in this way it can inspire his Apollonian, form-driven art, the second act shows the result of his realization that his

48

response to the boy is not only aesthetic but also psychological and physical. Dionysus makes his presence felt.

The fact that the aging, intellectual Aschenbach and the physically beautiful Tadzio inhabit different worlds is underlined in the opera by having the very verbal Aschenbach never able to communicate directly with the boy, who is played by a silent dancer, not a singer. As we shall see again in the next chapter, when the body dances it takes center stage for audiences as well as other characters. And, as already noted, in Act 1, scene 7, we witness, through Aschenbach's eyes, boys playing on a beach being transformed into a scene of Hellenic beauty in action, the Games of Apollo. The countertenor Voice of Apollo asserts that "he who loves beauty / Worships me." The Chorus sings of Tadzio himself in Greek mythic terms, twice referring to him as "[n]o boy, but Phoebus of the golden hair." After this reinforced link to Apollo as Phoebus, the Chorus then ominously recalls the story of Hyacinthus "[b]asking in Apollo's rays" and doomed by a "beauty that will fatal prove." Tadzio may well be, in Aschenbach's eyes, a creature of Apollo, but, like Hyacinthus, he is also a Dionysian object of desire. The Voice of Apollo alternates with the Chorus as the boys play on the beach, and both articulate Platonic philosophical concepts of love and its relation to beauty. They sing of how Phaedrus learned from Socrates that "[b]eauty is the only form / Of spirit that our eyes can see." It is in this way that beauty can bring "reflections of Divinity" to the soul of the lover.[23] Tadzio begins to dance at this point to musical forms that have been called "simple, tonal, elegant – musical analogues for the beauty in simplicity and form which Aschenbach seeks and has found in Tadzio."[24]

Apollo then announces the start of the "feasts of the sun" in which his "devotees" will "contest / In strength, agility and skill / The body's praise." The boys then compete in a variety of ordered, organized sports: running, long jump, discus and javelin throwing, and wrestling, in all of which Tadzio proves victorious. This is a long scene, originally choreographed by Frederick Ashton, and early reviewers commented both on its length and its seeming athletic inappropriateness in an opera that was largely introspective and unphysical.[25] But the main reason why Tadzio has to win the pentathlon (he does not in the novella)[26] and why the dance scene must be of a certain length is that the audience must be carried utterly and thoroughly into Aschenbach's imaginative vision: we must literally come to see Tadzio as he does – as both the incarnation of formal classical beauty *and* as a very attractive physical creature, as both Apollonian in form *and* Dionysian in the bodily desires he arouses. Only then will we understand Aschenbach's response. After Tadzio's victory and Apollo's Platonic assertion that "[b]eauty is the mirror of spirit," Aschenbach the writer claims he feels inspired in artistic terms by the boy's body. He sings, "His pure lines shall form my style":

> When thought becomes feeling, feeling thought . . .
> When the mind bows low before beauty . . .
> When nature perceives the ecstatic moment . . .
> When genius leaves contemplation for one moment of reality . . .
> Then Eros is in the word.

Sung to the music of Tadzio's theme in what has been called an "extended lyrical outpouring," as we have seen, this final high-minded aestheticizing of Aschenbach's response is revealed for the sublimation it is when the boy then passes close by him.[27] Unable to speak, as he had intended to, Aschenbach breaks down when Tadzio smiles at him:

> Ah, don't smile like that!
> No one should be smiled at like that.
> (*realizing the truth at last*)
> I – love you.

These final shattering words are sung to an E major triad, the "natural" key of Aschenbach.[28] This would suggest that, in admitting his love, Aschenbach is finally being true to himself or "natural." Eros may be in the word, but words fail when confronted with the reality of the erotic body.[29]

Words have rarely failed Aschenbach: a most talkative man, he is contrasted in the opera to the silent dancing Tadzio not only by his loquaciousness but also by his music. As we have already seen, Britten chose to give his introspective Apollonian writer figure a cerebral mode of expression. He originally intended to have the diary entries Aschenbach reads to the audience simply spoken to piano accompaniment but changed his mind after hearing Peter Pears, for whom he was writing the role of Aschenbach, sing Schütz's *Passions.* He then substituted a "freely declamatory vocal line, with pitch notation but no rhythmic indications" to create the stark effect of "the driest of recitative."[30] In contrast to this music, Tadzio is provided with a very different, exotic sound world that is symbolic of both his inaccessibility and the Dionysian possibilities of Aschenbach's attraction to him. Mann turned to the language of sculpture and visual images to evoke classical beauty (as would be appropriate for German readers of the novella who had inherited the ethos of that Winckelmannian classical revival); Britten chose to create his own version of a Balinese gamelan-style music that was traditionally associated with dance.[31] This percussive Eastern music is both relatively foreign and exotic to Western ears and, conveniently, associated with the East, the place from which Dionysus came. Like Aschenbach, the audience becomes immersed in the sensuality of this new musical world. A motive, played on the vibraphone and unlike anything we have heard thus far, comes to be associated with Tadzio; to the flute (mythically associated with Dionysus) and (Apollonian-linked) harp that accompany his movements, Britten gradually adds more exotic percussive instruments like the xylophone and glockenspiel (all percussive, and thus Dionysian, by tradition).[32]

Critics have differed on the effect of this use of tuned percussion. For some, the instruments' ability to play tunes – but only "mechanically, un-expressively, un-emotionally, un-humanly" – makes the percussion symbolic of Tadzio's remoteness; to others this orchestration is a sign of the boy's "unearthly, beckoning beauty." To still others, the music of this most bodily of characters has an "oddly disembodied effect."[33] These paradoxical responses are reinforced by the complexity of the mythic context as much as by the effect of the music itself. Apollo, whose voice presides over the games, is (among other things) the god of form and order, of divine distance and awe. It may therefore be appropriate that when Aschenbach wants to see Tadzio as Apollonian, the boy's music should seem ethereal, even disembodied. The exotic and sensual quality that many others perceive in the same music (because of the percussive instruments) represents the barely submerged lure of Dionysian desire that Aschenbach will soon have to confront. At this point such paradoxes are merely appropriate expressions of the complications of Aschenbach's reactions to such perfect corporeal beauty.

Camille Paglia has linked the Greek "Apollonian idealization of form" to the figure of the beautiful boy as an Apollonian ideal; yet, she also notes, Dionysus too is traditionally presented as "a voluptuously appealing beautiful boy."[34] Once again, the two gods are less different in some ways than we might expect. The difference lies in the response to bodily beauty implied in each: Apollonian aesthetic contemplation and Dionysian sensual desire. As Aschenbach tries to blame the heat of the sun for his inability to address the boy on the beach, the Dionysian reality of his physical passion crashes down upon him. As we have already seen, the rest of the opera proceeds to complicate and contest the Apollonian and Platonic concepts of order, beauty, and love to which Aschenbach has clung.

✲ The Marking of the Unbeautiful

The heritage of Plato's teachings about beauty as visible form is clear on the operatic stage. As we shall see in even more detail in the next chapter with *Salome*, but as *Death in Venice* also clearly reveals, the beautiful body can be the object of the sexualized gaze of not only characters on stage but the audience as well. But what about the unbeautiful body? It is less the object of the gaze than of the stare, the look away, or the furtive glance.[35] If the beautiful body is characterized by proportion, the ugly body is traditionally defined by its lack. In the *Timaeus*, Plato writes that the "body which has a leg too long, or which is unsymmetrical in some other respect, is an unpleasant sight, and also, when doing its share of work, is much distressed and makes convulsive efforts, and often stumbles through awkwardness, and is the cause of infinite evil to its own self."[36] The unbeautiful is often marked in our language in terms of its failure of form: de*form*ed, mal*form*ed. For Aquinas, deformed or mutilated bodies were ugly, "for they lack the required proportion of parts to the whole."[37] In the Platonic and Neoplatonic contexts, form is a sign of virtue, and the body's external shape is an indicator of its possessor's moral state. An absence of proportion therefore is believed to signal an absence of moral good, if not the presence of utter depravity. Like Plato, Cicero wrote of the danger of an imperfect body prejudicing the soul; Saint Augustine pondered the theological meaning of monstrous births; Saint Gregory the Great felt that deformed bodies were "spiritually incapable of experiencing the beatific vision or transcendental thoughts." By the eighteenth century, the science of physiognomy sought to study the inner human through outer appearances, arguing that "[t]he beauty and deformity of the countenance is in a just and determinate proportion to the moral beauty and deformity of the man. The morally best, the most beautiful. The morally worst, the most deformed."[38]

The Platonic inheritance lives on in this persistent view of the body as the visible sign of the nature of the soul. In an adaptation of another Thomas Mann story, *Mario und der Zauberer*, Harry Somers and Rod Anderson in their *Mario and the Magician* (1992) offer in the character of the hunchbacked magician, Cipolla, an image of the ugly man as the evil, unscrupulous demagogue. By symbolizing in his body the absence of the symmetry and proportion associated with beauty and virtue, Cipolla incarnates the absence of order, both aesthetic and moral. His body is marked. So too, and in similar ways, are racialized bodies on the stage marked bodies. Monostatos, the black villain of Mozart/Schikaneder's *Die Zauberflöte* (1791), experiences feelings of love that are denied him because of what he calls his "hateful" race ("Weil ein Schwarzer hässlich ist") in a society where white explicitly defines the beautiful ("weiss ist schön"). Operatic versions of Shakespeare's *The Tempest* have also used the racially marked body to signify otherness: John Eaton and Andrew Porter's 1985 opera casts Caliban as a female jazz singer whose low *tessitura* part "is heavily influenced by traditional blues and is accompanied by a jazz trio."[39] As these examples make clear, the marked body on stage always engages in complex ways this specular politics, the politics of the visible. The body that is not perfect, that lacks proportion or admirable form, may be considered unbeautiful or ugly, but it may also be what we today call physically disabled.[40] We now live in an age where a sensitivity to differences in physical ability has challenged that Platonic insistence on the consonance of interior and exterior. But it has not yet been dismantled completely. Disabled people are still said to suffer what Robert Murphy calls a "contamination of identity." Their disability is seen to be embedded in the very fabric of their physical and moral personhood.[41] Despite all the work done in recent years on the cultural construction of the body, disability has been largely neglected as an area of investigation, in part because of the concentration on the body as a locus of pleasure. The new field of disability studies has begun to correct this situation, especially through its emphasis on the designation of disability as both a social and a specular process. Drawing on feminist theory's critique of the power relations based on social categories that are grounded in the body, it situates disability explicitly in the context of the marked body and the construction of its meanings.[42]

Both the visibility of the disabled and the responses that it can evoke – horror, pity, fear, compassion, avoidance – are in a sense produced not by the disabled body in itself but by the reactions in the viewer, argues Lennard Davis.[43] This becomes clear in an opera such as Richard Strauss and Hugo von Hofmannsthal's *Die Frau ohne Schatten* (1919), where we are presented with three disabled, dependent brothers who quarrel and fight with one another: they are referred to in the libretto as the Hunchback, the One-Eyed Brother, and the One-Armed Brother. The woman married to their single able-bodied sibling is repulsed by them and treats them like the animals she feels they are. Her husband attempts to placate her, telling her why they need to be kept in the family home. As children they were normal, he explains: "[H]atten blanke Augen, / grade Arme, / und einen glatten Rücken" [They had bright eyes, / straight arms, / and a smooth back]. The malformation of humanity comes from life, he implies, not birth. It is society that deforms, not nature. Likewise, disability is not simply a medical condition invoking discourses of intervention and service; it is as socially constructed as is the dominant bourgeois concept of normality itself.[44] Just as the operatic characters' identities in this opera or in *Francesca da Rimini* are reduced to the single named trait of their individual disability, so other physically different characters in opera, as we shall see, are frequently reduced to their essential moral baseness: villains on the stage, as in literature, film, or television, are often scarred, mutilated, or deformed. Their corporeal shape is used to elicit responses from others, including the audience.

There is an historical dimension to these responses, however. As Davis argues, in preindustrial society the disabled were integrated into the social fabric.[45] This is well illustrated in mid-seventeenth-century Venetian comic operas that draw on the *commedia dell'arte* tradition of the stupid servant type-character, Pulcinella, who is often portrayed as hunchbacked as well as mentally simple.[46] It is not rare in this type of opera to find a figure such as Demo, the stuttering hunchback of Francesco Cavalli and Giacinto Andrea Cicognini's *Giasone* (1649). Proud of his deformity, Demo thinks himself absolutely perfect:

> Son gobbo, son Demo,
> son bello, son bravo;
> il mondo m'è schiavo.
> Del diavolo non temo,
> son vago, grazioso,

lascivo, amoroso.
S'io ballo, s'io canto,
s'io suono la lira,
ogni dama per me arde e so, so,
so, so arde, e so, so, so . . .

[I'm a hunchback, I'm Demo,
I'm handsome, I'm brave;
the world is my slave.
I don't fear the devil,
I'm charming, I'm graceful,
wanton, amorous.
If I dance, if I sing,
if I play the lyre,
Every woman burns for me and lang, lang,
lang, lang, burns and lang, lang, lang . . .]

His stuttering prevents him from completing his final "sospira" (languishes), but the fact of his social role is firmly established, even if the audience laughs at what they might see as the ironic disjunction between self-image and reality. In a similar way, Rigoletto, as we shall see shortly, is granted a social function as jester in the sixteenth-century court of Mantua.

In postindustrial society, Davis claims, this integration is replaced by the segregation and ostracization of the disabled, thanks to notions of standardization and normality defined by eighteenth- and nineteenth-century ideas of nationality, race, and gender. These ideas would, in some senses, culminate in the eugenics movement and its desire to breed out defective traits in the name of perfecting the body and thus the race and the nation.[47] It is not surprising that disability studies has turned to Erving Goffman's work in *Stigma: Notes on the Management of Spoiled Identity* to investigate the social process that makes the physically different into the deviant. Goffman implicitly points to the Platonic heritage when he notes that the Greek word "stigma" refers to the "bodily signs designed to expose something universal and bad about the moral status of the signifier."

These signs were usually made deliberately and ritualistically to mark "a blemished person, ritually polluted." This concept is given a positive context in the Christianizing of the idea in the stigmata of the saints or of Christ himself.

Today, however, as Goffman explains, the term "stigma" usually refers to "the situation of the individual who is disqualified from full social acceptance." Both ugliness and physical deformity constitute types of stigma, for they represent "an undesired differentness from what we had anticipated." Such a physical attribute threatens "the pleasure we might otherwise take in the company of its possessor."[48] As Andry wrote in the eighteenth century in his *Orthopaedia*, "[w]e are born for one another, and ought to shun having any thing about us that is shocking."[49] The malformed body disturbs system and order; in Kristeva's terms, it is the sign of the abject.[50] For this reason, in the Old Testament, the man who is blind, lame, "brokenfooted, or brokenhanded" or the one who has a flat nose "or any thing superfluous" is forbidden to approach the altar; also excluded are the "crookbackt, or a dwarf, or that hath a blemish in his eye, or be scurvy, or scabbed, or hath his stones broken" (Leviticus 21:18–20). These too were felt to defile and profane the beauty of the holy space.

What Goffman's theory and this long history both suggest is that, if beauty is in the eye of the beholder, then the negative responses of the beholder also produce the pejorative sense of difference experienced and then internalized by the unbeautiful. The internalized anxiety and hostility, the "social withdrawal and abnormal personality traits – produced by emotional reaction to physical deformity" has been called the Quasimodo complex. This has also been defined as "the self-perception of concealed and unconcealed deformities engendered from the implicit and explicit reactions of others."[51] This theory of the defining power of the stare of judgmental society is named after the one-eyed, bow-legged, deaf hunchback character from Victor Hugo's 1831 novel, *Notre-Dame de Paris, 1482*, who comes to feel the full weight of his physical ugliness only when the beautiful gypsy dancer, Esmeralda, to whom he is devoted, recoils at the sight of him, unable to understand how a body so awkwardly designed could possible exist.[52] But Hugo's presentation of Quasimodo's physical presence and its multiple meanings is much more complex than this limiting characterization would suggest, and it is worth considering that complexity in some detail in order to understand one of the major successful challenges to the Platonic tradition's denigration of the unbeautiful: the Romantic concept of the grotesque. Obviously, Western art and philosophy abound with alternative contestations, but it is Hugo's particular sense of the grotesque that makes possible the specifically operatic challenge.

✤ The Romantic Grotesque

Victor Hugo's influence on nineteenth- and twentieth-century opera is clear in the amazing number of librettos that were derived from his works. What was specifically important to opera's development was the fact that he and his followers "advanced *le grotesque* as the epitome of then-modern art, the antithesis of a decorum-defined classicism they called *le sublime*."[53] What defined the life-affirming (if transgressive) grotesque was not ugliness itself (as in the more commonplace usage of the word) but, rather, a coming together of elements that did not match (such as appearance and reality, or ugliness and beauty), creating "the sense that things that should be kept apart are fused together."[54] As Hugo wrote in his preface to *Cromwell*, the world is not uniformly beautiful, the ugly exists alongside the beautiful as the other side of gracefulness, and the task of the modern artist is to document this polarity – as he himself had done in Quasimodo and Esmeralda.[55] The grotesque was also tied both to physicality and to drama for Hugo: bodies visible on stage represent the essence of the tragic and the comic, and, for that reason, the deformed and the ugly must be presented in the theater along with the beautiful and the decorous.[56] His novel *Notre-Dame de Paris, 1482* demonstrates well how the discourses of the ugly and the beautiful still act as foils for one another as they had done in Platonic thought, but now to utterly different effect. The story's narrator offers the reader a detailed description of both Quasimodo's physical attributes and the response of beholders to them. He ends with a remark that, despite his deformities, the hunchback had a certain air of fearsome energy and courage, and this is said to be a strange exception to the generally accepted "universal rule" that asserted that strength, like beauty, results from harmony of parts.[57] But it is Esmeralda's radiant beauty that is the real foil for Quasimodo's ugliness: it is described as a more-than-human beauty that can lure a handsome man away from his fiancée and a priest from his God. (See figure 5.)

While Esmeralda is admired (even by those for whom her gypsy race provides an impediment), Quasimodo is feared because of his strength, his agility, and his temper. People feel that the spirit lodged in his misshapen body must itself be deformed and incomplete. But the novel makes clear that he has been formed in both moral and psychic terms by society, especially by the responses of women, who equate him with the devil and consider him to be as wicked as he is ugly. The narrator does not deny that the spirit might atrophy in a defective body, as he puts it, but makes it clear that Quasimodo was vicious because he avoided people, and he avoided people because he was ugly and therefore had to face the jeers and rejection of others.[58] He had found nothing but hatred around him as he grew up, and, as the text explains, he had finally picked up the weapon of hate with which he had been wounded in order to fight back. When he endures his painful time in the stocks, cruelly and publicly mocked by all (especially by the women), it is Esmeralda's act of mercy and kindness that sows the seeds of redemption in his soul. Described in this scene with inhuman, grotesque, animalistic metaphors, Quasimodo is later transformed when he, in turn, rescues Esmeralda from the public scaffold and takes her to the sanctuary of the cathedral: he is said at that moment to have a beauty all his own. He feels august and strong, able to look that rejecting society in the face and intervene for good in its machinations.[59] But notice that the discourse of beauty is indeed invoked here to give a sense of moral redemption: the Platonic tradition has not, perhaps, been destroyed, even if it has been challenged.

But challenged it has been: by the grotesque coming together of Quasimodo and Esmeralda in life and in death (years later, his skeleton, with its curved spinal column, head down between the shoulder blades, and one short leg, is found with hers). The tradition has also been contested within the novel itself by the figure of Phoebus (the other name for Apollo), the beautiful young man whom Esmeralda loves but who is morally corrupt and faithless. Quasimodo is shocked when he learns that being handsome on the outside is seemingly enough to win the love of a woman. He sings a song warning that the heart of a handsome young man might really be misshapen, but then adds:

> Ce qui n'est pas beau a tort d'être;
> La beauté n'aime que la beauté . . .
> La beauté est parfaite,
> La beauté peut tout,
> La beauté est la seule chose qui n'existe pas à demi.

> [Whatever is without beauty is wrong to exist,
> Beauty only loves beauty . . .
> Beauty is perfect,
> Beauty can do anything,
> Beauty is the only thing that does not live by halves.][60]

As the very existence of this song suggests, Hugo was not unaware of the operatic possibilities of his novel. Indeed, he wrote a libretto that was put to music by Louise Bertin, but the opera was not a success, perhaps because the complexity of the long novel is not easily reproduced on stage and in song. In the opera, the tenor Quasimodo is given an aria in which he sings:

> Triste ébauche,
> Je suis gauche,
> Je suis laid . . .

Dans mon âme
Je suis beau!

[Sad shape,
I am clumsy,
I am ugly . . .
In my soul
I am beautiful!]

Yet somehow, even with the music this might well fail to capture the complicated mutual implication of beauty and ugliness that the novel provides. Reduced to a minor character, Quasimodo pales in importance next to the beautiful Esmeralda and the story of her love for the now more conventional – that is, morally positive – and handsome Phoebus. Fittingly, Hugo named the opera version *Esmeralda*. The power of the grotesque had come from the novel's jarring conjunction of the ugly and the beautiful and of the equally jarring disjunction of the beautiful exterior of Phoebus and his inner corruption. If the inevitable simplification in this one operatic version destroyed that power, then the same is true of the numerous other operas that were written on Hugo's text, none of which has ever been successful for long on the stage.[61] In each of them, despite their different selection of plot details and endings, the deformed and dangerous Quasimodo appears, and in each he is redeemed by the beautiful Esmeralda. In none, however, is the real power of the grotesque retained; in none is the complexity of the causes of Quasimodo's alienation explored.

Where that power is captured and that causality is explored on (an admittedly odd version of) the operatic stage is in Philip Glass's *La Belle et la bête* (1994). Glass projects Jean Cocteau's 1946 film of this name onto a screen at the back of the stage. He replaces the soundtrack with his own music, which is played and sung live, more or less synchronized with the screen's actions and words.[62] The singers' bodies are on stage but function more as instruments than actors; when not singing to the audience, they turn and watch the film. The orchestra too is visible on stage in this self-reflexive "opera-tizing" of the surrealist film that retells Mme de Beaumont's famous fairy story of the beautiful girl and the half man/half beast figure who loves her and keeps her captive in his magical realm. A victim of the Quasimodo complex, La Bête knows that he is repulsive to La Belle in his ugliness but insists that his heart is good, even if he is a monster. La Belle reminds him that there are many men who are more monstrous than he is but who hide it. When he asserts that she flatters him the way she would an animal, without thinking she replies that he *is* an animal. Injured to the quick, he leaves and returns covered with blood from a recent kill; he then begs her forgiveness for being the beast, the animal that he is ("d'être 'Bête'"). The beautiful woman finally comes to realize that the monster is indeed good and that it is she and others who are monstrous. When she can finally look upon him not with repulsion but with love, he is transformed into a handsome man, telling her that love can make a man a beast but it can also make an ugly man handsome. ("L'amour peut faire qu'un homme devient bête. / L'amour peut faire aussi qu'un homme laid devienne beau.")

Until the end, the opera and film retain the grotesque fusing together of the dichotomies of the monstrous and the beautiful. In the final moments, however, the implied moral and aesthetic validation of the grotesque seems to be undone in the beast's transformation: in true Platonic fashion, the good soul must inhabit a beautiful body. Implicitly, the negative view of the unbeautiful therefore persists here, as indeed it has done in many other discourses before and after. It can certainly be found in nineteenth-century philosophical treatises, for instance: Schopenhauer tried to account for the force behind the individual sexual instinct in terms of a rejection of age, disease, and deformity. Singled out for repudiation were such things as "a stunted, dumpy, short-legged figure" and "a limping gait."[63] In theological discourses of the same time, bodily malformations were often seen as signs of divine punishment. And the strong medical interest in teratology (the study of physical abnormalities of development) flourished in this period and, with it, both a new desire to define the "normal" and a greater use of the increased capabilities of imaging (such as photographing) the abnormal as well as the normal.[64] But the evaluative weight was unchanged: giants were deemed evil, and dwarfs were demonized as trolls. It was, of course, this kind of negative evaluation that fed entropic theories of racial degeneration or that linked criminality and moral deviance to physiognomy.[65] Medical and moral discourses came together with powerful force.

One of the best-known medical cases is that of John Merrick, called the Elephant Man. In 1884 Frederick Treves, a lecturer in anatomy, saw Merrick on public display in an English shop. As he later wrote about his response to the pictorial sign announcing the exhibit, "[t]here was nothing about it of the pitiableness of the misshapened [*sic*] or the deformed, nothing of the grotesqueness of the freak, but merely the loathsome insinuation of a man being turned into an animal." In short, the terrifying situation of La Bête has moved from the fairy tale to real life. But so too has his final redemption, at least in metaphoric terms, for Treves comes to the conclusion that, "[a]s a specimen of humanity, Merrick was ignoble and repulsive; but the spirit of Merrick, if it could be seen in the form of the living, would assume the figure of an upstanding and heroic man, smooth browed and clean of limb, and with eyes that flashed undaunted courage."[66] In language, at least, the Platonic ideal is again asserted, as Treves comes to respect Merrick's courage and goodness.

ꙮ The Not-Quite-Human and the Not-Quite-Manly

This motif of the not-quite-human does not always appear in this positive context of real or even metaphorical redemption, as Goffman too has noted and as the operatic stage has explored.[67] From Oscar Wilde's *The Birthday of the Infanta*, Alexander Zemlinsky and Georg C. Klaren created yet another musical dramatization of this theme.[68] Changing Wilde's child into a beautiful but cruel young woman, they set up the conditions in *Der Zwerg* (1922) for the grotesque tension of opposites: the Infanta is presented with a dwarf as a birthday present. It may be true that this dwarf is not Wilde's "charming natural monster" but a "much more complex and indeed civilized being,"[69] yet in the opera he is clearly considered to be like an animal and thus a pet:

> Er hinkt, die Haare sind feurige
> Borsten, der Kopf hockt zwischen
> Schultern, die zu hoch. Ihn beugt eines
> Höckers Last, klein und verwachsen
> die ganze Gestalt, vielleicht kaum über
> zwanzig alt, vielleicht alt wie die Sonne.

> [He limps, his hairs are fiery
> bristles, his head squats between his
> shoulders, which are too high. The weight
> of a hump bows him down, small and
> deformed is the whole figure, perhaps barely
> over twenty years old, perhaps as old as the sun.]

What amazes the court is that the dwarf (after whom the opera is generically named) has no idea of his own ugliness. Therefore, when the Haushofmeister ironically introduces him as a hero, a knight, as well-shaped and beautiful as Narcissus, there is much laughter at the dwarf's expense, laughter he does not understand. The dwarf's music is often mock heroic, as if commenting on his delusion; so too are the direct textual echoes of Wagner's *Lohengrin*, for the dwarf sees himself as a "Ritter aus fernem Land." He wants to marry the Infanta and be her protecting knight; being called a frog and a turkey-cock does not seem to give him any hint of the perceived inappropriateness of his desires. Then, to violent dynamic contrasts in the music, the dwarf sees himself in a mirror and screams: "Es ist nicht denkbar, dass es so hässliches auf einer schönen Erde gibt!" [It isn't conceivable that anything so ugly could exist on a beautiful earth!].

Confirming his horrific (self-)discovery, the Infanta laughs and calls him an ugly, deformed creature, a monster, not a human: "Du bist ein Scheusal, bist kein Mensch!" In despair, he cries out that he is a dwarf and he loves her ("Ich bin ein Zwerg und liebe dich"), but she only wants him as a living plaything, a pet. Begging her again and again to tell him that he is actually beautiful, he collapses as the Infanta testily complains that her toy is already broken. The opera ends with what one critic calls "a final lurid wrench, a massive C minor chord in place of the D minor that might have been expected," as if the tonal plan of the work had also been "deformed."[70] Thematically too there is no redemption; there is only tragedy in this drama of dehumanization.

In opera, with its convention of strong narratives of love and death, the reduction of the unbeautiful to the less-than-human often, as with the dwarf, takes the form of a desexualization, even within a marriage situation. The grotesque marital pairing of the beautiful and the ugly has its mythical echoes in Venus and the limping Vulcan, of course. In Aare Merikanto and Aino Ackté's Finnish opera *Juha* (1922; 1963), there is a love triangle consisting of a handsome young pair and an old man named Juha, who is described as "kanttura," a word that in Finnish means clumsy and twisted but with connotations of animality.[71] He refers to himself as lame, crippled, bow-legged. It is he who is married to the young and beautiful Marja, who falls for the stranger whom Juha describes as well proportioned, slim, and handsome: he is said to be strong, straight, and graceful as a pine tree, with legs as straight and slim as an elk's. There are clearly age and fitness differences here but also implicit racial ones, since Juha is Finnish and the stranger, Shemeikka, is Karelian/Russian. The older, lame, desexualized man, who is reduced to being called a decrepit old bungler, is left in the end with no illusions about his beautiful wife's infidelity or about her handsome lover's moral corruption. With nothing to live for, he commits suicide.

The problematic sexuality of the unbeautiful man is most clear, perhaps, in *Porgy and Bess* (1935), composed by George Gershwin, with Du Bose Heyward and Ira Gershwin providing the libretto. As women pass him by on stage, the lame Porgy sings, "When Gawd make cripple, He mean him to be lonely." Yet it is Porgy, "a cripple and a beggar," who takes in the beautiful but scandalous Bess, abandoned by the others when her lover, Crown, is on the run after committing a murder. At this point, Porgy's tune literally changes. He may have "plenty o' nuttin'," but he is happy because "I got my gal." While the local women feel that "dat woman ain't de kin' for to make a cripple happy," Porgy expresses his newfound happiness again and again, and it is always in terms connected to being with Bess:

Two is strong where one is feeble;
man an' woman livin', workin',
sharin' grief an' sharin' laughter,
an' love like Augus' sun.

Bess knows that her affection is what keeps him alive: "He's a cripple an' needs my love." Later, having been reviled as less than a man and physically knocked down by Crown, Bess's younger lover, Porgy is ready when Crown returns for Bess: he stabs and then strangles him, laughing "Bess, Bess, you got a man now, you got Porgy." The elimination of this threat to his newly won masculine identity, however, is not enough to keep Bess with him, and the lame man is left alone at the end once again, heading off in desperation to New York City to try to find her: "Widout her I can't go on."

On the operatic stage, the gender politics appear clear: most deformed or disabled characters are gendered male, and in each case animal imagery is associated with what is presented as their less-than-human and less-than-manly identities in the eyes of others. Significantly, however, in each the inner moral evil that their ugly exteriors are assumed to reveal is linked to a refusal of love by a beautiful woman and a subsequent desexualization (at least in her, if not his, eyes). For example, in *Das Rheingold* (1869), Richard Wagner's first opera of the cycle of *Der Ring des Nibelungen*, the clumsy Nibelung dwarf, Alberich, comes out of the darkness of Nibelheim to play in the bright waters of the river with the Rhinedaughters. His vocal line contains awkward, reverse-accented dotted rhythms that reinforce both his awkward physical movements and the Rhinedaughters' resulting disgust and name calling: "Pfui! Der Garstige!" [Ugh! The foul creature!].[72] It quickly becomes clear that Alberich has amorous designs on the beautiful, graceful female creatures who tease and mock him. Finally, one of them tells him:

Pfui, du haariger,
höck'riger Geck!
Schwarzes, schwieliges
Schwefelgezwerg!
Such' dir ein Friedel,
dem du gefällst!

[Ugh, you hairy,
hunchbacked fool!
Black, callused,
sulfurous dwarf!
Look for a lover
who will please you!]

The implication here is: a lover who looks like you, not like us. Another Rhinedaughter claims to admire his beauty and then, with irony, describes his ugliness:

Deinen stechended Blick,
deinen struppigen Bart,
o säh' ich ihn, fasst' ich ihn stets!
Deines stachligen Haares
strammes Gelock
umflöss' es Flosshilde ewig!
Deine Krötengestalt,
deiner Stimme Gekrächz,
o dürft' ich staunend und stumm,
sie nur hören und seh'n!

[Your piercing eyes,
your rough beard,

may I always see and hold them!
    Your prickly hair's
    unruly locks,
may they flow around Flosshilde forever!
    Your toadlike shape,
    the croak of your voice,
O could I, astonished and mute,
hear and see only them.]

Alberich's pain at this ironic derision and rejection is evident in both his words – "Wehe! ach wehe! / O Schmerz! O Schmerz!" [Woe, O woe! / O pain! O pain!] – and in his music, with its descending chromatic sequence. Their deceitful teasing both enrages him and fills him with desire:

Wie ihr auch lacht und lügt,
lüstern lechz' ich nach euch,
une eine muss mir erliegen!

[Though you may laugh and lie,
lusting, I long for you,
and one of you must yield to me!]

But the desiring, toadlike, unnatural dwarf is not allowed to love or even to lust after the beautiful, graceful, natural, fishlike Rhine-daughters; it is their continuing mockery of his ugliness and the desexualization it implies (in their eyes) that, in the end, drive Alberich to choose power and evil over love: the magical Rhine gold can be fashioned into the ring of power only by someone who has forsworn love, and it is this course of action that Alberich chooses. In so doing, he at last makes his exterior ugliness consonant with his new interior malevolence. But the fact that he has been driven to this state by others – as was Quasimodo – conditions the moral guilt as it subtly challenges the Platonic equation of inner and outer. At this point, the audience in fact may well come to sympathize with Alberich, as we might with the giant Fasolt who loves the

68

beautiful goddess Freia: again, however, love is not allowed between mismatched grotesque opposites.

In the third opera of the cycle, *Siegfried* (1876), Alberich's brother, Mime, comes in for the same kind of comparative pejorative evaluation, but this time the ideal against which he is measured is the young hero Siegfried. The Nibelung smith, like Vulcan and the Nordic Völund of *The Poetic Edda*, limps, but he is also ugly, as the handsome Siegfried unkindly points out:

> Grade so garstig
> griesig und grau,
> klein und krumm,
> höckrig und hinkend,
> mit hängenden Ohren,
> triefigen Augen.

> [Just as ugly
> disgusting and gray,
> small and crooked,
> hunchbacked and limping,
> with hanging ears,
> dripping eyes.]

And, as Marc Weiner has put it, like the Rhinedaughters' music, "Siegfried's music moves evenly, but the Nibelungs' does not. It limps."[73]

The traditional interpretation of Alberich and Mime in the *Ring* is that they are inherently evil creatures, but the text is much more subtle and suggests a more complex invocation of the grotesque and thus the reconsideration provoked by it of the Platonic theory of beauty and goodness. Like Hugo's Quasimodo, Wagner's Alberich is driven to evil by the rejection and derision of others and by the dehumanizing and desexualizing at work in such responses. Therefore, what Plato would argue to be the inherent consonance of inner character and outer appearance is challenged, and the politics of beauty, here at least, are uncovered for what disability studies and feminism have argued they are: an ideological construct. As Francis Bacon wrote in his 1625 essay on deformity, the malformed will seek to "free themselves from scorn" either "by virtue or malice." That the turn to malice might make for more dramatic stage action is clear from this common theme in Western theater from the seventeenth century onward. Certainly the operatic examples suggest the power of this theme, but also its continuing and subtle attacks on the Platonic tradition.[74]

We can see this same kind of challenge in Ruggero Leoncavallo's one-act *verismo* opera *Pagliacci* (1892), in which the hunchbacked character Tonio provides another instance of the desiring but thwarted man whose hatred turns to evil as he attempts to avenge his rejection by a beautiful woman. This opera tells the story of a troupe of *commedia dell'arte* clowns, and it is self-reflexively framed by Tonio, who speaks as the incarnated voice of the Prologue. Tonio stresses that what we are about to see is how people actually act, even though it is a play; we shall witness how people really love, but also the sad fruits of hatred. In an anti-Platonic warning, perhaps, he specifically enjoins us not to be distracted by the characters' outer theatrical costumes but to think instead of their inner souls.

As the opera itself opens, the traveling players are introduced one by one to the village by their leader, Canio:

Vedrete di Tonio
Tremar la carcassa,
E quale matassa
D'intrighi ordirà.

[You will see Tonio's
Big bulk tremble,
And what a tangle
Of intrigues he'll devise.]

We soon learn that Tonio is in love with Nedda, the beautiful wife of the jealous older Canio. She, like everyone else, cruelly mocks the hunchback. His response to her contemptuous rejection of him is both moving and revealing, but it is preceded by a chromatic, tonally undetermined, ominous bass line:

So ben che difforme,
Contorto son io;
Che desto soltanto
Lo scherno e l'orror.
Eppure ha il pensiero
Un sogno, un desio,
Un palpito il cor!
Allor che sdegnosa
Mi passi d'accanto,
Non sai tu che pianto
Mi spreme il dolor,
Perché, mio malgrado,
Subito ho l'incanto,
M'ha vinto l'amor!
(*appressandosi*)
Oh! Lasciami, lasciami
Or dirti . . .

[I know well that I am deformed,
And misshapen;
That I arouse only
Derision and horror.
Yet my thought is
Of a dream, a desire,
A heartbeat!
So when you disdainfully
Pass me by,
You don't know what cry
The pain wrings from me,
Because, despite myself,
At once I feel the spell,
And love has conquered me.
(*approaching*)

Oh! Let me, let me
Now tell you . . .]

Nedda interrupts him playfully, laughing at his pain and his passion, and tells him to continue his declaration of love later that night when they are on stage together. His response marks his Alberich-like transformation:

No, è qui che voglio dirtelo,
E tu m'ascolterai,
Che t'amo e ti desidero,
E che tu mia sarai!

[No, it's here that I want to tell you,
And you shall hear me,
That I love you and desire you,
And that you shall be mine!]

Her reaction to his declaration of love, his attempts to kiss her, and his implied threats is to offer to box his ears, but Tonio warns her that she will regret her scorn. When she takes a whip to him, calling him "Miserabile," he swears she will pay for her actions and words. As he leaves, Nedda articulates the Platonic doctrine of inner and outer, without understanding that it is her mockery and rejection that have helped drive him to this evil:

Aspide! va.
Ti sei svelato ormai,
Tonio lo scemo!
Hai l'animo
Siccome il corpo tuo
Difforme . . . lurido!

[Viper! go.
Now you have revealed yourself,
Tonio the fool!
You have a soul
Like your body
Deformed . . . filthy!]

Using the dehumanizing animal imagery that so often accompanies desexualization and deformity, Nedda tells her lover, Silvio, in the next scene that Tonio has become dangerous in his bestial frenzy ("bestial / Delirio") but that she cooled the ardor of the filthy dog ("cane immondo") with her whip. It is when Nedda tells Tonio to his face that he disgusts her and makes her sick ("Mi fai schifo e ribrezzo") that he can say with mordant irony that he is at last happy ("Oh, non sai come / Lieto ne son!") and so can exact his fatal revenge on her and her lover through the jealous Canio.[75]

✈ Reconsidering the Platonic Heritage

This example of the staged grotesque offers yet another potent reminder of the social causes of moral deformation: there is no *necessary* Platonic correlation here between an ugly body and an evil character. These operas can all be read as showing how social rejection can induce hatred and anger. But societies under stress have contributed to the cultural linking of physical abnormality and evil in still other ways, that is, through scapegoating. As René Girard argues: "Physical deformity must correspond to a real human characteristic, a real infirmity. . . . Moral monstrosity, by contrast, actualizes the tendency of all persecutors to project the monstrous results of some calamity or public or private misfortune onto some poor unfortunate who, by being infirm or a foreigner, suggests a certain affinity to the monstrous."[76] The scapegoating of the physically abnormal has a long and inglorious history, one that is reflected in the theatrical popularity of the hunchback figure as a symbol of exclusion.[77] Hugo's fascination with this figure can be see in *Notre-Dame de Paris, 1482*, but also in his play of the same period, *Le Roi s'amuse* (1832). Based on an imagined episode in the life of Francis I of France, it was censored after only one performance and not revived for fifty years. What was as shocking to audiences as the scandalous portrait of the royal court, it seems, was the presentation on stage of the jester Triboulet as both a hunchback and the father of a beautiful daughter in a play in which the animality and ugliness of human physicality clashed violently with the language and style of elegance.[78] Hugo himself defended both the morality of his play and his grotesque character, arguing that Triboulet was deformed and a jester and *that* is what had made him evil: he hated the king and courtiers because of their rank, but he also hated anyone who was not misshapen like him.[79] The deformity was necessary, in other words, to motivate the work's social critique. The playwright was quick to point out the moral side of the drama: for his evil, Triboulet is cursed by a man he has mocked (a father whose daughter was dishonored by the handsome but unscrupulous king), and in the end Triboulet is punished. The reason his punishment is so very moving is that this deformed jester is also a man with a heart, a loving father.

When Giuseppe Verdi and Francesco Maria Piave decided to compose an opera based on this play, they ran into similar problems with the censors. First called *La Maledizione* (The curse), what we now know as *Rigoletto* (1851) required a change of setting to the more distant sixteenth-century Mantua. But the opera also encountered negative reactions to the very idea of having a hunchbacked jester as the protagonist of a tragedy. This was both a class and an appearance issue: the heroic world of tragedy was by convention both aristocratic and beautiful. Verdi's response to the first rewriting of Piave's libretto that *did* pass the censors was one of fury. As he wrote to the director and impresario of Teatro La Fenice in Venice in 1850:

> I see that they have avoided making Triboletto [later Rigoletto] ugly and a hunchback!! A hunchback who sings? Why not? . . . Will it be effective? I don't know. But, I repeat, if I don't know then they who propose this change don't know either. I thought it would be beautiful to portray this extremely deformed and ridiculous character who is inwardly passionate and full of love. I chose the subject precisely because of these qualities and these original traits. And if they are cut, I shall no longer be able to set it to music. If anyone says to me that I can leave my notes as they are for this new plot, I reply that I don't understand this kind of thinking, and I say frankly that my

music, whether beautiful or ugly, is never written in a vacuum, and that I always try to give it character.[80]

The end result was that the censor allowed the jester to remain deformed, though the first Rigoletto is said to have been afraid of being an object of audience derision for appearing as a hunchback.[81]

That the audience did not laugh but instead was moved by the disabled man's plight is a matter of record, even if some early critics still lamented the "French" taste for the grotesque conjunction of beauty and deformation.[82] Verdi persisted in thinking that both his subject and its sympathetic treatment were revolutionary. And so they were, and this could be seen in the changes from the French original, as well as in the (then still) daring portrayal of the grotesque on the operatic stage. Perhaps in part because of Verdi's music, Rigoletto is considerably more moving a character than Triboulet, and the result is that, instead of being the major instigator of evil in the court, he is seen more as its victim: "Rigoletto engages in acts of cruelty and hatred not merely because of his deformity or occupation, but in reaction to the contempt and degradation with which he is treated."[83] A typical scapegoat, he is both inside that community and excluded from it, distanced by his special isolating identity;[84] when the courtiers are angered by the actions of the handsome Duke, they take it out on his admittedly sharp-tongued jester, the target with the marked body. When one of the courtiers tells the others he has learned great news about Rigoletto, he is interrupted at once by mocking questions: "Perduto ha la gobba? Non è più difforme?" [Has he lost his hump? Is he no longer deformed?]. No, he reports, the news is even stranger than that: "Il gobbo in Cupido or s'è trasformato!" [The hunchback has been transformed into Cupid] and has a lover! The other courtiers register their shock in terms of the monstrous: "Quel mostro Cupido!" As we have seen, this desexualization is a constant in dramatized representations of hunchbacks.

Given this context, we are not too surprised in the next scene to find Rigoletto showing the spite and heartlessness that such mockery and social rejection can induce in their victims. Even the Duke finds his jester's verbal cruelty to the courtiers excessive at times; nevertheless, Rigoletto feels safe in his lord's protection. The irony, of course, is that it is the charming and handsome Duke himself from whom Rigoletto (and his beautiful daughter) will soon need protection. This vulnerability is signaled by the entry of Monterone, who protests the Duke's ravishing of his daughter; utterly unsympathetic, Rigoletto mocks his paternal pain and anger (in music "deformed" by chromatic tones) and is cursed for it. ("Tu che d'un padre ridi al dolore, / Sii maledetto!")[85] As the opera progresses, the music of the curse comes to be closely related to the music associated with Rigoletto's deformity: diminished seventh chords, ascending and descending chromatic lines, and broken melodic lines with rests and irregular rhythms.[86]

It is not until two scenes later that the audience realizes the deep and terrible irony of this moment and of the curse, for Rigoletto himself is the father of a daughter, Gilda, whom he loves deeply. Yet he does not seem to have identified in any way with Monterone or his pain, perhaps because he believes he can keep the sordid world of the court separated from that of his sequestered daughter.[87] That he cannot is one source of the tragedy; the other is his own scapegoated position in the court. In Act 1, scene 8, Rigoletto is given a moving aria full of bitter invective in which he denounces both society and nature for making him the nasty and cruel creature he has become:

O uomini! O natura!
Vil, scellerato mi faceste voi! . . .
O rabbia! . . . essere difforme! . . .
O rabbia! . . . essere buffone! . . .
Non dover, non poter altro che ridere! . . .
Il retaggio d'ogni uom m'è tolto . . . il pianto!

[O men! O nature!
Vile, wicked you made me! . . .
O rage! . . . To be deformed! . . .
O rage! . . . To be a jester! . . .
Not to be allowed or able to do anything but laugh! . . .
All men's inheritance is taken from me . . . to weep!]

In the next lines he contrasts both his person and his position to those of the Duke, who is young, charming, powerful, and handsome ("[g]iovin, giocondo, si possente, bello"). But he in turn blames not his spoiled and unscrupulous protector but rather the courtiers for his evil ("Se iniquo son, per cagion vostra è solo").

When his thoughts turn to his beloved daughter, a completely new lyricism appears in his music, and the "violent, rising attacks and agitated orchestration" of the invective disappear.[88] As he tells Gilda of her deceased mother's surprising love for him, his vocal line moves from the uneven and fragmented (when he describes himself as alone, deformed, poor) to the legato of that selfless love:

Ella sentìa, quell'angelo,
Pietà delle mie pene,
Solo, difforme, povero,
Per compassion mi amò.

[She felt, that angel,
Pity for my sufferings,
Alone, deformed, poor,
She loved me out of compassion.]

The contrast between the beautiful Gilda and her ugly father is brought to the fore by both the courtiers' plot to abduct her (for they still think she is his mistress) and by her attraction to a handsome youth who turns out to be the Duke in disguise. In the opera, as in the play, the beautiful young woman continues to love the Duke even after her abduction and the subsequent loss of her virtue to him. The text makes clear that this is in part simply because he is so handsome: in the play, she calls him "brave, illustre et beau," but in the opera he simply becomes "[b]ello e fatale." It is explicitly because of his Apollo-like good looks ("Somiglia un Apollo quel giovane") that he is spared in the end and Gilda becomes the sacrificial victim to her love and his physical beauty as she is murdered in his stead by the man hired by her vengeful father. The fact that he is not worth her sacrifice, that his corrupt inner reality does not match his attractive outer appearance, is part of both the dramatic horror and the grotesque's serious challenge to the Platonic tradition.

Given this establishment of visible extremes with significant thematic resonance, it is crucial that the casting for this opera be done with care. The Duke should be handsome, as Gilda should indeed be beautiful. Yet modern productions of *Rigoletto* are sometimes tempted to downplay the physical deformity of the protagonist – as did Jonathan Miller's famous updating of the opera to a 1950s New York setting. Rigoletto became the joking barman in a Mafioso club; his hump was slight, though his limp was noticeable. Here his difference or otherness was signaled mostly by his very sharp tongue. Sometimes, however, Rigoletto's physical body is emphasized, as when Nicholas Muni put him in a stylized wheelchair. When this production was first put on stage by the Canadian Opera Company in 1992, it was met with considerable discomfort by an audience sensitized to disability issues: suddenly people could not distance themselves from the character and his physical plight as easily as they might have wished.[89] The use of the wheelchair, however, made for at least one intensely dramatic stage moment: as Rigoletto approached the palace room in which Gilda was being held by the Duke, he threw himself in despair out of the chair onto the flight of stairs that rendered that room inaccessible to him because of his disability. Yet another cause of the unease that any production of this opera can evoke, however, is simply its lack of fit with still powerful Platonic notions. The presence of the handsome but vicious Duke belies the theory of the consonance of external and internal, as much as it does the conjunction of beauty and goodness. The foil for the Duke is the equally beautiful but this time morally good Gilda. She continues to love him because, unlike her vengeful father, she can forgive. That Rigoletto cannot is his – and her – tragedy.

The deconstructing of these familiar Platonic extremes is disturbing, in part because this challenge of the grotesque introduces ambiguities into a once stable system of dichotomies. In *Purity and Danger: An Analysis of the Concepts of Pollution and Taboo*, Mary Douglas has written of humans' social need to classify and systematize into ordered relations. Disability theorists like Rosemarie Garland Thomson have extended her concept of dirt (defined as "that which must not be included if a pattern is to be maintained")[90] into the idea of "social dirt" represented by human disabilities that are judged aberrant and thus outside the system or pattern. Douglas herself argues that such ambiguities create tension and can threaten the system and, thus, must be dealt with, either by reduction or elimination. The particular ambiguities of the deformed cruel jester who is also a loving father disrupt the pattern of the Platonic system. Therein lies their power to upset audiences; therein lies as well their attractiveness for the theater. As we have seen, Verdi found his hunchback hero moving and inspiring, and Hugo, in the preface to his play *Lucrèce Borgia*, elaborated further on this appeal: in Triboulet he wanted to take the most hideous physical deformity, the most repulsive and scorned of bodies, and place in it a soul with the most pure feelings ever given to man – paternal love.[91] The disturbing ambiguities of the grotesque are clearly at the core of his aesthetic and ethical conception of this work.

Likewise, but in reverse terms, Hugo describes his attraction to the character of the infamous poisoner Lucrezia Borgia: here it is the opposite case, that of the most hideous moral deformity, the most repulsive of human souls, being placed in the body of a beautiful woman. But the ambiguities proliferate, for he then adds to this disjunction a further complication: in her deformed heart are the most pure feelings ever given to woman – those of maternal love. In the monster, he asserts, there is a mother, and this changes everything.[92]

If paternity can sanctify physical deformity and maternity purify moral deformity housed in physical beauty, then the supposed Platonic correlation of inside and outside is rendered ambiguous for both ends of the spectrum of appearance. (See figures 6 and 7.) The possibility of a dangerous contrast between external beauty and internal moral turpitude may have seriously concerned medieval religious thinkers, but nineteenth-century writers for the stage saw the dramatic possibilities in precisely such ambiguities.[93]

If it is male characters in opera who are deformed, ugly, and often desexualized, it is (with a few exceptions) women who are conventionally beautiful.[94] Much work has been done by feminist historians and theorists on how female beauty has been tantamount to female identity at certain periods in Western culture.[95] But at the same time that the grotesque was complicating Platonic theories regarding the unbeautiful, the figure of the beautiful woman was also being rendered ambiguous. No longer of necessity – that is, manifestly, visibly – pure in spirit, she was becoming both sexualized and demonized, producing the familiar cultural dichotomies of the Madonna and the whore.[96] In the next chapter, we shall see in more detail how the construction of the *femme fatale* at the end of the nineteenth century influenced the stage presentations of Salome as beautiful and seductive but also dangerous and evil. In many ways Lucrèce Borgia is Salome's forerunner, a *femme fatale avant la lettre*: Hugo's early exploration of her moral and physical ambiguities may well have contributed to the creation of this contradictory female stereotype.

When Gaetano Donizetti and Felice Romani began working on their operatic version of Hugo's play *Lucrèce Borgia*, they obviously wanted to move in much the same direction as would Verdi and Piave with *Le Roi s'amuse*, that is to say, toward making their protagonist more sympathetic than Hugo's had been. Yet the opera *Lucrezia Borgia* (1833) does not avoid the obvious complexities and still presents her as both a vengeful poisoner and a loving mother. The first we *hear* of her, she is said to be an evil woman ("empia femmina") who causes suffering and pain to others, and the music that accompanies her name suggests horror through its knocking rhythms and diminished triad. But the first we actually *see* of her is as a loving mother watching her son, Gennaro, sleep (though the young man is unaware of his parentage). Her music seems designed to inspire sympathy, not horror. So too do her words: "M'aborre ognuno! / Pur, per sì trista sorte / nata io non ero" [Everyone abhors me! / Yet, for such a sad fate / I was not born]. Regretting her past, she wants to arouse pity and love ("un senso di pietade e amore") in her son.

When Gennaro awakens, he falls in love with this beautiful woman, recounting to her his life story largely because he feels he can tell from her face that she has a noble and beautiful soul ("alma cortese e bella / nel vostro volto appar"). The audience is aware of the irony of this invoking of the Platonic doctrine of consonance and soon so is Gennaro, for his friends arrive and denounce her, for all their families have been her victims: "Ella è donna venefica, impura, / vilipese, otraggiò la natura" [She is a baneful and impure woman, / she has degraded and offended nature]. In the next scene, the traumatized Gennaro announces that he would like to stamp her infamy on her brow ("Stamparle in fronte / vorrei l'infamia"), stigmatizing her and her beauty because of her many sins. Instead, in anger, he tears the B off her name on the palace crest, leaving the damning (and sexualizing) "ORGIA."

Although we witness Lucrezia's pain at Gennaro's rejection, we also watch as her evil character gradually asserts itself on stage through vengeful and willful behavior. The beautiful woman turns out to be quick to take offense and even quicker to avenge it. At the end, when she unwittingly poisons Gennaro along with his friends, he refuses to take the antidote offered him; in despair, she confesses to him, as he dies, that he is her son. The pain she feels is clearly meant to be taken as real:

Era desso il figlio mio,
la mia speme, il mio conforto;

ei potea placarmi Iddio,
me potea far pura ancor.

[He was my son,
my hope, my comfort;
he could have made God have mercy on me,
he could still have made me pure.]

The opera plays down the incestuous nature of Gennaro's conception (which the play makes clear), no doubt as part of the attempt to
make Lucrezia sympathetic, despite her crimes. But the ambiguities
can still disturb, as the Platonic uniting of beauty and goodness is
deconstructed before our very eyes and ears.

Today, however, we are much more likely than the original audience
to accept the separation of the physical and the moral when it comes
to beauty.[97] We do not really expect the attractive to be virtuous
anymore. This is likely why *Lucrezia Borgia* is, in the end, less
disturbing to us than *Rigoletto* might be, for, sadly, we have not
come quite as far in breaking the cultural linkages between the
unbeautiful and the reprehensible. Christopher Reeve, an actor who
played the handsome hero Superman, has devoted much effort in
the last few years to speaking out against popular cultural images of
the disabled as villainous: since suffering a spinal cord injury that
left him quadriplegic, Reeve is particularly well placed to see both
sides of this Platonic heritage operating in our culture. Yet there are
clearly still cases, even on the operatic stage, where we seem to want
to make the physical exterior fit the moral interior. For instance,
in Gian Carlo Menotti's opera *Amahl and the Night Visitors* (1951),
it is not a question of villainy but simply of consonance between
outer appearance and inner spirit. In this retelling of the Christmas
story, a poor twelve-year-old crippled boy generously offers to give
his home-made crutch – his only means of mobility – as an offering
to the three kings who are going to find the Christ Child. His act of
generosity and charity provokes a miracle. As the stage directions

make explicit, when he hands over the crutch, he discovers he can walk without it: there seems to be a need to make the body whole and healthy to match Amahl's inner spiritual goodness.[98]

Disability studies are showing us new ways of unpacking this less-than-appealing side of the Platonic legacy, but beginning in the nineteenth century, opera too began to reconsider and in part deconstruct that persistent theory by introducing the complicating ambiguities of the grotesque: as Hugo taught (and as many operatic composers and librettists learned from him), if the deformed were malign, it might well be because of society's cruel contempt and scorn, not because of any innate evil. And the handsome man or beautiful woman was just as likely to be false as true. In these ambiguities lay new dramatic possibilities with which to confront complacent operatic audiences. Today these operas may be jarring for us for different reasons, that is, because of our heightened sensitivity to the negative (and often continuing) history of the treatment of the disabled and the unbeautiful. But it has always been upsetting to witness on the stage the enactment of the pain of inhabiting a less-than-perfect body in a world that equates the aesthetic and the moral.

2

The Body Dangerous

As an art form, opera has always been self-conscious about singing, despite the fact that, as Carolyn Abbate and others have emphasized, the convention of opera is that the singers are actually deaf to the "music-drowned world" in which they live.[1] We have already seen that many early operas focused on Orpheus, the singing poet, and Wagner's *Tannhäuser* and *Die Meistersinger von Nürnberg* stand as nineteenth-century epitomes of opera about the singer. But dance – the Dionysian body in motion – has also been an important part of opera historically, from the days of the Renaissance precursors of opera, the *intermedi* and the pastoral plays, which involved both music and dance.[2] As we saw in the Prelude, the ending of Monteverdi and Striggio's *Orfeo* (1607) brought the story of the ascending Orpheus and Apollo back down to earth with a dance performed by the shepherds and shepherdesses. While dance here clearly reasserts the earthly and the bodily (that is, the realm of the audience), it is arguably not exactly central to the drama. While this relatively peripheral *divertissement* role persisted in seventeenth-century French and English court entertainments, by the eighteenth century, especially in France, operatic dance came to be used to express in bodily terms emotions that could not be expressed in words. While Italian *opera seria* never exploited this emotive power of dance, Gluck and Calzabigi's *Orfeo ed Euridice* (1762) certainly did, incorporating into the second act a ballet that did indeed further the dramatic action as well as heighten the emotional tenor of the work.

Classical ballet as a separate art form came into prominence in the nineteenth century, developing out of "the mute action of pantomime and melodrama – themselves accompanied by music – but with a much more highly codified set of conventions."[3] The French romantic context made possible the creation of what has been called an "erotics of looking" through the public performance and display of, primarily, the female dancing body. Although the history of ballet has been reinterpreted by feminist theorists in recent years, there is little doubt that the eroticized voyeurism of the audience played a role in the popularity of ballet in nineteenth-century opera as well.[4] Meyerbeer's grand operas were by no means the only ones to incorporate dance for a variety of uses, from enhancing the atmosphere with local color to incarnating and thus celebrating ritual. Interestingly, dancers were often cast in the roles of mute operatic characters: Fenella in Auber's *La Muette de Portici* (1828) and Silvana in Weber's 1810 opera that bears her name. It is as if dance became the literally embodied voice of the silent character: *Death in Venice* continues this long tradition in its portrayal of Tadzio as a dancer.

Opera histories usually note that it is not until the twentieth century that singers themselves are called upon to become dancers (for instance, when performing as Elektra, Daphne, Zerbinetta, or, of course, Salome). Arguably, however, this doubling up began in a sense in 1875 with Bizet's creation of the dangerous gypsy Carmen, whose vocal arias are deliberately named after dances – the *seguidilla* and the *habañera*. Susan McClary goes even further in asserting the link between the corporeality of dance and Carmen's stage appeal for audiences, then as now: "Bizet grounds Carmen's music in the physical impulses of exotic, pseudogypsy dance. . . . Her rhythms indicate that she is very much aware of her body. In fact, before she even begins to sing, her instrumental vamp sets a pattern that engages the lower body, demanding hip swings in response. Moreover, these rhythms are so contagious that they make José – and the listener – aware both of her body and also of their own bodies."[5] In Western culture, dancing women have long been suspect, in part because of those legendary Dionysian maenads or bacchantes, whose winter dance rituals culminated in the tearing to pieces and consuming raw of a sacrificial animal. Linked thus to the irrational as well as the corporeal, dance is said to take possession of the dancer, often without the consent of the conscious mind.[6] Therefore, dance was frequently prohibited because both religious and secular authorities recognized and feared its power. Nevertheless, it is also interesting that, in the West, dance has historically been seen as a representation either of such Dionysian madness and possession, excess and transgression (usually "foreign" or modern dance) or else of Apollonian order (baroque and classical ballet, with their emphasis on physical control and discipline).

❧ The Dionysian Body of Salome

This chapter examines one of the most provocative dancers in opera, Richard Strauss's Salome, and, through her, the role of the staged body in late-nineteenth- and early-twentieth-century concepts of social transgression, medical neurosis, and gender empowerment. Strauss's 1905 opera was based on the Oscar Wilde play of the same name (first published in Paris in 1893). It represents the decadent *fin-de-siècle* revision of the biblical story of the beautiful (and very young) princess of Judea who dances for the lustful Herod in order to possess – and kiss – the decapitated head of John the Baptist, in this version the object of her newly awakened adolescent passion. It was shocking then; it still manages to be so today.[7] However, critics at the time seem to have found the opera more shocking than the audience at large, who greeted the first performance with thirty-eight curtain calls; there were fifty productions within two years.[8] Wilde's play was originally written in French and then translated into English and famously illustrated by Aubrey Beardsley.[9] A planned production with Sarah Bernhardt was banned in London in 1892, ostensibly for portraying biblical characters on stage, but the play opened in Paris in 1896, the year following Wilde's famous trial and conviction. The German version premiered in 1901 in Breslau and found its perfect audience among the German avant-garde (who saw themselves as the supporters of the artist, persecuted by English law and English aesthetic conservatism): there were 111 performances in Germany in 1903 and 1904 alone. It was in Berlin at Max Reinhardt's Kleines Theater that Strauss saw the play in Hedwig Lachmann's prose translation (which he would later use for the libretto instead of a poetic version prepared by Anton Lindner). When someone at the performance suggested to him that it might make a good opera, he is said to have replied that he was already busy composing it.[10]

The opera he completed a few years later suffered a fate at times not unlike that of Wilde's play: it too was banned, this time in Vienna (at the state theater) for religious reasons. The Dionysian spectacle had to be bowdlerized in order to play in London, where Sir Thomas Beecham claimed: "we had successfully metamorphosed a lurid tale of love and revenge into a comforting sermon."[11] No synopsis of its decadent plot appeared in any Covent Garden program until 1937. The New York production was closed down by the daughter of J. Pierpont Morgan on moral grounds, with the press noting its "moral stench."[12] It would appear that the general taboo regarding respect for the bodies of the dead was broken too scandalously by Salome's necrophilic and almost cannibalistic kiss of Jochanaan's lips.[13] In general, though, Wilde's decadent and lyrically lush libretto (even in German translation) contributed to the moral and aesthetic shock response as much as did the powerful, radically new sounds of Strauss's music. Together the narrative, the text, and the music worked to place not so much the *voice* but the *body* of Salome front and center, where the audience members (like Herod) cannot take their eyes off her.

As Terry Eagleton so memorably puts it, today the body – "so obvious, obtrusive a matter as to have been blandly overlooked for centuries – has ruffled the edges of a bloodless rationalist discourse, and is currently *en route* to becoming the greatest fetish of all."[14] Perhaps he is correct, but for many, as we have seen in the Prefatory Note, the gains seem to outweigh such dangers of fetishism. Feminist and other theorists have turned our attention to the "somatophobia" of the Christian and Cartesian traditions, that is, their construction of the body as the source of danger to reason.[15] They have taught us that the body is a force to be reckoned with, a lesson that recent work on opera too has begun to heed. While it may seem obvious that the staged body is at the heart of any form whatsoever of theatrical representation, we have been arguing in this book that it is the disembodied voice that has come to dominate discussions of opera, especially since the arrival of those technological advances in audio recording and radio transmission examined in the Prelude.[16] In a related move, opera criticism too came to be dominated by considerations of the music that voice sings, usually separated from the libretto's verbal text and the dramatic staged narrative. Musicologists confidently assert: "It is after all the music that an opera-lover goes to hear."[17] But, speaking for these opera lovers, at least, we go to *see* as well as hear a performance, and that performance includes a verbal text and a staged dramatic narrative for which that (admittedly important) music was especially written. Our argument has been that opera is an embodied art form; it is the performers that give it its "phenomenal reality."[18] Indeed, we feel opera owes its undeniable affective power to the coming together of the verbal, the visual, and the aural and not to the aural alone. And it is specifically the body – the gendered, sexualized body – that will not be denied in staged opera. As Joseph Roach explains: "Self-evidently, the signifying body is central to theatrical representation in any form. The techniques whereby the body is prepared for performance, the particular bodily expressions whereby the public accepts the truth of performance, and the imagery whereby the body is eroticized in performance illuminate at any given cultural moment the relationships between sexuality and power."[19] No matter how much audiophiles of all sorts may like to forget it, the voice does come from the body, as we shall see in detail in chapter 3. But there are also moments in opera when the singers do not sing at all, and when bodily dance takes over from the voice as a means of expression. Herbert Lindenberger has pointed out that, in late-nineteenth- and early-twentieth-century operas such as

Schoenberg's *Moses und Aron*, with its dance around the Golden Calf, or Saint-Saëns/Lemaire's *Samson et Dalila*, with its appropriately named Bacchanale, the dance sequences display "brazenly contorted bodies accompanied by correspondingly brazen orientalist orchestral music."[20] As we have seen, the music of the athletic ballet sequences of Britten's *Death in Venice* is Orientalist in a similar way, thanks to the use of gamelan-style tuned percussion. Of course, both this particular choice of instrumentation and its associations with the Orient make the connection between Dionysus and dance all the stronger. In Strauss's *Salome* too the protagonist dances, and for about ten minutes the orchestra supports her moving body, not her voice.[21]

The body of Salome was the obsession of late-nineteenth-century European, especially French, culture.[22] Gustave Flaubert's 1877 story "Hérodias" created, in its portrayal of the sultry but strangely indifferent young dancer, the exoticized and Orientalized type that would so influence his compatriots. This Salome danced "like the priestesses of India, like the Nubians of the cataracts, like the bacchantes of Lydia."[23] The Dionysian connection with the dancing body is thus reasserted. The body of this exotic dancing princess soon became the subject of operas, poems, stories, plays, sculptures, decorative objects, ballets, films, and paintings.[24] No painter was more obsessed with Salome's body than Gustave Moreau, who left hundreds of oils, watercolors, and drawings as testimony to his fascination. In so doing he anticipated (and in part created) the tastes of a generation of writers, from Jules Laforgue to the young Proust, from Joris-Karl Huysmans to Oscar Wilde.[25] Two of Moreau's paintings from the year 1876 stand out from the others precisely because of Huysmans's immortalizing of them in his novel *A rebours* (translated as *Against Nature*). His hero, the dandy Des Esseintes, purchases these works in order to contemplate Salome's charms and dangers. One is an oil painting entitled *Salome Dancing before Herod*. (See figure 8.) It pictures the princess in an exotic, Orientalized setting (copied from the pages of the *Magasin pittoresque*), as described in great and lush detail by Des Esseintes. Curiously, his subsequent depiction of Salome's body puts the static painted image into motion: "she begins the lascivious dance which is to rouse the aged Herod's dormant senses; her breasts rise and fall, the nipples hardening at the touch of her whirling necklaces; the strings of diamonds glitter against her moist flesh . . ." and so on (and it does go on). Of all the painters who had portrayed Salome over the centuries, only Moreau, claims Des Esseintes, has captured "the disquieting delirium of the dancer, the subtle grandeur of the murderess." For this French male, Salome had become more than a biblical character or even a pornographic delight: "She had become, as it were, the symbolic incarnation of undying Lust, the Goddess of immortal Hysteria, the accursed Beauty exalted above all other beauties by the catalepsy that hardens her flesh and steels her muscles, the monstrous Beast, indifferent, irresponsible, insensible, poisoning, like the Helen of ancient myth, everything that approaches her, everything that sees her, everything that she touches." He imagines Moreau thinking of "the dancer, the mortal woman, the soiled vessel, ultimate cause of every sin and every crime," before moving on to contemplate his second possession – a watercolor called *The Apparition* that disturbs him even more. In this, the head of John the Baptist appears before the dancer, who tries, as he puts it, to "thrust away the terrifying vision which holds her nailed to the spot." This Salome upsets him because she is "a true harlot, obedient to her passionate and cruel female temperament; . . . here she roused the sleeping senses of the male more powerfully, subjugated his will more surely with her charms – the charms of a great venereal flower, grown in a bed of sacrilege, reared in a hot-house of impiety."[26]

If that sounds a bit overblown (not to say misogynistic) today, in terms of sentiment as much as rhetoric, we need to remind ourselves of two things: first, of the strategic value of exaggeration to the decadent aesthetic, and second, of the astonishing impact of that description on all subsequent representations of Salome, especially that of Oscar Wilde, whose Dorian Gray saw in Des Esseintes a prefigurement of himself: "For years Dorian Gray could not free himself from the influence of this book. Or perhaps it would be more accurate to say that he never sought to free himself from it. . . . The hero, the wonderful young Parisian, in whom the romantic and the scientific temperaments were so strangely blended, became to him a kind of prefiguring type of himself. And, indeed, the whole book seemed to him to contain the story of his own life, written before he had lived it."[27]

Huysmans's particular description of Moreau's paintings has been called the "principal engenderer" of Wilde's play *Salomé*, from which Strauss composed his opera.[28] Des Esseintes may have been attracted, in his words, to Moreau's "hieratic allegories whose sinister quality was heightened by the morbid perspicuity of an entirely modern sensibility," but we are attracted to another allegory suggested by the form (rather than the content) of Moreau's Salome paintings.[29] Art historians have commented on the radical disjunction in Moreau's oil paintings of this period between the large background blocks of color (developed in advance to get the chromatic harmony right) and the superimposed drawing of fine detail, often in India ink.[30] What is striking, however, is that the superimposed detailed drawing does not always coincide with the color blocks: the delicate tracery appears almost independent of the colored form it seems intended to define. We would like to suggest that it was the strange disjunction between this detailed precision and the ill-fitting blocks of colors (which offered suggestion rather than definition) that in part provoked the symbolist generation's dedication to Moreau's art.

Wilde's play could also be called a symbolist drama, or at least a British aesthete's version of what the French writers tried to do in capturing the fleeting, immediate sensations of inner life. This is where an allegorical reading, in the light of Moreau's formal disjunction, becomes possible. Wilde's delicate, "bejeweled" text is like Moreau's equally delicate India-ink tracery that covers the canvas surface with the effect of a kind of cloisonné enamel.[31] The large blocks of unruly color represent, in this allegory, the music Strauss composed for Wilde's text: strong, powerful music that feels at times utterly inappropriate for the delicacy of the libretto. If we were to imagine what the music of a truly symbolist opera might sound like, we should likely think of Debussy's suggestive, evocative music for Maeterlinck's play, *Pelléas et Mélisande.* Instead, here the subtle, erotic, sophisticated prose of Wilde's (translated) text contrasts with the often abrasive orchestration, with what have been called its moments of "lewd bestiality" that respond more to the psychological implications than to the actual language of the play text.[32] However, like Moreau's disjunction of detailed drawing and large color blocks, the lack of fit between Wilde's text and Strauss's music is in some ways, we would argue, the very cause of the disturbing power of the work. The Apollonian's clashing with the Dionysian can be as powerful as their conjoining.

Caught trying to reconcile the delicate text and the brutal music, critics are quick to point to this lack of fit, condemning one side or the other, depending on their preferences.[33] Arguably, however, it is the disjunction itself that contributes to the impact in performance. Without Strauss's music, Wilde's play remains an ornate lyric, a ballad – but not, on its own, all that dramatic: it takes the uneasy conjunction – and disjunction – with Strauss's music (astonishing in its "audacity of raw excitement and [at times] extreme compositional crudity") to make the play into a drama.[34] Strauss's instinct for the theatrical has subsequently been made clear, but in *Salome* the music's emphatic and dramatic vocabulary of harmonies, rhythms, and instrumentation often clashes with the luxuriant, voluptuous vocabulary of the verbal text.[35] And when the two opposites come together, as in Moreau's paintings, the power to disconcert lies in their noncoincidence.

✧ Pathologizing the *Femme Fatale*

There is a direct analogy here with the equally disconcerting disjunction within the character of Salome herself: she incarnates and embodies on the stage a *psychic* lack of fit that makes her powerful and finally, perhaps, terrifying. But she does not begin that way. The Salome we first see on stage is quite different: an attractive if willful young girl. Wilde intended his Salomé to be both the embodiment of sensuality and a chaste virgin, and all Strauss did was to accentuate the contradictions. Actual productions of the opera, though, have tended to emphasize either the virgin or the whore, rather than sustaining the ambivalence Wilde seems to have intended: the virginal Birgit Nilsson performed the role differently than did the vampish Teresa Stratas.[36] Salome is obviously the typical *femme fatale* in the long operatic tradition of Carmen, Kundry, Dalila, and, later, Lulu – the demonic beauty who could lure men to damnation and therefore aroused in her beholder fear along with attraction, terror along with desire.[37] Traditionally characterized by her almost oppressive physical presence as seductress, the *femme fatale* usually took on the identity of an historical or mythic character – like Salome – likely in order to stress the universal or archetypal nature of her appeal. As Patrick Bade points out: "This preoccupation with evil and destructive women is one of the most striking features of late nineteenth-century culture. The theme was all pervasive, appealing to men of opposing artistic creeds, symbolists and realists, rebels and reactionaries, and penetrating deeply into the popular consciousness."[38] The placing of these women in exotic, often Oriental locales offered European audiences not only heightened mystery and complex associations of the physical and the spiritual but also "easy, imaginative projections of sexual desires."[39]

As a negative, misogynistic version of the "eternal feminine," this time embodying death more than life, the *femme fatale* was viewed as "deadlier than the male, coolly indifferent or aggressively lethal."[40] But while Salome might well have been, to use Lawrence Kramer's term, "everyone's favorite *fin-de-siècle* dragon lady," this is a *femme fatale* with a difference: as Ken Russell captured well in his film, *Salome's Last Dance*, she is an adolescent and a virgin.[41] We only come to see the contradictions as the opera progresses, as her character is unveiled as surely as the famous Dance of the Seven Veils reveals her body. But the Salome of the opening is young and beautiful; she is an impulsive spoiled child who must have her own way, a pampered princess who lives very much in her own world, as befits the narcissism of the young.[42] Yet it is this same pubescent girl who develops an obsessive (and ultimately lethal) passion to kiss the lips of Jochanaan (the opera's Germanic-Hebraic name for John the Baptist). Indeed, upon first seeing his body, she sings a very sensual hymn of praise to its beauties that is rare in opera, a dramatic genre always ready to talk of love but rather reticent when it comes to frank expressions of physical desire. But, again, part of the impact on audiences, then and now, derives from the fact that this frankness is articulated by and therefore associated with a chaste pubescent female body.

However, it is Jochanaan who first introduces the language of sexuality into both the play and the libretto: when he is brought out of his cistern-prison at Salome's request, he begins a tirade against her mother, Herodias, in terms of her sexual misdeeds, which seem to range from looking at pictures of men to giving herself to Syrian captains and the young men of Egypt and, of course, to the abomination of her incestuous bed (for she has wed her husband's half-brother). He then addresses Salome as the daughter of Babylon and Sodom whose mother has filled the earth with the wine of her lust. It is only after this sexualized attack that Salome herself begins to use sexual and sensual language in her seductive depiction of Jochanaan. She begins with an extravagant description, built upon biblical similes, of the whiteness of his body, of which she says she is enamored ("Ich bin verliebt in deinem Leib") – a description that ends with her request to touch his body ("Lass mich ihn berühren deinen Lieb"). At this point the motif of Herodias echoes in the music, identifying the daughter with the mother's condemned sexuality.[43] Jochanaan's response to Salome is an (implicitly sexualized) attack on all womankind for first bringing evil into the world. His rejection of her advances causes Salome to respond this time with a series of hideous images of his body, which she now says she hates. The music shifts at this point and takes on a new dissonance. Having thus disposed of his white body, Salome turns her attention to his black hair. Her fulsome description and his subsequent rejection are followed, once again, by a revised depiction of his hair as a tangle of black serpents writhing around his neck, prefiguring the Medusa image that the final scene will also powerfully evoke, as we shall see. Her attention then becomes fixed on the redness of his mouth, and she concludes her praise by asking to kiss it. His continued rejection of her sensual advances is met with her stubborn will: "Ich will deinen Mund küssen, Jochanaan" [I will kiss your mouth, Jochanaan], she insists.

Gustave Moreau was not alone in seeing in the young, willful Salome a representative of generic Woman, that is, associated at that time with sensuality and unhealthy curiosity.[44] To understand both Salome's appeal to her earliest audiences as well as the thrilling danger she incarnated, we need to understand the context of gender politics of the time, a time different in many ways from our own. Today, conditioned by feminist arguments, we are likely to find it distressing that, in this earlier period, the medical and social discourses were all too content to reduce women to morally underdeveloped, childlike creatures. In this way, for Strauss and Wilde's contemporaries, the dangerous Salome could come to stand, even in her youth, for all women.[45] Cesare Lombroso articulated this view rather forcefully in his study of the "female offender" at the end of the nineteenth century: "women are big children: their evil tendencies are more numerous and more varied than men's, but generally remain latent. When they are awakened and excited they produce results proportionately greater."[46] Female libido was therefore taken to be "volatile, capricious, even rampaging . . . inherently dysfunctional, dangerous even." Gender and criminality were clearly connected in *fin-de-siècle* medical thinking.[47] Nevertheless, the impact of Salome's actual youth is not to be discounted, for it is one of the sides of the psychic lack of fit that makes her so disturbing. There was another medicalized discourse at the time that specifically linked "the insanity of puberty" in females to "a destructive tendency" comparable to pugnacity in males.[48]

In addition, female criminal violence came to be directly associated with female menstruation. Control, according to Havelock Ellis, was "physiologically lessened at the menstral [sic] period even in health, while it is much more lessened in the neurotic and imbalanced."[49] Ellis draws here on a longer nineteenth-century tradition of associating pubescent women, menstruation, sexuality, and insanity that is articulated most fully (and relevantly, for Salome's characterization) by Henry Maudsley in *The Physiology and Pathology of Mind*, in the second edition of the work, dated 1868:

> Where the heritage of the insane temperament exists . . . if the individual is placed under conditions of great excitement, or subjected to a severe mental strain, the inherent propensity is apt to display itself in some repulsive act of violence. The great internal disturbance produced in young girls at the time of puberty is well known to be an occasional cause of strange morbid feelings and extraordinary acts; and this is especially the case where the insane temperament exists. In such case also irregularities of menstruation, always apt enough to disturb the mental equilibrium, may give rise to an outbreak of mania, or to extreme moral perversion more afflicting to the patient's friends than mania, because seemingly willful. The stress of a great disappointment, or any other of the recognised causes of mental disease, will meet with a powerful co-operating cause in the constitutional predisposition.[50]

Indeed, the connecting of insanity to gender, youth, and menstruation is a recurring theme in the medical literature of the nineteenth century.

In this context, the obsession with the moon in both the play and opera takes on a new and sinister meaning beyond even the usual notion of lunacy. The moon's role has been interpreted in many ways: as the favorite lighting for the decadent movement's nocturnal settings, as a symbol of mythic mutability, or even as a representation of the feminine extremes of the crone (Hecate) and the virgin (Diana).[51] But the moon's insistent presence here may also symbolically engage that contemporaneous medical discourse of female periodicity following puberty and its physical dangers for others. The moon dominates the stage as the curtain rises; each character who enters looks at it and projects upon it his or her own feelings at that moment – usually feelings related to the body of Salome. As the lovestruck Syrian Narraboth admires Salome's physical beauty, the nervous Page compares the moon to a woman coming out of a grave ("Wie eine Frau, die aufsteigt aus dem Grab"). But Narraboth sees in the moon a small dancing princess, with feet like white doves ("Wie eine kleine Prinzessin, deren Füssen weisse Tauben sind. Man könnte meinen, sie tanzt"). To this the Page responds once again, in stark contradiction, that the moon more resembles a dead woman ("Wie eine Frau, die tot ist").

The role of the moon as a psychic screen upon which characters project their desires and anxieties is affirmed as Salome herself enters and admires it in terms of a silver flower that is cool and chaste ("kühl und keusch") with the beauty of a pure virgin ("einer Jungfrau, die rein geblieben ist"). She will shortly associate the moon's chastity with that of Jochanaan's pale ivory body: "Gewiss ist er keusch wie der Mond." And, indeed, the moon becomes a constant point of reference in her hymn to his bodily beauty. His eyes are said to be like lakes upon which mad moonlight flickers ("irres Mondlicht flackert"); his black hair is like the dark nights when the moon is hidden. When Herod enters, seeking Salome and arguing with Herodias, who scolds him for staring at her daughter too much, he too ends up looking at the moon, which he then sees as a mad drunken woman looking everywhere for lovers ("eine wahnwitziges Weib, das überall nach Buhlen sucht . . . wie ein betrunkenes Weib"). The more down-to-earth Herodias refuses such blatant psychic projection, asserting that the moon is like the moon, and that is all it is ("der Mond is wie der Mond, das ist alles").

This constant reference to the moon in a context of lovers, chastity, death, and danger suggests another connection to that medical discourse of menses, but this time associated with abnormal sexuality, specifically with hyperaesthesia (or exaggeration of the sexual appetite). In one physician's terms at the time: "In women it is during or after menstruation that the sexual appetite and consequently sexual hyperaesthesia are generally strongest."[52] These medical contexts can fruitfully be considered here, alongside the familiar symbolic ones, in interpreting this odd stage feature of the moon as the focus of everyone's attention. As a pubescent female verbally linked to that moon, Salome is directly associated with menses and indirectly, therefore, with these various contemporaneous medical discourses of the pathological that link the menstruating woman with violence and increased sexuality.[53]

As the opera progresses, as layers of Salome's character are revealed, she becomes more and more disturbing. It will surprise no one that the woman whom Huysmans's Des Esseintes called "Goddess of immortal Hysteria" has indeed been interpreted as an hysteric or even a psychotic by post-Freudian critics.[54] But the contemporary discourses – of Richard von Krafft-Ebing and Havelock Ellis, not to mention Jean Martin Charcot, Pierre Janet, and Freud himself – offer another context in which Salome would have been constructed *at the time* in terms of pathological sexuality. Even before Freud, the associations of women with hysteria included heightened suggestibility, emotional irritability and instability, hyperaesthesia, and impulsiveness.[55] Maudsley once again provides a canonical articulation that is suggestive for the opera's portrayal of Salome: "An acute attack of maniacal excitement, with great restlessness, perverseness of conduct, loud and rapid conversation. . . . An erotic element is sometimes evinced in the manner and thoughts; and occasionally ecstatic states occur. The symptoms are often worse at the menstrual periods."[56]

Such a list offers a kind of thumbnail character sketch of the willful young Salome, who must have her own way, who reacts as strongly to first seeing Jochanaan's body as to being rejected by him. Her lability is clear in that rapid oscillation we have seen between praise for his corporeal beauty – his body, his hair, his lips – and disgust at the same when he rejects her advances. To underline the psychic oscillation, the music shifts at the point of rejection, offering "disturbingly heterogeneous orchestration, dissonant harmony and more angular vocal lines."[57] While today it may be more fashionable to interpret hysteria, as does Elizabeth Grosz, as a form of resistance, when the opera and play were written the pathological dominated the medical (and cultural) discourse of female sexuality.[58] And, as we shall see shortly, that pathology directly linked hysteria to the Dionysian dancing body.

If the assumed norm at the time for women was, in fact, asexuality, as doctors claimed, and women who sought men were deemed anomalies, imagine how transgressive Salome would appear.[59] Her open display of sexual desire for Jochanaan would have been seen by most as a sure sign of mental disease and proof (in the "elementary force" with which she was attracted to him) of her nymphomania. The contemporary discourse on the excitable, insatiable women who, from their early youth, "throw themselves onto men" would have provided another significant context for interpreting Salome.[60] Today we are more likely to believe, with Bram Dijkstra, that male desire created the image of the insatiable nymph and that male scientists then "discovered her existence as a medical fact," but at the time, to Krafft-Ebing nymphomania was a "syndrome within the sphere of psychical degeneration," and this belief would then account for what another physician called the nymphomaniac's loss of "all sense of shame, all moral sense, and all discretion, as regards the object of her desires."[61]

Certainly, by the finale of her body-unveiling dance, when Salome makes her demand for the head of the prophet, her character too is unveiled in what, at the time, would have been seen as all its pathological glory. Presumably this is what led the first Salome, Maria Wittich, to protest what was asked of her: "I won't do it, I am a decent woman," she exclaimed.[62] Salome's dramatized psyche caused Romain Rolland to write to his friend Strauss that Wilde's play "has a nauseous and sickly atmosphere about it: it exudes vice and literature. This isn't a question of middle-class morality, it's a question of health." He went on to call Salome "unwholesome, unclean, hysterical," as did many of the early critics of the opera, protesting in the name of health but likely also reflecting the impact of Wilde's scandalous reputation and recent sodomy trial.[63] But the verbal signs of the influence of those medical discourses of pathological female sexuality are present nonetheless in that vocabulary of hysteria and unhealthiness.

Yet the power of Salome as a character comes from her progressive staged embodiment of that perverse disjunction between the pathological, dangerous sexuality of the castrating *femme fatale* and the innocence and willfulness of this young girl – and her biblical story.[64] That willful character can be seen in her stubborn repeating of her desires. When she decides she wants to see Jochanaan's body she reiterates this wish three times, moving progressively from benign "Ich möchte" (I would like to) to the more assertive "Ich wünsche" (I want to) and finally to the peremptory "Ich will" (I will). Four times she insists she will kiss Jochanaan's mouth. Eight times she repeats to Herod her demand for Jochanaan's head as the payment for her dance. In her final monologue to that severed head, her childlike willfulness comes together with the dangerous pathology in all its power. She again repeats several times that she has said she wanted to kiss his mouth and now she is going to do so, for she is alive while he is now dead. When she does kiss him, she sings: "Was war ein bitterer Geschmack auf deinen Lippen. Hat es nach Blut geschmeckt? Nein! Doch es schmeckte vielleicht nach Liebe . . . Sie sagen, dass die Liebe bitter schmecke" [There was a bitter taste on your lips. Was it the taste of blood? No! Then perhaps it was the taste of love . . . They say that love has a bitter taste]. The vampiric associations with the *femme fatale*, preying on men "ill-equipped for the onslaught,"[65] here unite with representations of the willfulness of the child who decides she doesn't really care: "Allein, was tut's? Was tut's?" [What does it matter?]. The important thing is that she has had her way, as she twice exultantly notes.

What would have been seen as pathological physical desire comes together with adolescent female power, as the orchestra plays what has been described as the "most sickening chord in all opera."[66] Throughout, the music has mirrored the paradoxes of Salome's character. One of the few vaguely complimentary things Theodor Adorno ever said about Strauss was about his "ability to compress the plenitude of emotions, including those which are incompatible, into isolated complexes, to fit the up and down oscillation of feeling into a single instant."[67] Musically, Salome's entire final monologue is grounded in C major/minor, the keys of "violence and death which are opposed to the C sharp major/minor world of desire." The ambivalence of her character is shown by her participation in both keys.[68] But by the end of the opera, as Salome kisses Jochanaan's mouth, the violence, death, and desire all come together and contrast with the text's emphasis on the willfulness of the chaste virgin who has learned the meaning of power.[69] Even before her famous Dance of the Seven Veils, Salome has used her knowledge of that power, a power inseparable from her physical body. That dance is a calculated move in a game of exchange with Herod, one in which she offers her body as a sensual, sexual spectacle to his eyes in return for a promise that will fulfill both her lethal willful stubbornness and her consuming sexual obsession to kiss the mouth of the resistant prophet.[70]

❧ Gazing at Salome Dancing

The Dance of the Seven Veils is the best-known part of the opera and play. Wilde's text, like the Bible, leaves the dance undescribed, though Wilde does name it. Marjorie Garber argues that "[i]n its non-description, in its indescribability lies its power, and its availability for cultural inscription and appropriation."[71] That may be true for the play, but for the opera the music is much more explicit, here as elsewhere: "Its Hollywood-exotic contours, bedizened with motifs from the opera proper, sometimes tempt directors to make an elaborate production number, far beyond the rather chaste little scenario that the composer sketched to guide himself."[72] In that scenario, Strauss had Salome posing specifically like Moreau's *Salome Dancing before Herod* and then provided her with a rather stylized choreography, with "menacing steps or lively paces" to go with certain bars of the music.[73] The dance's embodied representation on stage is probably guaranteed to be a failure for many viewers because "no staging can be the Dance in all its mythic force."[74] Strauss himself came to feel that many productions went "beyond all bounds of decency and good taste": "Salome, being a chaste virgin and an Oriental princess, must be played with the simplest and most restrained of gestures, unless her defeat by the miracle of a great world is to excite only disgust and terror instead of sympathy." He felt that the music offered enough "turmoil," and so the acting should be "limited to the utmost simplicity."[75] At least in Strauss's eyes, this was not intended to be what Kramer calls "the first operatic striptease in history."[76] Why, then, did he write the physically provocative music he did? It is not hard to imagine that it was the music that drew Peter Hall to direct (his wife) Maria Ewing to end up naked at the end of the dance (at Covent Garden) and Atom Egoyan to have his dancing Salome (at the Canadian Opera Company) naked behind a screen, with large menacing shadows of Herod and other men looming over her. (See figure 9.) Admittedly, if our viewing experience over the years is any indication, most directors come closer to the kind of choreography Strauss favored, preferring a dance of sometimes mere swaying, leaving most to the imagination. Of course, as we shall see, these days, increasingly, it all depends on the dancing skill as well as the appearance of the singer.

Dance is, of course, of all the art forms the most insistently bodily, and bodies are decidedly sexed and gendered. The dance is the moment in the opera when the "sensual is made visible" as well as audible.[77] The wild music that signals the start of the Orientalized dance is quickly subdued by Salome herself. The slow, seductive, at times waltz-like music (complete with Orientalist castanets) speeds up again by the end, causing the bewitched Herod to cry out in delight, "Herrlich! Wundervoll, wundervoll!" Drawing on authentic Oriental music (as modified by European clichés about it), Strauss set up a tension between distance and recognition for the audience. Familiar waltz music is interwoven with Oriental(ist) sounds that, to a turn-of-the-century European audience at least, would have connoted sensuality – not to mention the luxury and cruelty associated with the Eastern "other."[78]

In fin-de-siècle Europe, however, dance had a particular cultural resonance that contributed to the memorable quality of Salome specifically as dancer. Not only did dance in general become "an emblem of the perfect work of art that fuses sensuousness and thought into one," but it took on a more medicalized and pathological meaning through its association with hysteria.[79] Charcot's famous photographs of the "attitudes passionnelles" and his colleague Paul Richer's drawings of the body of the female "grand hysteria" patient are strikingly reminiscent in their posing of the positions of modern dance.[80] As such, they are very different in form and effect from the Apollonian controlled, disciplined form of classical ballet. If hysteria is indeed "written on the body," the medical discourses and Dionysiac dance come together in interesting ways at this moment in cultural history.[81] As Felicia McCarren argues: "Dance and medicine resemble one another remarkably in their histories of 'discovering,' or constructing, new realities for the body, new understandings of what the body does, and, especially, how it means. The two disciplines depend on the idea that the body means inherently, without language, but that the meanings of its movements, signs, or symptoms can be interpreted as a language. The traditions of interpretation of the body in these two domains intersect in the long-standing link between dance and hysteria in medical history, dance history, and the cultural imagination."[82]

This conjunction may help explain the fashion in these years for modern dances on the theme of Salome by the likes of Loïe Fuller and Maud Allan.[83] Fuller's dances, it has been argued, consciously attempted to confront the medical stereotyping of the "performative hysterical" female body, established by Charcot's famous Tuesday *leçons,* which were attended by members of the general public as well as medical practitioners.[84] Elizabeth Dempster points out that modern dancers like Isadora Duncan and Ruth St. Denis "constructed images and created dances through their own unballetic bodies, producing a writing of the female body which strongly contrasted with classical inscriptions. These dancers, creating new vocabularies of movement and new styles of presentation, made a decisive and liberating break with the principles and forms of the European ballet."[85] But to do so, they turned to representations of hysteria. It is not surprising, then, that productions of *Salome* have almost always used modern and/or Orientalized choreography for their dances.[86]

Given the literally embodied nature of dance, a singing Salome is not necessarily going to look convincing as a dancing Salome, and actual productions of the dance can vary from the laughable to the mesmerizing. At the 1907 Metropolitan Opera premiere, the dancing Salome was portrayed by a diminutive dancer (Bianca Froelich), while the singing Olive Fremstad weighed in at about 250 pounds. As one unkind critic noted, it was as if "some antifat remedy had worked wonders for a few minutes and then suddenly lost its potency."[87] In our current age of increased theatrical realism, the appearance of the singer is more of an issue than ever before. Nevertheless, no matter what the size, the dancing body has always been hard to ignore. Indeed, from the early Church Fathers on, one strong tradition was that dance was Dionysian: hedonistic, instinctual, physical, and consequently dangerous.[88] However, in the prelude, we have already seen a different interpretation of this Dionysian power in Nietzsche's assertion of the centrality of dance and music to the very birth of tragedy. While Salome's dance could be (and indeed has been) interpreted as a Dionysian dance of the body, it is also explicitly presented in the opera as a token in an economy of exchange. Salome uses her dancing body sensually in a Dionysian manner and also as a means to an end: the fulfillment of her obsessive desire and her strong, childlike will.[89]

In the opera, as in the play, the body is the focus of the attention – and the eye – of both audience and characters.[90] The dancing Salome is certainly the object of the gaze, particularly the male gaze, as she had been from the Bible onwards. In general, though, the visual or, more specifically, the act of looking (as both surveillance and spectacle) is so omnipresent in the opera and play that this has been called the "tragedy of the gaze."[91] As Martin Jay has convincingly shown, "ocularcentrism," or the dominance of the optic or visual, has a long and complex history in Western thought. The visual has been considered superior to the other senses, in part because it is detached from what it observes.[92] For this reason, the observer has the power of objectifying what is observed, of mastering and controlling through distancing. Because of this connection between the act of seeing and power, the privilege of vision has been linked to sexual privilege. The gaze has thus often been gendered male, leaving women as the objects of the gaze, either as exhibitionists or as the passively displayed.[93] Garber describes the "binary myth of Salome": "the male gazer (Herod), the female object of the gaze (Salome); the Western male subject as spectator (Flaubert, Huysmans, Moreau, Wilde himself) and the exotic, feminized Eastern other."[94] In more general terms, argues Laura Mulvey, the representations of women in opera, as in film, are "coded for strong visual and erotic impact so that they can be said to connote *to-be-looked-at-ness*." This coding means that to be looked at is a negative, a position of powerlessness.[95]

Salome the character and *Salome* the opera turn this now widely accepted view utterly on its head. Here, to be the object of the gaze is to have great power, as if "to-be-looked-at-ness" is what conveys mastery and control.[96] This is certainly an opera obsessed with the acts of looking and even staring. It opens with the Syrian guard

Narraboth staring at Salome as the Page tries to distract him; the soldiers stare at Herod, wondering what he is looking at; Salome enters, worrying about why her mother's husband stares at her the way he does.[97] The verb "ansehen" – to look at – dominates the text. Salome then stares at the moon as Narraboth continues to stare at her. The one person evading the gaze at this point is Jochanaan, imprisoned deep in a cistern by Herod, who obviously knows the power of being seen and wants to deny it to his enemy and harshest critic.[98] But Jochanaan evokes in others – first in the Cappadocian and then in Salome – the desire to see him. Knowing the erotic power of being looked at, Salome seduces Narraboth with the promise of a future glance at the lovestruck guard: "Ich werde dich ansehen." This is a young woman who is not objectified by the gaze but instead is empowered by it: she commands Narraboth to look at her, and when he does, he gives in at once to her request to bring Jochanaan out of the cistern, against Herod's orders.

Jochanaan too, however, knows the power of the visual and refuses to look at the staring Salome. In this scene the gaze is female, not male; in addition, the power once again is in the beheld and not the beholder. Jochanaan refuses to give Salome the mastery that would come from his gaze: "Ich will dich nicht ansehen," he tells her, and demands to be taken away from her staring eyes. It has been suggested that this refusal to look at her is a metaphoric refusal to recognize her as a person, independent of her mother.[99] But, more significantly, it is a refusal to grant her the power of the "gazed upon," a power already central to this young woman's sense of personhood. In Atom Egoyan's 1996 production for the Canadian Opera Company, Jochanaan in fact is made to cover his eyes with a black band, a band that Salome places over her own eyes at the end before she dies.

In visual terms, Salome's dance is a triumph, as all of us – the audience as well as Herod – bestow power on her as we gaze.[100] Salome therefore does not reverse the centrality of the male gazer as powerful, as John Paul Riquelme argues, but, rather, she alters the very power dynamics of the gaze itself: the person – of either sex – who gazes grants power to the one – of either sex – gazed upon.[101] When Salome demands her reward in the form of Jochanaan's head on a silver plate, Herod the tetrarch tries to offer her instead a number of strangely gendered visual treats that suggest a surrender of male visual control: jewels that, significantly, her mother had never seen and a crystal into which no woman had ever looked. But Salome refuses, for she knows well wherein lies the power of the gaze. It is this knowledge, however, that is the cause of the tragedy of both Salome and Jochanaan. When she later addresses his decapitated head with its closed eyes, she asks why he never looked at her when alive, in other words, why he never granted her the power that others did. Her narcissistic fury at being thwarted in her visual power (the power that comes from being looked at) is clear in the thrice-repeated personal "mich, mich, mich hast du nie gesehn" [me, me, me you never saw]. The tragic in this, for Salome, lies in her belief that, had he but looked at her, he would have loved her ("Hättest du mich gesehn, du hättest mich geliebt"). Such had indeed been the beautiful young princess's experience thus far in life. In despair, she again asks why he did not look at her ("Warum sahst du mich nicht an?"), knowing that being looked at is as much a fulfillment of desire as the act of looking can be. According to the libretto, no one (including the audience) ever actually sees Salome kiss the lips of the prophet: the act should occur in darkness as torches are put out and the moon (which itself had been gazed upon by everyone) disappears. The impact of Salome's invisible act is left to the imagination and to the aural power of the music and voice, as we then hear Salome sing of having kissed his mouth at last.

This interpretation – that Salome has attained mastery not so much of the gaze but of the "being-gazed-at" (and that therein lies real power) – is the contrary of the influential views of both Lawrence Kramer, who sees her as losing at the end the power of the gaze she usurped during the dance, and Carolyn Abbate, who sees her as a constant object of the gaze.[102] The male gaze has not been usurped because the power was never with it in the first place. Rather, in this case, to be the *object* of the gaze is to be empowered. This is an opera full of obsessive voyeurs and warnings of the dangers of looking, but in stark reversal of the traditional theory, to look is to grant power – to the one observed.[103]

To render in this way the visual more complex in its empowering dynamics is to suggest the need to rethink the relation between the aural and the visual in operatic performance, especially from the point of view of the audience: we gaze at Salome's body as well as listen to her voice, granting her the power Jochanaan refused her. An early reviewer implicated the audience by suggesting a certain hypocrisy inherent in any moralistic response: "[t]he public stares hypnotically, like slaves of the tetrarch, at the bloodthirsty music, then throws the shield of indignation over it."[104] Whether today we feel guilty pleasure or moral disgust at the end of *Salome*, the combination of the two extreme possibilities seems to have been central to the decadent aesthetic of both Wilde's play and the libretto: "the last pages of the opera are surely the apotheosis of decadent malaise. They capture that crucial moment for the decadent aesthetic, the moment when ecstatic experience of forbidden pleasures transforms into revulsion."[105]

In dramatic terms, the final scene (in which Salome kisses Jochanaan's mouth and Herod, in disgust and terror, orders her death) functions in complicated ways. We are perhaps as shocked by his act as by hers, but, given the growing horror that has likely accompanied the gradual unveiling of Salome's character, her death may allow the audience of any historical period to experience a satisfying cathartic release: the embodiment of the terrifying *femme fatale* is no more. In Susan McClary's strong formulation, in musical as well as narrative terms, the "monstrosity of Salome's sexual and chromatic transgressions is such that extreme violence seems justified – even demanded – for the sake of social and tonal order."[106] With the aid of what has been described as a music of "exposed nerve ends" that nonetheless has a strong erotic charge, the audience is both shocked and appeased.[107] It is, above all, implicated.

The audience has actually been implicated well before this, of course. Ted Chamberlin suggests that this ambivalent response characterizes the audience's reaction to the play's dance scene too: "we watch Salome's dance with appropriately perverse fascination, unable to avoid a shivery sense that *Salome* embodies something to which we are mysteriously vulnerable, something like the inseparability of Beauty from Decay and Death. And we develop a set of strategies for maintaining ourselves in a kind of delicious moral and rational suspension in the face of this mystery."[108] With the opera, we have been implicated by the music as much as the drama or the words of the text. Herod's first invitation to Salome to dance had launched "generously into a tune that never comes, foundering equally upon Salome's indifference and Herod's short concentration-span." But the dance, when it does come, assuages our disappointment, "thus deftly aligning the audience at once with Herod's desires and Salome's knowledge that she possesses the means of steering them towards the realisation of her own."[109] Her means, of course, include both her body and the power gained from having it gazed upon.

In *A rebours*, Huysmans too had made his hero identify with the gazing Herod: "Like the old King, Des Esseintes invariably felt overwhelmed, subjugated, stunned when he looked at this dancing-girl," the one in Moreau's watercolor.[110] His construction of her as the sign of the predatory, hysterical, but irresistible temptation of the flesh suggests that at least part of Salome's appeal was in her contradictoriness: as Gustave Klimt's paintings inspired by the opera suggest as well, the deadly young dancer was as much a degenerate object of misogynist fears as a sadomasochistic erotic ideal.[111] Huysmans's description also focuses the figurative eye of the reader on her body – though here in ekphrastic representation – just as surely as Wilde's and Strauss's construction of her focuses the literal eye of the audience of the staged versions on the performer's

Dionysian body. And, like that of the dancing bacchantes, Salome's performance ends with a ritualistic sacrificial death.[112]

Part of the unease of watching and listening to *Salome* may come from this implication in a relationship of empowerment that has fatal consequences. But for decades audiences have kept going to this opera, to see and hear the deaths of Salome and Jochanaan over and over. Abbate argues that, at the end, Salome's "musical speech drowns out everything in range, and we sit as passive objects, battered by that voice."[113] But we are always affected by more than the aural, and we are not passive: like Herod, we too have been active in the granting of power to this contradictory and complicated woman – the vamp *and* the virgin – whose body we too have stared at for almost the full ninety minutes of the opera. We heard of her physical beauty in the first moments, and then she appeared; we did not take our eyes off her body until the shields of Herod's soldiers crushed her to death. Shields are unusual weapons of execution, but they serve to recall the myth of Perseus and the Gorgon Medusa, already signaled in Salome's earlier description of Jochanaan's hair as being like serpents. Like Perseus, the soldiers have been protected from the sight of a female body that commands the deadly power of being-gazed-upon. Salome's death, seen in this context, is part of a complex structural irony as we remember Medusa's fate: decapitation by Perseus.[114]

As audience members we had no shields. We watched her dance, but we also watched her die. As a staged work, *Salome* does not allow its audience to remain passive or distanced: our gaze, like Herod's, does not objectify but instead empowers this woman. In fact, it may be the reversal of the power of the gaze that contributes to the anxiety that Salome manages to inspire. Repelled, perhaps, but also fascinated, we return and re-create again and again this contradictory story of virginal innocence and murderous passion as told through the troubling configuration of a delicately "bejeweled" text set to brutally powerful music. In the politics of the gaze, Salome is like Medusa: to look upon her is to feel her power. Salome causes the beheading of Jochanaan, rather than being beheaded herself (though Wilde actually considered this the best way to end his play), but, significantly, it is the Gorgon's physical presence that has the power to turn people to stone: her body's power, like Salome's, lies in being gazed upon.

ACT 2

Real Bodies

What is imagined by the playwright, incarnated by the performer, and witnessed by the audience is the living act itself, not the textual blueprints or remnants.

– William Storm

While the last two chapters dealt with represented bodies, in this part of the book we turn to real bodies, specifically those of the performers and the audience. There are, of course, other bodies in staged opera: animal bodies, for instance. The notorious stories of animal behavior and misbehavior in certain productions are the stuff of operatic lore. They are certainly important distractions for audiences – as are children's bodies – because of the Dionysian suggestions of the contingent and uncontrollable. Then there are the (almost) unseen bodies of the skilled musicians who make up the orchestra and without whom live opera would not really exist. Like almost all books on opera, this one too leaves these bodies in the darkened orchestra pit, to be considered at a later date. We turn instead to the most obvious and visible of bodies: those of the performers on the stage.

It just might be possible to ignore the physicality of the act of singing if we are listening to a disembodied voice on a recording, but to watch someone sing in the flesh is to be made instantly aware of not only the Apollonian control and discipline required but also the brute Dionysian corporeality of voice production. In chapter 3 we will examine some of the many ways in which we are made aware of the bodily realities facing the performers on stage. This involves not only questions of physical health and the often frightening fragility of the human voice as a musical instrument, easily abused by accident or bad judgment, but it also means considering the impact on the voice of things as varied as hormones and the choice of roles to sing. The psychological state we call stage fright is, of course, also mostly manifest in physical ways as the body becomes the battlefield of psychic conflicts.

Another aspect of the performer's body that we cannot usually ignore in actual live performance (though, again, on recordings we can) is its appearance. The singing body is either visually appropriate to the role in which it is cast, or not. In the 1990s a large and aging Pavarotti could still sing the part of the starving young writer, Rodolfo, in the Parisian garret of *La Bohème*, but people would have been more apt to comment on it than earlier. While opera is a dramatic form of a certain excess and artifice, where the willing suspension of disbelief has functioned more often and more successfully than in spoken theater, the increasing use of video technology has brought the demands for realism from television and film to the operatic stage. As we shall see, when Maria Callas famously lost weight, new respect for her acting abilities was widely expressed, as were new doubts about her "thinned-down" voice.[1] Size is not the only issue here, of course. Age too is relevant: how long can aging mezzos sing those young male trouser roles? Or, on the other end of the scale, consider the plight of young baritones like Dmitri Hvorostovsky whose voice range condemns them to playing much older men.[2] Race, of course, is also an issue: why is it that the gypsy Carmen and the Philistine Dalila are among the few roles consistently sung by black singers today?[3] Why did a French director, in his attempt at realism in the film version of Puccini's *Madama Butterfly*, feel comfortable casting a Chinese singer in the Japanese Cio-Cio-San's role for the consumption of Western audiences?

The final chapter, "The Perceiving Body," will move from our earlier focus on the implied audience to consider the various Apollonian and Dionysian responses of those who actually perceive opera in the flesh. What happens as we sit in the dark, still and silent, but paradoxically busy both interpreting and responding, often physically, to the multisensorial and communal experience of being part of the audience of live opera? While we participate in making meaning of what we see and hear, we also laugh and weep; we feel a pleasurable frisson; we boo and we cheer; we cough and we fidget.[4] For better or worse, the solitary listening to a recording in our living room cannot duplicate the public experience of being part of a larger audience interacting with the bodies both around us and on the stage.

The energy of a live performance is felt physically by audience members as much as by performers. In *The Absent Body*, Drew Leder reminds us that "[f]rom the most visceral of cravings to the loftiest of artistic achievements, the body plays its formative role." But, as he goes on to note, we usually ignore it, "paying little attention to . . . physical sensations or posture."[5] Never is this more true than when we are sitting in an audience. It is not that we are not prey to physical reactions; we just do not necessarily think about them very much. Nietzsche argued that the perceivers of tragedy (and Wagnerian opera) experienced an "internal bifurcation": they were "receptive in [their] Dionysiac state" to the potentially destructive power of the sensuous music but protected by the Apollonian control of aesthetic formal beauty.[6] Rejecting the Aristotelian theory of tragic catharsis as unaesthetic "pathological discharge" more appropriate to medicine, Nietzsche argued for a version of what we earlier saw as a balancing of the Apollonian and Dionysian impulses as the ideal or appropriate audience response.[7]

We became acutely and amusingly aware of the distinctions between real and represented bodies once when we were visiting lecturers in an English Department. Many audience members attending our illustrated talk on the cultural history of syphilis were themselves working on topics of research involving "the body." Knowing that people today, since the invention of penicillin, have the luxury of not having to recognize the bodily signs of syphilis, but also believing that it would be difficult to understand the operatic and literary representations of the disease without that knowledge, we projected a photographic image of a syphilitic gumma on a real human leg. The sudden intake of breath in the room at the sight of this horrific wound made us suddenly extremely conscious of the difference between talking about the body in the abstract (or even as represented) and seeing the body in the flesh, even if mediated by photography. We offer in this section no such shocking images but simply an interest in how the production and reception of opera are intensely bodily acts.

3

The Performing Body

In the last chapter we saw how the Dionysian dancing body of Salome was positioned front and center on the operatic stage, a body not to be ignored. But what happens if the vocal Salome does not match the physical Salome? The first interpreter of the role, Maria Wittich, did not perform the dance herself; not until a year later did Fanchette Verhunc become the first to both dance and sing the role. It has been said that *Salome* did much to make the concept of the *physique du rôle* a prerequisite for singers, yet it clearly presented a problem at the time: "Salome is a dramatic soprano rôle, and those who sang it were almost all rather stout, to ensure the power and endurance of the voice."[1] But the larger question here is this: Is stoutness really necessary for power and endurance? Or is this a great operatic myth? If so, what is the source of the obviously potent mystique of size of body correlating with size of voice? These are among the questions that this chapter addresses.

Another is the paradox in which operatic singers (and directors) today are caught: Should performers look right for the role or sound right? If both are not possible, which should prevail? Either way – visually or aurally – it is a question of the body. And either way, audiences today face a similar paradox: accustomed as we are to film and television realism, do we want to see opera as credible drama, in which characters look as well as sound appropriate for their roles? Or do we accept the conventions of operatic artifice that have so often worked to separate what we see from what we hear? It is not simply the ascendancy of the opera director today that has brought this question to the fore; it has been an issue for a long time.

Mary Garden's commanding physical presence earlier in this century led a Parisian critic to remark that she portrayed Salome with an "untamed sensuality" and "acted the whole opera with bare arms, heaving loins and voluptuous legs." Her performance of this role in Milwaukee was vetted by a committee of presumably incorruptible men over the age of seventy-five, but evidently her reputation was more sensational than the reality. Yet her 1921 premiere in Chicago was greeted with such storms of protest for being obscene and immoral that she canceled the rest of the performances.[2] It goes without saying that it was not her voice that produced this particular reaction.

✦ The Physicality of the Embodied Voice

It has been argued that all live music is corporeal, that there is a physicality to "music making itself (the sight of the body's labors to make sound)," but never is this more evident than when the instrument being played is the body itself.[3] The physical activity involved in vocal production is clear when we watch a tenor go red in the face while he strains for that high C or when a singer cancels because she has a cold. Opera is a performed, enacted, and embodied art form; therefore, it is both heard and seen by an audience. As Maria Callas famously taught audiences, on stage the singer is an actor: body language – gesture, facial expression, eye contact, posture – can sometimes communicate as strongly as the music and the words being sung.[4] But singers as singers always have to work within the limits of their anatomical endowment, as enhanced by vocal and acting technique. As mezzo soprano Dolora Zajick puts it: "The greatest artists are sublimators . . . *and* technically oriented. When you're connected technically, you empty out all the energy that is in you – that *is* you. All the anguish, joy, everything. *That*'s what people pay to see."[5]

Audiences also pay to experience the excitement and, frankly, the unpredictability of live opera: the body and the voice may be sublime, or they may fail. The voice in performance is not disembodied or transcendent; it is anchored in the real, and fragile, human body. Catherine Clément recounts being at a performance of *Don Giovanni* in which the protagonist tumbled head over heels down an enormous staircase: "Doubtless my memory amplifies the incredible noise. Doubtless the audience barely breathed a sound then . . . ; they concentrate on forgetting the accident, they blot it out. But this is the image of Don Juan my ears remember: the seducer betrayed by balance, the awkwardness of an actor stricken with dizziness or fear, the myth that loses countenance for a thunderbolt second, and shows its underside."[6] It also shows its corporeality.

Today people are likely to blame directors for the mad things they demand of their singing actors on the stage. At his Bayreuth *Ring* in 1988 and 1989, Harry Kupfer had Peter Hofmann, his Siegmund, race about 80 meters down the stage, hang from a raised bar almost 20 feet off the ground, drop and land on his feet, and then begin to sing the opening words of *Die Walküre*. Sometimes it is the costume designer who comes in for criticism, as did Rosalie for her 1994 Bayreuth *Ring* designs. Some of her visually striking costumes blocked the singers' hearing as well as inhibited their movement. But this is not new: back in 1948 Kirsten Flagstad complained bitterly about having to wear Brünnhilde's heavy winged helmet during *Ring* rehearsals at La Scala.[7] Singers have always had to deal with the demands made on their bodies and voices as well as the sometimes stubborn recalcitrance of those bodies and voices. It would seem that, throughout the centuries, they have always thought about how they looked as well as sounded: singers at Mazzocchi's singing school in Rome in the early seventeenth century are said to have practiced in front of a looking glass "so that they might be certain they were making no disagreeable movement of the muscles of the face, of the forehead, of the eyes, or of the mouth."[8] Looks and voice are both inescapable parts of the operatic experience and inescapably physical.

As an art form, opera has a history of calling attention to the real corporeal body: think of the importance of the *castrati* to its beginnings. Castrated before puberty, young boys with promising voices grew up to become the stars of seventeenth- and eighteenth-century opera, especially in the papal states, where women were banned from the stage. Unhampered by the (vocal) interruption of adolescence, these young men continued in school, receiving intensive training that no woman would ever have received, given the suspicion and moral disapprobation associated with the female sex on the stage. Not surprisingly, the *castrati* were exceedingly able in technical terms, and that fact, as much as physiology, might account for such things as their vocal agility and wide range. Yet there were physiological results of the castration that clearly affected the voice: "The operation ensured that the thoracic cavity developed greatly, sometimes disproportionately (leading to a form of gigantism), while the larynx and the vocal cords developed much more slowly and had considerable power brought to bear on them."[9] *Castrati* combined adult lung capacity with the brilliance and power of the high treble voice to create what commentators consistently referred to as a "disembodied" sound with an "unearthly" timbre. This verbal attempt to transcend the body – the body that had paid the price for this vocal beauty – was not fully successful, in part because *castrati* were also thought of as *all* body. Called capons, geldings, half-men, they became man-made monsters who were paradoxically highly sexualized in the audience's eyes.[10] Our contemporary popular culture has exploited precisely this sexual tension in films like *Farinelli* and novels like Anne Rice's *Cry to Heaven*.

The history of opera continued to concentrate attention on the physical body, however, even after the *castrato* went out of fashion. As we have noted, the culmination of this interest in the twentieth century was no doubt the career of the most famous of the acting singers, Maria Callas, who lost over sixty pounds and went from being a large diva to a slim glamorous one in the 1950s. (See figures 10 and 11.) The debate still rages over what effect this change of size had on her singing voice. Given the number of books and articles already written about her, it is tempting to agree with the sardonic view that "[t]hank God there was only one Callas."[11] But it is also true that no single performer has done more to focus public attention on the relation of the body to the voice than the charismatic Callas. The reviews testify to the physicality of her performing power: "you can't take your eyes off her," they repeatedly assert. As we shall see, especially after her weight loss, the visual aspect became increasingly important. As one biographer put it, "[N]ot only would it serve to reveal her dramatic talents to their best advantage, but it would also help distract attention from her increasing vocal frailty."[12] To a large extent, it was *seeing* Callas that made her so exciting; it was also seeing her that distracted people from the increasingly obvious flaws in her voice.

The size of the body in relation to the size, quality, and stamina of the voice is not the only corporeal issue that Callas's career raises. This was a woman both blessed and cursed by her physical body. Intensely myopic in the days before contact lenses, she had to memorize movements, tempi, and cues, for she could not see the conductor. But because she could not see the audience either, her concentration on the stage action and her role was utterly complete. Hence her dramatic power. From her early years, Callas was prey to all sorts of illnesses, and increasingly these affected her ability to perform. As she became famous, her stage fright increased to a pathological level, and its physical manifestations became more evident. Toward the end of her career, she also experienced the inevitable effects of aging, though recording impresario Walter Legge claimed that she never could accept the fact that "after fifty no woman can expect to have the upward range and facility she had at thirty."[13] In short, Callas lived intensely the physical problems faced by all singers, in part because she lived them very publicly. For that reason, she will be an inevitable touchstone for this chapter. But Callas also had the ability to make her audience acutely aware not only of her body but of their own bodies as well. As Wayne Koestenbaum rapturously explains:

Callas took in breath dramatically, audibly, as if she were gasping. Loud breathing gave the listener a sensation of knowledge, even of participation: the audience could hear where the phrase began, could measure how much effort its production entailed. . . . She turned the need to breathe into an expressive opportunity. A Callas trademark, the gasping for breath before a climactic utterance ("Numi, pietà"), a gasp she refused to conceal, followed by a rending, dangerous, phlegmy note, calculated to pierce, demystifying singing. Exposing the voice's reliance on breath, she implicitly asked the audience to forgive her instrument's shortcomings, and to recognize that air, and vocal resilience, inevitably diminish. Musical lines, like sentences in conversation, need to be stitched from the body's substance; they are an economy, with raw materials, labor, and a product. The intake of breath fills the audience with compassion for the singer's struggle, and with admiration for her accomplishment. The gasp is the audible price tag on the expensive garment of the aria.[14]

Callas never let herself – or us – forget the embodiment of her voice, even if she, like so many other singers, always thought not of "my voice" but of "the voice" as something both of her body and separate from it, not to say out of its control.[15] Apollonian distance on the Dionysian body may be a survival strategy for singers.

If anatomy is destiny for women in general, it is even more the case for singers of either sex. Born with a particular set of vocal cords, a specific pair of lungs, and a unique configuration of facial bones, each singer inevitably has fixed limitations – and advantages – within which to work; in other words, technique can probably only go so far. Legge claimed that there were specific anatomical reasons for Callas's particular voice: "the extraordinary formation of her upper palate, shaped like a Gothic arch, not the Romanesque arch of the normal mouth. Her rib cage was also unusually long for a woman of her height."[16] And when singers talk about what happens when they sing, they are relentlessly physical in their descriptions. In Marilyn Horne's words: "[W]hen I breathe, my diaphragm goes out, the whole rib cage fills, and the back muscles are absolutely engaged to their fullest." Joan Sutherland states the importance of physical support of the voice in this very corporeal way: "You make your chest cavity as large as possible – and hold it. You breathe only with your diaphragm. Your chest and shoulders never move. You feel as though you're holding up this long column of air on which the voice is resting."[17]

Like all musicians, singers have to master their instruments technically, but when those instruments are physically housed in their own bodies, they are particularly exposed to and reliant upon the vagaries of their human bodily existence.[18] To train the voice is to train the body. Voice manuals have always been based in the physical – at least what was understood of the physiology and anatomy of the time. Interestingly, the basic exercises have not changed much over the years, despite a change in understanding of the voice. Renaissance voice teachers such as Maffei in the mid sixteenth century utilized physiology as they received it from Galen, Aristotle, and Avicenna.[19] One of the most important modern physiologically based theorists was the famous teacher Manuel García (1805–1906), who presented his *Mémoire sur la voix humaine* to the Académie des sciences in Paris in 1840. His *Traité complet de l'art du chant* of the same year soon became a standard text for singers and teachers alike. What made García particularly important was that he invented the laryngoscope, an instrument that enabled observations of the workings of the larynx and made possible the medical discipline of otolaryngology. His subsequent study of the vocal cords was presented to the Royal Society in London in 1855.[20] It was his pioneering anatomical and physiological work that led to further scientific studies of musical acoustics and the mechanisms of singing.

García made his students undergo a medical and vocal examination and demanded that they submit to special treatments if their larynx appeared to require it.[21] Among his students were the famous "Swedish songbird," Jenny Lind, as well as Mathilde Marchesi, who would herself later become a celebrated teacher. Like

García, Marchesi's advice to singers was always physically based and physiologically informed.[22] In time, the ideas put forward in her *Theoretical and Practical Vocal Method*, especially those about different vocal registers (chest, medium, head), were tested and in part verified by experiment, but it was not, as she believed, three resonators that were involved but, rather, laryngeal adjustments.[23] In the nineteenth and twentieth centuries, there has been an increased capability of understanding vocal production as technologies have developed that allow imaging of the vocal apparatus (such as X-rays, xeroradiography, and endoscopy), improved concepts of respiratory tract physiology, and new techniques to evaluate vocal output. As scientific evidence changed, some teachers moved from theories of "placement and support" of the voice (involving breath control and resonance) to theories of laryngeal function, applying acoustic laws to the voice.[24] Increasingly, whole body awareness became part of teaching voice: with the work of Feldenkrais and Laban and with the Alexander Technique and Yoga came a growing sense of the corporeal complexity of the act of singing.[25]

A look at scholarly and scientific journals such as the *Journal of Research in Singing and Applied Vocal Pedagogy* reveals surveys and experimental studies on topics ranging from vocal cord pathology (polyps) to the impact of physical exercise on voice and from the importance of the position of the epiglottis to theories of "vocal ecology."[26] Technology has increased the ability to test, and often disprove, age-old physiological theories.[27] But the science often seems strangely imprecise; the power of tradition and mystique seems strangely strong. Perhaps Apollo and Dionysus are in tension here and in more ways than one, for it is also clear that singing not only demands top physical condition but also top psychological condition. In stressing the corporeal we do not want to give the impression that the psychic state of the singer on stage, open to intense public scrutiny and competition, is not of crucial importance, for it obviously is. But that psychological state often has physical manifestations, and these will be the particular focus of this chapter.[28]

As we have seen, the voice is a physically embodied instrument, one that is endowed with a motor, a vibrator, and a resonator. Or, to use another metaphor, it is like a wind instrument: it has a bellows (the lungs), a windpipe (the bronchi and trachea), a reed (the vocal cords), resonators (the closed cavities in the cranium and face), and a speaking trumpet (the mouth).[29] As Anna Russell rather unkindly described the physiology here: "singers have resonance where their brains ought to be."[30]

Sound itself results from the "regularly repeated interruption of airflow through the glottis, caused by the valving action of the vocal folds."[31] The intensity of the sound is proportional to the pressure developed below the cords, while the pitch depends on the frequency of vibration and is related to the length, mass, and tension of the cords themselves.[32] The sound is continuously modified by changes in the larynx to provide what we perceive as changes in intensity, pitch, and quality.

Since we are as concerned with how people talk about the embodied voice as we are with the actual physiology, it is interesting to note that when voice is discussed, different things are stressed, depending on the person's particular physiological theory.[33] Nevertheless, the complete bodily activity that is the act of singing is perhaps stated best by Marilyn Horne describing her first low note in *Norma*: "I just think that right into my nose with a tremendous amount of support, the buttock muscles are tight, and I place it there dead ahead of me, and bong, I just hit that bull's-eye-right-over-*there*."[34] There is certainly agreement over the fact that "support" of the voice is critical for a singer. As Louisa Tetrazzini, that famous diva from the past, said, "A shaky, uncontrolled breath is like a rickety foundation upon which nothing can be built."[35] But of what does this "support" consist? For many years it has been attributed to the diaphragm. This view has been recognized within the singing world, as seen in an interview with Marilyn Horne: "When I breathe, my diaphragm goes out. . . . It's as if the whole thing just opens up, an automatic mechanism that happens by pushing out the diaphragm," she says. To this her interviewer, Jerome Hines, replies, "By diaphragm you mean the stomach area underneath the ribs?"[36] However, while the diaphragm is the primary muscle of inspiration, singing is an expiratory activity. Nevertheless, it would seem that the myth of singing from the diaphragm has persisted for about as long as people have been singing. This is perhaps because, while certainly misleading from the viewpoint of mechanism, it was useful to voice teachers as a descriptive term.[37]

This "support" for singing actually requires building up pressure below the vocal cords, which themselves act as a variable resistor to the air that is forced through them. The pressure is supplied in part from the lungs themselves, which are elastic in nature and exert a pressure when inflated. This pressure decreases, however, as the lungs deflate and as lung volume diminishes, so that muscular activity is required for steady subglottic pressure in a proportion that compensates for the changing contribution from the lungs. This stable base support is provided by the contraction of abdominal muscles. The more rapid changes in pressure required for singing are achieved by superimposed activity of other muscles, such as those between the ribs.[38]

The muscle activity utilized by a trained performer in singing is different from that used in speaking as well as from that of an untrained person singing. According to one experiment involving male singers, there is also some variation among performers that "may depend in part on how the subject has learned on his own to use his own muscular system most effectively against the passive mechanical properties of his respiratory apparatus."[39] Nevertheless, in the singers investigated in another study, "the rib cage was relatively more and the abdomen was relatively less expanded than they were in the relaxed state at the same lung volume" because of abdominal muscle contraction creating the pressure for support and also lifting the chest wall.[40] These observations support the advice of teachers of the past, including that of Manuel García, who suggested that in singing the body should be held erect, the shoulders thrown back and the arms crossed behind, thus opening the chest to bring out the voice, and that of Sbriglia, who had belts made for both male and female singers to assist in holding up the abdomen, claiming that "you must have intestinal fortitude to support your *point d'appui* or the focal point in your chest."[41] Clearly, the act of singing is a complex physiological event.

Willa Cather captures some of this complexity and physicality in her novel *The Song of the Lark* when the musician and teacher, Harsanyi, persuades his piano pupil, Thea Kronberg, to sing for him. He holds his hands on her throat, "placing the tips of his delicate fingers over her larynx." As she begins, we learn that "[h]e loved to hear a big voice in a relaxed, natural throat, and he was thinking that no one had ever felt this voice vibrate before." He is startled that he had not realized before that she should have such a fine voice: "Everything about her indicated it – the big mouth, the wide jaw and chin, the strong white teeth, the deep laugh. The machine was so simple and strong, seemed to be so easily operated. She sang from the bottom of herself."[42]

People talk about opera, however, as a "marathon art": even if we do not consider the psychological demands or the musical and dramatic ones, the physical exertion alone warrants singers' designation as the Olympic athletes of the voice world.[43] If conductors can have major changes in heart rate, respiration, muscle tension, and temperature when at work, imagine what happens to singers. Herbert von Karajan's pulse rate was said to correlate with his emotional responses to the music he was conducting, as if he felt the music through his body.[44] The same is likely true of singers, for they use their bodies during performances in even more complex ways. Margaret Harshaw tells the story of being on stage with Zinka Milanov in the first act of *La Gioconda* and suddenly finding herself playing an interesting role in another singer's physical production of sound. Milanov had to sing a long pianissimo B-flat and move while holding it, so she placed her hand on Harshaw's shoulder and sang the note, and then they moved together downstage: "She was using me for support as she sustained the tone," said Harshaw.[45] The voice is certainly a most embodied thing.

✥ The Fragility of the Voice

The voice is also a most delicate thing, however, and singers know this all too well. Baritone Robert Merrill explains: "The life of a singer is incredibly fragile: It hangs by two thin cords in the throat, approximately the diameter of buttonhole thread. If not used correctly, they stretch and lose their elasticity." Luciano Pavarotti echoes these worries: "The voice is a fragile instrument that is vulnerable to many physical ailments that will damage the singing. Young singers must get into the habit of treating themselves like babies."[46] Singers know that illness or stress, allergy or overuse can make their voices lose tone quality or heft. In baritone Tito Gobbi's words, "[T]he singer – unlike every other musical performer – is his or her own instrument. If the singer is sick, so is the voice. If the singer is under a great strain, so is the voice. If the singer is shaking with terror, only the most reliable technique will save the voice from doing the same."[47] The singing voice is unpredictable, but even more importantly, it is, by definition, a passing phenomenon. It is tied inextricably to the unreliable body, "subject as it is to disease, decay, and violence of every sort."[48] This is why Koestenbaum can call "vocal crisis" a "physiological emergency, a bodily catastrophe": "A broken voice has brought the self's private woe, the body's history and flaw, into the Olympian art of singing."[49]

Maria Callas was said to transcend for a time "the shackles of a vocal apparatus that was recalcitrant from the start."[50] But there was more to it than that, for the fragility of the body's health cannot but affect the voice: Callas's letters as a young singer are full of tales of influenza, swollen legs, and inflamed throats. Yet she almost always sang nonetheless; the infamous cancellations began only later, when her vocal problems became more evident and her sense of control over her voice diminished.[51] In those later years, she was plagued with serious sinus infections that affected her hearing and her right jaw, "preventing her resonance chambers from working correctly."[52] She also developed a hernia related to an appendix operation, and this would actually have had a negative effect on her voice; as we have seen, the integrity of the abdominal wall is essential for the stable pressure base support for the voice from the abdominal muscles.[53] Even her harshest critics in those later years have had to admit the impact on the voice of her many health problems.

People offered other reasons too, of course, for her extended difficulties, including vocal abuse. It was said of Callas, as it is of some young singers today, that she rushed into certain roles, giving into the demands of her career.[54] She also mixed different repertoires. When in January 1949 she took over the soprano role in *I Puritani* from the ailing Margherita Carosio, conductor Tullio Serafin said, "Maria is involved in *Walküre*, a strenuous opera with an entirely different tessitura from that of *I Puritani*. It's impossible for her to sing these operas alternately."[55] Of course, she did, with great success. Given Callas's famous range and adaptability of voice, she was able to do what few singers before or after have done. But did it take its toll? And did some of the roles she sang early on contribute to the decline of her voice? The received wisdom in opera circles is that young singers should not take on certain roles for fear of placing too great demands on their vocal mechanisms too early: for tenors, Otello, Tristan, and Siegfried, for instance, and for sopranos, Norma, Brünnhilde, and Isolde.[56] Note the strong Wagnerian representation in those lists. Celebrated teacher Mathilde Marchesi was firm in her belief that the size of the Wagnerian orchestra caused singers to strain excessively. Wagner was "of the opinion that every voice should be at the composer's command," she exclaimed. "I, on the contrary, held that the composer must take into consideration the compass of the different voices, by which interpretation, pronunciation, and declamation must naturally benefit. Wagner remained true to his principle, and so, alas! many voices have been ruined through his music, and many talented singers, both male and female, have been lost to art."[57] No doubt the notion of the destructive quality of Wagnerian roles has its origins in the singing-related deaths of some of their early interpreters: the first Tristan, Ludwig Schnorr von Carolsfeld, who died shortly after the opera's premiere, and Hedwig Reicher-Kindermann, who died of a heart attack at the age of thirty while singing Wagner on a tour that "over-strained her both physically and psychologically," or so it was said.[58]

Wagnerian roles are certainly demanding, and vocal abuse is certainly real. Some say that "powering" the voice will destroy it; some claim that voluminous voices generally wear out more quickly than smaller ones. But the reality is that many singers have acute vocal trouble at one time or another, even famous ones like Renata Tebaldi, Jessye Norman, Elisabeth Schwarzkopf, Mario del Monaco, and a long list of others.[59] And while the causes can be psychological as easily as physical, the result is always corporeal. Jenny Lind is said to have done considerable damage to her voice in her early years, "partly through overstrain, partly through ignorance of the true principles of voice-emission."[60] For centuries, rival singing teachers and schools have claimed that voices have been ruined out of ignorance or from following the wrong pedagogical principles. While this has been denied by some, others assert that at least half of identifiable vocal pedagogies are built upon false physiological assumptions about diaphragmatic/chest wall action.[61] Significantly, however, from the ancient world to our present one, teachers have been acutely aware of the many different dangers to the voice, dangers that are both natural and self-inflicted.[62] Obviously, allergies and infections are the biological enemies of the human voice that singers fear most. Illness and indisposition are the major reasons why singers cancel performances. No wonder they are frightened of getting infected. Caruso was only the most flamboyant of those singers who take extreme measures to try to ward off infections.[63] But all the vocal hygiene in the world cannot keep infections at bay forever: vocal health is dependent on bodily health.[64] And chance and bad luck play their roles here too.

Let us look now at some of these many and varied physical problems – beyond the obvious one of infections – in order to get a clearer sense of just why the human voice is in some ways such a fragile instrument. The voice obviously goes through various changes in pitch and range over time, from childhood through adolescence and young adulthood and into old age. This is because of changes in, among other things, vocal cords, as well as lung capacity and elasticity. Vocal deterioration is said to be less audible in people who are in good overall physical shape and who practice sound voice training methods: *vox sana in corpore sano.*[65] Although the vocal shift that characterizes male puberty is the most obvious of the many hormonal changes humans undergo, it is women singers who are most affected by hormones, likely because testosterone levels do not fluctuate very much from day to day and female hormones do. Aging women and women undergoing androgen treatments do, however, often get what are called "virilized" voices. When female hormones are reduced in menopause, vocal cords can swell or dehydrate, causing permanent vocal changes that can spell the end of a singing career.[66]

Even in their early years, female singers must deal with hormonal issues because of their monthly menstrual cycles. Singer Carol Neblett put it rather emphatically: "A woman sings with her ovaries – you're only as good as your hormones." Joan Sutherland's more measured terms make the same point, as she notes that "at certain times of the month for a woman, a cloudiness, or fuzziness gets on the voice."[67] Though some claim that the connection between menstrual cycle and the voice has not been conclusively proved, others have strongly argued that there is a real vocal change caused by what is called laryngopathia premenstrualis, that is, by vocal cord swelling that leads to hoarseness and loss of power and flexibility in the voice.[68] Otolaryngologist Jean Abitbol and gynecologist Beatrice Abitbol have shown parallel cellular changes in the vocal cords and the cervix during the menstrual cycle, suggesting that the larynx is indeed hormonally affected.[69] The surprising inconclusiveness of the perceptions reported in actual auditory experiments involving singers would seem to be, in part, because the vocal changes are much more apparent to the singers – because felt by them in their bodies – than they are to the listeners.[70] So strong is this belief, however, that some European opera houses have for years traditionally granted their singers "grace days" before and in the early days of their menstrual periods.

Voice production can obviously be affected adversely not only by endocrinological problems but by the physical condition of the body's other various systems. The musculoskeletal system gets involved when dysphonia (that is, an undesired change in voice) is caused by tension and fatigue in the larynx and supporting structures.[71] The gastrointestinal system's most dangerous contribution to vocal problems is reflux, or what is commonly referred to as heartburn. This can cause a persistent cough, hoarseness, and sore throat; it also always involves the risk of aspirating when something "goes down the wrong way." Neurological problems such as muscle weakness or tremors can obviously affect the muscles that control the larynx and thus the voice.

Among the greatest terrors for singers, however, are those growths on the vocal cords called nodules or polyps, for these can temporarily or permanently damage the voice. It has been said that, for most opera singers, "it would be more acceptable to be diagnosed as a typhus carrier than the owner of a nodule."[72] Lucrezia Bori was such an "owner," and in order to ensure a successful operation for the removal of the nodules, she took four years of rest from the stage and, for one of them, was utterly mute.[73] As we have seen, Callas felt that her sinus problems were one of the major causes of her vocal deterioration in her later performing years, and this makes some sense, medically speaking. When the ears, nose, or throat are affected, the voice can be altered. Alfred Tomatis developed an interesting theory to explain the change in the voice of Enrico Caruso that occurred around 1902: he hypothesized that Caruso must have had an accident that partially blocked his Eustachian tubes. Indeed, it seems that the singer had a surgical operation in that year that damaged the tubes and caused a loss of hearing, especially of low frequency sounds. The rich and beautiful voice that Caruso then developed, argued Tomatis, turned this seeming handicap into the key to his greatness, because the tenor was forced to learn primarily through bone conduction.[74] Not all singers, of course, are this lucky. Ear, nose, and throat problems can cause permanent damage to the human voice.

Though in a somewhat different kind of category than nodules or sinus problems, the impact of sexual activity on the voice – most often, the male voice – has long been an obsession of singers (and audiences): even in the early period before the rise of opera, we can find warnings to singers about the dangers of sexual excess.[75] Pavarotti wonders: "Why is everyone so interested in sex and its effects on the voice? Maybe it's because singers have always looked for excuses when they are not in voice and too much lovemaking is a noble excuse. Or maybe it's because everyone is interested in sex and will use any pretext to bring it up."[76] He then proceeds to tell tales of singers who are convinced that sex helps their performance on stage, so they arrange a little something before or during the breaks. Others, especially tenors, evidently believe that sex damages the high notes. While we could find no scientific evidence to prove one view or the other, some singers continue to believe that it is wiser not to indulge a day or two before a performance. Robert Merrill recounts the story of Mario del Monaco's wife accusing Rudolf Bing of the Metropolitan Opera of ruining her sex life because he was using her husband in two or three shows a week.[77]

Moving from the humorous to the serious, however: stage fright is usually considered a psychological state, but its effects are decidedly corporeal. Maria Callas was one of many singers who were not at all nervous on stage at the start of their careers but who became increasingly terrified as they became famous and more was at stake: expectations were higher, and audiences were more partisan. As she remarked: "The audience's slightest reaction affects you. At times you feel enormous, bigger even than the theatre. Then at other times you feel tiny, ashamed, terrified. All you want to do is run away."[78] When she felt this way, Callas needed someone in the wings with her before going on stage to lend physical as well as moral support: "she would cling to that unfortunate person's arm with a strength that was positively frenzied," claimed one such unfortunate person. Another described being with her, holding her "icy hand and whispering encouragement while rivulets of perspiration would be running down her neck and the edge of her dress." She herself claimed that she would feel as if her heart had suddenly stopped beating in terror.[79]

Yet performers are among the first to admit that there is a positive side to a controlled version of this adrenaline rush, and studies have shown that singers feel it to be essential to the "edge" of their performance. On a more mundane level, some singers even find it clears their nasal passages: a stuffed nose disappears as soon as one has to sing on stage in front of an audience.[80] But the more debilitating bodily effects of stage fright are responses that even the most famous of performers have to learn to deal with. Pavarotti describes his preperformance nerves as they build after he is dressed and made up: "Now you must only sit and wonder how you ever got into this profession where you, a grown man, must get yourself dressed up in a funny costume, walk out onto a stage before thousands of people who may or may not wish you well, and risk making a complete fool of yourself or causing an artistic scandal." He has to find a bent nail on the stage floor to ward off evil and assure good luck, but just before he walks onstage, not even that helps: he sits with sweat rolling down his neck, hating his job, praying. Yet when he actually goes before an audience, all is suddenly well: "something clicks in my mind. I become the character, and everything else leaves my head."[81]

Singers fight their terrors by various means: infamously, Caruso used smoking and alcohol. They know that their physical and technical performance can be seriously affected by stage fright.[82] This may be a generic fear of performing in front of an audience, or it might be a nervous anticipation of problems at some particular point in the opera. It might even be a more generalized catastrophic fear of public voice loss or ruin. "Spook thoughts" like these have real physical manifestations.[83] The heart races and the rate of breathing increases, causing lightheadedness; skeletal muscles become tense and soon fatigued, leading to rubbery limbs; the adrenaline rush leaves one feeling trembling and shaky; perspiration increases; the face becomes pale; one might feel urinary urgency or nausea; the voice can be impaired by insufficient hydration in the mouth and throat that can lead to "red, edematous membranous tissue in the vocal tract."[84] An overall "body block" can even occur, as muscles "armor" against fear of failure. A common anxiety reaction to these bodily symptoms is memory loss – the singer's terror.[85] Some also report a strange sense of disembodiment as they helplessly watch themselves perform from a distance.

Invoking a good many of these symptoms are the extravagant stories told of Rosa Ponselle's stage fright before singing her first ever opera performance:

> Ponselle was a fiasco of nerves by the afternoon of the night before. "What in the name of God have I gotten myself into?" She tries to take a walk; cannot move. She crazes a companion into calling a doctor for a sedative; it doesn't take. She thinks she'll try a brush-up march through the score and pulls that special diva-*in-extremis* bit wherein she cannot recall half the notes. Backstage at the Met on The Night, she discovers she has Completely Lost Her Voice. She envisions a heart attack, complete with headline: "VAUDEVILLE SINGER DIES AT MET DEBUT."[86]

Panic takes many bodily forms.

Stage fright leads to sometimes quite elaborate superstitious rituals as singers try to ward off the dangers. Some learn to deal better with the psychological sense of vulnerability and exposure that opera singing entails as they become more experienced, though in Callas's case it was quite the opposite. Beniamino Gigli explained that he had to learn to separate the fear that is "*the result of doubting one's own abilities*" from the necessary fear that every artist "should feel and experience."[87] For some singers, techniques such as visualization and relaxation training help performance anxiety; for others, deep breathing brings some relief. For still others, drugs such as propranolol can be effective in reducing symptoms such as increased heart rate, but there are significant side effects.[88] While it is true that, "[l]ike any other athletic endeavor, optimal and safe singing and acting require unimpaired physiological response to the physical demands of performance," anxiety can obviously inhibit that physiological response.[89]

Even the most simple of medications can be problematic for singers, it seems. A common drug like aspirin has an effect on blood coagulation, causing slight hemorrhages of the small blood vessels on the membranes of the vocal cords that could result in hoarseness or loss of voice. Like decongestants, antihistamines can cause a dry mouth; diuretics can obviously do the same.[90] Despite the experience of famous singers like Caruso and Sir Charles Santley who smoked regularly yet still had wonderful voices, tobacco (and pot) smoking has obviously not proved of positive medical value for a singer's vocal apparatus (not to mention the lungs).[91] The same is true of excessive alcohol, though most singers admit to indulging in moderate drinking. Because cocaine shrinks the tissue in the nasal and pharyngeal cavities, it can cause a severe nasality in the voice.[92]

Though, as we shall see, opera plots like that of Verdi and Boito's *Falstaff* may celebrate the Dionysian glories of excess in food and drink, opera singers, on the contrary, are urged to indulge only in Apollonian moderation. In earlier times, thinned wine was considered safe, especially in the summer months. Later, people began to talk of light wines as being safest to use "as food" or to lift the spirits while warning that such stimulant use should never become a habit.[93] Overindulgence in food has clearly helped to produce some large singers over the years. Caruso was famous for his prodigious appetite, especially at his legendary lunches at Pagani's, but his own advice to singers was to eat good food in moderation and never before a performance: "when the large space required by the diaphragm in expanding to take a breath is partly occupied by one's dinner the result is that one cannot take as deep a breath as one would like," and tone suffers.[94] Santley too advised moderation: "Overfeeding produces a disordered stomach, which, acting on the voice and brain, robs both of their brightness."[95] And many singing manuals have repeated this warning over the centuries, arguing that singers' diet is in part responsible for their vocal health. Some studies have localized certain foods that can cause difficulties for singers, echoing teachers' lore over the centuries.[96] While overeating is a much discussed issue, it is not usually condemned outright, despite new knowledge about health risks: the power of the mystique of the big singer and the big voice remains strong.

✒ Body Size and Voice Size

Of all the issues involving the operatic body, no doubt the one most talked about is that of size: Does the operatic body have to be large to ensure vocal power and stamina? To be sure, there have been many stout singers past and present; in fact, Beverly Sills claimed that Callas's greatest practical contribution to opera, when she shed her sixty pounds in the 1950s, was in "erasing the image that all opera singers are fat with horns growing out of their heads."[97] Yet the idea persists that a large body is required to have the stamina and volume needed for today's large opera houses. Fighting this notion, though, is the new demand for verisimilitude in dramatic performance: directors today are sometimes as likely to cast for body type as voice type in an attempt to bring the realism of television and film to the operatic stage. The struggle between these two positions was never more clearly visible than in the responses to Callas's spectacular weight loss: public opinion was utterly polarized – and still is. (See, again, figures 10 and 11.) For some, the loss of pounds caused or, at the very least, coincided with the loss of voice; for others, there was absolutely no relationship because they felt that either her voice had been flawed from the start or the real problems came later.

Even before but certainly after her dramatic physical transformation, Callas was known as a performer you had to *see* as well as *hear*: words, music, and acting were all of a piece for her.[98] Recordings never, therefore, did her justice. As *Time* magazine put it in 1977 when she died: "She could act with her voice and sing with her body, like a great tragedienne. Especially in her later years, that voice could be edgy and even ugly. But that did not matter." Walter Legge felt her greatest strength was her power of projection in the theater, her ability to communicate with her body as well as her voice.[99] But for some that power came mostly when she slimmed down: the physique then fit the glamour of the voice; the outer and the inner images were at last in harmony.[100] Certainly no one could help but be curious about the effect of such a dramatic loss of weight on her voice: the audience at her 1957 *Norma* in London is said to have wondered, "In the absence of those unsightly but reassuring sixty pounds, where would those remembered tones of opulence originate?"[101]

Those "tones of opulence" seem to have characterized Callas's voice from the start, when she was a young beginner obsessed with learning to sing. A lonely child, she claims to have turned to food in compensation, in part assisted by both the mystique of size and voice and also the simple fact that the heavy singer was the norm in the 1940s. In her own words, "Using the excuse that in order to sing well one needs to be hefty and blooming, I stuffed myself, morning and night. . . . I was rotund and rosy." Her husband was a little less kind in his description of the young Callas: "Her lower extremities were deformed. Her ankles were swollen to the size of calves. She moved awkwardly and with effort."[102] Myopic, shy, and clumsy, she did not seem destined for stardom. But in 1953 the ugly duckling – to repeat the image everyone felt obliged to use – was transformed into a beautiful diva with a model's slim figure and a new taste for glamorous fashion.[103] How she achieved this loss remains a mystery: a relative by marriage claimed it was from eating his "physiological pasta"; Callas herself once told reporters she had a tapeworm but then denied both that claim and any notion that she had any secret means.[104] She asserted that she effected this major change in her bodily shape not only because of constant health problems but because of her desire to be a more striking singing actor. It is her first Medea, in Florence in 1953, that is credited with this transformation: she felt her face looked too soft and rounded for the Medea she wanted to portray; her chin needed more definition so that she could act the part more effectively. For anyone who has seen Callas on stage or in the few video recordings of her performances, it is clear that she communicated with her face and body as much as with her voice. Directors were clearly delighted at the new dramatic possibilities as Callas refined her artistry.

All was not perfect, of course, despite the Cinderella-like change into an Audrey Hepburn look-alike. (After seeing the film *Roman Holiday*, Callas had fixated on Hepburn's body and look as her ideal.) Her punishing schedule of performances in the 1950s often left her not only thin but shaky, on the edge of anorexia. Zeffirelli tells of directing her in *Il Turco in Italia* at La Scala in 1955: "During rehearsals we had a little argument because she kept tightening her corset and then would ask me to have the tailor take in the waist even more. She'd say, 'I suffered so much to get thin and now you put me onstage and make me look fat!' So I would have the seams pulled in and the waistline lowered to please her."[105] Critics were often dismissive or condescending of her weight loss. Noel Goodwin wrote in the *Observer*: "Buried inside the slim and hugely successful singer is a fat little girl still desperately compensating for an unhappy childhood: and the fruit of this compensation has been the metamorphosis of an unloved child into the greatest prima donna of today."[106] No one could ignore the bodily change; what they disagreed about was its relation to her voice.

Looking back on the reviews of performances in the mid-1950s, what becomes clear is that there had been a major break in how people *talked about* Callas. While earlier reviews had certainly discussed vocal difficulties, now these problems were always linked to her weight loss. This happened even when she was being praised, as for her performance in *Iphigénie en Tauride* in 1957 at La Scala: "her singing caused none of the momentary discomfort that has sometimes seemed to go with her slimmer figure."[107] Similarly, her 1956 Met *Norma* was greeted by *Time* in positive terms that nonetheless suggest the continuing power of the mystique of size: "the Callas voice rose from her slender frame with dazzling endurance. No doubt, other great sopranos can coax out of their ample, placid figures tones that esthetes call more beautiful." Yet in the same year, the *Saturday Review* called her "the most voluptuous sounding Tosca, the most ample in vocal volume," noting that she was "slight in appearance but commanding in manner."[108] After the weight loss, the same performance, such as her Covent Garden *Norma*, would elicit extreme claims: that she sang worse than ever before or better than ever before.[109] Ears, it would seem, are amazingly subjective organs of evaluation and are more connected to the eyes than we might think.

What is evident, years later, is that Callas was used by both sides of the debate to prove their points: she was the evidence they needed either to prove the correlation between bodily size and power/quality of voice or to demystify that linkage completely, since, to some, her voice actually improved with the bodily change. Koestenbaum puts the dichotomy nicely: "Callas, who lost 62 pounds in two years, is often cited as proof that a great voice needs girth to support it; supposedly, she sacrificed her power with her weight, and yet it seems that the slim Callas had a consolidated tone, with less abrupt breaks between registers."[110] Claudia Cassidy wrote in the *Chicago Tribune* of Callas's 1954 *Norma*: "to me her voice is more beautiful in color, more even through the range, than it used to be."[111] In 1956 *Time* pronounced: "To a world laboring under the impression that a prima donna must be corpulent to be operatic, Callas' sensational slimming has caused much shaking of heads and predictions of vocal perdition. But the newly glamorous Maria, thin, relaxed and even daring to taste the pleasures of the idle rich (she sang all night in a Vienna café last summer, for sheer pleasure), has lost not a decibel of power, a note of range, a mote of sweetness."[112] Yet even those who did not see a direct link between her weight loss and her increasing vocal difficulties still had to deal with the manifest changes in her voice over the years. The voice that had once had great agility, size, and a wide range (from A below the treble staff to E-flat above it), that had once been very adaptable, even with its three distinct registers, was altering.[113] Its tone, size, and security were different – and variable – from performance to performance.

For some, her voice had likely been forced from the start from incorrect training, and its deterioration was inevitable once the damage had begun: "The biggest flaw from the beginning was her inability to keep her voice free and unconstricted as it rose in pitch, and her willingness to compensate by main force. . . . Callas also had the bad habit, widespread in Italy in her day, of carrying the chest voice too high, like a Broadway belter. That, too, involves strain; and her slimming could well have accelerated the process by sapping her strength. But the strain, the roughening, was already there."[114] Commentators also blamed the flaws on natural imperfections in the instrument itself, claiming that her voice had always had the potential to become ugly or wobbly in the upper register. Or they looked to her selection of uncongenial roles for a scapegoat.[115] And indeed she stopped singing both Turandot and Wagnerian roles, though to the end she did not believe that singing Wagner could hurt the well-trained voice.[116] As we have seen, it was argued that she damaged her voice by switching roles often, especially those associated with different kinds of female voices: "Could the voice last indefinitely when alternating verismo with bel canto, neoclassical declamation and Verdian expressionism?"[117] Some pointed to her health difficulties, as we have also seen, and the sad fact that "Callas herself aged well, but her voice, alas, did not."[118] She did change her lifestyle during her affair with Aristotle Onassis, but whether this was a compensation for her vocal crisis or its cause is not clear.[119]

From the mid-1950s on, people talked more and more about the unsettling wobble in her upper voice, a wide tremolo or undulation.[120] As *Time* put it, in its characteristically vivid terms, in 1956: "Few rate the Callas voice as opera's sweetest or most beautiful. It has its ravishing moments. In quiet passages, it warms and caresses the air. In ensembles, it cuts through the other voices like a Damascus blade, clean and strong. But after the first hour of a performance, it tends to become strident, and late in a hard evening, begins to take on a reverberating quality, as if her mouth were full of saliva."[121] And most people could not help feeling that the weight loss must have had something to do with this loss of power and control.[122] What is striking is that when some critics describe her voice, they do so literally in the language of her reduced body: by the summer of 1956, writes Michael Scott, her voice no longer has the "weight of tone"; it is "thinner." It is not the "weighty voice" it once was; at times it is "thin and raw," "slimmed down": "I remember how diminished her voice was. . . . And it was impossible to ignore how her voice was reducing in size, how its range was contracting." Even her mother lamented the loss of her "rich and round" tones.[123]

Whether we look to the continuing power of the mystique of size or to actual physiology, it is impossible not to notice how often her critics and biographers speak of the physical causes of her vocal crisis, and most look to her reduced physical strength from dieting. Her "too-slim" body was said to lack the capacity to support or sustain the voice; the "slim figure just cannot meet all the demands the singer puts on the voice"; she no longer had "sufficient strength to be able to support" the voice, they said.[124] Callas herself dismissed all this as rubbish: "first you *must* have the voice. Then and *only* then you must look for the appearance. What is outside is *not* inside! If you're fat outside, your diaphragm does not necessarily work well *inside!*"[125]

With the loss of weight did come a change in body image and thus an increase in confidence for Callas and, consequently, an increase in dramatic power on stage. She helped make opera visually as well as aurally credible to a new generation whose ideas of spectacle were in the process of being formed by film and television.[126] By transforming her body, Callas became a role model, especially (but not only) for women: "Bodies can't always be altered, but Callas' self-revision, like a sex change, makes us believe in the power of wish."[127] As we saw in the first chapter, much has been written about the "culture of slimming" in our current Western world, a culture in which "the loss of weight, the exile of fat, the erosion of bulk are but preludes to a change of personality. Either the dieter will develop a personal confidence, retrieve a dynamic youth or discover a vital new self."[128] Callas certainly gained personal confidence and, in a sense, created for herself the dynamic youth she had never had, while constructing a vital new self for the world to see and admire.

Not everyone in the operatic world, however, has proved willing to surrender the mystique of size. Thinking of Anna Moffo and, no doubt, Callas, Joan Sutherland explicitly blames slimming for vocal loss: "the ones that slim down to look glamorous really tend to lose their voices and there's no two ways about it."[129] In the popular imagination as much as in singing lore, a big body is associated with a big voice – unless you are a very high soprano or a mezzo-soprano like Frederica von Stade, who sings trouser roles.[130] There are many who still argue that the lowest voice ranges need larger physical size, indeed corpulence, to accommodate chest voice.[131] But how then to account for the deep voice of the thin Samuel Ramey or Robert Lloyd? Science is not at all conclusive on these questions, but that has not stopped the speculation (often presented as asserted fact). The great tenor Caruso is said to have had large and thick vocal cords (usually characteristic of those in the basso range), but he also had the tenor's typically broad and rounded chest.[132] But what about today's slim Roberto Alagna?

While exceptions can probably always be found, the fact remains that the size mystique is powerful in part because it seems so very commonsensical. Orchestras have increased in size and sonority thanks to Wagner and Strauss, among other composers; theaters have become larger and larger. Big voices are needed, and "logically," big voices, with great stamina, must come from big bodies: Maria Wittich, Lauritz Melchior, Ben Heppner, Jane Eaglen. This mystique is strangely enshrined in the clichéd proverbs of the English language, such as "The opera ain't over until the fat lady sings."[133] Size does not always mean only fat, of course. People speak of Joan Sutherland's "unusual physical endowment": "She is a tall woman of almost heroic size, with a voice to match. It is not impossible, but certainly highly unusual, to find a large, dramatic voice housed in a small frame. One would expect a woman of such proportions to have larger than normal vocal cords."[134] And, apparently, she does. But most of the time, size means fat.

In an editorial in *Opera Quarterly*, Bruce Burroughs argues that obesity is in fact a requirement of the truly excellent vocal instrument and does so on grounds that this is common sense and, indeed, self-evident: "[I]f every single human being . . . were properly and completely trained as an acoustical singer, it would invariably be those (regardless of ethnic background, level of education, or propensity for musical or artistic expression) with the hefty, squat bodies, barrel chests, thick necks, broad, not-so-pretty faces, and genetic tendencies toward weight problems, who would turn out to have the great voices. It is simply a self-evident fact that this is the kind of body in which the very greatest vocal instruments have historically dwelt."[135] But even he has his limits: Rita Hunter's three hundred plus pounds give her an "outrageous size and mobility problems" that drive him to joke cruelly: "that's not Norma, it's Enorma."[136]

Are some singers large because they too believe in the correlation of size and voice? The power of this mystique is not to be underestimated, even if there are enough exceptions around to make one seriously question its physiological basis. Despite a society that values thinness almost to excess, opera culture today remains stubbornly recalcitrant. Marilyn Horne tells Joan Sutherland: "It's like a rocket, dear! The bigger the satellite they want to get up, the bigger the rocket. The bigger the voice, the more behind it!"[137] The value of a large "ideal sounding-board [and] resonating chamber body" would indeed seem hard to challenge.[138] Richard Klein, in his "postmodern diet book" called *Eat Fat*, goes even further and asserts: "Fat is beautiful, sexy, and strong. Politicians cultivate it, singers require it, gourmets appreciate it, and lovers play with it." He claims that extra weight on someone like Jessye Norman "contributes in ways, known and unknown, to exuding the sweet power of the sound we love" and suggests that singers derive physical and psychological strength from fat.[139] On the other side of the debate, fat is seen either as a sign of moral laxity and flawed character (in North America) or as an aesthetic failing (as in France). Peter N. Stearns opens his *Fat History: Bodies and Beauty in the Modern West* with a remark on the change in the last century to our slim concept of beauty: "the results are wide-ranging, from a desperate quest for slimmer opera stars to a huge new commercial literature and product line designed to aid slimming."[140]

Yet in recent years, the big female body, or at least the diva's body, has taken on immense symbolic significance in the work of gay and lesbian critics. For Susan Leonardi and Rebecca Pope, the diva has become an image of woman not as victim but as independent and empowered; for Koestenbaum, she offers "the uncomfortable and antipatriarchal spectacle of a woman taking her body seriously – channeling, enjoying, and nourishing it."[141] According to Michael Moon, she radiates the bodily authority and pleasure associated with another age: "the diva's body has never lost its representational magnetism for many of us [gay men] as an alternative body-identity fantasy, resolutely embodying as it does the otherwise almost entirely anachronistic ideal, formed in early nineteenth-century Europe, of the social dignity of corpulence, particularly that of the serenely bourgeois matron."[142]

To Koestenbaum, the heavy diva is a symbol of what we might call Dionysian larger-than-life excess: "Singers are supposed to be fat. The body must be huge. The body must spill over, embarrass itself, declare immensity."[143] Similarly, to Sam Abel, the large diva

145

"is the imposing visual representation of opera's fleshly materiality, an evocation of its immensity and that of the huge opera houses and grandiose personalities that signify opera in popular discourse." In short, she is the camp embodiment of opera itself, signifying both "glorious plenitude and embarrassing excess."[144] Yet the characters the divas portray are not themselves meant to be particularly larger than life, at least in physical terms: often they are young and seductive like Salome or fragile in their illness like Mimì or Violetta. Yet, Abel argues, this is the value of opera's artifice: the soprano's large size prevents realism and at the same time "provides a visual metaphor that allows us to believe in the potency of the singing body."[145]

The often extravagant symbolic meanings given to the large body by gay and lesbian theorists depend, however, in the end on the common-sense basis of the mystique. But can such a self-evident correlation between size of voice and body be proved scientifically? In order to try to decide, let us return briefly to how the voice makes its sounds.[146] Air moves from the lungs to the vocal cords, two triangular folds of tissue inside the larynx or voice box. The cords come together and the air forces them to vibrate, not unlike the reed of a clarinet. Sound comes from the resulting waves of air: the more rapid the waves, the higher the pitch. For middle C, they will vibrate about 250 times a second; a high note for a soprano will cause a vibration of more than 1,000 times a second. As the air (and this tone) makes its way up the vocal tract, texture, color, and vowel sounds are added. It is the shape of the vocal tract that reinforces certain harmonics in tones produced by the cords: this is why a diminutive soprano can sometimes be heard in every corner of the largest house, and why José Carreras's voice seems as loud as Pavarotti's. Another theory holds that it is the laryngeal pharynx that contributes most to the reinforced overtone area that gives the voice the power to soar over an enormous orchestra in a large hall.[147] Male singers, especially, can lower the larynx in the throat – this must be taught, however, since it is natural to raise it – in order to reinforce some of the upper harmonics in their voices that lie in "a unique range of pitch just above where most of the orchestra is massed."[148] This lowering takes little energy but is said to result in a great change in volume. Notice that size of body does not seem to feature in any of these accounts of how a powerful sound is produced.

The passageway between the vocal cords and the lips can be expanded, contracted, stretched, or compressed simply by smiling, moving the tongue, or opening the mouth wider; each configuration reinforces three or four different pitches, and, when the harmonics in the note sung are close to them, they become louder. So a soprano can open her mouth wider and change the shape of the vocal tract so that it resonates with the voice and adds volume – up to 30 decibels more. Power, some argue, has nothing at all to do with the shape or strength of the vocal cords of a Caruso or a Sutherland and more to do with "particularly favorable conditions within the resonance area."[149] But the scientific evidence for all these theories would appear to be imprecise, causing one critic to exclaim that "the only thing one can say is that beauty and strength of the voice are due to some lucky shape of one resonance area or another."[150] Does this "resonance area" mean the whole body, and therefore is size crucial? It is unclear. The most people seem willing to commit themselves to is the belief that certain natural anatomical advantages help and that a "technically accomplished handling of the organ" can do wonders.[151] Yet Jean Abitbol feels that fatter women singers may have an easier time with menopause, since fat cells store estrogen and convert male hormones to estrogen; if that is the case, their voices may last longer.[152]

Some claim that physical strength and fitness may be more significant than body size for vocal power. As we have seen, it is common to speak of singers as athletes; the prima donna was once even compared to a "racing mare."[153] Not only must singers keep their bodies healthy, but they must keep them fit. Yet brute athleticism does not necessarily make for beautiful music. Take this account of an unnamed German post-Wagnerian singer who was said to compensate for his vocal deficiencies in the face of new challenges by sheer force. He would take "particular delight in asking his admirers to note the expansion of his chest, and test the tension and power of his diaphragm while he is breathing or singing. A wonderful display of brute force, of course, performed by ignorant screamers who feel proud of their athletic achievements, and who never seem to have observed the little nightingale who can sing so beautifully, for hours at a stretch, his voice carrying to great distances, but whose diaphragm is only proportionate to his diminutive size."[154] Clearly more physiological research is needed into the mechanism of voice production to determine exactly what *is* crucial to the power and stamina of the human singing voice.

In the meantime, however, today's audiences are still caught in a paradoxical position: they know that there is a long operatic tradition that tacitly accepts overweight as the norm, and yet they are also aware of both the modern fashion of slenderness and the dramatic demands for realism on stage. The tradition that supports the mystique of size has been strangely reinvigorated by the fetishizing of the disembodied voice in the wake of technological changes and, in a way, also by the continuing valuing of music over drama by some musicologists writing about opera. As one asserts: "One of the pleasures of opera is the schism between what we see and what we hear – the possibility of an escape from verisimilitude, and the magic of an 'impossible' voice."[155] Another's way of putting this position is: "True opera lovers – as opposed to habitual scoffers – don't much care if a singer conforms to some conventional standard of physical beauty or even if she or he matches a character's physical 'type.' *La Bohème* becomes ludicrous not if the consumptive Mimì is rotund but if she is *vocally* and *interpretively* overnourished (or, worse, undernourished)."[156] And yet the heavy Fanny Piccolomini was laughed at in the premiere of *La Traviata* precisely because she did not look like a thin consumptive. At the end of the nineteenth century George Bernard Shaw would mock the ludicrous appearance of heavy and aging singers performing in inappropriate roles by suggesting that all spectators could do was lie back in their seats and close their eyes.[157] But today, the situation is even more difficult for audiences and singers alike. In the West, the thin female body has become the ideal, if not the norm, and the operatic stage has difficulty distancing itself completely from this general social context. A look at earlier photos of opera's stars, especially before World War I, confirms the suspicion that thin was not always the norm. But the recent combination of social disapproval, new knowledge of the health risks of obesity, and increased exposure to (or vulnerability in) the visual media seems to have made many large singers today self-conscious about their weight.[158] Pavarotti hates being photographed or seeing himself on television: "If people think I am happy about my weight, they are wrong. I am happy *in spite* of my weight. That is very different."[159] This may be nothing new, of course: there are earlier stories like those of the large Marie Wilt, the turn-of-the-century Viennese singer who was driven to suicide by the malicious barbs and caricatures of the press.[160] But it is hard not to believe that things are even more difficult for singers today.

Of course, there have always been small singers whose fragility has been part of their appeal. Malibran was clearly one of these: "Given her frail constitution and the fact that she had been taught by her father [Manuel García] to ignore all limitations, the fascination she exerted on her audience must have stemmed from the sense of danger she seemed to communicate."[161] But today, when television, films, and advertising bombard audiences with images of the slender body, especially the slender woman's body, audiences might well experience less a thrilling sense of danger than a comforting sense of normality in such physical fragility. What Albert Innaurato has lamented as the general "miniaturization of beauty" cannot but affect opera.[162] As we saw in the first chapter, concepts of beauty have a long and continuous history, but they are also responses to the social context of the day. So many of opera's plots stage the beautiful body that the issue of a singer's physical appearance becomes crucial if the work is to be experienced as drama and not simply as music.

Most obviously, Turandot would ideally be attractive enough to help an audience understand why men are willing to die to win her; Salome would be lithe, sexy, and athletic enough to perform the Dance of the Seven Veils so convincingly that we would understand why Herod is willing to give her anything, even, in the end, the head of Jochanaan. Strauss himself chose the sensual and seductive Mary Garden to play Salome in Paris. An acting singer like Callas, Garden used her entire body to perform her roles, claiming: "My voice is no more important to me than my shoulders. Everything about me is a vital part of the scheme of things. My voice is a means to an end. I use it to express the emotions, just as I use my hands or my eyes or my shoulders."[163] So much for the fetishizing of the voice!

There have always been small or normal-sized singers with "sex appeal" who project passion and fascinate audiences well beyond the effect of their voices: think of the vampish Maria Jeritza earlier or the dynamic Waltraut Meier today. But they have usually been the exception and not the norm, despite the fact that the history of women on the operatic stage is one that closely linked their sex to the erotic and the immoral: singers and actresses were said to radiate "an aura of licentiousness."[164] But today's media-driven demands for fashionably thin beauty, combined with the importance of theatrical values (especially once audiences can understand what is happening on stage with the help of surtitles), mean that when Radames sings "Celeste Aida, forma divina," it would help immensely if his Aida really had at least a conventionally attractive, if not divine, physical form. And if our experience is any indication, it really does. It is a fact that "[w]hen Renée Fleming sings Desdemona, something happens onstage that simply wouldn't happen if she were plain," no matter how beautifully she might sing.[165] It is simply too easy to say that the singer's body does not matter; for many audiences, it does. There was a time when the adjective "Junoesque" might have been taken as a compliment by a soprano, but that time is not now.[166] Yet, yet . . .

There are still many stout singers: Pavarotti, Ben Heppner, Gary Lakes, Jane Eaglen, Sharon Sweet, Alessandra Marc, Debra Voigt,

Margaret Price, and the list could go on. Does this in part represent the continuing force of the mystique of size? Does opera offer a kind of legitimation of size? Is weight, as some claim, a way to combat feelings of vulnerability on stage or anxiety about performing?[167] Is it simply a consequence of the "diva syndrome" – a set of maladaptive eating behaviors based on singers' strange lifestyles?[168] Is it a question of genetic inheritance, in some cases? We suspect the answer is highly individual and highly complex, and there is little doubt that even a large body can be dramatically powerful on stage.

The heavy singer's body will likely not disappear from the opera stage, even in this culture of slimness, and the audience watching and listening may well continue to be caught between the allowances of operatic artifice and the demands of theatrical realism. On the one hand, opera is and always should be larger than life, it is argued. Catherine Clément celebrates Monserrat Caballé's heft against Callas's thinness: "she weighs so much that she is incapable of expression; fixed superbly in her song, attentive to vocal perfection alone, she sings as if she sought to banish the memory of the one who sacrificed her voice to the perfection of a body that finally conformed to death. Oh Caballé, deformed idol, never get thin. Stay buried in life . . . an imposing matron, be able to stay ugly."[169] But, on the other hand, it may take courage and fortitude to do that, given today's corporeal climate. Directors look for the convincing body as much as the convincing voice: they cast the small or even average-size body of a Ljuba Kazarnovskaia as their Salome or a Beatriz Urzo-Monson as their Carmen, a Renée Fleming for their Desdemona or a Hildegard Behrens for their Brünnhilde. When, in *Don Carlos*, Princess Eboli sings "O don fatal et détesté," lamenting her fatal and hated beauty, comprehending audiences (reading surtitles) may well scrutinize the body they see before them in a new way. Opera is a staged, public art form, and, as such, it is always and inevitably a part of the culture in which it is performed as well as the culture in which it was first produced. The audience members are the ones who decide its success, and it is to their bodies that we now turn.

4

The Perceiving Body

Opera was born with the astonishment of its first audience: imagine the original fan, the original blush, the first ecstatic response to opera!
– Wayne Koestenbaum, *The Queen's Throat*

"At the opera, what does your body do?" asks Wayne Koestenbaum. "Clap until your hands hurt . . . Yell 'brava'" is his response.[1] But the sensual impact of being a participant in the shared experience of a live opera performance provokes your body to do other things besides applaud and shout, and it does so *during* the opera, not only *after* it is over: you laugh and you weep at what you see and hear; you feel the hair stand up on the back of your neck when the soprano sings a certain note; your feet feel like tapping; your heart races or feels as if it is standing still; your breathing speeds up. Of course, your body can do other things too: it can fidget out of boredom or excess of stimulus or simply because of an uncomfortable seat; it can yawn and even doze off; it can cough and set off a chain of acoustic contagion in the bodies that surround it; it can remind you that perhaps you should not have had that glass of wine right before the curtain went up. You might glance – or stare – at your neighbor for talking or rattling jewelry or unwrapping candy; you might simply look out of curiosity.

In short, your body is very busy at the opera. Writing about all staged theater, Marvin Carlson reminds us that the "roots of the words 'theatre' (from *theatron*, a place for seeing), 'spectator'

(from *spectare*, to watch), and 'auditorium' (from *audire*, to hear)
all reflect the necessary physicality and presence of the theatre
experience."[2] Music is said to be experienced within and through
the body: through the ears, most obviously, but also through the
skin and bones, as vibrations are carried through our seats or the
floorboards.[3] But there are two other things for us to consider. First,
opera is more than just music: there is a verbal text and dramatized
action on the stage.[4] And, second, our perceiving selves consist of
more than just physical bodies. The embodied story we perceive, one
that is taking place before our eyes and ears, has the power to involve
us physically – but also emotionally and intellectually – in ways
that exceed most other art forms. This is part of the extravagance
and excess of live opera. The sensory overload experienced in an
operatic performance combines with the powerful immediacy of the
enacted narrative to affect and, at times, to overwhelm the perceiver.
Etymologically, the perceiver is the one who becomes aware through
the senses. Witness the famous story of the great eighteenth-century
castrato Gasparo Pacchierotti singing Bertoni's *Artaserse* in Forli in
1776. He was supposed to sing "Eppur son innocente," which was
to be followed immediately by an instrumental passage, but when
the performer stopped singing, the orchestra remained utterly silent,
enraptured by "the beauty of the situation, the music, the expression
of the singer."[5]

Think of how literature has represented the experience of being
in an opera audience, for (as we shall see throughout this chapter)
it has done so with great relish. In Willa Cather's *The Song of
the Lark*, Dr. Archie, the hometown Colorado patron and mentor
of the singer, Thea Kronberg, finally gets to hear her sing at the
Metropolitan Opera in New York. He finds that, as he nervously
awaits her appearance on stage, he twists his gloves into a string;
terrified, he compares his feelings to a hunter's paralysis in front of
a buck elk. But when she begins to sing he finds himself "drifting
along on the melody" in a state of "exalted calmness" and distance.
Nevertheless, he later describes his reaction in physical terms (after

all, he is a physician): "it gave me a pulse."[6] The body seems anything but passive in this audience experience.[7]

❧ Apollonian Minds in Dionysian Bodies

If Dionysus might appear to triumph in our multiple and powerful corporeal responses to opera, Apollo – the god of form and control, rationality and music – is never far from our experience either. Any dictionary of musical quotations will provide example after example of statements by composers or critics about the relation of music to both the intellectual and the sensuous life.[8] And it probably does not require all the philosophical baggage of phenomenology to convince most opera audiences of both the mental and the sensory nature of perception.[9] We are busy interpreting both the form and content of what we see and hear, even as we are affected physically and emotionally by it all. Once again, the Apollonian and the Dionysian prove to be complementary impulses. If, in this chapter, we tend to emphasize the physicality of the audience's experience, it is simply as part of our more general attempt to restore the lost balance between the Dionysian and the Apollonian. Thanks to the kind of (admittedly important) musicological work that has so firmly entrenched the rational analysis of form as one of the dominant discourses about opera, there is a need today both to think about and to give value once again to the actual experience of the perceiving audience, an experience that is both intellectual and sensuous.

We should recall Nietzsche's remark that his response to Wagner's music was "physiological": "I breathe with difficulty as soon as Wagner's music begins to act upon me." That same music once even provoked Wagnerphobic Italians to claim that listening to it could cause jaundice and bring on diseases like smallpox and cholera.[10] Both opera's music and text make demands on the ear, as the staged performance makes demands on the eye. And all this sensory information is, of course, decoded and interpreted by the brain, as we shall see in a later section of this chapter: even the intellectual has a physical basis, of course. But let us look first at a few of the things that happen to our bodies when we go to the opera. In Gustave Flaubert's novel *Madame Bovary*, Emma Bovary attends a performance of *Lucia di Lammermoor* and is entranced from the moment she enters the opera house. Admiring the fashionable young men, the lights, the musicians warming up, her heart begins to race and her senses are aroused. As the opera begins, she is carried back to the romantic world of her youthful reading: "She gave herself up to the flow of the melodies, and felt all her being vibrate as if the violin bows were being drawn over her nerves." But it is the arrival of the famous tenor Lagardy that provokes her strongest bodily as well as imaginative responses: "Emma bent forward to see him, scratching the velvet of the box with her nails. Her heart filled with these melodious lamentations that were accompanied by the lugubrious moanings of the double-basses, like the cries of the drowning in the tumult of a tempest . . . and when they [the lovers in the opera] uttered the final farewell, Emma gave a sharp cry that mingled with the vibrations of the last chords." Emma then attempts aesthetic distance but fails, and, as the curtain falls, it is her body that responds to everything around her: "The smell of gas mingled with the people's breath and the waving fans made the air even more suffocating. . . . [S]he fell back in her armchair with palpitations that choked her."[11]

Not long after Flaubert wrote this novel, French scientists began trying to explain the physiological responses Emma and many others experienced. While people had always written of the Dionysian power of music over the body, at the end of the nineteenth century we find experimental studies of the effect of music on respiration, the heart, and capillary circulation. These studies claimed to have demonstrated that both heart rate and breathing accelerated, independently of the kind of music experienced, but that the rhythm of breathing tended to adapt itself to that of the music. Brusque opening music was said to produce vasoconstriction (contraction of blood vessels).[12] Since this early work, much more has been learned about the impact of music on autonomic function, and not only on pulse and respiration but also on things like muscle tone.[13] Anyone who has been to a live rock concert knows about the physical impact of loud, powerfully rhythmic music on the body. In a different way, in studies carried out in medical environments, it was demonstrated that music could reduce autonomic cardiovascular reactivity – that is, heart rates – and thus improve performance in surgeons, for instance, just as it can work to diminish stress and anxiety in patients.[14] These physiological responses may be independent of the mental attitude taken by the perceiver.[15]

If that is the case, the issue raised is whether the physiological response to music is a learned response or an inborn one. Experimental studies suggest that infants are biologically prepared to find consonance perceptually more attractive than dissonance, and that certain musical intervals (combinations of two tones) with simple ratios are more pleasing (and thus are found most often historically and cross-culturally in music). Even Apollonian appreciation of form, then, may well be biologically grounded.[16] But on the other hand, there is considerable evidence that the relationships brought into existence by performed music – relationships both among the sounds heard and among the audience members – are in fact given meaning by the culture in which the hearing occurs: these are learned and not universal.[17] As one psychobiologist puts it, it is as if we grow a cultural ear to accompany our physiological one. This ear would be the product of the interaction of the individual and acoustic stimuli specific to a certain physical and sociocultural "sonorous environment."[18] But opera likely requires us to posit a cultural eye as well as ear, for, as Roland Barthes explains, its enjoyment involves "mobilizing many of the senses, many sensual pleasures." However, these pleasures depend on certain cultural reflexes.[19] Two people may see and hear the same opera but have very different physical and intellectual responses to it because of differences in previous experience, background knowledge, taste, and a host of other cultural variables.[20]

What seems evident is that, whether the physiological and mental responses are learned or innate, they are real. For this reason, claims have always been made for the therapeutic value of music to soothe and even heal both the body and the mind. While rather extravagant assertions about the healing powers of listening to music have been made, there is considerable evidence that the so-called Mozart effect (now rather audaciously trademarked by Don Campbell in his *The Mozart Effect*™) does have some validity in the areas of stress reduction, where mind and body most strikingly come together.[21] As Franco Zeffirelli once wrote to Maria Callas: "Dear Maria, yesterday evening Marlene Dietrich, one of your rabid admirers, spoke constantly of you. She says that in American hospitals they play your records continuously because they have discovered that your voice helps those who are ill, giving them confidence, calming them, and helping them to recover from what ails them. That is not surprising – we have known that for quite a while."[22]

There are other therapeutic functions for music besides tranquilizing and soothing. When Michael Nyman composed on opera based on Oliver Sacks's story "The Man Who Mistook His Wife for a Hat," what was embodied on the operatic stage was the story of the power of music to help organize and integrate the brain, "to knit or reknit a shattered world into sense." The first "neurological opera," as Sacks himself called it, allowed the audience to hear as well as see how the patient built for himself a system in which music acted as a substitute for his lost visual cognition.[23] In the words of the libretto, "He had no body image, / He had body music."

As we keep insisting, opera is not just music, however, and so the physiological and intellectual responses of the audience at a live opera, in particular, are reactions not only to the musical sounds but to the words we hear and interpret. To this must be added the reactions to what we see on stage, where a theatrical world has been constructed for us through sets, costumes, lighting, and all the other aspects of the mise-en-scène or staging. We react to all these elements, both alone and in concert with each other: we may laugh or cry not only at the music we hear but at what a character on stage says or does. Laughter and tears are among the most complex combinations of the physical and the mental we can experience, and both have been shown to have therapeutic values rivaling those of music itself. Therefore they too need to be examined in this overview of what the body does at the opera.

Comic opera is, of course, not the only kind that provokes mirth: inadvertent incongruities or slips of the tongue (or foot) can always induce an unplanned laugh at the most inappropriate of moments in the performance of a tragic opera too. It is a rare performance of the third act of Wagner's *Siegfried* that the hero's naive exclamation, upon removing the breastplate of the sleeping Brünnhilde, of "Das ist kein Mann!" [That is no man!] does not elicit some snickering or even guffaws from the audience. But laughter, however caused, is a very bodily thing: as a muscular phenomenon, laughter involves the facial muscles, but it is also a very complex respiratory event. There is a long history of the claims made for laughter in terms of release of tension and establishing of psychic equilibrium; it is restorative and relaxing. Physiologically, the act of laughing is said to stimulate the circulatory, respiratory, and sympathetic nervous systems, for it involves the diaphragm, thorax, abdomen, heart, and lungs.[24] Afterward, it is argued, blood pressure is lowered, digestion is enhanced, and muscle tension and even pain are reduced, thanks to the release of endorphins. The immune system may even be affected.[25] Back in 1790 Immanuel Kant had echoed many before him in claiming that laughing furthered the "vital bodily processes" that had a "favorable influence on health," and modern science suggests he was correct.[26]

Certainly laughter and humor have been shown to have positive effects in palliative and critical care situations. They appear to relieve both physical pain and the sense of loss; they reduce stress at a physical and psychological level. The explanations for these effects range from theories (Freudian and other) of physiological release causing a liberating effect (that would have made Dionysus proud) to theories of brain function and hormone release.[27] But laughter has psychosocial as well as physiological results, and these are important for the audience of opera as a public art form. Laughter has been shown to reduce isolation and increase communication: not only does shared laughter bring people together, but the sense of physical relaxation after a laugh has actually been related to the creation of a sense of group fellowship. As we all know from experience, laughter is contagious, facilitated by the presence of others, and it has been argued that groups that laugh together cohere better and rate the shared activity higher in affective terms.[28] Dionysus was the god of public emotion, and such laughter is one of his signs.

If laughter is shared, tears are more private, but the physiological reactions underlying both are similar; indeed, we often weep when we laugh. If our own personal experience is any indication, people are much more likely to cry at an opera than at a symphony concert or even a play. A powerful combination of the music, the words, and the live action on the stage is potentially capable of provoking tears; in fact, we are most likely to respond in this way when all three come together with particular emotional force. In 1877 Tchaikovsky wrote about having recently seen Bizet's opera *Carmen*: "I cannot play the last scene without weeping; on the one hand, the people enjoying themselves, and the coarse gaiety of the crowd watching the bullfight, on the other, the dreadful tragedy and death of two of the leading characters whom an evil destiny, *fatum*, has brought together and driven, through a whole series of agonies, to their inescapable end."[29] As we shall see in a later section of this chapter, there is a real cathartic value to such a response. While music clearly has its independent effects on the body, there are other responses to the verbal text and the dramatized action of opera (and to the combination of all three) that should not be ignored when considering the impact of live opera on audiences. And it is worth noting, before we leave it, that the Dionysian and the Apollonian come together in Tchaikovsky's account, as the body responds not only to the memory of the live performance, as he plays the music on the piano, but to intellectual analysis.

✺ Two-way Communication

While we see as well as hear an operatic performance, there is arguably a certain striking immediacy to the act of hearing. When a singer's voice enters our ears, our bodies respond. One of the more flamboyant accounts of such a response is, as usual, that of Wayne Koestenbaum:

> A singer's voice sets up vibrations and resonances in the listener's body. First, there are the physiological sensations we call "hearing." Second, there are gestures of response with which the listener mimics the singer, expresses physical sympathy, appreciation, or exaltation: shudder, gasp, sigh; holding the body motionless, relaxing the shoulders, stiffening the spine. Third, the singer has presence, an expressive relation to her body – and presence is contagious. I catch it. The dance of sound waves on the tympanum, and the sigh I exhale in sympathy with the singer, persuade me that I have a body – if only by analogy, if only a second-best copy of the singer's body.[30]

This experience is not unlike that of watching the Olympic competitions: we can run, as we can sing, but we cannot run and sing quite like that! We become aware of our own physical limitations, even as our bodies respond to the music and the "presence" of the singer. The kinesthetic response, as the conscious perception of our own body through our muscles and our inner ear is known, is not a one-way affair, however. As theorists of theater have long argued, just as the bodies in the audience influence each other (as, most obviously, in the case of contagious laughter), so too they have an impact on the bodies on stage.[31] As we sit in the audience, we react to the body language of the singers; we thrill to sublime moments in the music; we may even get a sore throat out of sympathy with a strained or strident voice.[32] But the communication process does not stop there; our responses get passed on to the performers on stage. Just as Maria Callas could sing an aria "with every ounce of strength she could summon, driving it like nails into the consciousness of the audience," so too that audience could make every performance into a battle for her. The myopic singer's response to the claque at La Scala was defiant: "As long as I hear them stirring and hissing like snakes out there, I know I'm on top. If I heard nothing from my enemies, I'd know I was slipping."[33] Even if the audience is not quite this audibly expressive, other performers' experiences confirm Brecht's assertion of audience power: "The effect of an artistic performance on the spectator is not independent of the effect of the spectator on the artist. In theatre, the audience regulates the performance." Certainly Anna Moffo warns singers never to project their performance anxiety over the footlights: "When the audience feels you're nervous, it's all over. They can smell it, and you make *them* nervous" – and the singer cannot but feel that audience reaction.[34]

In other words, live opera is not one-way communication, a simple stimulus from the stage followed by a response from the audience. As novelist Robertson Davies wrote in his novel *The Lyre of Orpheus*, "the magic of a great theatrical moment is created by the audience itself, a magic impalpable but vividly present, and . . . what begins as trickery of light and paint is enlarged and made fine by the response of the beholders. There are no great performances without great audiences, and this is the barrier that film and television, by their utmost efforts, cannot cross, for there can be no interaction between what is done, and those to whom it is done. Great theatre, great music-drama, is created again and again on both sides of the footlights."[35] Kier Elam's semiotic modeling of theatrical communication gives a good sense of the circularity of this two-way process. In *The Semiotics of Theatre and Drama*, he shows how, from a variety of sources (librettist, composer, director, designers, technicians), an idea is transmitted through the body or voice (or costume, set, prop, lighting). This sends a signal (a movement or sound, for instance) that travels by means of physical channels (light waves or sound waves). It is then picked up by receivers (our eyes or ears) and converted into a message (speech, music, gesture) that is interpreted by the receiver. But the circuit continues, for the receiver's hands, face, or voice can become transmitters in turn, sending a signal through a physical channel that is converted into a message: applause, whistling, booing, walking out of the theater. Such messages are communicated from the audience to the performers on the stage.[36] As Pavarotti explains: "The aria goes well and the audience makes me aware of them with their applause – nothing wild, but cordial, bordering on warm. It is amazing how you can feel audience reactions to you even before the applause. It is something you sense in an almost psychic way. I have rarely been surprised by the audience's response at the end of a piece – its coldness, its indifference, or its whole-hearted enthusiasm. I can feel it before they show it."[37]

In Jean-Jacques Beneix's 1981 film *Diva*, the opera singer Cynthia Hawkins refuses to record her voice, because singing is, for her, a two-way communication with a live audience, and she needs to feel the spectators' bodily presence. Refusing both the separation of body and voice and the subsequent fetishizing of the voice that such a separation facilitates, she is like Callas, who "seemed to draw the sap of life from the performance itself and the audience's reception."[38] There are similar tales of famous conductors who have completely lost the dynamism, the exciting quality of their performances when they moved from the concert hall into the recording studio: without the other half of the communication circuit, something is missing. The immediacy and the corporeality of live performance are two-way phenomena.

In emphasizing the physical here, once again, we simply want to restore the balance between the Dionysian and the Apollonian that is upset when music is considered only as an intellectual aesthetic pleasure. As we saw in the prelude, for Nietzsche opera was both corporeally based, rooted in our Dionysian bodies, and also appreciated, understood, and made bearable through Apollonian form. Despite the long history of debate, there is no reason why music, and especially opera, must be interpreted in an either/or fashion, as primarily either abstract form or physiological pleasure, for it clearly involves both. For many composers and critics like Igor Stravinsky and Eduard Hanslick, music is primarily form or structure and should be responded to, and thus approached, cerebrally. What we might call Apollonian musicology shares this view. Others, like Paul Hindemith, feel music to be expressive and rooted in bodily rhythms and movement, especially when tied to words.[39] The Dionysian power of music over the body has long been suspect. Plato's Socrates would only allow music played on Apollo's instruments, the lyre and cithara, into his ideal republic, and warned of the danger faced by the soldier who abandons himself to music: "the effect begins to be that he melts and liquefies till he completely dissolves away his spirit, cuts out as it were the very sinews of his soul and makes himself a 'feeble warrior.'" Yet music should be taught and taught properly, argued Socrates, because of this very power: "because more than anything else rhythm and harmony find their way to the inmost soul and take strongest hold upon it, bringing with them and imparting grace, if one is rightly trained, and otherwise the contrary."[40]

As Philip Brett notes, this legacy of moral ambiguity has been passed on through the Christian suspicion of music, from the anguish experienced by St. Augustine when he is moved more by the voice than by the words of a song to the strong attacks of the Calvinists: "Lurking beneath the objections against music, the ethical question surrounding it, is the long tradition of feeling that it is different, irrational, unaccountable."[41] Its ravishing of the senses, its Dionysian power to arouse the body, can appear suspect when Apollonian control is what is valued. Brett sees musicological formalism and abstraction as having developed as ways to rescue music from "its own irrationality" and, we would add, in the case of opera, from its own bodily excess. But both the intellectual and the sensuous are involved in the experience of perceiving live opera.

It is interesting that the same was said of the experiencing of one of opera's forerunners, the oral poetry of ancient Greece: it produced a total response, "not just the distanced, intellectual response of the visually oriented, read poetry to which we are accustomed. The highly formulaic and formalized, ritualized patterning and repetition of meter and diction in early oral poetry reinforces this total effect. These formal qualities act through the motor responses and psychosomatic mechanisms of the audience, producing an identification, at the physical as well as mental level, with the rhythmic movements and structure of the poet's song."[42] The close relationship between the Apollonian formal patternings and the Dionysian motor responses that opera shares with this early performed poetry mirrors the increasingly tight relationship between the two deities in ancient Greece. While the Olympian Apollo and the "stranger god" Dionysus came to share not only space at Delphi but devotional time and festivities, they each also began to take on the characteristics of the other. As Dionysus became somewhat tamed through traditionalization and ritualization, the aloof and sober Apollo accepted the Dionysian *ekstasis* into his own religion.[43] If, as we have seen, Apollo remained the god of music, associated with certain string instruments, Dionysus was the god of the dance and of the music of the flute and drum.

However, he was also the god of collective emotion. The Dionysian ritual had a cathartic social function as an outlet for what E. R. Dodds calls "collective hysteria." The bacchantes in Euripides' *Bacchae* – and the opera based upon it, *The Bassarids* – exhibit a strong group consciousness.[44] Sitting in the opera audience, we too experience music's documented power to intensify crowd feeling. We may not take to the streets like the audience of the 1830 Brussels production of *La Muette de Portici* (1828; by Daniel Auber and Eugène Scribe/G. Delavigue). This performance "so excited its audience that they rushed out to storm the courthouse, and so began the national revolution that finally established Belgian political independence."[45] But even on a more reduced scale, something collective does happen in a theater audience: spectator to spectator communication can stimulate laughter, confirm our individual responses, and integrate us all into a larger responding unit.[46] It was in part because he was the god of mass emotion that Dionysus had an altar in the theater of Dionysus in ancient Athens, the site of the great drama festivals.

❧ The Busy Activity of Perception

In the prelude, we noted the theory that the origins of Greek drama were in the even earlier Athenian religious festivals of Dionysus. Here the physical presence of the statue of the god or an actor playing him on stage helped eliminate any physical or spiritual barrier between performers and audience in the sense that "[s]tage, orchestra [where the chorus stood] and auditorium formed a single unit and so too did actors, chorus and spectators, all of whom were sharing in a common act of devotion."[47] Being a member of an audience at a Dionysian rite meant having an active role, but many have argued that there has been a gradual but constant move away from this participatory activity to the silence and passivity that are said to characterize the modern theater audience. However, neither silence nor passivity describes the audience of opera in, for example, eighteenth-century Italy, as Georg Joseph Vogler witnessed it: "The public doesn't take the slightest interest [in the stage action]. . . . People yawn during the recitatives and chat during the vulgar arias. Nobody listens; they play games in the loges, drink coffee, eat supper. Sometimes, out of sheer disgust, they even close the window to the theatre [in their box], until the highlight of the concert moves them to silence for perhaps five minutes, eliciting scattered applause."[48] Apparently the performers were not insulted by this lack of attention and chatted among themselves and with the audience during the performance. Even into the nineteenth century in a European opera house, the crowd would only quiet down when a famous singer appeared on stage.[49] The stage was certainly not the only attraction: as Mary Cassatt's famous 1879 painting *At the Opera* vividly suggests, the audience was there to be observed as well as to observe. (See figure 12.)

According to one historical argument, the new theater designs of the nineteenth century – such as that of Bayreuth – worked to change this kind of audience behavior: rows of publicly visible seating rather than (or in addition to) the more private boxes made contact with fellow spectators into a different kind of experience. But the body did not suddenly become passive as a result. It is true, as Richard Leppert argues, that the spectator "may move toes in time to the beat but not hum, stomp feet, sway the torso, or bob the head: bodily reaction to music in the concert hall [and opera house] must be neither audible nor visible. To give oneself over to any of these reactions invites rebuke." This new social contract with other audience members does not, however, mean "a socially required passivity of reception," as Leppert claims.[50] As we have seen, the body still responds physiologically. What is usually meant by passivity here is Apollonian physical control: relative stillness and quiet. But the Dionysian can still be perceived at a micro level as we experience music kinesthetically in our bodies: "It seems that we use our musculatures to *represent* music, modeling the most important features of musical patterns by means of physical movements large and small. At one extreme, we bounce up and down to a pulsing beat. At the other, we are immobile yet are racked by anticipations of movement, experiencing the impetus toward motions that we do not actually initiate."[51] But sometimes the corporeal experience is more visible and much more obvious.

In Willa Cather's story "A Wagner Matinée," the narrator takes his Aunt Georgiana, who is visiting Boston from Nebraska, to a symphony concert with an all-Wagner program. At the first strains of *Tannhäuser*'s Pilgrims' Chorus, she clutches his sleeve. When it ends, she lets go and stares "dully," immobile, at the orchestra through the next number, "though her fingers worked mechanically upon her black dress, as if, of themselves, they were recalling the piano score they had once played." When Walter's Prize Song from *Die Meistersinger* begins, he recounts, "I heard a quick drawn breath and turned to my aunt. Her eyes were closed, but the tears were glistening on her cheeks, and I think, in a moment more, they were in my eyes as well."[52] Even in a silent, dark auditorium we react, because the human body is open to forces outside it: the live music, the reactions of those around us, and, in performed opera, the dramatic action and the

167

words. As Cather's story goes on to make clear, however, we are also open to forces from the inside: the associations and memories provoked by what is seen and heard. If listening is "the process of unpacking the musical-theoretical, musical-historical, cultural, psychoanalytic, and personal dimensions of music," then the act of perceiving an opera is an even more complicated unpacking process.[53]

We experience through the body, but we interpret through the mind. In other words, we listen as well as hear: "We hear the sounds, which means that we perceive the aural images that form in our minds as the result of certain concrete physical events, namely, vibrations of the air as they impinge on our ears, and we perceive their aural characteristics. What we do *not* hear is the relationships between them," because these formal relationships are not physical but mental.[54] This activity of perceiving relations is not passive, however, even if we sit quietly in our seats. We do not have to perform music to interpret it actively in both a corporeal and a cognitive way.[55] Reflecting the fact that Apollo and Dionysus are the complementary deities of the experience of the opera audience, Suzanne Langer has linked music to what she called the "pattern, or logical form, of sentience," the "form of feeling," and those twinned Apollonian-Dionysian terms capture well the complex duality of the audience experience.[56] Opera is music with a text; it is music with dramatic action. These other, defining components cannot be ignored or written off as mere "references to this messy world of human conflict" – even if some defiant listeners try to do so.[57]

What live opera does is engage in a very immediate way the emotions of the audience. We have avoided using the word emotion very often until now in our attempt to focus on the purely corporeal. But the interpretive activity of our perceiving mind and the physical reactions of our perceiving body come together in our emotional response, as we all know from our own experience and as we saw in Cather's story. For the narrator's aunt, Wagner's music is emotionally connected to her past and to a young man who had sung in the chorus at Bayreuth; for each of us, the connections are inevitably equally personal and individual. Yet in earlier centuries composition teachers taught their students how to produce "passionate responses in listeners through rhetorical manipulation."[58] And if Hindemith is to be believed, composers do indeed still know how to generate certain emotional reactions in their listeners. While admitting that one could never be completely sure of the emotional effect of one's music on the audience "when using complex materials," he claims that the composer, "by experience and clever distribution of this material, moreover with frequent references to those musical progressions that evoke the uncomplicated feelings-images of sadness or gaiety in an unambiguous form, . . . can reach a fairly close approximation to unanimity of all listeners' reactions."[59]

The ability of music, especially live music, to stir the emotions in this way has been attributed to many things, but one of the most common theories is a psychoanalytically inspired one that argues that these responses are not rationally explicable but are rooted in the unconscious and specifically in our relationship with our mother's body: "music is able to simulate that state when the infant still feels itself to be coextensive with the mother's body, a state in which all sensation appears to be authentic – before the alienating codes of language and culture intervene, before one is even aware of being an individual separate from the mother." For some, though, it is specifically the high female voice that has this direct link to our emotions through memory of the maternal relationship.[60] Whatever the reason for the emotional impact of music, it is undeniably felt by most people at some time or other, even if science has had a difficult time studying it: "although a good deal is known about the neuroanatomical and neurophysiological substrate of emotion we do not know why music moves us as it does."[61]

In *The Greeks and the Irrational*, E. R. Dodds discusses at length how the Dionysian rituals used music and dance to purge the irrational impulses: the ecstatic release brought about through the music had a cathartic effect, in both psychological and social terms.

Aristotle's famous audience-centered definition of catharsis as the purging of pity and fear provoked by watching tragic drama would seem to derive in part from this earlier practice, but it is particularly interesting for us because of Aristotle's implicit mixing of the Dionysian and the Apollonian: drama excites the emotions of pity and fear but also regulates, controls, dispels, indeed purges those emotions, in part through the distancing effect of the staged action. Yet many have seen only the Dionysian aspects of this notion of catharsis, and so such theatrical response has continued to be suspect, from Plato to the Church Fathers and well beyond. Opera is thus even more dangerous: "the peril of theatre and its 'impurities' was aggravated in opera by the effect of even more insidious seductions: voice, dance, harmonies. . . . It was the trap where the Tempter lay in wait for souls in order to take possession of them."[62] In the eighteenth century, Jean-Jacques Rousseau refused to accept Aristotelian catharsis as morally purifying, sharing Plato's distrust of the arts but for different reasons: the Enlightenment philosopher believed that reason was what was needed to achieve virtue, and the theater was the realm of emotion and not reason.[63] Diderot and Lessing tried to argue that later eighteenth-century bourgeois drama could turn passion into virtue and that, through the pathetic and the sublime, the emotions could be put to good work. Schiller and Goethe linked catharsis to the form of the art work itself.[64] Whatever the approach, all seem implicitly to feel that the power of theater to arouse emotion cannot be denied; with the addition of music, opera simply upped the ante.

As we sit in the audience at the opera, we are simultaneously distanced and involved. In a sense, we never forget completely that we are sitting watching a performance of a highly conventionalized art form: after all, people are singing instead of talking. Patrice Pavis argues that any theater spectator "remains the chief manipulator, the stage-hand for his [and her] own emotions, the craftsman of the theatrical event."[65] Such Apollonian control is shared by the spectator of opera. But we also, at times, find ourselves surrendering to the passion of the opera, even identifying emotionally with its characters, as Puccini's Cio-Cio-San dies by her own hand in *Madama Butterfly* or Berg's Wozzeck by his. And what we feel, in that surrender, is both cerebral and corporeal. As Judith Peraino explains it: "A physical catharsis for the opera audience transpires through literally sympathetic vibrations resulting from the music and the vision of the singers. This catharsis combines with the engagement of the emotions and the aesthetic experience of identification – that is, a vicarious/empathetic experience of the sentiment displayed by one or more characters. Opera is a unique artform that provides for an intertwining of emotional/physical rapture – a complete catharsis that unites the mind and the body."[66] While many would argue that church Gospel singing and certainly rock concerts can do the same, the point is simply that, although such sympathetic identification can be linked (and has been, by Camille Paglia) to the Dionysian, it clearly involves the Apollonian as well.[67] The activity involved in the multisensorial perception of live opera cannot be accounted for completely if either is denied.[68]

However, in both aesthetics and musicology, there is a history of attempting to sever the bonds between these two complementary aspects of musical experience. Cognitive theories argue that music is not primarily a physical stimulus to pleasure but is a "perceived and cognized object for the ear," an "object of perceptual consciousness" that can only be enjoyed when intellectually understood. From this perspective, we are said to respond with the intellect and not the nerve endings, as Peter Kivy puts it.[69] But the physiology of listening suggests otherwise, as we have seen. The competing theory, the arousal theory, is based on a stimulation-response model and has a long history, from Plato (on the negative side) through Descartes's *Compendium of Music* and *Passions of the Soul* in the seventeenth century, in which the philosopher argues that music positively stimulates the "animal spirits" that induce the human emotions.[70] One of the reasons that the Florentine Camerata rejected complex polyphony in music and created a new monodic vocal style for opera was because "solo song could arouse, so they thought, the individual emotion of the text it expressed – hope, love, fear, anger, and the like – while polyphonic music in four, five or more parts could not."[71]

Arguably, what these competing cognitive and arousal theories reflect is really only a different emphasis or a different way of articulating what is most important to a particular person when experiencing music. And some part of that determination of what is important is likely a learned response: for instance, Leppert argues that men have been encouraged to approach music cognitively, in an abstract and scientific manner, while women have historically been encouraged to make actual music: "Music is understood to be of the body – feelings – not of the mind."[72] But from our own personal experience, we know that, however we may value the different parts of the experience (physical, intellectual, emotional), they are all present and accounted for. Can we ignore the gooseflesh, the racing pulse? But are we really distracted by these sensuous responses from thinking about what we are seeing and hearing, as some claim?[73]

There is certainly a great amount of sensory information bombarding us when we sit in the opera house: the music and the voices, the bodies of the performers acting out a narrative on stage, the sets, props, and costumes, the lighting, and so on. But the human brain does deal with all that information, though it does so in different ways: in general terms, the right hemisphere or right brain, as it is usually referred to, processes tonality and melody; the left brain processes language.[74] As both music and words, opera thus engages both sides of the brain. As a staged art form, it also demands both visual and auditory processing. The complexity of vision is well known: it involves particles of light drawing responses from receptor cells in the retina and then being interpreted by the brain. But it is also a very physical and muscular activity: muscles are used to look at something and then to align the eyes to see a single image; the lens changes shape, depending on focal length; the iris expands or contracts, depending on ambient light; and so on. Hearing too is a muscular activity. Molecules of air vibrate and shove at the eardrum. Before that, though, the outer ear has amplified the sound by funneling it into the ear canal; both the outer ear and the canal resonate and boost certain frequencies. When the air molecules meet the eardrum, it vibrates, pushing against the malleus bone, which then trips the incus and stapes, all of which have muscles that tug at them with each sound. The motions then reach the fluid-filled inner ear, where they meet up with the body's nervous system, and the complex brain processing begins. Sounds, like sights, are in fact sensed and sequenced in different parts of the brain.[75]

There is yet another complication. Hearing is not the same as listening: as Roland Barthes has explained, the first is a mechanical and physiological phenomenon, the second is a cognitive and psychological one that deciphers, decodes, makes meaning.[76] Hearing is passive; some auditory processing does go on, but it is automatic and takes place in the brain stem. In contrast, listening to music, for instance, is active: "We automatically *hear* every note or simple figure, but must *listen* for larger structures."[77] This processing occurs in the cerebral cortex, which searches for patterns and familiar devices in music; listening is therefore guided by anticipation and memory. This is perhaps what accounts for the power of Wagnerian *Leitmotiven*, those musical phrases that recur throughout a complex work like *Der Ring des Nibelungen*, gaining meaning with each repetition and development. The brain pays attention to things like this, we are told. We may actually have a "cognitive preference" for certain kinds of music because their structure complements our particular listening skills: we may be attuned, for instance, to the melody and words (if we teach literature), or to the harmony (especially if we are professional musicians), or to the meter/beat, or to the larger musical structures. It would seem that this preference is a complex matter of brain biology, acculturation, and training. Listening has, in fact, been called a "performance skill" in which "the listener inwardly reproduces many features of a piece by anticipating them, and thereby better prepares himself to perceive them."[78]

It would seem that music – and opera – can both order the brain and overwhelm the body. The applause and the shouting we engage in at the end of a live performance is perhaps a sign of both our cognitive appreciation and our need for physical release of emotional tension. As Willa Cather writes at the end of her story "A Wagner Matinée," when the music ended, "the people filed out of the hall chattering and laughing, glad to relax and find the living level again."[79] To some members of the audience, such a sudden break from the emotional world of the opera is an abomination. At the end of a production of *Madama Butterfly*, Catherine Clément is driven to protest the rupture of her emotion: "All around you people are applauding; they stand and Butterfly is revived in the night lights. She is not a Japanese woman; she is plump, she can laugh, and she is alive. . . . Wake up, follow the rules, hit your two hands against each other; shout, if you dare, the word bravo."[80] The unwillingness to relinquish this surrender to the world of the opera is something every spectator has no doubt experienced at some point. But we may also have felt a need for some form of physical release, not to mention an immediate desire to express our appreciation or to communicate our discontent to those responsible for what we have just seen and heard.

On a personal, anecdotal level, our own strongest experience of this response took place in Paris a few years ago at the Théâtre du Châtelet's performance of Wagner's *Ring* cycle. Over the course of the four operas we came to feel increasing irritation at what appeared to be a cynical production (made primarily for radio broadcast and thus with little concern for coherent staging). The interpretation – such as it was – lacked motivation and even sense at times. During the final intermission of *Götterdämmerung*, after speaking with other members of the audience who felt as we did, we decided that, should the director, Pierre Strosser, come on stage, we would vocally express our displeasure. When Strosser did appear, he was met with what we can only call a verbal wall of angry abuse: several thousand spectators were on their feet with us, booing and screaming in many different languages. The crowd fed on its shared anger, the adrenaline made the heart beat faster and the yelling louder, and for a moment we understood those theater and opera riots we had read about. This Dionysian experience was far from pleasant, but it was intense enough to make us understand Clément's image of the "wild rite" of postperformance audience behavior that "gives opera a savage dimension where something other than a simple representation is being celebrated."[81]

Even without discounting the possibility of pathology, opera's fans have always been rather extreme. The stars of opera – from the *castrati* to the divas – have been the objects of adoration and adulation. Opera books are full of stories of the intense enthusiasm of the fans of Maria Malibran, Jenny Lind, and Pauline Viardot; in 1913, a nineteen-year-old woman shot herself when refused a meeting with soprano Mary Garden.[82] London is said to have suffered from "Galli-Curci fever," and San Francisco was the site of Adelina Patti "mania."[83] We have long known of the existence of opera "claques," that is, groups of people either paid or given complimentary tickets to ensure either calculated applause or the booing of a rival singer.[84] But even more innocent partisanship lines have always run deep in opera: in 1834, when Malibran dared to sing Norma, a role "owned" by Giuditta Pasta, at La Scala, "her life was threatened and, during the second performance, the audience rioted."[85] Renata Tebaldi fans at La Scala were merciless with Maria Callas. During the 8 January 1955 performance there of *Andrea Chénier*, when her voice wobbled on a climactic high B, her enemies were openly hostile: "As hoots and whistles combined with the applause of Callas's admirers, the soprano maintained her composure." When she did not complete a performance of *Norma* in Rome three years later, an angry crowd gathered and threw rotten fruit and eggs. When she arrived back in Milan, she found several tons of farm manure dumped in front of her house, and human excrement had been used to write "filthy slogans" on the doors and windows.[86] Assuming fans are sane, then what drives them to such extremes of behavior? What does opera offer that other art forms do not seem to provide? In a word: ecstasy.

ॐ *Ekstasis*

Call it ecstasy, call it rapture. But whatever we call it, it seems that opera audiences experience it – and talk about it in this way – more often than audiences at any other kind of live performance art. This state of extreme arousal is more than just "a condition of heightened alertness, awareness, interest, and excitement: a generally enhanced state of being."[87] Ecstasy is something more powerful than this, and it is no accident that the drug taken by young people attending "raves" is called Ecstasy: the dancing that ensues may well be a modern manifestation of Dionysian *ekstasis*. For an opera audience, ecstasy is physical; it is also emotional and even intellectual. But the language used to describe it is inevitably more visceral, more Dionysian in its associations. In the story "Paul's Case," Willa Cather writes of how a young man feels a "peculiar intoxication" and a "delicious excitement" at the sound of operatic music: "all stupid and ugly things slid from him, and his senses were deliciously, yet delicately fired."[88]

Opera is doubly liable to provoke this kind of extreme arousal because it consists of both drama and music. Linda Williams uses the term "body genre" to describe films that are sensational and excessive in offering "a body caught in the grip of intense sensation and emotion" with the hope of inspiring the same response in the viewer. Body genres include pornography, horror films, and what she calls melodramas or "weepies." As we have seen, operatic drama too could be seen as a body genre, for its excess also induces in its audience some kind of rapture.[89] When we add to this the power of (especially live) operatic music, which, as we have seen, has direct physiological as well as emotional and cognitive effects on the listening body and mind, then we can begin to understand how operatic ecstasy can be so powerful. Think of how people describe their reactions to exciting performances: they talk of feeling tingly, as though they have touched a live wire; of being kept on the edge of their seats and being left limp afterward; of being electrified; of being turned to quivering jelly; and so on. Or they talk of being overwhelmed by the sound, drowned in it.[90] The physicality of the descriptions is striking: Dionysian *ekstasis* is a bodily thing, first and foremost, though in a complex and even paradoxical way. As we can see in *The Bacchae* and *The Bassarids*, ecstasy involves the transporting of the self outside the self, outside even the body sometimes. The exaltation of the senses could lead to a transcending of the body through the very excitement of the body.[91] Music seems the most immediate of the arts and so is perhaps the most readily able to provoke ecstasy in this Dionysian sense.

Just as, in ancient Greece, the Apollonian forms of worship gradually absorbed the visionary and ecstatic elements of the Dionysian rites, so the intellectual response to opera is somehow also involved in this rapture, even though we tend to describe it in intensely physical ways. The perception of and response to Apollonian formal order and aesthetic beauty are not only means to the Platonic good, as we saw in the first chapter, but they have been seen as part of the intense pleasure we are calling ecstasy:

When music is written with genius, every event is carefully selected to build the substructure for exceptionally deep relations. No resource is wasted, no distractions are allowed. In this perfect world, our brains are able to piece together larger understandings than they can in the workaday external world, perceiving all-encompassing relations that go much deeper than those we find in ordinary experience. . . . As our brains are thrown into overdrive, we feel our very existence expand and realize that we can be more than we normally are, and that the world is more than it seems. That is cause enough for ecstasy.[92]

As described by many, ecstasy can involve a sense of mental or spiritual expansion, of merging with external reality, which itself is endowed with a sense of intense personal significance: "This peculiar transcendental state of cosmic consciousness may at times sweep over an orchestral conductor, and occasionally a singer. The ecstatic or near-ecstatic feeling is compounded of several factors beyond the four criteria mentioned by [William] James [transiency, passivity, ineffability, noetic quality]. They also include loss of time-sense, derealisation, depersonalisation, . . . specular illusions . . . , and also subjective aberrations in corporeal awareness."[93] One possible reason why we describe what we feel in bodily terms rather than in intellectual or spiritual ones is connected to what the brain does when it experiences music: it is said to produce the body's natural opiates, endorphins.[94]

Yet when listeners speak of ecstasy, they often have in mind one particular physical sensation, variously described as a *frisson*, gooseflesh, chills, thrills, skin orgasm, a rush, a tingling in the spine, or the hair standing up on the back of the neck. This is what some audience members wait for. Studies have shown that this sensation is provoked in particular circumstances and by particular sounds: the most intense and dramatic crescendos in the music; a piercing crescendo against a background mood of melancholy or sadness; certain sustained high-frequency notes, sung (or played) by a solo performer, often a cappella. Our bodily response to these physical stimuli is seemingly affected by such things as familiarity with the music, personal meaning or memory associated with it, its perceived emotional content, and how much we actually like the music.[95] In live opera, where we listen in the context of a dramatized story that usually has strong emotional resonance, this feeling is likely to be produced more often than, let us say, in a symphony performance.

Why do we feel this *frisson* of pleasure? There are theories that suggest that these chills are neurochemically similar to the chills engendered by social loss; others look to our childhood or infancy for psychoanalytic reasons for this feeling that occurs on our skin, that is, on the boundary separating our bodies from the rest of the world; still others look to the adrenaline rush – the "fight versus flight" response – or to those released endorphins.[96] Neurological theories about the phenomenon of synaesthesia – the perceiving of one sense in terms of another – suggest that sensory overflow might be the cause of the ecstatic physical response, that music may be loaded with emotional content both in itself and because of associations.[97] In the case of the complex multisensorial nature of live opera, this would seem an interesting possibility.

In Balzac's novella *Sarrasine*, a young man at the opera finds that the performance is having an ecstatic effect on him: his senses are described as "lubrifiés" (lubricated), as he feels a "ravishing ecstasy." By the end he feels completely intoxicated, loses contact with his surroundings, and succumbs to what the text calls convulsive delights: orgasm, perhaps, by any other name. As Barthes comments on this response in *S/Z*:

> This music's erotic quality (attached to its *vocal nature*) is here defined: it is the power of *lubrication*; *connection* is a specific characteristic of the voice, the model of the lubricated is the organic, the "living," in short, seminal fluid (Italian music "floods with pleasure"); singing (a characteristic generally ignored in aesthetics) has something coenesthetic about it, it is connected less to an "impression" than to internal, muscular, humoral sensuality. The voice is a diffusion, an insinuation, it passes over the entire surface of the body, the skin. . . . Music, therefore, has an effect utterly different from sight; it can effect orgasm.[98]

Can it? Is the *frisson* the same as the orgasm? Or do we simply lack a language other than the erotic in which to speak of the body's ecstasy?

Sex is certainly the metaphor of choice for many critics who attempt to describe this sensation. For Koestenbaum, in the work we have cited so often, *The Queen's Throat*, subtitled *Opera, Homosexuality, and the Mystery of Desire*, listening to opera – live or recorded – is a visceral process, one he calls "a sanctioned, invisible autoeroticism." But Sam Abel, in *Opera in the Flesh*, goes one step beyond metaphor and argues that, in live performance, "[a]betted by the love story, the opulent surroundings, and especially by the eroticized body of the singer, a purely musical climax becomes a full-fledged sexual consummation."[99] Much opera is about sex, he claims, but some parts are all sex. What exactly does he mean by this, though? Sometimes he seems to be speaking metaphorically, such as when he defines Aristotle's catharsis as "a dramatic orgasm, the moment when the tensions of the narrative find their release." Yet at other times Abel seems to be more literal: through the physical contact of sound, "operatic orgasms" happen to audiences, he asserts. The "constant barrage of visual and auditory stimuli" overwhelms the senses and "leaves little room for objective contemplation."[100] Without denying opera's Dionysian impact on the body, we nevertheless find it reductive to believe that the mind is somehow crowded out of the operatic response completely. Yet Abel clearly feels that the power of live opera is sensual and, more specifically, erotic, not verbal or intellectual.

David Levin has dubbed this kind of commentary "critical Neo-Lyricism" and attacks its "seemingly unmotivated hyperbole and proto-ritualized sentimentalization," along with its melodramatic "new world of libidinal stratospherics."[101] But the question remains: Why is the sexual the language of choice to talk about operatic ecstasy?[102] For gay men like Abel and Koestenbaum, it is in part an understandable choice to revel in the sexualized body, in what was once closeted, silenced. Same-sex passion also finds a language through operatic ecstasy in Marcia Davenport's 1936 novel *Of Lena Geyer*, in which a young woman describes what she feels when she hears a soprano sing: "the pulse in my throat choked me. I sat letting it rush through me like electricity, completely unconscious of ever having lived before." What she constantly refers to as a "physical thrill" is clearly also a sexual thrill.[103] But gay and lesbian writers have not been the only ones to use this erotic language; for example, we find psychoanalytic discussions of the voice as a libidinal object that can sweep away the audience.[104] And for a feminist critic like Susan McClary, the link between the sexual and the musical is again direct and corporeal: "[T]o say that one hears sexual longing in the *Tristan* prelude is not to introduce irrelevant 'subjective' data into the discussion of the opera, and we are missing the point if we fail to understand that. The process by means of which Wagner's music accomplishes this is not at all mystical. In part, his music draws on his own (excessively documented) experiences in the sexual realm, and we as listeners perceive longing in his music likewise because we are human beings with bodies who have experienced similar feelings firsthand."[105] While many are happy enough to accept the sexual as an analogy or metaphor, that is clearly not always what a critic like Abel intends. Both opera and sex may arouse intense emotions and physiological responses; both may leave us feeling satisfied and at peace afterward. However, as Anthony Storr points out, sports enthusiasts may feel the same thing watching championship tennis: "The pattern of arousal followed by relaxation is ubiquitous – an inescapable aspect of both human and animal life."[106]

Yet how often do we read of music's ability to create in its listeners tensions and frustrations of desire, to instill expectations and then tease us by withholding the resolution until the climax?[107] Given this musical discourse, it is not hard to see why the analogies with sexual desire and its release are made. If we add the thematic content of much opera – love (or in its more extreme forms, as Abel sees it, sexual taboos) – then the linking is even easier to understand. This does not mean it should be the final word, however. Equating operatic ecstasy with sex is severely reductive of the notion of human bodily pleasure. Even Freud's Eros was a larger, life-driving force. Yet what such a reduction does manage to capture that *is* important is a sense of the bodily nature of this ecstatic response. If this "critical Neo-Lyricism" came into being to counter the Apollonian force of musicological analyses of form, then it has succeeded in its balancing act: the two poles are now clearly defined. Left in the middle, responding emotionally, physically, and intellectually to what we see and hear on stage, are the members of the opera audience. We do not have to be tied to the masts of our ship to listen to the seductive song of the operatic sirens; we listen, we feel, we comprehend. The Dionysian *frisson* and emotional charge are accompanied by Apollonian understanding and appreciation of the opera's story and music.

1. Dionysus, the god of excess, with his drinking
cup and thyrsus, accompanied by a flute-playing
satyr and a dancing maenad. Courtesy of the
Royal Ontario Museum.

2. Apollo, the god of music, with his lyre. Courtesy of the Royal Ontario Museum.

3. Susan Marie Pierson as the defiantly dancing Elektra, 1996. Photo by Brian Campbell, Canadian Opera Company. © D. Brian Campbell 1996.

4. Kenneth Riegel as the German writer Aschenbach and dancer Jeffrey Edwards as the beautiful dancing Tadzio in *Death in Venice* (1984). Photo by Robert C. Ragsdale, Canadian Opera Company.

5. Quasimodo and Esmeralda from *Notre-Dame de Paris* (Paris: La Librairie Ollendorf, 1904). Courtesy of the Thomas Fisher Rare Book Library, University of Toronto, Canada.

6. The unbeautiful Rigoletto, performed by Brent Ellis (1992). Photo by Michael Cooper, Canadian Opera Company. Courtesy of Michael Cooper Photographic.

7. The beautiful Lucrezia Borgia, performed by Beverly Sills (1976). Photo by Beth Bergman, New York City Opera. © Beth Bergman 1999.

8. Gustave Moreau, *Salome Dancing Before Herod*, 1876. Oil on canvas, 56 1/2 in. × 41 1/16 in. The Armand Hammer Collection, UCLA at the Armand Hammer Museum of Art and Cultural Center, Los Angeles, California. Photo by Robert Wedemeyer.

9. The dancing Salome. Photo of the Atom Egoyan production (1996) by Michael Cooper, Canadian Opera Company. Courtesy of Michael Cooper Photographic.

10. Maria Callas, before her weight loss, in *Norma* (1952). Photo by E. Piccagliani, Teatro alla Scala, Milan.

11. Maria Callas, after her weight loss, in *La Vestale* (1954). Courtesy of Photofest.

12. Mary Cassatt, *In the Loge*, 1879. The Hayden Collection.
Courtesy, Museum of Fine Arts, Boston.

13. "A Moral and Physical Thermometer," in Dr. Benjamin Rush,
M.D., *An Inquiry into the Effects of Ardent Spirits upon the Human
Body and Mind* (New York, 1811). Courtesy of the Thomas Fisher
Rare Book Library, University of Toronto, Canada.

A MORAL AND PHYSICAL THERMOMETER.

A scale of the progress of Temperance and Intemperance.—Liquors with effects in their usual order.

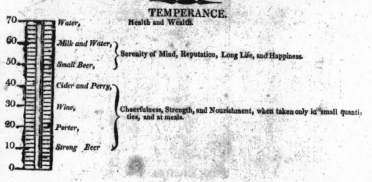

TEMPERANCE.

70	Water, — Health and Wealth.
60	Milk and Water, ⎫
50	Small Beer, ⎬ Serenity of Mind, Reputation, Long Life, and Happiness.
40	Cider and Perry, ⎫
30	Wine, ⎬ Cheerfulness, Strength, and Nourishment, when taken only in small quanti-ties, and at meals.
20	Porter, ⎬
10	Strong Beer ⎭
0	

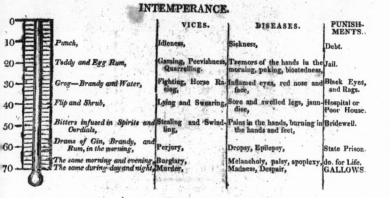

INTEMPERANCE.

		VICES.	DISEASES.	PUNISH-MENTS.
0				
10	Punch,	Idleness,	Sickness,	Debt.
20	Toddy and Egg Rum,	Gaming, Peevishness, Quarrelling.	Tremors of the hands in the morning, puking, bloatedness,	Jail.
30	Grog—Brandy and Water,	Fighting, Horse Ra-cing,	Inflamed eyes, red nose and face,	Black Eyes, and Rags.
40	Flip and Shrub,	Lying and Swearing.	Sore and swelled legs, jaun-dice,	Hospital or Poor House.
50	Bitters infused in Spirits and Cordials,	Stealing and Swind-ling,	Pains in the hands, burning in the hands and feet,	Bridewell.
60	Drams of Gin, Brandy, and Rum, in the morning,	Perjury,	Dropsy, Epilepsy,	State Prison.
70	The same morning and evening, The same during day and night.	Burglary, Murder,	Melancholy, palsy, apoplexy, Madness, Despair,	do. for Life. GALLOWS.

14. Falstaff, performed by Timothy Noble (1995),
enjoying his restorative drink of wine. Photo
by Robert C. Ragsdale, Canadian Opera
Company.

A Toast to Opera's Bodies

If my dearest wish were granted me
I'd demand that Bacchus planted me
Deep inside a lake of wine.

Supping water's quite unthinkable –
Only Bacchus knows what's drinkable:
I'm a worshipper at his shrine.

In these words, the rain-soaked Elviro, in Handel's *Xerxes* (1738), praises the comforts and delights of wine.[1] Of course, he is not alone in opera in voicing his feelings about the gift to humankind made by Dionysus. The satyr who opens Rameau's *Platée* (1745) likewise sings of Bacchus as the veritable soul of pleasure ("âme des plaisirs"). The harvesters who then echo his words add associations of fertility and abundance to the god they praise. Thespis, the author of the drama who claims to be inspired by Bacchus, calls him "dieu de la liberté, / père de la sincérité" [god of liberty, / father of sincerity]. And all this takes place at the foot of a mountain whereupon sits a temple to Bacchus. The god's many roles that we have seen in earlier chapters are succinctly invoked in this opening scene: Dionysus not only presided over dramatic performances, but he was also the god of the vine and of exuberant life. On one level, then, these characteristics all make him from the start the perfect deity to be a patron of the excessive art form called opera.

Opera's penchant for Dionysian toasts (*brindisi*) and drinking songs has not gone unnoticed: Franco Onorati's playful account of drinking and eating among musicians, composers, and operatic characters is called *"Libiamo, libiamo . . ."*, recalling one of the most famous of *brindisi* – that of Alfredo and Violetta in *La Traviata* (1853). But there are literally dozens and dozens of others he could have recalled, including another toast from the same composer and librettist, Verdi and Piave. In the operatic version of *Macbeth* (1847), Lady Macbeth, of all people, sings another typical *brindisi* to distract her guests from her husband's terror at seeing Banquo's ghost:

Si colmi il calice
di vino eletto;
nasca il delitto,
muoia il dolor.
Da noi s'involino
gli odi e gli sdegni,
folleggi e regni
qui solo amor . . .

[Let the goblets be filled
with select wine;
pleasure is born,
pain dies.
From us fly away
hatreds and scornfulness,
here makes merry and reigns
only love . . .]

Operas often call attention to such arias by marking them as what is called "phenomenal song," that is, as a self-conscious performance: in *La Traviata*, Alfredo is quite specifically asked by the partygoers, including Violetta, to sing a *brindisi*. While few operas are totally centered on the Dionysian experience of drinking, equally few are without either a drinking song that celebrates the virtues and pleasures of drink or some sort of toast that consecrates love, life, or health.

Does Dionysus reign alone, then, over this particular aspect of operatic excess? Historically, Greek drama grew out of the dithyramb, the improvised cult-songs in honor of Dionysus that were sung at banquets by those struck by the inspiration of wine. Yet after these songs to Dionysus, a paean to Apollo was often performed as well, a solemn choral lyric of invocation. Once again proving to be complementary as much as opposing forces, Dionysus and Apollo meet as well in the operatic representations of drinking in interesting ways that mirror Western cultural habits. In this Postlude, we would like to look at a few of these stagings of the drinking, singing body as a final toast to the "bodily charm" of opera: to real bodies, but especially represented ones. Obviously, performers do not actually drink real alcohol on stage, but they sometimes have to represent, that is, to incarnate the intoxicated body with a certain verisimilitude for the audience. The physiological effects of drink on the human body (including on the singer's body) have been well documented throughout the ages – by individual personal experience as much as by scientific research.[2] And opera represents those effects in its staged dramatizations of inebriated characters in ways that audiences from different places and times will all recognize as familiar – that is, if the performers can manage to be convincing.[3]

✥ Dionysian Excess and Apollonian Control

Wine, the gift of Dionysus, would seem the appropriate subject, then, with which to conclude our study of the return of Dionysus from the dual exile of audio technology's fetishizing of the disembodied voice and of some musicologists' Apollonian neglect of the staged and thus the physical aspects of opera. Historically, we know that most early societies made their own alcoholic beverages and used them for personal and social ceremonials, usually either for hospitality or to mark rites of passage.[4] It seems that priests or shamans could reach states of ecstasy through alcohol and that power was then attributed to the gods. In Greco-Roman culture, the god in question was Dionysus, of course, and we have seen that his bacchantes, or women worshipers, did indeed consume wine as an important element of their rituals. The Dionysian ecstatic exaltation of the senses through music, dance, and intoxicating drink was a way to enter into communion with the god.[5]

From the start, however, people seem to have experienced considerable ambivalence about alcohol consumption, as the Apollonian urge for order and control exerted its power over Dionysian excess. The Judeo-Christian world accepts moderate drinking but condemns excess; Islam has banned alcohol entirely. The elaborate rules societies have developed to control alcohol use have very much depended upon whether people judged its effects on the mind and body to be positive or negative ones: just as there are contradictions within the legends' characterizations of Dionysus, so too drinking his wine has been seen both as a source of collective festive pleasure and as a form of individual antisocial behavior.[6] And these Dionysian dualities multiply: alcoholic beverages have been viewed as both energizers and tranquilizers; for some people, they have been medicines, while for others, food; in certain situations they become sacred symbols, while in others they are what have been called "super-ego solvents."[7]

While the wisdom and virtue of Apollonian moderation have consistently been sung along with the risks and dangers of Dionysian excess, the dual or contradictory nature of Dionysus himself is not to be forgotten, for it is evident in the very terms used to talk about his gift to humankind: *aqua vitae*, the water of life, has its dark equivalent in *Schnapsteufel*, the brandy devil.[8] Charles Baudelaire articulated this internal dualism well when he wrote of wine as being like humankind – capable of both sublime deeds and monstrous deceits: "What man has never known the profound joys of wine? Whoever has had a grief to appease, a memory to evoke, a sorrow to drown, a castle in Spain to build – all have at one time invoked the mysterious god who lies concealed in the fibers of the grapevine. How radiant are those wine-induced visions, illuminated by the inner sun! How true and burning this second youth which man draws from wine. But how dangerous, too, are its fierce pleasures and debilitating enchantments."[9]

The horrors – both social and personal – of excessive drinking have been documented throughout the ages and include such things as madness, anarchy, and physical and moral degeneration.[10] The Old Testament argued that excess leads to, among other things, shameful deportment, dishonor, vulnerability, impaired judgment, and ungodly behavior.[11] Yet when the drinkers in Mozart and Stephanie's *Die Entführung aus dem Serail* (1782) sing the praises of alcohol – "Vivat Bacchus!" – it is not these horrors but the positive, convivial celebration of community that is being evoked. Again, Baudelaire put this position rather well, this time rather operatically adopting the voice of wine itself: "Can you hear the powerful refrains of ancient times, the songs of love and glory, resounding and echoing within me? I am the soul of our native land, half soldier and half gentleman. I am Sunday's hope. As *work makes for prosperous days*, so wine makes for joyful Sundays. Pay me proud tribute, with your shirtsleeves rolled back and your elbows leaning upon the family table, and you shall know true contentment."[12] And in Massenet's *Werther* (1892), two characters dutifully sing to precisely such a joyful Sunday: "Vivat Bacchus! Semper vivat! C'est dimanche!"

However, well before this, beginning in the eighteenth century, Europe also initiated a particularly Apollonian campaign to regulate Dionysian excess: it began to treat the excessive consumption of alcohol in terms of disease. Theoretically, this medicalization signaled a move from making moral judgments to seeking, through a biological model, physical mechanisms and rational explanations.[13] Yet medical positions were often enlisted and exploited in the many temperance campaigns that were born in these same years. Physicians were in a decidedly conflicted position: since Galen, they had used alcohol for its anesthetic and therapeutic properties. While the medical belief in alcohol's positive medicinal value reached its height in Europe by 1700, in popular culture it continued long after.[14] In 1851 Baudelaire wrote that wine "stimulates the digestion, fortifies the muscles, and enriches the blood."[15] And this view also continued in medical culture: despite changes in *physiological theories* about alcohol (its nutritive value, its role in body temperature regulation, its stimulant effect, and so on), *clinical use* did not change much at all.[16] Alcohol was used to stimulate depressed and lethargic patients and to treat those with fevers; its anesthetic power could ease the pain of wounds or prepare a patient for surgery.[17] In 1836 William Lee published a pocket edition of "that Most Useful and Popular Work Entitled *Brandy and Salt: Being an Effectual Remedy for Most of the Diseases which Afflict Humanity*." And well into the twentieth century, brandy was still being touted as a therapy for digestive problems, including diseases like cholera.[18] It should be noted that there is some truth to some of these beliefs, as modern medicine has discovered: whatever damage alcohol may do to the liver, wine has proved to be successful in tempering some risk factors of cardiovascular disease.[19]

Nevertheless, as early as 1774 doctors were warning of the consequences of excessive drinking for pregnant women and the elderly.[20] Focusing on problems, not Dionysian pleasures, they outlined what they saw as the dangers of excess – and those dangers were often more than physical ones. In 1811 Benjamin Rush visualized these perils in his "Moral and Physical Thermometer," which graphically lined up "intemperance" libations with vices, diseases, and punishments and nonalcoholic drinks with serenity, strength, long life, and (at the top) "Health" and "Wealth." (See figure 13.) Given this moral turn, religious leaders vied with physicians for influence: the Reverend Benjamin Parsons, in his 1840 "Anti-Bacchus" essay, claimed that over forty diseases were directly caused by alcohol.[21]

While there were a good many Apollonian temperance novels and even temperance stage melodramas in the nineteenth century, there were, to our knowledge, absolutely no "temperance operas": indeed, the term itself is rather an oxymoron.[22] Instead we find the lusty Dionysian celebrations of the glories of drink in a work like Johann Strauss's *Die Fledermaus* (1874, to a libretto by Haffner and Genée after a French *spirituel vaudeville* called *Le Réveillon*). This opera manages to expose and exploit many of the long-held beliefs and long-cherished customs of drinking. Early in the opera, for instance, a lover tries to seduce with wine:

Trinke Liebchen, trinke schnell,
trinken macht die Augen hell
. . . gibt der Wein dir Tröstung schon
durch Vergessenheit!
. . . trink mit mir, sing mit mir.

[Drink, my love, drink quickly,
drinking makes the eyes clear
. . . wine gives you comfort
through forgetfulness!
. . . drink with me, sing with me.]

Then, at a party at the home of the Russian Prince Orlofsky, the host virtually demands excessive behavior of his guests, asking that they drink with him and never be so rude as to stop. He then toasts "Champagner . . . König aller Weine," and all join in a chorus of "long live Champagne the First," that king of wines. To a sentimental waltz tune, the guests are led in a song of drinking and brotherhood, a staged enacting of verbal and liquid social bonding. With inhibitions lifted by the wine, all sing of love and alcohol as granting blissfulness. The upper classes may imbibe champagne at the prince's party, but the local jailer gets happily drunk on a less noble drink, the "verdammter Slibowitz" that he both enjoys immensely and conveniently blames for everything. And although the champagne too gets blamed for escapades that are really only more socially elevated forms of misbehavior, all ends happily with yet another Dionysian chorus to the majesty of that sparkling wine.

❧ Celebrating Dionysian Excess

One of the reasons for the age-old injunction not to indulge in excessive drinking – from Hippocrates and the Old Testament to the present – is the fear of what happens when inhibitions are lifted.[23] Yet some, like Plato, for instance, felt that drunken excess could have positive moral training value, if administered in carefully controlled situations.[24] And much early medical theory saw wine as allopathic and cathartic, and so getting drunk was one way of purging the body.[25] In short, the positive as well as negative results of drinking have been debated from early times to the present.

If ever there was a dramatic character who incarnated the more positive values of Dionysian excess in food and drink, it is Falstaff – both Shakespeare's original creation and, even more so, Boito's operatic version for Verdi's 1893 opera named after its protagonist. We know that there has been a long line of passionate apologists for Falstaff and that he and his drinking mates were favorites with audiences from the start.[26] Among the other operas written about him are Antonio Salieri/Carlo Prospero Defranceschi's *Falstaff o sia le tre burle* (1798), M. W. Balfe/S. M. Maggioni's *Falstaff* (1838), Ralph Vaughan Williams's *Sir John in Love* (1929), and Otto Nicolai/Salomon H. Rosenthal's *Die lustigen Weiber von Windsor* (1849).[27] In the latter, Falstaff as major drinker is featured prominently, beginning his day drinking *Sekt,* his "old friend" that has always helped him forget the fearsome hardships ("die fürchterlichen Strapaze") of life. In fact, he gets into a drinking contest with the local Windsor burghers, knowing that it is wine that creates community, that keeps people together ("hält den ganzen Menschen zusammen"). Between rounds of the contest, he sings a drinking song about how he learned to love that sparkling wine at his mother's breast, a song that ends with

> Trinken ist keine Schand',
> Bacchus trank auch, ja,
> Bacchus trank auch
>
> [Drinking is no disgrace,
> Bacchus drank too, yes,
> Bacchus drank too.]

While the complexity and ambivalence of Shakespeare's character from the *Henry* plays and *The Merry Wives of Windsor* are lost in this particular operatic version, Boito restores both. He did, however, make major cuts to the play texts and thereby changed the balance of character presentation. His opera's Falstaff is more active, less victimized; he is certainly less mercenary but perhaps a bit more self-satisfied than the Shakespearean original. In the seventeenth-century English context, it may well be the case that "[r]iotous behavior is frowned on and any form of excess, even excess in pleasure is considered disruptive. Falstaff is excessive in body as in behavior and he arouses most vilification."[28] But the late-nineteenth-century Italian opera offers a more tolerant take on the excessive Dionysian protagonist who nevertheless shocks the Apollonian mores of the English gentlefolk of Windsor. As one commentator put the difference, "The great critical debates about whether Falstaff is a sordid vice-figure or an inspired jester have been decisively arbitrated by Verdi and Boito in favour of the latter," and another has noted that to Romantic writers Falstaff was heroic *because of* his excesses, "which cause failure but also ensure distinction."[29] It is true, as Peter Conrad argues, that Boito "repatriated" Falstaff from "puritanical England to sensual Italy," but he also moved from a staged play to a staged opera – with its very different conventions for and tolerance of excess.[30]

Falstaff opens, in an adaptation of the play's first scene, with a focus on drinking and its consequences. Dr. Caius appears at the inn, accusing Falstaff's men, Bardolph and Pistol, of having made him drunk and robbing him. This is almost an inversion of the traditional *brindisi*, this time emphasizing the bad rather than the good things that can happen when you drink. The two comic drunks agree they all did drink together, thereby accounting for their own considerable hangovers ("che dolore! . . . Ho l'intestino guasto"), but they deny the robbery, claiming that Caius simply holds his drink badly: "Costui beve / poi pel gran bere / perde i suoi cinque sensi" [This one drinks / then with excess of drink / loses his five senses]. It seems Caius ended up falling asleep under the table. In disgust, the doctor swears that if he ever gets drunk at an inn again, he'll do it with honest, sober, civil, and pious people ("gente onesta, sobria, civile e pia"). His phrases here are punctuated in the music with pretentious brass fanfares that underline the ludicrousness of his oath.[31]

Falstaff is presented with his bill by the innkeeper and immediately blames his companions for *their* excessive drinking, which costs him too much, while *he* proceeds to order yet another bottle of wine. The self-satisfied knight here prides himself on his excessive body size, and Bardolph and Pistol encourage him with supportive cries of "Falstaff immenso!" and "Enorme Falstaff." This is another of those operas in which we cannot ignore the body. The Shakespearean emphasis on cunning and money is here replaced with an operatic celebration of drink and its benefits. Patting his paunch, Falstaff announces that it is his kingdom, and he will work to make it larger ("Questo è il mio regno / Lo ingrandirò").[32]

The plot of the opera basically follows that of the play. The cunning, broke, but amorous knight has sent love letters to two married women, Alice Ford and Meg Page, in a covert bid for financial support. The women plan to trick and humiliate him while still teaching Alice's jealous husband a lesson. When Falstaff pays a secret amatory visit to Alice, she hides him from her enraged husband in a laundry basket, which is then tossed into the waters of the Thames. Act 3 opens with Falstaff recovering from this dunking, suddenly and movingly aware of his size and age as negatives, as if for the first time.[33] The Host of the Garter Inn brings him a cup of heated wine, which turns out to be just the thing to restore his forces. (See figure 14.) This comforting beverage provokes a song in praise of wine's positive effects on the human body:

Buono. Ber del vin dolce
e sbottonarsi al sole, dolce cosa!
Il buon vino sperde

le tetre fole dello sconforto,
accende l'occhio e il pensier,
dal labbro sale al cervel
e quivi risveglia
il picciol fabbro dei trilli;
un negro grillo che vibra
entro l'uom brillo.
Trilla ogni fibra in cor,
l'allegro etere al trillo guizza
e il giocondo globo squilibra
una demenza trillante!
E il trillo invade il mondo!!!

[Good. To drink sweet wine and
unbutton oneself in the sun, a sweet thing!
Good wine dispels
gloomy tales of dejection,
lights up the eye and the thought,
from the lip it goes up to the brain
and there awakens
the little maker of trills;
a black whim that vibrates
within the drunken man.
Every fiber of the heart trills,
the happy air flashes to the trill,
and the joyous globe is thrown out of balance
by a trilling madness!
And the trill invades the world!!!]

During the Italian word play on "grillo"/"brillo"/"trillo" (whim/drunk/trill), actual trills predominate in the music, and on that final line about their universal invasion "the whole orchestra resolves into a gigantic unison trill."[34] As Falstaff warms up with his wine, the music heats up as well.

While it is true that, as in the play, the operatic Falstaff is scapegoated and ritually mocked at the end, he retains his Dionysian joy in excess: he responds to his tormentors' insults and threats with repeated requests to save his "abdomen" ("Ma salvagli l'addomine") – that paunch that constitutes his kingdom and his identity. In contrast to Herbert Lindenberger's sense that Falstaff is an operatic character in a "relatively unoperatic context,"[35] we would argue instead that the operatic version of the character is perfectly in keeping with the genre's Dionysian celebration of excess. This is not to deny that, for many cultures, excessive consumption is associated with gluttony and self-indulgence in a negative sense, and, of course, operas reflect that as well.[36] Sometimes it is the violence induced by drink itself that is used to dramatic effect in opera, in part because it fractures the audience's social notions of companionship and community associated with people drinking together.

✎ The Dark Dionysus

If operas like Wagner's *Parsifal* and *Götterdämmerung*, in their different ways, show how the sharing of wine can establish a symbolic bond of brotherhood, others (like Mascagni's *Cavalleria Rusticana*) demonstrate how such bonds can also be broken through the machinations of drink.[37] In medical terms, studies of the neurophysiological and endocrinological consequences of alcohol do indeed show how it acts on brain mechanisms directly associated with aggressive behavior, and many sociological investigations have supported these findings.[38] Court records, of course, document at length the relationship between drink and arguments leading to violence, but the conclusions drawn are sometimes surprising. For certain cultures at certain moments in history, intoxication has actually been considered a legal defense: the inebriated were not deemed responsible for their behavior.[39] In Gershwin's *Porgy and Bess* (1935), Crown is seen by all to be "cock-eyed drunk," and therefore "he don' know what he's doin'." As the rest of the plot reveals, the loss of control that is assumed to come with the release of inhibition through drink is seen as threatening to the social order.

It is this dark side of Dionysus that the Apollonian is most often called upon to bring to order.[40]

However, Dionysus himself, as we have seen, is a most contradictory god who can stand for life and death, creation and destruction. So too the god of wine can inspire in his devotees both that celebratory social bonding or aggressive violence. In Italy, as in Germany, excessive alcohol consumption has been seen as a cause of criminal behavior, dangerous to public order.[41] For precisely this reason, it also became a useful plot device that could be counted on to work in theatrical terms on the operatic stage. Again adapting a Shakespearean play, Verdi and Boito created in their *Otello* (1887) a drinking situation loaded with multiple symbolic meanings that draw not only on the dramatic tension between the Apollonian and Dionysian but on the contradictory identity of Dionysus himself. The villain, Iago, is jealous of Cassio's command (as Captain) and plots to use alcohol as a means to entrap and disgrace him. To this end, he invites Cassio to drink in celebration of their leader Otello's recent victorious arrival. The Captain resists, saying that his brain burns from only one glass ("Già m'arde il cervello / Per un nappo vuotato"). But Cassio is caught in a double bind: he is about to go on duty and knows he must not drink, but there is a very strong social obligation not to refuse to drink to his leader's health. This tension is orchestrated and manipulated by Iago, who knows that, if Cassio becomes inebriated, he will be ruined ("S'ei s'inebria, è perduto").

In order to get him to drink more, Iago sings a memorable and diabolically effective drinking song. In subject matter, it begins as a simple *carpe diem* – drink while you may – but musically other signals are being given to the audience: its "snakelike" chromatically descending scale tells another story.[42] An early reviewer called that scale (descending from F to G-sharp) "outright sinister and fatal," and in a sense he was right.[43] This is a devilish drinking song whose "striding melody with its vigorous bass line is as heady as the wine which it celebrates."[44] It also breaks all the *brindisi* conventions, for its formal strophic structure is broken up by Cassio's increasingly drunken interventions, resulting in broken lines and the laughter of the chorus. The "disposizione scenica" (production book) of the original La Scala performance describes these interventions in revealing detail: as Cassio begins to totter and to become more animated as he drinks, he suddenly recalls Iago's *brindisi* and "would like to start the first tune up again, but he does not remember it. Holding himself up with his legs somewhat spread apart and facing the audience with a glass in his hand, he persists in looking for the line with which Jago [*sic*] began his *brindisi*."[45] He continues in these efforts, stammering to a hiccuping accompaniment in the music, coming in early, forgetting words, and stumbling around the stage.[46] Throughout, Iago holds an amphora of wine and fills Cassio's glass as well as those of the chorus members. Throughout, he repeats his invitation to drink with him, with increasing excitement in the orchestra and chorus: "Beve, beve con me!" The high A on the "Beve" gives, as one critic puts it, a "flavour of excess."[47] Iago taunts all to drink even more or risk showing themselves to be cowards and hypocrites:

Fuggan dal vivido
nappo i codardi
che in cor nascondono
frodi . . .

[They flee from the bright
glass those cowards
who in their hearts hide
crimes . . .]

Another early reviewer was also right on the mark when he noted that the plot "hinges on this Bacchic scene: Cassio must become tipsy so that his drunkenness leads to quarrels, scandal, and Otello's fury."[48] According to the first Iago, Victor Maurel, once everyone has become carried away with drink, Iago "begins to weave his plot while Cassio leaves his reason in the bottom of his glass."[49] Dionysus defeats Apollo. Provoked into a violent fight, Cassio not only is a threat to public order but proves himself to be in no shape to do his job, that is, to take his turn on the watch. Iago deliberately makes matters worse by announcing that Cassio is often drunk like this. Just before Otello himself enters to restore order and strip Cassio of his rank (in Iago's favor), the complexity of the music gives a strong effect of "confusion, urgency, intensity" worthy of the culmination of this unorthodox *brindisi* that "swaggers with lusty *camaraderie*."[50] In this scene we can see many of the social conventions associated with drinking, some of them Dionysian – hospitality, social bonding, the obligation to drink to the health and happiness of the one toasted – and others, Apollonian – the demand for sobriety on the job. We find associations with bravery and manliness but also violence and lack of control.[51] Like its source text, *Otello* enacts on stage the tensions between the two impulses and within the Dionysian itself. But, of course, not all release of inhibitions necessarily leads to negative results.

❧ Liberation through Intoxication

There is a long literary tradition of "Bacchus Liber" – the Romans' liberated and liberating god – that Rabelais, that connoisseur of excess, linked to the god Pluto, the one who reveals hidden truths. Erasmus wrote generically of the truth to be found through drink ("in vino veritas"), but Rabelais believed that wine was simply the mirror of the individual soul: the god of wine took away inhibitions and revealed the more personal truths beneath.[52] These old Dionysian traditions have their roots, of course, in real physiological responses: in alcohol's indirect effect in suppressing the function of inhibitory brain centers. In addition, because alcohol suppresses anxiety, it can also lead to a gradual removal of social inhibitions.[53] This is why drinking, even when considered a bad habit, has sometimes been seen as a positive, even as an attractive and gratifying one.[54]

While few operas are actually centered on the Dionysian act of drinking, one certainly is: Benjamin Britten and Eric Crozier's *Albert Herring* (1947). The differences between the opera and its source text, Guy de Maupassant's short story "Le Rosier de Madame Husson," illustrate well the differences, among other things, between operatic and literary representations of drinking. The story is written in the context of the France of the 1850s, when social concern about alcoholism and degeneracy was beginning to surface. It tells the tale of Isidore, a young, very simple, timid, and innocent man who is chosen king of the local May festivities because no pure girl could be found. He drinks too much at the fête, gives in to temptation, and escapes with his prize money to Paris; disheveled and still intoxicated, he returns a week later, ends up being thrown out by his mother, and ultimately dies of delirium tremens. In contrast, *Albert Herring*, the later Anglicized version of the tale, makes Albert sheltered, naive, bullied by his teetotaling mother, but longing to escape the chains of respectability and repression. Set in Suffolk in 1900, this opera is more a social comedy about the victory of Dionysus than a moral lesson about the effects of alcohol. In this version, it is the butcher's assistant, Sid, and his girlfriend, Nancy, who offer both foils and models for Albert: early in the opera, Sid sings about the Dionysian pleasures of a pint of ale and flirting with the girls and then addresses Albert's need to break those maternal apron-strings. It is at the May festival, where Albert is going to receive a large prize of money for his virtuous life, that Sid decides to become actively involved in helping his friend make that break. Knowing that Albert is in a mood to rebel, he spikes his lemonade with rum ("Just loosen him up, / And make him feel bright"), and the music wittily and ironically cites Wagner's *Tristan und Isolde*: the spiked rum becomes a love potion (or at least a threat to chastity) by comic inappropriateness of association. Yet the echo is perhaps fitting in other ways: like the Wagnerian potion, this too is a substitute for an expected beverage, and it results in a real transformation of the drinker. Consuming his first ever alcoholic beverage, Albert gets the hiccups and announces: "I feel brisk like a rocket, / Going up with a *Whoosh!*" The music at this moment again recalls *Tristan und Isolde*, as does the ending of the choral hymn of celebration of Albert's chastity and innocence: "Albert the good / long may he reign / to be re-elected / again and again."[55] That dispiriting prospect, as much as his actual drinking, may explain why he remains speechless when awarded his prize.

At the end of the festivities, Albert returns to his mother's greengrocer's shop, as the stage directions put it, "not exactly drunk, but in a hilarious mixture of excitement and cheerfulness, stimulated by the rum." He happily recalls the taste of the (spiked) lemonade as he thinks about pretty Nancy (again accompanied by the *Tristan* echo) and envies Sid his directness and confidence in matters sexual. From the symbolic location of the *inside* of the shop, he hears Sid and Nancy *outside* sing of Albert's need to sow a few wild oats, and he responds with "indignation, excitement and embarrassment combining in him in a kind of nervous rage."[56] Screwing up his courage, Albert takes his prize money and leaves.

Act 3 opens with the village search for the missing Albert, assumed dead by all except Sid, who believes he has simply liberated himself at last: Bacchus Liber. In their grief, all sing a most moving threnody that is widely regarded as the musical climax and high point of the opera.[57] Then, anticlimactically, Albert reappears: "dirty, dishevelled and stained with mud." His account of his Dionysian night on the town is pretty innocuous compared to Maupassant's week of dissipation.[58] Albert recounts at least what he can remember: he had decided, he tells them all, "To try a taste of certain things / The Prayer Book catalogues among its sins." First he tried drink – beer, rum, whisky, and gin:

> Before very long, I was pretty far gone –
> Reeling about, beginning to shout,
> Disgustingly drunk! – a nuisance to everyone! –
> So they threw me out of *The Dog and Duck*
> To lie in the gutter and sober up!

At the next bar he was thrown out because he "started a fight 'cos they said I was tight." That, he announces, is but a general sample of a night "that was a nightmare example / Of drunkenness, dirt, and worse."

The "worse" is left implicit, but the Wagnerian echoes have prepared us for the fact that, as Albert has to admit, he did not spend all £3 on alcohol alone. The man whose chastity made him May King seems to have managed to spend some of the money making sure he would never be elected again for the same reason. He claims that he did all this because, in his words, his mother "squashed me down and reined me in, / Did up my instincts with safety-pins / . . . My only way out was a wild explosion!" – made possible by alcohol. He admits it was not much fun, but "sooner or later it had to come." It is hard not to agree with those who find that Albert's account of his night of sin to be less than convincing, even if his rebellion against his mother is real enough.[59] But this judgment assumes that alcohol alone is involved in the (by definition, chaste) May King's liberation. As one critic puts it: "we cannot really believe that being thrown out of three public houses and spending three whole pounds on drink can have transformed Albert's character and liberated him from his own timidity."[60] But the text is clear: the drink simply allowed the release of inhibitions, and that is what made possible both the psychological emancipation and the subsequent sexual initiation (heterosexual or homosexual – and the debate continues).[61] The final pleasant string melody is "descriptive perhaps of Albert's newly gained self-assertion."[62] Critics have pointed to the echoes in the libretto of *carpe diem* themes from Marvell's "To His Coy Mistress" and Eliot's "The Love Song of J. Alfred Prufrock."[63] However, these literary themes are also directly associated with sexuality and occur, here in the opera, in the specific context of the liberating effects of alcohol, as once again Dionysus, briefly at least, claims victory over the Apollonian forces of social order.

✸ The Alcoholic Imagination

Like the well-known and time-sanctioned operatic link between the realms of Bacchus and Venus, there is also a longstanding direct relationship between wine and artistic inspiration.[64] Visionaries –

be they poets, artists, or saints – came to be associated early on with either the effervescence or the melancholy induced by alcohol: Ovid's Bacchus was the god of illusions as well as wine.[65] For the German Romantics, wine became the symbol of cosmic union with the deity and with nature, dissolving egoism and building community. A stimulant for the body, spirit, and imagination, wine became the subject of art as well as its inspiration. The figure most discussed in this context – especially by the French – was the hard-drinking German jurist, composer, artist, and fantasy writer E. T. A. Hoffmann. Not surprisingly, his *Kreisleriana* collection was a favorite of Baudelaire. In the essay on wine we have been citing, the French poet admiringly refers to Hoffmann's ideas about which wines were best for composing certain kinds of music: champagne for comic opera, Rhine or Jurançon for religious music, Burgundy for patriotic music. Such exquisite notions, felt Baudelaire, could only come from the passionate feelings of a real drinker ("le sentiment passionné d'un buveur"), one who had developed a "psychological barometer" that allowed him to observe the varying atmospheric phenomena and temperatures of his soul – a soul inspired by alcohol.[66]

Baudelaire's "divine Hoffmann" himself became the fictionalized subject of a French opera, Offenbach's 1881 *Les Contes d'Hoffmann*, based on a successful French play written thirty years before by Jules Barbier and Michel Carré. The opera's three central acts – developed from three of Hoffmann's tales – are framed by a tavern scene that recalls many others in opera, though this time with a specific focus on the poet and his liquid inspiration. The curtain goes up on Luther's tavern in Nuremberg, the scene of a rather startling chorus actually sung by the spirits of wine and beer:

Glou! glou! glou! je suis le vin!
Glou! glou! glou! je suis la bière! Ah!
Glou! glou! glou! nous sommes
les amis des hommes;
nous chassons d'ici

langueur et souci:
Glou! glou!

[Glug! glug! glug! I am wine!
Glug! glug! glug! I am beer! Ah!
Glug! glug! glug! we are
the friends of men;
we chase from here
boredom and worry:
Glug! glug!]

Not content to let singers on stage sing their praises, the punningly conceived alcoholic "spirits" celebrate themselves. It is actually out of a barrel of this heady stuff that the figure of the Muse comes, calling on the spirits to aid her in winning Hoffmann back from the distractions of love: "Vous, flacons et tonneaux, secondez mon ouvrage, / votre ivresse fait oublier" [You, bottles and barrels, help my work, / your drunkenness makes one forget]. Certainly the students who then enter the tavern are ready to help out: they plan to drink beer and wine until dawn. Hoffmann announces that he too will drink – to oblivion – and is encouraged in this by the Muse, now disguised as his young friend Nicklausse, who, needless to say, also finds it much more reasonable and practical to drink than to be in love. It is in this convivial context of drinking and smoking together that Hoffmann tells the three tales of his unhappy loves. At the end, the woman he has been awaiting, the opera singer Stella, finds him in a drunken stupor: Hoffmann has indeed consecrated himself to his Muse ("Muse aimée, je suis à toi!").

To the French Romantics, Hoffmann (no matter what the actual biographical facts) became the very image of the inspired drunk who could write so well about drinking because of his own experience.[67] The mythification process of creating "Hoffmannism" – of which this opera would be the culmination – began with the first translations into French in 1829 in which the translators took up an idea from Julius Eduart Hitzig's 1823 biography and then ran with it, citing Walter Scott's 1827 denunciation of Hoffmann for his excessive drinking. From there, Baudelaire and others aggrandized his alcoholic consumption, creating the myth of the alcoholic imagination and inspiration.[68] No doubt the positive French associations of intoxication ("ivresse") with Dionysian ecstasy, rapture, and exhilaration owe much to this history.[69] The world of drink seems to have provided a kind of exotic subculture for Paris in the nineteenth century, one that has been vividly captured in images like Manet's absinthe drinker.[70] For Baudelaire, it was wine and hashish that offered humans a way to provoke the divine in themselves: of wine, he wrote, "certain beverages immeasurably augment the personality of the thinking being and create, as it were, a third person through a mystical operation whereby natural man and wine, the animal god and the vegetal god, representing the Father and Son of the Trinity, combine to engender a Holy Ghost, the superior man, who proceeds equally from the two."[71] For Baudelaire, it was not simply wine but excess of wine that brought on the desired "excessive poetic development" of humanity. And other French thinkers have followed his line of reasoning. Gaston Bachelard, for instance, argues for the importance of studying the "alcoholic unconscious": "One is mistaken if one imagines that alcohol simply stimulates our mental potentialities. In fact, it creates these potentialities. It incorporates itself, so to speak, with that which is striving to express itself. It appears evident that alcohol is a creator of language. It enriches the vocabulary and frees the syntax." Referring to Hoffmann, he goes on to assert that "a whole area of phantasmagorical literature is dependent upon the poetic excitation of alcohol."[72]

The difficulties of actually proving such an assertion are self-evident. Many of the great alcoholic writers also suffered from other diseases that might equally have affected their art: Maupassant and Baudelaire were syphilitic; Dostoyevsky was epileptic; Hoffmann may well have been what today we would call schizophrenic as well as syphilitic.[73] Nevertheless, the history of alcohol's collusion with creativity is a long and venerable one, dating from the

Dionysian worship at those great Greek drama festivals to Horace's *Epistles*, which confidently assert that "no poetry written by water drinkers would ever achieve immortality,"[74] and from Syrian legends of prophetic intoxication to the imagery of the Jewish mystical tradition.[75] And, of course, as many delight in pointing out, a very high percentage of American writers who have won the Nobel Prize for Literature were alcoholics; perhaps that is why so many writers escaped to Europe during the Prohibition years in the United States.[76] Whatever it is about alcohol's properties – its ability to promote fantasy or an increase in self-confidence, its relaxation potential, its lowering of inhibitions – something attracts artists of all kinds to it. Alban Berg's 1929 concert aria "Das Wein" is a musical setting of Stefan George's translations of (not surprisingly) three Baudelaire poems in which wine is presented as the solace for careworn folk, as an incentive to love, and, finally, as the inspiration of the poet.[77]

In opera, it seems that Dionysus is victorious when it comes to drinking, both when it is celebrated and also when it leads to violence and the resulting loss of control that we witness in *Otello*. Opera is obviously attracted to the narrative possibilities of staging excess, and the effects of the Dionysian release of inhibitions on the staged body offer many a dramatic plot possibility. As a result, for opera audiences, when the excessive body drinks on stage, it always signifies.

When Wagner wrote disparagingly of Rossini's "narcotic-drunken melody," he was questioning the composer's seriousness by reducing his music to intoxication, that is, to excess and virtuosity.[78] As Herbert Lindenberger has pointed out, opera is an extravagant art form – larger than life, addictive, excessive. He links the operatic to such terms as "*histrionic, extravagant, gestural, ceremonial* and *performative*."[79] In other words, Apollonian moderation would not appear to be opera's reigning mode; on the contrary, Dionysian excess is.

Mario Castelnuovo-Tedesco wrote a one-act folk opera called *Bacco in Toscana* in 1931, and in it he brought together scientists, scholars, and aristocrats from Pisa and Florence along with Bacchus and his satyrs to celebrate the glories of Tuscan wine.[80] It is in this same spirit that we offer a final toast to the charm of opera's bodies, both real and represented ones. As we have been arguing throughout this book and as Nietzsche insisted from his very different philosophical point of view, Dionysus and Apollo play their complementary operatic roles. But it is under the sign of the Dionysian that opera's bodies can be fully restored: the unbeautiful body, the dancing body, the drinking body owe much to his power, and so, too, we have been suggesting, do both the performing and perceiving bodies that take part in live staged opera. *Pace* the audiophiles, operatic bodies are still living, breathing, and present. *Pace* audio technology, the operatic voice is still an embodied voice.

Notes

꙾ Before We Begin . . . An Introductory Note

1. Brooks, *Body Work*, xi.
2. Starobinski, "The Natural and Literary History of Bodily Sensation," 353.
3. Elizabeth Grosz believes that the fascination with the body in the 1980s, while "presenting itself as a celebration of the body and its pleasures, . . . bears witness to a profound, if unacknowledged and undiscussed, hatred and resentment of the body" (*Space, Time, and Perversion*, 1).
4. See Phelan, *Mourning Sex* (1997) on the "catastrophe and exhilaration of embodiment," including trauma (2). The pleasurable discourse continued into the nineties too, however. See Frueh, *Erotic Faculties* (1996). In this section, we will include dates of publication to signal the timing of the issues raised.
5. See, for example, Dollimore, *Sexual Dissidence* (1991). Caroline Bynum's comment comes in her important survey of body criticism and her critique of the essentializing that goes on in this work when everyone from Plato to Descartes and onward is labeled as dualist and misogynist ("Why All the Fuss," 5).
6. Eagleton, *The Illusions of Postmodernism*, 69.
7. Foucault, *An Introduction*, 12.
8. Feher, Naddaff, and Tazi, eds., *Fragments* (1989).
9. Examples of collaborative work: in order to challenge the Cartesian dualism of mind and body, psychologists and philosophers work together to see how the body is integral to certain aspects of self-consciousness (see Eilan, Marcel, and Bermúdez, "Self-Consciousness and the Body," 1); literary and film theorists, postcolonial commentators, and queer and feminist critics collaborate in an attempt to "rethink, to reconceptualize, explore, disentangle or recomplicate sexual

bodies" as either resistant or compliant (Grosz and Probyn, eds., *Sexy Bodies* [1995]). Other scholars explore the place of the specifically female body in the Western imagination or the role of the body in general in the thought of one particular time, such as the medieval period. See, respectively, Suleiman, ed., *The Female Body in Western Culture* (1986), and Kay and Rubin, eds., *Framing Medieval Bodies* (1996). Individual scholars working indisciplinarily have tackled topics such as the medical and aesthetic history of perception as a sensory experience from the Enlightenment onward (Stafford, *Body Criticism* [1991]) or the relations between power and the body from political, anthropological, and philosophical perspectives in order to determine both parallels and differences among tribal and modern societies (Gil, *Metamorphoses of the Body*). The body has also been examined as the site of the production of ideologies, particularly in response to cultural crises (Wilson and Laennec, eds., *Bodily Discursions* [1997]).

10. *Food for Thought* (1989).

11. Mirzoeff, *Bodyscape* (1995).

12. See, respectively, Korte, *Body Language in Literature* (1997), and Ruthrof, *Semantics and the Body* (1997).

13. See Beal and Gunn, eds., *Reading Bibles, Writing Bodies* (1997).

14. See Grosz, *Space, Time, and Perversion*, in which she argues the need to rethink the entire notion of subjectivity and, with it, "space and time, materiality, exchange, knowledge, power, pleasure, social and cultural production" – in short, all the humanities and the social sciences (2–3). Her *Volatile Bodies* is an important part of this refiguring of the body as the very "stuff" of subjectivity (ix). For many others, too, the study of the philosophical underpinnings of representations of the sexed body in Western culture involves looking at social, political, and ethical understandings of those bodies (see Gatens, *Imaginary Bodies* [1996]).

15. Grosz, *Space, Time, and Perversion*, 2.

16. Kramer, "The Musicology of the Future," 7.

17. See the bibliography for the works of these important feminist critics.

18. Leonardi and Pope, *The Diva's Mouth* (1996), 8.

19. McClary, *Feminine Endings*, 57.

20. McClary, *Feminine Endings*, 4.

21. Adorno, "The Curves of the Needle," 54. See also: "Only there where the body itself resonates, where the self to which the gramophone refers

is identical with its sound, only there does the gramophone have its legitimate realm of validity: thus Caruso's uncontested dominance" (52). This may be less of an ideological statement than it appears. Witness Jürgen Kesting, in *Maria Callas*, on why Caruso became famous in the age of the gramophone: "his dark-toned tenor voice fitted perfectly into the frequency spectrum which the acoustic recording method could achieve at the time, and could be reproduced better than female voices demanding higher frequencies, which often sounded disembodied, stiff, and lacking in vibration" (63).

22. McClary, *Feminine Endings*, 50.

23. Dunn and Jones, eds., *Embodied Voices* (1994), 3. They also note the feminist use of the term "voice" in relation to "cultural agency, political enfranchisement, sexual autonomy, and expressive freedom," all of which were historically denied to women (1).

24. Clément, *Opera, or the Undoing of Women*, 45.

25. Brett, Wood, and Thomas, eds., *Queering the Pitch*, ix.

26. Wood, "Sapphonics," 27.

27. See Abel, *Opera in the Flesh*, and Koestenbaum, *The Queen's Throat*.

☙ Prelude. Restoring Opera's Bodies

1. For more on the history of the relationship between Apollo and Dionysus, see Burkert, *Greek Religion*, esp. 224–25.

2. In his 1755 *Gedanken über die Nachahmung der griechischen Werke in der Malerei und Bildhauerkunst*, Winckelmann presented a definition of the ideal beauty that helped generate the neoclassical movement in the arts. For him, Greek sculpture (which he knew only from later Hellenistic work and Roman copies) was characterized by noble simplicity and quiet grandeur. His 1764 *Geschichte der Kunst des Altertums* had a further impact not only on art and its study but on philosophy (Herder, Lessing) and literature (Goethe) and is generally said to provide important background to the (Apollonian) Age of Reason or Enlightenment.

3. At the time of writing *The Birth of Tragedy*, Nietzsche was in the process of liberating himself from the influence of Arthur Schopenhauer's work, though he still used the language and many of the concepts of that philosopher to articulate his rebellion. Our very different twenty-first-century interdisciplinary context will lead to different language but also different theoretical perspectives. What we share is a sense

that Apollo and Dionysus interact in the experience of the operatic performance.

4. In *Nietzsche and Wagner*, Joachim Köhler points out that while *The Birth of Tragedy* was not credible as scholarship, it was influential nonetheless: "Its antithesis of Apollonian and Dionysian became part of the vocabulary of cultured conversation, while its interpretation of Greek antiquity, which moved beyond the frontiers of orthodox scholarship, culminated in an encomium of Wagner's *Gesamtkunstwerk*" (76).

5. The citations are from, respectively, Conrad, *A Song of Love and Death*, 32; Lindenberger, *Opera: The Extravagant Art*, 78; McClary, *Feminine Endings*, 82. The latter sees this tension dramatically enacted in operatic madwomen, showing "how their dementia is delineated musically through repetitive, ornamental, or chromatic excess, and how normative procedures representing reason are erected around them to serve as protective frames preventing 'contagion'" (81).

6. See, for instance, from Ottavio Rinuccini's libretto *Euridice*, Jacopo Peri's (1600), and Giulio Caccini's (1600, but performed 1602). At least a dozen other operas on that theme from the seventeenth century are extant.

7. Many have commented on the association of Apollo with the masculine world and manliness. See Otto, *Dionysus*, 142; Leppert, *The Sight of Sound*, xxvi; McClary, *Feminine Endings*, 47; Koestenbaum, *The Queen's Throat*: "Apollo tries to make a man of Orpheus; father accuses son of effeminately yielding to emotion. Their duet might have convinced its first listeners that this new genre of *dramma per musica* would cure male fragmentation, harden the soft male interior, unify father and son, bind heaven and earth, and balance the oppositions seething in the listener's breast" (178).

8. In "'The Wound Is Healed Only by the Spear That Smote You,'" Slavoj Žižek sees the transformation of Eurydice as a consolation and thus sublimation (178). Of course, even in the other versions of the myth, when Apollo does not intervene, what remains at the end is the bodiless head of Orpheus, singing on the sands of the shores of Lesbos. As Burkert notes in *Greek Religion*, if the report of the content of Aeschylus's Orpheus tragedy *The Bassarids* can be trusted, it "told how Orpheus scorns Dionysos and at sunrise prays from the mountain

top to the sun god alone, whom he calls Apollo. Thereupon Dionysos sends a swarm of maenads, the Bassaridai, who tear Orpheus limb from limb; the Muses of Apollo gather the remains and bury him" (225).

9. See Turocy, "The Dance Was at the Root," 31.

10. For an intriguing instance of the disavowal of the body, see Girouard, *Life in the English Country House*, 245–66, on the development of the privy. And in *Vision and Painting*, Norman Bryson points out how Western representational painting deliberately concealed the "work" that went into its creation, because to distance the palpable corporeal body is to show how civilized one is (159).

11. Dodds, "Introduction," Euripides, *Bacchae*, xlv. Dodds refuses to see Pentheus, as some have, as the martyr of enlightenment and reason. Instead, he argues, he is "typical tragedy-tyrant" with no self-control, a willingness to believe the worst on hearsay evidence or none at all, a brutality toward the helpless, a reliance on force to settle spiritual problems, a foolish "racial pride," and "the sexual curiosity of a Peeping Tom." He concludes: "It is not thus that martyrs of enlightenment are represented" (xliii).

12. In *Violence and the Sacred*, René Girard argues, however, the contrary, that in the Greek play there is nothing attractive about Dionysus: "Throughout the play the god wanders from place to place, engendering violence and crime with the artfulness of a satanic seducer. Only the quixotic masochism of our own age, the result of a long immunity to the violence that threatens primitive societies, allows us to see anything attractive in the Dionysus of *The Bacchae*" (132). The opera, however, is very much a product of the 1960s with its specific ethos.

13. Dodds is right to insist that Dionysus is more dangerous and significant than would be suggested by the god of wine that the Alexandrines and Romans tamed him into being: "He is the principle of animal life . . . , the hunted and the hunter – the unrestrained potency which man envies in the beasts and seeks to assimilate" ("Introduction," xx). However, our postlude will explore how even that tamer incarnation can have complex aesthetic and social consequences in opera. See Younger, *Gods, Men, and Wine* on the "Early Dionysus," the god of nature, the "Middle Dionysus," the god of wild and fertile nature, the "raging god" tamed by Orpheus, and finally the "Late Dionysus," the pleasurable god of wine tamed by Olympian religion (123–25). The

long and continuing history of the both positive and negative impact of this Bacchic drink on the human body forms the subject of our postlude.

14. Ariadne's story was very popular as an operatic subject in the seventeenth and eighteenth centuries (e.g., Claudio Monteverdi/Ottavio Rinuccini's 1608 *Arianna* or Nicola Porpora/Paolo Antonio Rolli's 1733 *Arianna in Nasso*) and again in the twentieth (e.g., Darius Milhaud and Henri Hoppenot's 1927 *L'Abandon d'Ariane*).

15. On the contradictions inherent in Dionysus, see Kerényi, *Dionysos*; Padel, *Whom Gods Destroy*, 26; Dodds, "Introduction," xliv; Pater, "A Study of Dionysus"; Henrichs, "Loss of Self," 238–39; Faraone, "Introduction," 1–3.

16. As such, the Dionysian is related to what Mikhail Bakhtin, in *Rabelais and His World*, calls the medieval grotesque body, with its associations of disorder, energy, excessiveness, unfinished becoming, and the communal: "The body discloses its essence as a principle of growth which exceeds its own limits only in copulation, pregnancy, childbirth, the throes of death, eating, drinking, or defecation" (20). In contrast, the "modern" or new (or Apollonian) body as defined by Bakhtin is balanced, measured, closed, individual, and private: its head is supreme (321).

17. Girard, again in *Violence and the Sacred*, reads the Dionysiac cult as a consequence of major political and social upheavals and Dionysus as the god of mob violence (134). We will see in chapter 4 a more positive way to interpret Dionysus as the god of communal emotions when we examine the power of live opera on the bodies of the members of the audience.

18. In "Loss of Self," Henrichs outlines how the "Renaissance Dionysus," the god of enjoyment of the senses, was transformed into the "Romantic Dionysus," the deity who represented both light and darkness, and finally, with Nietzsche, into the "modern Dionysus," associated with loss of self, suffering, and violence. Typical of this later view is the position of Girard, as we have seen, who claims that Dionysus "has no proper being outside the realm of violence. All his attributes are linked to violence; if he is associated with the gift of prophetic inspiration, it is because prophetic inspiration is part of the sacrificial crisis. And if he later appears as the god of wine, that is probably a more sedate version

of his original designation as the god of homicidal fury" (*Violence and the Sacred*, 133). In *The Greeks and the Irrational*, Dodds discusses the origins of the sacrificial story of the Titans, who trapped the infant Dionysus, tore him to bits, and then devoured him (155). He also links this to the maenadic rites of sacrifice (of a live animal) ("Introduction," xvii). See also Friedrich, "Everything to Do with Dionysos?" on how the "genial god of wine, the theatre, and vitality" in the ancient world (258) came to be associated with the "dubious" obsessions of the post-Romantic period: "the primitive, the savage, the irrational, the instinctual, the collectivist" (257) and thus "bloodshed, cannibalism, savagery, violence, death-cult, irrationalism, and madness" (258).

19. Dodds, *The Greeks and the Irrational*, 76.

20. Otto, *Dionysus*, 176. Girard argues that this association of Dionysian delirium with women was "reassuring to male dignity and authority" (*Violence and the Sacred*, 141). Tellingly, in both opera and play, Pentheus dresses in women's clothes to spy on the Bacchantes and in the end is torn apart by the women. As Christine Battersby argues in *Gender and Genius*, in the nineteenth century the romantic male "genius" chose to differentiate himself from other men by uniting feminine imagination with masculine reason (the Dionysian and the Apollonian, in our terms here). Camille Paglia is perhaps the most flamboyant of recent critics to associate Dionysus with "liquid nature, a miasmic swamp whose prototype is the still pond of the womb" (*Sexual Personae*, 12) and Apollo with the male principle that offers form and shape to the world.

21. Of great importance, however, is the challenge to the idea that Dionysus is a late entry into the Greek pantheon, an arrival from the East, from Thrace; his name appears among the Hellenic divinities around 1250 BCE, listed on the Linear B tablets from Pylos. Similar oppositions exist among female deities, of course. Charles Segal, in "The Gorgon and the Nightingale," points out that Athena, sprung from the head of Zeus, is a male-oriented goddess associated with Apollo. Wearing body armor, she is associated with control and aestheticizing artistry. In contrast, Medusa stands for "flux, process, and animality" (21), as well as fleshiness and sexual vitality.

22. On the Greek distinction between the mortal, visible, dissoluble, and human body (*soma*) and immortal, invisible, indissoluble, and divine

soul (*psuche*) in Plato, see Loraux, "Therefore, Socrates Is Immortal," 15–17. On the Platonic denigration of the body, see Perniola, "Between Clothing and Nudity," 239.

23. See Grosz, *Volatile Bodies*, 6, and Bordo, *Unbearable Weight*, 145. The complex relations of the body to Christian doctrine have been the subject of important studies such as Bottomley's *Attitudes to the Body in Western Christendom* and Brown's *The Body and Society*.

24. See Porter, "The Body and the Mind," 237–38. Thomas Szasz, in *The Myth of Mental Illness*, argues that Freud breathed new life into the obsolete Cartesian dualism, with its Platonic and Christian roots. For more, see Porter, "The Body and the Mind," 234. See Bordo, *Unbearable Weight*, 2–5, on the particular problems this causes for women.

25. Theater historians dispute Nietzsche's ideas about the direct links between tragedy and Dionysian rites. See, for instance, Wise, *Dionysus Writes*, 1, 13, and Storm, *After Dionysus*, 9. Yet most accept that Greek drama developed out of the seventh-century BCE choral lyric poetry known as the dithyramb, the improvised song in honor of Dionysus that was sung at banquets (and, interestingly, followed by a paean, a solemn choral lyric of invocation to Apollo). As the "Master of Illusions," Dionysus became the patron of the new art of theater in the sixth century BCE (Dodds, *The Greeks and the Irrational*, 94, n. 82; Storm, *After Dionysus*, 9) and gave his name to the Athenian Great Dionysia festival as well as to the temple and theater beneath the Acropolis. The three days of dramatic performances were part of a larger, complex ritual in the god's honor. His altar was placed in the center of the "orchestra" where the chorus stood. In "Everything to Do with Dionysos?" Friedrich shows how the Dionysian festival provided "the institutional framework for the tragic performances" (268) and how the rituals of Dionysus, with their mythic narrative plots, also offered a complex enough structural antecedent for secularized drama (269).

26. In *The Birth of Tragedy*, Nietzsche writes that music and tragic myth are both "expressions of the Dionysian capacity of a people . . . both transfigure a region in whose joyous chords dissonance as well as the terrible image of the world fade away charmingly; both play with the sting of displeasure, trusting in their exceedingly powerful magic arts" (143); in the German: "Ausdruck der dionysischen Befähigung

eines Volkes . . . beide verklären eine Region, in deren Lustakkorden die Dissonanz ebenso wie das schreckliche Weltbild reizvoll verklingt; beide spielen mit dem Stachel der Unlust, ihren überaus mächtigen Zauberkünsten vertrauend" (*Werke*, 133).

27. Nietzsche, *The Birth of Tragedy*, 143; in the German: the "Schönheitsschleier" covers the "ewige und ursprüngliche Kunstgewalt" (*Werke*, 133).

28. Nietzsche, *The Birth of Tragedy*, 46; in the German: the "[Kunst] die in ihrem Rausche die Wahrheit sprach" (*Werke*, 34). Nietzsche's roots in Schopenhauer's views of music (as the art that represents the universal noumenon, or will) are clear in his descriptions of this process in *The Birth of Tragedy*: "Language can never adequately render the cosmic symbolism of music, because music stands in symbolic relation to the primordial contradiction and primordial pain in the heart of the primordial unity, and therefore symbolizes a sphere that is beyond and prior to all phenomena" (55); in the German: "Der Weltsymbolik der Musik ist eben deshalb mit der Sprache auf keine Weise erschöpfend beizukommen, weil sie sich auf den Urwiderspruch and Urschmerz im Herzen des Ur-Einen symbolisch bezieht, somit eine Sphäre symbolisiert, die über alle Erscheinung und vor aller Erscheinung ist" (*Werke*, 43–44). See Paglia, *Sexual Personae*, in which she ignores this aural dimension utterly in her assertion that Greek tragedy was Apollonian because it captured and distanced Dionysus, "binding down nature to be *looked at*" (104). Nature (or, rather, culture) was also *listened to* on stage. Greek theater was an "exercise [not only] of the eye" but of the ear as well, and indeed of the entire body.

29. Later, in his madness, Nietzsche would sign his letters Dionysus, and in 1888–89 he composed a collection of poems entitled *Dionysos-Dithyramben.* He decorated his apartment in Turin like a Greek temple and used it to stage "Dionysian orgies for his own delight," claims Köhler in *Nietzsche and Wagner*, 6. In January 1889 the philosopher invited his friend Franz Overbeck to witness this Bacchanale, and Overbeck wrote that it "symbolized in the most gruesome manner the orgiastic frenzy that lies at the root of Greek tragedy" (Köhler, *Nietzsche and Wagner*, 7).

30. Nietzsche, *The Birth of Tragedy*, 124; in the German: "Ja, meine Freunde, glaubt mit mir an das dionysische Leben und an die Wiedergeburt

der Tragödie . . . [K]ränzt euch mit Epheu, nehmt den Thyrsusstab zur Hand und wundert euch nicht, wenn Tiger und Panther sich schmeichelnd zu euren Knien niederlegen. Jetzt wagt es nur, tragische Menschen zu sein: denn ihr sollt erlöst werden. Ihr sollt den dionysischen Festzug von Indien nach Griechenland geleiten! Rüstet euch zu hartem Streite, aber glaubt an die Wunder eures Gottes!" (*Werke*, 113).

31. Nietzsche's language is specifically Wagnerian here: the German spirit, like Siegfried from *Der Ring des Nibelungen*, will one day awaken and "will slay dragons, destroy vicious dwarfs, wake Brünnhilde – and even Wotan's spear will not be able to stop its course!" (*The Birth of Tragedy*, 142); in the German: "dann wird er Drachen töten, die tückischen Zwerge vernichten und Brünnhilde erwecken – und Wotans Speer selbst wird seinen Weg nicht hemmen können" (*Werke*, 132). Later, of course, Nietzsche would call Wagner a "sickness" and a decadent degenerate whose characters were hysterics. See *The Case of Wagner*, 155–66. But the influence of the older composer on the young philosopher at this early stage in his thinking has been commented on by many: see, for instance, Lindenberger, *Opera: The Extravagant Art*, 98, 98 n.; Grey, *Wagner's Musical Prose*, 5. It should be pointed out, however, that the common denominator in both men's thinking at this stage is the work of Schopenhauer.

32. See Burkert, *Greek Religion*, 224.

33. See Blau, *Blooded Thought*. As early as 1849, Wagner was writing in "Art and Revolution" that Apollo, inspired by Dionysus, would join the "bond of speech" to measure and harmony and bring forth "the highest conceivable form of art – the DRAMA" (33); in the German: "das kühne, bindende Wort . . . das höchste erdenkliche Kunstwerk, das Drama" (*Frühe Prosa und Revolutionstraktate*, 275). Köhler notes in *Nietzsche and Wagner* that Wagner reminded his young friend that the Apollo/Dionysus opposition was *his* and could be found in his early revolutionary writings (82).

34. Nietzsche, *The Birth of Tragedy*, 64, 104; in the German, *Werke*, 52, 92–93.

35. Nietzsche, *Thus Spoke Zarathustra*, 34.

36. See Sutcliffe, *Believing in Opera*: "Every great operatic composer has felt himself to be the servant of theatre, and most (by no means just Wagner) have seen themselves as servants with vital revolutionary

programmes of theatrical improvement to put into effect. Dissatisfied with the operatic theatre they inherited, they have wanted to create something more powerful and real, better able to convey their compelling metaphysical burden. Handel's detailed stage directions reveal how important theatrical realization was to him, and the same can equally be said of Gluck, or Berg" (8). In *Richard Wagner's Music Dramas*, Carl Dahlhaus notes: "The central category in Wagner's aesthetic theory of musical drama is 'realization.' A Hegelian by upbringing, Wagner believed that what is interior has to externalize itself, to take on a form if it is not to be void. Whatever the poetic intention, the meaning locked away in the heart of a work, the important thing is the realization of that intention, the form in which it is presented to the perception of others. Wagner spoke of dance, the representation of mankind in its true, physical nature, as the 'most real' of all the arts. He regarded stage action as a 'form of dance imbued with ideals,' so that movement and gesture on the stage can also come under the heading of the 'art of realization' – which for Wagner was the essence of art itself" (157).

37. Abel, *Opera in the Flesh*, 164.
38. See Hepburn, "Icons." In "The Replay's the Thing," Peggy Kamuf notes that in his *Nixon in China* (libretto by Alice Goodman) John Adams's "rhythms and harmonics . . . are perfectly adjusted to these effects of telegraphic and televisual media, although one ought not invoke here any mimetic or representational model" (84).
39. Machover worked with fifty artists and scientists at the MIT Media Lab to create an interplay of sensory perception, musical structure, and language (Marvin Minsky's text) for this one-of-a-kind interactive musical event (in New York in 1996 and then subsequently around the world). Working with sound and image, three performers shape, select, and interpret precomposed and audience-created elements using special hyperinstruments. Thanks to Michael Doherty for bringing this spectacle to our attention.
40. See Hayles, *How We Became Posthuman*. Operas also exist in cyberspace, of course. The first telecollaborative, totally Internet opera, *Honoria in ciberspazio*, was seen and heard on 21 March 1998. For more on cyberspace and the body, see Hayles, "The Seductions of Cyberspace," and also Waller, "If 'Reality Is the Best Metaphor,' It Must

Be Virtual": "The old nineteenth/twentieth-century (Euro-American) body, with its vestigial sensorium and markers of race, gender, mortality, and other 'constraints' of identity and situation, is replaced by one or a series of new navigating identities, now obediently and flexibly *allied with*, rather than opposed to, spirit/mind, which is, it should be noted, more than ever in charge" (101).

41. See Engh, "Adorno and the Sirens," on the idea of the panic that ensued when "humanity encountered its technologically disembodied voice" (121). Robert Jourdain, in *Music, the Brain, and Ecstasy*, reminds us of the chronology here: Thomas Edison and Alexander Graham Bell's early work in recording voice in 1877 was followed by the Victor and Columbia companies' marketing of the gramophone in 1897. In 1903 the first complete opera recording (of Verdi's *Ernani*) appeared on forty single-sided platters. The electric phonograph was invented in 1925, and the long-playing record in 1948. The sixties brought stereo technology; the seventies, the tape cassette; and the eighties, the CD (243–45). Jourdain adds: "Where music once nourished a healthy appetite, whether in the concert hall or the village square, now a perpetual banquet of song serves only to soothe a blunted palate. We live in an age of widespread musical obesity" (245).

42. During test screenings, of course, audiences can influence films more or less directly, as Michael Doherty has pointed out to us.

43. Sutcliffe, *Believing in Opera*, 59. Earlier he explains: "The television director's editing suppresses a great deal in terms of lighting, atmosphere, incident and reaction that the *audience* in an opera-house is accustomed to *absorb effortlessly* or subliminally" (8, emphasis his).

44. Levin, "Introduction," 13. He draws the analogy between opera and a very physical form: professional wrestling, as described by Roland Barthes in *Mythologies*. On operatic excess, see Lindenberger, *Opera: The Extravagant Art*, and Peraino, "I Am an Opera," 132.

45. Levin, "For the Record," 30, about Theodor Adorno, "The Curves of the Needle."

46. Adorno might have been amazed at the sexualization of the domesticated listening experience in the work of gay opera critics like Wayne Koestenbaum, for whom solo listening is "masturbatory" (*The Queen's Throat*, 57), and Sam Abel, who writes: "When I listen to an

opera recording, the erotic experience becomes a private masturbation fantasy" (*Opera in the Flesh*, 168).

47. Adorno, "Opera and the Long-Playing Record," 64.
48. Adorno, "Opera and the Long-Playing Record," cited in Levin, "For the Record," 44.
49. Schopenhauer, *Schopenhauer*, 163.
50. Storm, *After Dionysos*, 6.
51. Adorno, "Opera and the Long-Playing Record," 63 and 64, respectively.
52. Barthes, "The Grain of the Voice," in *The Responsibility of Forms*, 277, his emphasis.
53. Legge, "La Divina," 11. Sutcliffe in *Believing in Opera* adds: "And modern recording technology (not to mention the recording companies' promotion departments) invites the implicitly definitive or 'perfect' performance: manufacturers naturally purvey only the best!" (47).
54. See Christiansen, *Prima Donna*, 150.
55. Kehler, "Questionable Embodiment," 14–15.
56. Koestenbaum, "Callas and Her Fans," 6.
57. Philip Glass explained to the Toronto audience of his collaboration with Robert Wilson entitled *Monsters of Grace* that in earlier performances the singers were offstage, so that the audience would focus attention on the 3-D visuals. But the opera did not work for him, he claimed, and the singers were therefore brought onstage to make a connection with the audience.
58. Storm, *After Dionysos*, 10. On Dionysus as the litmus test for obsessions, see Padel, *Whom Gods Destroy*, 26.
59. Scott, "Electra after Freud."
60. Since Greek myths themselves were not single tales but had multiple versions, "when Hofmannsthal and Strauss used Sophocles' *Electra* they were doing what Sophocles himself had done in relation to Aeschylus and possibly even in relation to Euripides," claims P. E. Easterling in "Electra's Story," 15. On the playwright's desire to write a "modern Nietzschean tragedy of Dionysian depth," see Adams, "'Elektra' as Opera and Drama."

In the various Greek versions of the story, Electra and her brother, Orestes, avenge the murder of their father, Agamemnon, at the hands of his wife, Clytemnestra, and her lover, Aegisthus. The reasons given for the murder are multiple: Agamemnon had killed Clytemnestra's first husband and one of her children before taking her as his wife; he had sacrificed their daughter Iphigenia in order to placate the gods and allow the Argive fleet to sail for Troy; he had murdered the stepbrothers of Aegisthus. (See Mann, *Richard Strauss*, 75–76.) In Aeschylus's trilogy *The Oresteia*, the second play (called *The Libation Bearers*) focuses on Orestes. Electra appears amid a chorus of captured Trojan women, lamenting Agamemnon's death and praying that it be avenged. When Orestes returns from exile, Electra disappears from the stage. In Euripides' *Electra* she is given a much larger role, as the title suggests, but she is far from sympathetic as a character: vain and self-pitying, as well as vengeful and morbidly fixated on her dead father, Electra falls short of being a tragic figure. Her worries are about marriage and about the loss of her ancestral home and social position. Clytemnestra is allowed to voice her potent reasons for killing Agamemnon, thereby helping the audience, if not Electra, understand her actions. When Orestes returns, it is Electra, however, who must firm up his resolve to do the matricidal deed, and she takes an active role in luring her mother to her death.

61. Forsyth, "Hofmannsthal's 'Elektra,'" 21; see also Mueller, "Hofmannsthal's *Elektra*," 75–80.

62. See Wilhelm, *Richard Strauss*, 120. Hofmannsthal condensed and tightened Sophocles' plot and made it into a one-act play with considerably more dramatic tension. He reduced the male roles and developed both Klytämnestra and Chrysothemis (Elektra's sister) as foils for the protagonist. The reduction of the part of Orest resulted in a much less complex character, one with no doubts at all concerning his role in the avenging. Hofmannsthal removed the mediating and moderating voice of the chorus and replaced it with a number of maids in the opening scene who squabble and recount stories about, but never comfort, Elektra, as they do in the Greek tragedy. Elektra is therefore more isolated than in the other plays, and she remains the center of attention and action from beginning to end. For more on the move from play to opera, see Bales, "*Elektra*."

63. Tenschert, *3 x 7 Variationen*, 94.

64. Holloway, "The Orchestration of 'Elektra,'" 137.

65. We learn of the sounds she makes – her howling ("heulen") and moaning ("stühnen"). We are told of her behavior: she is said to watch

everyone like a wild cat ("wie eine wilde Katze") and to spit like one too. She is called a demonic creature but is clearly physically mistreated, made to eat with the dogs, beaten, dressed in rags. We are also told of Elektra's actual words, even before she comes onstage to sing, for the maids quote her at length. And what they quote are her strange, sensually and sexually obsessed words attacking the maids for enjoying her pain: she tells them to eat fat and sweet things and go to bed with their husbands; she curses their children, conceived and born in such a house of horror.

66. Arnold Whittall, in "Dramatic Structure and Tonal Organization," claims, "In its sheer relentlessness, this is one of the most harrowing episodes in twentieth-century music" (63).

67. Holloway, "The Orchestration," 132.

68. The fact that Elektra will use a similar image when Orest finally murders their mother, and the added fact that the maids have quoted Elektra as saying that they should not sit on her wounds ("Sitzt nicht auf meinen Wunden!") both suggest that mother and daughter share more than their pale bodies. Indeed, musicologists have analyzed the similarities in their music as well. See Carpenter, "The Musical Language," 85.

69. Brooks, *Body Work*, 3.

70. See Stafford, *Body Criticism*, on Winckelmann's "disquisitions concerning the pampered fluvial skin of ancient sculpture" (284). As noted at the start of this chapter, this is the influential view of both Greece and the body that Hofmannsthal was writing against in his play and opera. It is also significant that physical signs on the skin of the human body (of leprosy, smallpox, and syphilis) have been taken as "stigma of moral violation" for many centuries (294).

71. See Dodds, *The Greeks and the Irrational*, 271–74, on the maenads' Dionysian dance. He argues that dance is especially powerful because it is a form of "self-surrender" that is hard to stop once begun (272). The communal round dance is mentioned in Sophocles' play and actually done at the end of Euripides' work. On the dance in Hofmannsthal's play and opera, see Schlötterer, "Elektras Tanz," 47–49. Bryan Gilliam, in "Strauss's Preliminary Opera Sketches," outlines Strauss's sketches, which reinforce the differences between the two modes of dance and the music written either to suggest or to accompany them.

72. Schlötterer, "Elektras Tanz," 49.

73. The ritualistic, theatrical traditional dance of death, so richly portrayed in the German visual art tradition, had its musical counterpart in works like Camille Saint-Saëns's tone poem "Danse macabre" and Jean Sibelius's "Valse triste." See Meyer-Baer, *Music of the Spheres*.

74. The ironic and distorted waltz motif used throughout stops. By the ending, the various motifs mix together and underscore Elektra's complicated mix of emotions: triumph, vindication, love. See Wintle, "Elektra and the 'Elektra Complex,' " 76. On the level of tonality, there are cumulative references to and moves toward C throughout the opera, from the monologue to the recognition scene, but each is undercut and never resolved. See Gilliam, *Richard Strauss's Elektra*, 209. This tension is only released in the last four bars as the music is "wrenched" into C major after the brutal juxtaposition of the E-flat minor of the waltz meter and C minor. See Whittall, "Dramatic Structure and Tonal Organization," 72. The final resolution in C major has been interpreted in radically different ways. Some see it as a sign of her victory (e.g., Whittall, "Dramatic Structure and Tonal Organization," 72), while others see it as her undoing, since C major has no tonal complement and is therefore indissoluble (Carpenter, "The Musical Language," 105).

75. See Greene, *Listening to Strauss Operas*, 37.

76. Paglia, *Sexual Personae*, 94. Paglia's definition of the Dionysian is worth citing at length: "Dionysus liberates by destroying. He is not pleasure but pleasure-pain, the tormenting bondage of our life in the body. For each gift he exacts a price. Dionysian orgy ended in mutilation and dismemberment. The Maenads' frenzy was bathed in blood. True Dionysian dance is a rupturing extremity of torsion. The harsh percussive accents of Stravinsky, Martha Graham, and rock music are cosmic concussions upon the human, volleys of pure force. Dionysian nature is cataclysmic. Our bodies are pagan temples, heathen holdouts against Judeo-Christian soul or mind" (94–95).

77. The usefully precise terms used here – performed theater vs. textual drama, performance texts vs. dramatic texts – are those used throughout Keir Elam's *Semiotics of Theatre and Drama*. He defines the theater (and its performance texts) in terms of the performer-audience transaction, the production and communication of meaning within

the performance itself. On the contrary, drama is defined as a mode of fiction designed for stage representation and constructed according to dramatic conventions (2).

78. Mirzoeff, *Bodyscape*, 3.

79. See Iser, *The Implied Reader*.

80. Thesander, *The Feminine Ideal*, 8. She continues: "We exist through our bodies, but it is the formed and moulded body that signals our social position and cultural affiliation" (9).

81. Connerton, *How Societies Remember*, 72.

82. Brooks, *Body Work*, 21. Brooks also notes that the rise of the novel, with its penchant for realism, was important in the development of a different interest in the body (3); arguably, staged drama and opera would already have accomplished this in a more immediate way because of the actual bodies on stage. Elizabeth Grosz writes in *Volatile Bodies* of all "bodies as networks of meaning and social significance" (117).

83. See, for instance, Weiner's *Richard Wagner and the Anti-Semitic Imagination* for an argument about the differences over time and place in the meanings given to staged bodies.

84. See Foucault, *The Birth of the Clinic*: "The structure, at once perceptual and epistemological, that commands clinical anatomy, and all medicine that derives from it, is that of *invisible visibility*. Truth, which, by right of nature, is made for the eye, is taken from her, but at once surreptitiously revealed by that which tries to evade it. Knowledge *develops* in accordance with a whole interplay of *envelopes*; the hidden element takes on the form and rhythm of the hidden content, which means that, like a *veil*, it is *transparent*" (165–66). In *Volatile Bodies*, Grosz discusses Michel de Certeau's work on this subject (118). See McCarren, "The 'Symptomatic Act' circa 1900," 771, on the extension of this idea (that is, of medicine as reading the body's surface to show what is beneath) in relation to hysteria.

85. See Norbert Elias's two volumes of *The Civilizing Process*, *The History of Manners* and *Power and Civility*, on the raising of the threshold of shame and embarrassment up to the nineteenth century. He argues that certain aspects of the body were projected onto the "bestial" lower orders and then expelled from elite culture. See Greenblatt, "Filthy Rites," on how tears become the only acceptable body fluid to mention in polite society.

86. See Porter, "The Body and the Mind": "Cultures, groups, and individuals respond in different ways to life's pains and pressures; idioms of suffering and sickness can be more or less expressive; direct or indirect; emotional, verbal, or physical; articulated through inner feelings or outward gesture. Varied repertoires clearly register the tensions, prohibitions, and opportunities afforded by the culture (or subculture) at large, reacting to expectations of approval and disapproval, legitimation and shame, to prospects of primary penalty and secondary gain" (228).

87. Phelan, *Mourning Sex*, 3.

88. Rouse, "Comment," 394.

89. See Gil, *Metamorphoses of the Body*, 106–7.

90. Adorno, "Bourgeois Opera," 39.

91. Brooks, *Body Work*, 286.

92. Respectively, Gilman, *Disease and Representation*, 155; Weiner, *Richard Wagner*, 1.

93. On music's powers, see Kerman, *Opera as Drama*, 11.

94. Koestenbaum, *The Queen's Throat*, 192. Earlier he notes that the "physiology of opera singing is a set of metaphors; when we hear an opera, we are listening not only to the libretto and to the music, but a story about the body" (155).

95. In "A Voice for Reconstructing the Theatre," Guy Coutance writes: "The modern mise en scène was born, in this mid–twentieth century, of two particular and distinct trajectories: the revelation of a space, that of Wieland Wagner, and the revelation of a body and of a presence, those of Maria Callas. The two meet. Opera is nothing without the miracle and mystery of the voice, just as the dramatic theater is nothing without the actor's body" (169). In the case of Callas, as we shall see in chapter 3, the acting body and singing voice had a very strange and fascinating relationship in the eyes of her fans and critics alike.

96. For an opposing yet complementary view, see Leppert, *The Sight of Sound*: "Paradoxically, texted music acts in discursive excess of words by inscribing the effects of words and music on the mind and body together, but in a hierarchy opposite to that culturally sanctioned: the body excels. Music betrays the very paucity of the words it sets, or rather it makes emphatic the severe limitations of a reason that valorizes a rationality divorced from embodiment" (87). We will return to this

opposition in the next section in our discussion of the Dionysian embodiment and Apollonian rationality in opera. See also Lacoue-Labarthe, *Musica Ficta*, on music "putting itself at the service of the word to reinforce its power . . . , itself translated or expressed, that is to say imitated, the affects or passions, even ideas, whose verbal signifier was already understood as sensual presentation or expression" (xvii).

97. On the reciprocal motivation of different sensory fields in opera, see Kittler, "World-Breath," 220.

98. In *The Sight of Sound*, Leppert makes this argument for the performance of all music, not only dramatic forms of vocal performance, claiming that all music is "an embodied practice, like dance and theater" (xxi).

99. See Bennett, *Theatre Audiences*, 164–65; see also Brooks, *Body Work*, 9, on the erotic investment of the male gaze. David Schwarz in *Listening Subjects* talks of the gaze as "an overdetermined look; it often bears an uncanny sense of looking and *being looked at*" (64).

100. Brett, "Musicality, Essentialism, and the Closet": "allegorization became the only way to neutralize Aschenbach's potent cry to Tadzio of 'I love you' at the climax of act 1; and so music critics fell over themselves to adopt and elaborate upon the Apollonian/Dionysian allegory with which Mann himself had clouded some central questions" (21). The overreliance in these interpretations on Nietzsche's *The Birth of Tragedy*, however, may be one of the unexamined causes of this neutralization: the philosopher's imagery for the union of Apollonian and Dionysian was the decidedly heterosexual one of the duality of the sexes needed for the propagation of the species (*The Birth of Tragedy*, 19).

101. For the general, rather than specifically Mannian, artistic terms, see Paglia, *Sexual Personae*: "Apollo makes the boundary lines that are civilization but that lead to convention, constraint, oppression. Dionysus is energy unbound, mad, callous, destructive, wasteful. Apollo is law, history, tradition, the dignity and safety of custom and form. Dionysus is the *new*, exhilarating but rude, sweeping all away to begin again. Apollo is a tyrant, Dionysus a vandal. Every excess breeds its counterreaction" (96–97).

102. Respectively, Mann, *Death in Venice*, 8, 11, 8, 13; in the German: "Die Vermählung dienstlich nüchterner Gewissenhaftigkeit mit dunkleren,

feurigeren Impulsen liess einen Künstler und diesen besonderen Künstler erstehen" (*Der Tod in Venedig,* 68–69); "die bleiche Ohnmacht, welche aus den glühenden Tiefen des Geistes die Kraft holt" (72); "der leidenschaftlichen Abhandlung über 'Geist und Kunst,' deren ordnende Kraft und antithetischen Beredsamkeit" (68); "von jeder Sympathie mit dem Abgrund," "Wunder der wiedergeborenen Unbefangenheit" (74).

103. On the Apollonian, see Carnegy, "The Novella Transformed," 172. On the allusions in the Mann text to Euripides' *The Bacchae,* see Gillespie, "Mann and the Modernist Tradition," 100–101. On Mann's annotations in his copy of Erwin Rohde's *Psyche,* see Lehnert, "Thomas Mann's Early Interest in Myth." It is interesting that Rohde was a close friend of Nietzsche in their youth.

104. Mitchell, "*Death in Venice*: The Dark Side of Perfection," 244.

105. Dodds, *The Greeks and the Irrational,* 273. The positive potential of the Dionysian release is also explained by Dodds: "The psychological effect was to liberate the instinctive life in man from the bondage imposed on it by reason and social custom: the worshipper became conscious of a strange new vitality, which he attributed to the god's presence within him" ("Introduction," xx).

106. Michael Wilcox, in *Benjamin Britten's Operas,* makes the connection between Greek athletics and the ethos of British public schools: "The homoerotic, Dionysian character of such narcissistic display was officially seen as something dangerous and morally corrupting in those august institutions, however much the homoerotic element was unofficially enjoyed by boys and staff alike. And so it is with Aschenbach, whose initial worship of Tadzio's beauty tries hard to be aesthetic as opposed to lustful" (93).

107. This interpretation of idealism is argued by Hindley, "Contemplation and Reality," 512, and implied by Mitchell, "*Death in Venice,*" when he argues that the formalized, "slightly aloof" music of this scene is appropriate, for it is the last moment of serenity before Aschenbach admits his passion. Carnegy, in "The Novella Transformed," argues that Aschenbach's control is destroyed in this scene, and he "is plunged into Dionysiac passion and the waiting abyss" (173).

108. Corse and Corse, "Britten's *Death in Venice,*" 359.

109. See Evans, "Synopsis," 81.

110. See Palmer, "Britten's Venice Orchestra," on how the drums sound the "way to the abyss. This is the dark side of passion, the swamp, the black beast" (131).

111. Piper, "The Libretto," 51.

112. Evans, "Twelve-Note Structures," traces the transition in the games scene from the Apollonian to the Dionysian and further argues that in the dream the "exchange between the gods is at first distinguished by alternating four-sharp and one-flat key signatures. As the conflict comes to a head, the two regions come into closer bitonal conflict, the voices now in duet. But E major is triumphant and as Apollo fades away, his final phrases, punctuated by tolling bell clusters, surrender to the major/minor ambivalences now accorded to the region of A" (107).

113. Schmidgall, *Literature as Opera*, 331, see also 341.

114. The singer who performs the Voice of Dionysus is the same as the one who sings the other ominous and threatening characters, such as the Traveller, the Elderly Fop, the Old Gondolier, the Hotel Manager, the Hotel Barber, and the Leader of the Players. The fact that Apollo was sung by a countertenor in Matthew Locke's seventeenth-century semi-opera *Psyche* may have influenced Britten's choice of vocal range here. Our thanks to Caryl Clark for this reference.

115. These are Roseberry's terms in "Tonal Ambiguity in 'Death in Venice,' " 94–95.

116. Evans, *The Music of Benjamin Britten*, 330. See also Evans, "Twelve-Note Structures": "The conflict between the Dionysiac E and the Apollonian F which was first resolved in favour of E, now achieves a shattering resolution in A major as Aschenbach receives the sacrifice of Tadzio at the climax of the Dionysiac orgy" (109).

117. Palmer, "Britten's Venice Orchestra," 135.

118. Mann, *Death in Venice*, 65; in the German: "liessen die Kultur seines Lebens verheert, vernichtet zurück" (*Der Tod in Venedig*, 146).

119. Evans, "Twelve-Note Structures," 114. Our thanks to Erika Reiman for pointing out that the inspiration for Britten's choice of music for these monologues – Schütz's *Passions* – has an Apollonian association as well. As a student of Giovanni Gabrieli in Venice, Schütz would have known well the monodic style of opera composition, including such works as Monteverdi's *Orfeo*. That Aschenbach was meant to sound somewhat like Apollo, then, is not impossible.

120. Our position is, therefore, different from that of Philip Brett, who draws an analogy between the ending of E. M. Forster's *A Passage to India* and the opera: "For two generations of upper-middle-class Englishmen, training in the humanist liberal tradition that promised so much and performed so little, the climax of their creativity coincided with a scene of denial and pessimism" ("Eros and Orientalism," 252).

121. In *Sex, Art, and American Culture*, Paglia created a new sport of listing popular artists who managed the same balance: Robert Mapplethorpe "unites sharp-edged Apollonian form with melting Dionysian content" (45); Madonna "has both the dynamic Dionysian power of dance and the static Apollonian power of iconicism" (12); Ingmar Bergman's style "respects both Apollo and Dionysus" (104).

122. T. J. Reed, in "Mann and His Novella," writes: "Mann had peered once more into the abyss and bound Dionysus with the spell of Apollo" (167).

123. On the parable notion, see Mitchell, "An Introduction": "His last opera unfolds, parable-like, his long-standing preoccupation with the problems and perils of the artist, dangerously poised between the Apollonian heights and the Dionysian abyss" (22). See, on the music, Schmidgall, *Literature as Opera*, 345–46.

124. Evans, "Synopsis," 85.

125. Cited in Evans, "*Death in Venice*," 107.

126. Whittall, "*Death in Venice*," 1096.

ꙮ Act 1. Represented Bodies

1. See Hutcheon and Hutcheon, *Opera: Desire, Disease, Death*. Arianna Stassinopoulos, in *Maria Callas*, recounts how Callas explained to Derek Prouse what she was trying to do in order to represent the consumptive Violetta in a 1955 *La Traviata*: she tried "to create a sickly quality in the voice of Violetta; after all, she *is* a sick woman. It's all a question of breath, and you need a very clear throat to sustain this tired way of talking or singing. And what did they say? 'Callas is tired. The voice is tired.' But that is precisely the impression I was trying to create. How could Violetta be in her condition and sing in big, high, round tones? It would be ridiculous" (143).

2. Stafford, *Body Criticism*, 291, 329–32.

3. The monstrous body was anything but "asignifying," as José Gill claims in *Metamorphoses of the Body* (153). It signified in very strong and

powerful ways, as we shall see. See Said, *Orientalism*, on "the intricacies (as well as the macabre fascination) of teratology" and the issue of deviations possible within a biological system (144). His long note (number 54) offers an excellent introductory bibliography (339–40).

4. See Aschheim, *The Nietzsche Legacy*, 59–62.

✥ 1. The Body Beautiful

1. Critics have read this story in biographical terms, both involving E. T. A. Hoffmann (who was short and concerned with his physical "inferiority") and Offenbach (who looked like Hoffmann). See Kracauer, *Orpheus in Paris*, 84, 346–47; Hewett-Thayer, *Hoffmann*, 8–9; Plaut, "Offenbach's *The Tales of Hoffmann*," 200; Jeanvoine, "Hoffmann dans les *Contes d'Hoffmann* d'Offenbach," 338, 341. Other critics read the song allegorically as the victory of discourse over the body, poetry over the erotic, in defining identity. See Neumann, "Der Erzählakt als Oper Jules Barbier-Michel Carré," 66–69.

2. The citation is from Lindenberger, *Opera: The Extravagant Art*, 60. See also his *Opera in History*, 15–39, on G. M. Artusi's attack on Monteverdi's deviations from sixteenth-century contrapuntal conventions in his madrigals vs. later musical historians' praise of him for liberating dissonance from its usual strict constraints. Many found Monteverdi's harmonic violations frankly ugly; they were "shocks to the ear" (39).

3. Lindenberger, *Opera: The Extravagant Art*, 43.

4. Douglas, *Purity and Danger*, 35.

5. Respectively, Plato, *Symposium*, 206d, and *Republic* III, 402d. For more on the body/soul relationship in Platonic and Neoplatonic thought, see Alliez and Feher, "Reflections of a Soul"; on physiognomics and the assumption of solidarity between inner and outer dimensions, see Magli, "The Face and the Soul."

6. See Marwick, *Beauty in History*, 15–16.

7. Plato, *Phaedrus*, 250d.

8. Donington, *The Rise of Opera*, 32–33. The earlier citation is from Donington as well (21).

9. Respectively, Plato, *Timaeus*, 69b, 87c–d.

10. See Eco, *Art and Beauty in the Middle Ages*, 37–38; Adams, "Neoplatonic Aesthetic Tradition," 21.

11. Cited in Eco, *Art and Beauty in the Middle Ages*, 25.

12. Our thanks to Suzanne Akbari for pointing out to us that in Virgil, *Eclogue* 5, l. 44, and *Georgics* I, 219, and in Ovid, *Metamorphoses* I, 612, and *Ars Amatoria* I, 296, "formosa" is the term used.

13. Cited in Eco, *Art and Beauty in the Middle Ages*, 28 and 70, respectively.

14. Andry, *Orthopaedia*, 63.

15. Wolf, *The Beauty Myth*, 2.

16. Buss, "The Strategies of Human Mating," 249. See also Gangestad, Thornhill, and Yeo, "Facial Attractiveness," and Gangestad and Thornhill, "The Evolutionary Psychology of Extrapair Sex."

17. "Men could solve the problem of identifying reproductively valuable women if they attended to physical features linked with age and health, *and* if their standards of attractiveness evolved to correspond with these features," according to Buss, "The Strategies of Human Mating," 244.

18. Eco, *Art and Beauty in the Middle Ages*, 36. Marinus of Samaria writes of the ancient Greek philosopher Proclus in precisely these terms: "For as the former [temperance] consists in the harmony and mutual agreement of the faculties of the soul, so the latter physical beauty [handsomeness] may be discovered in a certain symmetry of its organic members. His appearance was most agreeable, for not only did he possess the beauty of just proportions, but from his soul exuded a certain living light, or miraculous efflorescence which shone over his whole body, and which is quite indescribable" (17–18). Our thanks to Brian Stock for this reference.

19. See Woods, *A History of Gay Literature*, 74.

20. As we mentioned in the previous chapter, biographically oriented critics have been quick to point out the links between Britten and Aschenbach. After all, Britten himself wrote to Peter Pears during the composition of the opera that he was "getting rather attached to Aschenbach, not surprisingly" (in Carpenter, *Benjamin Britten*, 539). Most have seen Britten's Aschenbach as the "public and performing face of his own private and secret passion for boys" (Wilcox, *Benjamin Britten's Operas*, 92), but critics differ in the interpretation of the ending. Like Aschenbach, Britten was facing death as he composed the opera, but what was he offering as an interpretation of his own life? For some, the opera is "an anguished autobiography by Britten, an account of the tension and guilt he had experienced because of his feelings for

boys; also an *apologia pro vita sua* which answers those who . . . had assumed the worst of him" (Carpenter, *Benjamin Britten*, 553). For others, the opera marks the realization by both the composer and his protagonist that "a huge and important part of their lives has been stunted by repressive laws" (Wilcox, *Benjamin Britten's Operas*, 94).

21. Where Mann would call on the German context of the Winckelmannian classical revival in the visual arts to frame his Aschenbach's intellectualized response to Tadzio, the opera's librettist chose to translate that context for an English-speaking public through Elizabethan Neoplatonic language. See Piper, "The Libretto," 51. For a detailed analysis of the novella and the libretto from a Platonic perspective, see Hindley, "Contemplation and Reality," esp. 514–20.

22. Helene J. F. de Aguilar, in "Dangerous Faith," argues that Britten had an "unflagging fascination with beauty, desire, and evil" (168), as can be seen not only in the other operas but in his song cycle *Socrates and Alcibiades*: "It is no accident that Socrates' hunger for physical beauty is expressed in a melody of austere purity unadorned and unhurried. The love of the beautiful is unrelated to time, activity, or change. It is at all times perfect" (168).

23. Later, in scene 16, toward the end of the opera, Aschenbach recalls again Socrates' discussion but now stresses the Dionysian dangers of the "abyss" for the lover who perceives only physical beauty:

> Socrates knew, Socrates told us.
> Does beauty lead to wisdom, Phaedrus?
> Yes, but through the senses.
> Can poets take this way then
> For senses lead to passion, Phaedrus?
> Passion leads to knowledge
> Knowledge to forgiveness
> To compassion with the abyss.
> Should we then reject it, Phaedrus,
> The wisdom poets crave,
> Seeking only form and pure detachment
> Simplicity and discipline?
> But this beauty, Phaedrus,
> Discovered through the senses
> And senses lead to passion, Phaedrus
> And passion to the abyss.

24. Corse and Corse, "Britten's *Death in Venice*," 360.

25. See Peter Heyworth's review in the *Observer*, 24 June 1973 (in Mitchell, *Benjamin Britten*, 194–98), and Desmond Shawe-Taylor's in the *Sunday Times*, 24 June 1973 (in Mitchell, *Benjamin Britten*, 191–94).

26. In Mann's text Tadzio is "the passive recipient of everyone's love earned not through excellence but through innocence and beauty" (Rorem, "Critical Reception," 191).

27. The citation is from Whittall, "*Death in Venice*," 1095.

28. For more on the musicological relationship of keys here and elsewhere, see Evans, "*Death in Venice*," 109–14.

29. Mann's text draws more fully on Plato's work to show how homosexual attraction "might inspire or debase, provide the spiritual impetus to see all beauty through a single form or the spiritual limitation of pursuing only beauty's single exemplar" (Reed, "Mann and His Novella," 166).

30. Schmidgall, *Literature as Opera*, 346. See also de Aguilar, "Dangerous Faith," 158.

31. See Cooke, "Britten and the Gamelan," 117–25, on this theme.

32. See Evans, "Synopsis," on this motive: "spanning a major seventh, [it] is supported on harmony compounded of its melody notes" (79). Schmidgall, in *Literature as Opera*, sees the motive as possessing "an ominous quality of suspended animation" (347). See also Carnegy, "The Novella Transformed," on the "A major–ish theme with its prominent major seventh, A–G#, scored for vibraphone and other percussion," which creates "quite literally a shimmering, vibrant and vibrating sound aura" (175).

33. Respectively, Palmer, "Britten's Venice Orchestra," 131, and Carnegy, "The Novella Transformed," 175. For more musicological detail on Tadzio's "aloof" and remote music, see Evans, "*Death in Venice*," 111. The "oddly disembodied effect" theory is that of Evans, "Synopsis," 79. This effect may in part be caused by the fact that Tadzio's motive does not develop over the course of the opera, and therefore it has a "very arresting quality all of its own" (Evans, "*Death in Venice*," 111).

34. Paglia, *Sexual Personae*, 106, 124.

35. On responses to the facially disfigured, Elisabeth A. Bednar writes in "Self-Help for the Facially Disfigured" of "the initial stare, then the look away, before a second, furtive glance inevitably puts the beheld

immediately in a separate class" (53). On the disabled, see Thomson, *Extraordinary Bodies*, 26.

36. Plato, *Timaeus*, 87e.

37. Cited in Eco, *Art and Beauty in the Middle Ages*, 78.

38. The final citation is from Johann Kaspar Lavater as cited by Carey in "The Quasimodo Complex," 32. Carey's article also offers a more detailed discussion of these various articulations (31).

39. Morgan, "*The Tempest*," 685. There is also a 1922 version by Felice Lattuada and Arturo Rossato, in which Caliban is killed for conspiring against the King of the Island, and, before that, we find a masque composed in 1712 by John Weldon.

40. Not all ugly bodies are disabled, of course: there is always the example of the fat Falstaff, insulted as such by the "merry wives of Windsor" in the various operas written about him, as we shall see in a later chapter. Catherine Clément, in *Opera, or the Undoing of Women*, calls him "old, fat, dirty, ridiculous, obscene" (125). Sander L. Gilman, in "The Fat Body," has linked this particular figure to the *buffo* tradition but also to what he calls "fat boy" music.

41. Mitchell and Snyder, introduction to *The Body and Physical Difference*, 3.

42. See Thomson, *Extraordinary Bodies*, 15–16.

43. Davis, *Enforcing Normalcy*, 12–13.

44. Davis, in *Enforcing Normalcy*, argues that it was industrialization, with its need for bodies to function as and with machines, that created the need for standardized bodies (129–31).

45. Davis, *Enforcing Normalcy*, 3.

46. On this *commedia* figure, see Lea, *Italian Popular Comedy*, 90–100.

47. Davis, *Enforcing Normalcy*, 3, 24, 31, 36.

48. The citations are from Goffman, *Stigma*, 1, 5, and 50, respectively. In *Eat Fat*, Richard Klein argues that fat has this role as "sign of some moral deficiency" today in North American society: "Aesthetically, physically, and morally, fat is a badge of shame" (22).

49. Andry, *Orthopaedia*, 36.

50. Kristeva, *Powers of Horror*, 4. See also Girard, *The Scapegoat*: "The human body is a system of anatomic differences. If a disability, even as the result of an accident, is disturbing, it is because it gives the impression of a disturbing dynamism. It seems to threaten the very

system. Efforts to limit it are unsuccessful; it disturbs the differences that surround it. . . . Difference that exists outside the system is terrifying because it reveals the truth of the system, its relativity, its fragility, and its mortality" (21).

51. The first citation is the original coining by Masters and Greaves in 1967; the second is Carey's later reformulation (both cited in Carey, "The Quasimodo Complex," 28). In his essay on "The Tyranny of the Normal," Leslie Fiedler discusses his thesis that so-called normals are fascinated with congenital malformations because they are symbols of both "the absolute Other and the essential Self" (3).

52. In the French: "Elle ne pouvait comprendre qu'un être si gauchement ébauché existât" (Hugo, *Notre-Dame de Paris, 1482*, 367). Quasimodo is named as he is in the novel because of the day on which he was discovered in the cathedral as a four-year-old foundling but also because the "quasi" in the name suggested the degree to which his body was unfinished and incomplete: "il voulût caractériser par ce nom à quel point la pauvre petite créature était incomplète et à peine ébauchée. En effet, Quasimodo, borgne, bossu, cagneux, n'était guère qu'un *à peu près*" (147). Hugo's obsession with the hunchbacked body will become clear in this chapter. In his life he seems to have been fascinated by this figure and by that of the dwarf. See Robb, *Victor Hugo*, 71, 90, 123–24, for anecdotes about his concerns with his own body image. For other biographical speculations, see Übersfeld, *Le Roi et le bouffon*, 96 (on the young Hugo's hunchbacked servant), and Beaudoin, *Psychanalyse de Victor Hugo*, 73–74 (on his "mutilation complex").

53. Harpham, *On the Grotesque*, 20. *The New Grove Dictionary of Opera* entry on Hugo by Christopher Smith lists eighty-nine different composed or projected operas on Hugo's works both by major composers (Verdi, Bellini, Donizetti) and by others (765).

54. Harpham, *On the Grotesque*, 11. Harpham traces the history of the term *grotesque* and its appearance in earlier visual art (Bosch) and literature (Dante) as well as later (xv–xviii).

55. Hugo, preface to *Cromwell*, 69.

56. In the French: "Ainsi, que les pédants prétendent que le difforme, le laid, le grotesque ne doit jamais être un objet d'imitation pour l'art, on leur répond que le grotesque, c'est la comédie et qu'apparemment

la comédie fait partie de l'art" (Hugo, preface to *Cromwell*, 79). In *S/Z*, Roland Barthes also points out that, in the romantic mind, "ugliness connotes genius, by the intermediary stage of a sign, a sign of exclusion" (103).

57. In the French: "et, avec toute cette difformité, je ne sais quelle allure redoutable de vigueur, d'agilité et de courage; étrange exception à la règle éternelle qui veut que la force, comme la beauté, résulte de l'harmonie" (Hugo, *Notre-Dame de Paris, 1482*, 52).

58. These paraphrased passages in the original French read: "l'esprit qui était logé dans ce corps manqué avait nécessairement lui-même quelque chose d'incomplet" (Hugo, *Notre-Dame de Paris, 1482*, 69); "Il est certain que l'esprit s'atrophie dans un corps manqué" (150); "Il était méchant en effet parce qu'il était sauvage; il était sauvage parce qu'il était laid" (150–51); "il s'était vu conspiré, flétri, repoussé" (151).

59. The two passages referred to here, in the original French, read: "En grandissant il n'avait trouvé que la haine autour de lui. Il l'avait prise. Il avait gagné la méchanceté générale. Il avait ramassé l'arme dont on l'avait blessé" (Hugo, *Notre-Dame de Paris, 1482*, 151); and "en ce moment là Quasimodo avait vraiment sa beauté. Il était beau, lui, cet orphelin, cet enfant trouvé, ce rebut, il se sentait auguste et fort, il regardait en face cette société dont il était banni, et dans laquelle il intervenait si puissamment" (349).

60. Hugo, *Notre-Dame de Paris, 1482*: in the French, 378; in the English translation, 407.

61. Alexander Sergeyevich Dargomïzhsky adapted Hugo's own libretto, and a new text for the music was provided by Z. Shilyayev and E. Kaplan in the 1950s; A. Goring Thomas composed the music for an English libretto called *Esmeralda* by Theo Marzials and A. Randigger (1883); in the early years of the twentieth century, Franz Schmidt created the music for a libretto (in the veristic style) written by himself and Leopold Wilk of *Notre Dame* (performed 1914), and a new "musical opera" appeared in 1993 called *The Hunchback of Notre Dame* (John T. Wallace/Gary L. Sullivan). Yet another opened in 1998. But there are at least twenty other produced or at least sketched operas on this text listed by Smith ("Victor Hugo," 765).

62. The original film score was by Georges Auric, a member of Les Six, and was only heard in the scenes in the Beast's domain and

in love scenes. See Jeongwon Joe's doctoral dissertation, "Opera on Film, Film in Opera," in which she also points out that Glass uses music mimetically or representationally in a way that Cocteau would not have approved of (275–76). Erika Reiman has pointed out to us that it is difficult to write "ugly" minimalist music, since the redefinition of consonance/dissonance is such an important feature of this style.

63. Schopenhauer, *The World as Will and Representation*, 2: 543.

64. See Jan Bondeson's *A Cabinet of Medical Curiosities* for a fascinating perspective on this interest.

65. See Cesare Lombroso's work on the criminal man and woman in Lombroso and Ferrero, *The Female Offender*. See also Hurley, *The Gothic Body*, 4–6, on how Darwinian theories of evolution rendered the sense of the body unstable and thus open to monstrous becoming. This was often associated with animal imagery.

66. Treves, *The Elephant Man*, 2, 36–37, respectively.

67. Goffman argues: "We construct a stigma-theory, an ideology to explain his [the person with the stigma's] inferiority and account for the danger he represents" (*Stigma*, 5). Interestingly, in the visual arts, the term *grotesque* also came to be used to describe mixed forms, including those of human and animal. The same associations were carried into operatic representations, as we shall see.

68. The autobiographical links with Zemlinsky's own lack of attractiveness have been remarked upon by many. It should be noted here that this work was not rediscovered until 1980. There are some differences in text and music between the Hamburg State Opera production version and the later restoring of the original texts with revisions by the composer (from the autograph score) by James Conlon for his 1996 EMI recording, which we have used here.

69. Clayton, "*Der Zwerg*," 1250.

70. Clayton, "*Der Zwerg*," 1251.

71. Our thanks to Heta Pyrhönen for her assistance with the connotations in Finnish.

72. Our thanks to Erika Reiman for her assistance in the musical analysis of this section.

73. Weiner, *Richard Wagner*, 282. His interpretation of this difference is in racial terms, however. See his chapter 4 for an extended discussion

of the limping figure in Wagner and its association with mythological characters, the devil, and Jews.

74. Bacon is cited in Carey, "The Quasimodo Complex," 39. Predictably, perhaps, there have been several operas on Shakespeare's *Richard III* (by A. Schweitzer in the 1770s, Wolkmann in 1872, J. E. German in 1889, and A. J. S. Federman in 1872), but none of them has made it into the standard repertoire, despite the political and thematic resonance the librettos might have.

75. Another way to read this moment is as the point where he goes from being outcast by others to embracing abjection and experiencing joy (Hurley, *The Gothic Body*, 4).

76. Girard, *The Scapegoat*, 34.

77. See de Van, *Verdi*, 285.

78. See Übersfeld, *Le Roi et le bouffon*, 134.

79. Hugo's preface to *Le Roi s'amuse*: "Triboulet est difforme, Triboulet est malade, Triboulet est bouffon de cour, triple misère qui le rend méchant . . . Triboulet haït le roi parce qu'il est roi, les seigneurs parce qu'ils sont des seigneurs, les hommes parce qu'ils n'ont pas tous un bosse sur le dos" (4). See also Conati, *Rigoletto*, 82.

80. *Letters of Giuseppe Verdi*, 76–77.

81. Keates, "Introduction," 12.

82. See Conati, *Rigoletto*, 305, for the positive reviews of the opening night from *L'Arte* (Florence) and *L'Italia musicale* (Milan). The *Gazzetta Ufficiale di Venezia* is the source of the lament. See Conati, *Rigoletto*, 303, and Osborne, *Rigoletto*, 26.

83. Edwards and Edwards, *The Verdi Baritone*, 66.

84. See Girard, *Violence and the Sacred*, 160–64, 252–53, 272–73.

85. "Deformed" is the term used in "Alcune osservazioni sulla struttura delle opere di Verdi" by Roman Vlad, who goes on to call this melodic line modally hunchbacked ("vere e proprie gobbe modale") (500).

86. Again, thanks to Erika Reiman for her assistance with the musicological analysis throughout this section.

87. Jean-Pierre Ponnelle's 1983 filmic version of the Vienna production of the opera does, however, make the identification between Rigoletto and Monterone on stage. Not only does the opening scene of Rigoletto with Monterone's daughter echo visually the final one of him with his own daughter, Gilda, but Ponnelle uses the same singer

for both Rigoletto and Monterone: the curse then becomes eerily self-directed.

88. The citation is from Edwards and Edwards, *The Verdi Baritone*, 65; Parker writes of the shift to a "lyrical, 'paternal' vein" in "The Music of 'Rigoletto,' " 18.

89. The wheelchair figures as an obvious semiotic marker in staged representations of disability in recent opera. John Adams's and Alice Goodman's *The Death of Klinghoffer* (1991) is based on the actual takeover of the cruise ship, the *Achille Lauro*, by Palestinian revolutionaries, during which an American Jew, Leon Klinghoffer, was executed and his body thrown overboard, still sitting in his wheelchair. The opera introduces this character early on through his friends' worries about how he'll manage on the ship with all its stairs and ladders, since he is confined to a wheelchair after a stroke. During the occupation of the ship, the wheelchair is visible and a subject of discussion by both Klinghoffer and the crew. As Klinghoffer is shot (as an example to Syria for its "betrayal of the Palestinian people"), his wife is heard worrying about his paralysis and the lack of serious medical research into conditions like his. In the sometimes odd politics of the opera, the victims of various forms of political machinations – from revolution to imperialism – are somehow equated with the disabled man.

90. Douglas, *Purity and Danger*, 35.

91. In his preface to *Lucrèce Borgia*, Hugo writes: "Prenez la difformité *physique* la plus hideuse, la plus repoussante, la plus complète; placez-la là où elle ressort le mieux, à l'étage le plus infime, le plus souterrain et le plus méprisé de l'édifice social; éclairez de tous côtés, par le jour sinistre des contrastes, cette misérable créature; et puis jetez-lui une âme, et mettez dans cette âme le sentiment le plus pur qui soit donné à l'homme, le sentiment paternel. Qu'arrivera-t-il? C'est que ce sentiment sublime, chauffé selon certaines conditions, transformera sous vos yeux la créature dégradée; c'est que l'être petit deviendra grand; c'est que l'être difforme deviendra beau" (11).

92. Again in the preface to *Lucrèce Borgia*, Hugo writes in parallel terms: "Prenez la difformité *morale* la plus hideuse, la plus repoussante, la plus complète; placez-la là où elle ressort le mieux, dans le coeur d'une femme, avec toutes les conditions de beauté physique et de grandeur royale, qui donnent de la saillie au crime; et maintenant mêlez à toute

cette difformité morale un sentiment pur, le plus pur que la femme puisse éprouver, le sentiment maternel; dans votre monstre, mettez une mère; et le monstre intéressera, et le monstre fera pleurer, et cette créature qui faisait peur fera pitié, et cette âme difforme deviendra presque belle à vos yeux" (11).

93. Eco, *Art and Beauty in the Middle Ages*, 9. Harpham, in *On the Grotesque*, notes that the Northern Reformation (e.g., Erasmus) exploited the irony of the false beautiful exterior and the genuine interior as part of the Protestant rethinking of the Christian Neoplatonism and its assertions of their consonance (6).

94. One of these exceptions that prove the rule is the ugly but vain marsh-nymph after whom is named Jean-Philippe Rameau's *Platée* (1745). Jupiter pretends to marry her to cure his wife, Juno, of her jealousy: when his wife finally sees the unbeautiful Platée, she is easily convinced of how needless her jealousy has been. Interestingly, the role of the nymph was a *travesti* role, written for a countertenor. Another related consideration here would be the classical tradition of the paradoxical encomium, the praise of the ugly beauty. See Dubrow, *Echoes of Desire*, 163–210.

95. See, for example, Pacteau, *The Symptom of Beauty*, and Stratton, *The Desirable Body*.

96. See Psomiades, *Beauty's Body*, 5.

97. In *On Beauty and Being Just*, Elaine Scarry suggests we have moved in the opposite direction, and we need reminding that beauty and justice are connected in various ways.

98. The stage directions are: "(Amahl lifts the crutch. There is a complete hush in the room. The boy takes one step toward the Kings, then realizes that he has moved without the help of his crutch.)" He then sings: "I walk, Mother . . . I walk, Mother!" The stage directions continue: "(Step by step, Amahl very slowly makes his way toward the Kings, the crutch held before him in his outstretched hands. The Mother rises and draws back, almost fearful of the miracle she beholds.)" The Kings greet this as "a sign from God," as the stage directions call for Amahl to "jump and caper about the room."

✌ 2. The Body Dangerous

1. Abbate, *Unsung Voices*, 119; Cone, *Music: A View from Delft*, 125.

2. The subsequent overview of the role of dance in opera offered here

is derived from Schmidt, "Dance: 1, 2," and Wiley, "Dance: 3, 4" in *The New Grove Dictionary of Opera*, 1: 1058–67. For more on baroque dance, see Turocy, "The Dance Was at the Root," esp. 31–32.

3. Brooks, *Body Work*, 259.

4. The citation is from Brooks, *Body Work*, 259. On the feminist recasting of the history of dance, see Banes, *Dancing Women*.

5. McClary, *Feminine Endings*, 57.

6. Dodds, "Introduction," xv. See Rohde, *Psyche*, 283–84, on Bacchic dance worship and the resulting ecstatic communion with the god. He argues that this has a continuing tradition in European "dance-mania."

7. On the shock value, see Carroll, "Eros on the Operatic Stage," 43. The biblical story can be found in Mark 6: 14–29 and Matthew 14: 1–12. For a sense of the complexity of biblical and historical accounts of Herod Antipas, Herodias, Salome, and John the Baptist, see Meltzer, *Salome and the Dance of Writing*, 29–41. See also Girard, "Scandal and the Dance," 311–24. For Meltzer's reaction, see "A Response," 325–32.

8. For an extensive discussion of the first reviews, see Messmer, ed., *Kritiken*, 30–68; Gilliam, ed., *Richard Strauss and His World*, 333–47; Williamson, "Critical Reception," 131–44. Julius Korngold suggested, in 1907 in Vienna, that the popular success of the opera was proof of its inferior musical quality: great art "that is truly original and profound generally requires a longer period to put down roots" (cited in Gilliam, ed., *Richard Strauss and His World*, 343). Strauss's personality was also at issue in the responses to the opera: he was no late Romantic interested in "angst and introspection" (Holloway, "'Salome': Art or Kitsch?" 152). A craftsman, occupied with the business of music, and perhaps a worldly wise opportunist when it came to audience response, Strauss did have his defenders, however: "Strauss was not just a scat playing, money grubbing, haute bourgeois opportunist," Kurt Wilhelm assured his readers (*Richard Strauss*, 199). But the combination of his personality and his taste for writing mimetic music made those with other musical tastes recoil: Joseph Kerman calls the opera "insincere in every gesture, meretricious" (in *Opera as Drama*, 212).

9. On Beardsley's decadent attraction and "Japanese grotesque" response to the shocking nature of the play, see Snodgrass, *Aubrey Beardsley*, 52–54, 87, 276.

10. Cited in Puffett, "Introduction," in *Richard Strauss:* Salome, 4.
11. Cited in Jefferson, *The Operas of Richard Strauss,* 46.
12. See Fludas, "Fatal Women," 15.
13. See Hamard, "La Femme fatale," 40.
14. Eagleton, *The Illusions of Postmodernism,* 25.
15. See, for instance, Grosz, *Volatile Bodies,* 5. For others, see Huyssen, *Twilight Memories,* 165, especially the discussion of Peter Sloterdijk's *Critique of Cynical Reason* and his position that the Enlightenment had not been able to include the body and the senses in its emancipatory project.
16. See Roach, *The Player's Passion,* on the theatricalization of the human body and its relation to medical and physiological discourses.
17. Puffett, "Introduction," in *Richard Strauss:* Salome, 8.
18. Abbate, "Opera; or the Envoicing of Women," 234.
19. See Roach, "Power's Body," 101.
20. Lindenberger, *Opera in History,* 186.
21. Compare one musical commentator's "pudeur" about the body in Salome's famous dance: "Une voix nue, non un corps 'strip-teasé,' chante l'absence, hurle le silence, déroule l'écheveau du mystère" (Vieuille, "La Voix de Salomé," 140). The body is referred to as a "corps/voix" when it is significant; the body's voiceless dance is called a pseudo-dance (146).
22. Pym, "The Importance of Salomé," 312–13, offers statistical proof of this: 82 percent of the Salome images (in various art forms) appeared between 1860 and 1920, and Paris was the center of this activity. The height was at the turn of the century. See also Meltzer, *Salome and the Dance of Writing,* 15–16, on how Salome has tended to rise into cultural consciousness at "decadent" moments. Richard Bizot in "The Turn-of-the-Century Salome Era" argues that Salome's "prominence at the outset of the century was symptomatic of two major strains of cultural influence just then intersecting: orientalism, with its overtures of 1890s decadence, and feminism" (85).
23. In the original French: "Elle dansa comme les prêtresses des Indes, comme les Nubiennes des cataractes, comme les bacchantes de Lydie" (Flaubert, *Trois Contes,* 130).
24. Jules Massenet's 1881 opera *Hérodiade* is based on this story as scripted by Paul Milliet and Henri Grémont, but it eroticizes (by increasing

Herod's lust for Salome) and sentimentalizes the plot considerably, making Salome into a daughter seeking the mother who has abandoned her and falling in (chaste) love with John the Baptist, who persuades her to love him "comme on aime en songe." He does eventually confess his love for her just before his execution, forbidding her to follow him in death. This Salome dances but does so in order to beg for mercy for a John the Baptist sentenced to death. When the execution takes place nonetheless, Salome attacks Hérodias with a dagger but turns it on herself when she learns that Hérodias is the mother she has been seeking. An opera about lust and religion, about erotic obsession and spirituality, it has some of the paradoxes we shall see in Strauss's opera, but Salome's relation to John here is chaste, spiritual, and sentimental – in short, a far cry from the later version.

25. On Moreau's fascination, see Kaplan, *The Art of Gustave Moreau*, 58–67. On the literary impact, see Mathieu, *Gustave Moreau*, 16, 250, and "La Religion," 16–17. In the reverse direction of literary/artistic influencing, see Meltzer, *Salome and the Dance of Writing*, 17–18, on how Flaubert's *Salammbô* had influenced Moreau's depiction of Salome. Moreau did 120 drawings of this work, 70 of them of Salome's body alone. See Mathieu, *Gustave Moreau*, 122.

26. Respectively, the textual citations are from Huysmans, *Against Nature*, 64, and in the French: "elle commence la lubrique danse qui doit réveiller les sens assoupis du vieil Hérode; ses seins ondulent et, au frottement de ses colliers qui tourbillonnent, leurs bouts se dressent; sur la moiteur de sa peau les diamants, attachés, scintillent" (*A rebours*, 143); *Against Nature*, 65, and in the French: "l'inquiétante exaltation de la danseuse, la grandeur raffinée de l'assassine" (144); *Against Nature*, 66, and in the French: "elle devenait, en quelque sorte, la déité symbolique de l'indestructible Luxure, la déesse de l'immortelle Hystérie, la Beauté maudite, élue entre toutes par la catalepsie qui lui raidit les chairs et lui durcit les muscles; la Bête monstrueuse, indifférente, irresponsable, insensible, empoisonnant, de même que l'Hélène antique, tout ce qui l'approche, tout ce qui la voit, tout ce qu'elle touche" (144–45); *Against Nature*, 66, and in the French: "la danseuse . . . la femme mortelle . . . [le] vase souillé, cause de tous les péchés et de tous les crimes" (146); *Against Nature*, 67, and in the French: "repousse la terrifiante vision qui la cloue, immobile, sur les

pointes" (147); *Against Nature*, 68, and in the French: "Ici, elle était vraiment fille; elle obéissait à son tempérament de femme ardente et cruelle . . . ; elle réveillait plus énergiquement les sens en léthargie de l'homme, ensorcelait, domptait plus sûrement ses volontés, avec son charme de grande fleur vénérienne, poussée dans des couches sacrilèges, élevée dans des serres impies" (148).

27. See Wilde, *The Picture of Dorian Gray*, 147. For more on the impact of Huysmans's descriptions of Salome, see Becker-Leckrone, "Salome©," 239–40.

28. Ellmann, *Oscar Wilde*, 321. Wilde's acquaintance with Mallarmé, who was writing his "Hérodiade" at the time, was another factor, as was his reading of J. C. Heywood's dramatic poem, published in England in 1888, which retold Heine's *Atta Troll* (where the phantom Herodias kisses the head of John the Baptist). He also studied many other visual representations of Salome (321–23).

29. Huysmans, *Against Nature*, 69. In the French: "ses hiératiques et sinistres allégories aiguisées par les inquiètes perspicuités d'un nervosisme tout moderne" (*A rebours*, 149). Not surprisingly, perhaps, others have been attracted to other allegorical readings. In *Salome and the Dance of Writing*, Meltzer reads Huysmans's descriptions of these two works as an allegory of the ontology of writing: "The Salome of Moreau and her verbal rendition by Huysmans, then, is a mimetic elaboration, both ideological and figural, of the logocentrism informing the writings of the Gospels" (43).

30. Lacambre, *Gustave Moreau*, 34; Mathieu, *Gustave Moreau*, 200.

31. The term "bejewelled" is that of Murray, "Richard (Georg) Strauss," 569.

32. Schmidgall, *Literature as Opera*, 250–51; Patricia Kellogg-Dennis in "Oscar Wilde's *Salomé*" suggests that Strauss may actually have been doing a "brilliant pastiche of turn of the century Decadent art" (225).

33. For instance, Lawrence Kramer in "Culture and Musical Hermeneutics" sees Wilde as stagy and Strauss as sensationalist (284). Robin Holloway in " 'Salome': Art or Kitsch?" sees the music as fleshing out Wilde's "flashy insubstantiality" (155). Robert Hirschfelt, in 1907, cited in Gilliam, ed., *Richard Strauss and His World*, says: "Oscar Wilde's poetry is moonlight. In this airy magic, Richard Strauss installs the spotlights of his leitmotifs" (334).

34. See Lewis, "Salome and Elektra," on the play as an "extended lyric" (127); Wilde himself thought of it as a ballad (see the letter to Lord Alfred Douglas from 2 June 1897 in which he discusses his aim to make drama as personal as lyric poetry), but so have critics since. See Specht, *Richard Strauss und sein Werk II,* who opens his discussion of the piece with "Eine Ballade. Kein Drama." The final citation here is from Holloway, " 'Salome': Art or Kitsch?" 150.

35. Also to be considered in the impact, of course, would be the cuts Strauss made to Wilde's text (or, rather, to Lachmann's German translation of it), reducing the subplots, repetitions, political maneuverings in the name of structural symmetries and formal groupings of events. See Tenschert, "Strauss as Librettist"; Carpenter, "Tonal and Dramatic Structure," 89–93.

36. On the disquieting erotic appeal of Salome as young girl, see Ganz, "Transformations of the Child Temptress," 13. On Wilde's intention, see Ellmann, *Oscar Wilde,* 232, 255. On the different performative possibilities, see Puffett, "Postlude: Images of Salome," 161–63.

37. The biblical Salome was not always portrayed this way, of course, and the history of these representations illuminates the choices made by Wilde. In the New Testament accounts, the dancer is simply referred to as the (unnamed) daughter of Herodias; her function is simply to be the tool of her mother's desire to have John the Baptist executed. There is no mention of the play's incestuous attraction of Herod to Salome or of her violent desire for John the Baptist. But the biblical Salome takes on more character, so to speak, over the centuries, with the increased veneration of John. By the fourth century, she had become a symbol of evil for her role in his martyrdom, though the major focus in both the literary and visual arts is on the death of the Baptist, of which she is simply the agent. The Church Fathers used her story to underline the evils of dancing, as explained by Merkel, *Salome,* 2–3, and Zagona, *The Legend of Salome,* 20. By the Middle Ages, the dancing scene was inspiring religious artists who used it as a moral warning; by the Renaissance, however, Salome had simply become the image of the graceful young dancer. It was not, in fact, until the late nineteenth century that Salome took on her *femme fatale* identity, thanks to that post-romantic French obsession with her and her body.

38. Bade, *Femme Fatale*, 6. See also Hamard, "La Femme fatale," 29, on the mythic characters adopted. On the danger element, see Stott, *The Fabrication of the Late-Victorian Femme Fatale*.

39. Fludas, "Fatal Women," 15.

40. See Kluckhohn, *Die Auffassung der Liebe in der Literatur des 18. Jahrhunderts und in der deutschen Romantik*, 213–14, on the German *Sturm und Drang* construction of woman as either "das einfache natürliche Weib" or "*das Machtweib*," or *femme fatale*. The citation here is taken from Fludas, "Fatal Women," 15; see also Hamard, "La Femme fatale," 46.

41. Kramer, "Culture and Musical Hermeneutics," 271. In *Femme Fatale*, Bade in fact calls her "the paedophile's femme fatale" (16). See also McCracken, "Redeeming Salome," on the links between the nineteenth-century notions of children and the twentieth-century Lolita figure. For him, Salome is the "Ur-nymphet."

42. See Chamberlin, *"Ripe Was the Drowsy Hour": The Age of Oscar Wilde* on both the narcissism of Wilde's Salomé (105, 175–76, 178) and her contradictions: "the confusion of evil and pride and beauty and horror" (179).

43. Mann, *Richard Strauss*, 54.

44. See Moreau, *L'Assembleur de rêves* on *Salome dansant devant Hérode*: "Cette femme que représente la femme éternelle . . . à la recherche de son idéal vague, souvent terrible. . . . C'est l'emblème de cet avenir terrible, réservé aux chercheurs d'idéal sans nom, de sensualité et de curiosité malsaine" (78). Interestingly, modern French commentators on the opera use similar language. See Petitjean, "Symbolisme et sacrifice": "Définir Salomé par la banale perversion d'une cruauté capricieuse serait n'en rien saisir. Salomé représente au vrai l'idéal féminin, porté à sa dimension métaphysique la plus effroyable. . . . [E]lle crée l'angoisse totale" (132).

45. See Dijkstra, *Idols of Perversity*, 283. For a very different view of Wilde's Salome as sexually as well as morally ambivalent and therefore related to the androgyn in *fin-de-siècle* associations of both virginity (and sterility) and lechery, see Chamberlin, *"Ripe Was the Drowsy Hour,"* 173, 175–76. We feel that the operatic Salome is definitely coded as *female* and also as young (rather than androgynous), given the resonance with contemporary medical discourses, as we shall explain.

46. Lombroso and Ferrero, *The Female Offender*, 151. On the importance of Lombroso and the Italian School of Criminal Anthropology to this view of women in general, see Harris, "Melodrama, Hysteria and Feminine Crimes of Passion," 32.

47. The citation is from Porter, "The Body and the Mind," 251. For more on this, see Harris, "Melodrama, Hysteria and Feminine Crimes of Passion," 32, 52.

48. Ellis, *Man and Woman*, 307, paraphrasing Dr. Clouston's "Developmental Insanities."

49. Ellis, *Man and Woman*, 256. See also Ellis's remark: "Whenever a woman commits a deed of criminal violence, it is extremely probable that she is at her monthly period" (255).

50. Maudsley, *The Physiology and Pathology of Mind*, 341. For further articulations of this linkage, see, for instance, John Haslam, *Considerations on the Moral Management of Insane Persons* (1817), 4–5, and George Man Burrows, *Commentaries on Insanity* (1828), 146, as discussed in Porter, "The Body and the Mind," in which he also cites German psychiatrist Wilhelm Griesinger on the linking of the erotic and menstrual to hysteria (254–55).

51. "The Decadent movement was nocturnal and avoided the harsh light of conscience. Its unspeakable acts and intoxicating dreams required the cover of dark. What light the Decadents needed the moon could supply," according to Schmidgall, *Literature as Opera*, 254.

52. Forel, *The Sexual Question*, 225–26. For further discussion, see Campbell, *Differences in the Nervous Organization*, 200, and Ellis, *Man and Woman*, 254, on erotomania. The Mosher survey in the United States also looked at this conjunction at the same time. See Mosher, *The Mosher Survey*.

53. As if to underline the connection, Wilde has his Jochanaan offer an apocalyptic vision of the day the moon would appear as red as blood, an image Herod appropriately recalls – and twice repeats – just before Salome begins her infamous dance.

54. See Newman, *More Opera Nights*: "In a final ecstasy of perversion her mind cracks" (36); Kennedy, *Richard Strauss*, 143–44, sees the opera as "a study in obsession." See also Tranchefort, "Le Mythe subverti," 127, on her "psychose délirante."

55. The list is that of Ellis, in *Man and Woman*, referring to Conolly

Norman and Charcot (281). Cf. Pierre Janet's somewhat different linking (in 1907) of hysteria to a variety of psychic symptoms, from somnambulism to suggestion, in *The Major Symptoms of Hysteria*. However, Charcot's private belief that hysteria was "toujours la chose génitale" was never really publicly admitted. See Evans, *Fits and Starts*, 26–28. For a full history of the meanings of hysteria from ancient times to Freud, see Gilman et al., eds., *Hysteria beyond Freud*.

56. Maudsley, *The Physiology and Pathology of Mind*, 287.

57. Banks, "Richard Strauss and the Unveiling of 'Salome,' " 11. The music itself has been called nervous and even neurotic. See Adorno, "Richard Strauss, Part II," on Strauss's "artistic morality of nervousness": " 'Nervous' was a catchword of the modern style. It covers what since Freud has been called 'neurotic,' pathogenic disturbances resulting from repression, as well as Ibsen's doomed utopia of hysterical women who, foreign to the reality principle and powerless, protest against the *contrainte sociale*. Nervousness becomes a sign of prestige, denoting the greatly intensified and differentiated reactive capacity of the person who becomes his own precision instrument, who is defenselessly abandoned to the world of sensation and who, through this defenselessness, accuses the gross way of the world" (115).

58. Grosz, *Volatile Bodies*, 157–58, in response to Foucault's interpretation of the "hystericization of women's bodies." See also Showalter, *The Female Malady*. Susan McClary in *Feminine Endings*, 99, uses Showalter's thesis of nineteenth-century madness as a "female malady" to read Salome's mental state as explicitly linked to excessive female sexuality. In "Hysteria, Feminism, and Gender," Showalter shows how both the treatment and historical accounts of hysteria as the potential condition of *all* women have been informed by traditional gender roles in which the male is the therapist and the female, the patient. See also Micale, "Hysteria Male/Hysteria Female," 200–239, and Evans, *Fits and Starts*, esp. 2–3.

59. "The sexual instinct is very much less intense in woman than in man," claims Harry Campbell in *Differences in the Nervous Organization of Man and Woman*, 210. In *Psychopathia Sexualis*, Richard von Krafft-Ebing adds: "Woman, however, if physically and mentally normal, and properly educated, has but little sensual desire" (14); Eric Trudgill in *Madonnas and Magdalens* explains the medical profession's role

in promoting anxiety about sex in the nineteenth century, in part by assuming women to be asexual and willing to submit to their husband's sexual needs only to please them and to procreate (50–63).

60. On nymphomania, see Szasz, *Sex*, 16. The citation is from Forel, *The Sexual Question*, 97.

61. The citations are from, respectively, Dijkstra, *Idols of Perversity*, 249; Krafft-Ebing, *Psychopathia Sexualis*, 483; Forel, *The Sexual Question*, 227.

62. As recounted by Strauss himself in "Reminiscences," 151.

63. Rolland is cited in Williamson, "Critical Reception," 131, 131–32. For an acute and pointed analysis of Wilde's reception, especially in Germany and Austria, and of the links between Wilde's homosexuality and the Jewish theme of the play and opera, see Gilman, "Opera, Homosexuality, and Models of Disease: Richard Strauss's *Salome* in the Context of Images of Disease in the Fin de Siècle," in his *Disease and Representation*, esp. 156–62.

64. See Adam and Worms, "Salomé au pays des hommes," 156, on the fear of symbolic castration that Salome represents.

65. Pearsall, *The Worm in the Bud*, 85.

66. Schmidgall, "Imp of Perversity," 13. David Murray in *"Salome"* describes the orchestra here as adding "one gross dissonance like an obscene jeer" (148).

67. Adorno, "Richard Strauss, Part II," 117.

68. Ayrey, "Salome's Final Monologue," 117. Ayrey quite bizarrely connects these keys with the "moralistic and repressive world of orthodoxy" (which he strangely associates with the decadent court of Herod) and "sincerity and innocence" (118–19).

69. See Clément, "Désir de sainte," 124, on the chaste but desirous Salome.

70. Kathy Alexis Psomiades, in *Beauty's Body*, argues that Wilde's Salomé "circulates herself to get what she wants": "Her performance is from the start something purchased; her body as she dances is already set into equivalency with John's severed head. She uses her performance to acquire the object she wants, in an exchange that is like the exchange of sex for money" (196).

71. Garber, *Vested Interests*, 341. While the literary tradition had been silent about the details of the dance, the visual arts had filled in the blanks admirably. Salome's dance had altered with the changing

conventions of the times – from medieval Dionysian maenadic frenzy to Renaissance innocent elegance. Moreau and other nineteenth-century artists took the unnamed biblical dancer and made her into the demonic *femme fatale* we know today. See Hausamann, *Die tanzende Salome*; Devynck, " 'La Saulterelle déshonnête,' " 18; Merkel, *Salome*, 13. On the entry of the sexual into the representations in the nineteenth century, see Serrou, "Mille et un regards sur Salomé," 18. The name of the dance is said to be from the Babylonian myth of Ishtar. See Becker-Leckrone, "Salome©," 254–55.

72. Murray, "*Salome*," 147. On the Hollywood aspects and what is seen as failed exoticism, see Goldet, "Commentaire littéraire et musicale," 88–89.

73. See appendix to Puffett, *Richard Strauss*: Salome, 165–66.

74. Abbate, "Opera; or the Envoicing of Women," 241.

75. Strauss, "Reminiscences," 151. For the most interesting description of the music and its "turmoil" as vulgar, mediocre, and frankly bad, as "bargain-basement orientalism" that works dramatically nonetheless, see Holloway, " 'Salome': Art or Kitsch?" in which it is argued that by "sheer genius" Strauss raises "[s]ustained, masterly, deeply-thrilling" (149) kitsch to the level of "*Kunst*" (157).

76. Kramer, "Culture and Musical Hermeneutics," 281.

77. Banks, "Richard Strauss and the Unveiling of 'Salome,' " 15. On gender and dance, see Dempster, "Women Writing the Body."

78. For an extended discussion of this tension between the familiar and the exotic, see Schatt, *Exotik in der Musik des 20. Jahrhunderts*, esp. 18–22. Of course, it goes without saying that luxury and cruelty are *not* the only associations with the East at this or any other time in history: spirituality was another, and very different, connection.

79. Kramer, "Culture and Musical Hermeneutics," 279. See Chamberlin, "*Ripe Was the Drowsy Hour*," 177, on the associations in nineteenth-century Europe with dance as "pessimistic and diseased."

80. On these representations, see Gilman, "The Image of the Hysteric," esp. 359–74.

81. The citation is from Brooks, *Body Work*, 226.

82. McCarren, "The 'Symptomatic Act' circa 1900," 748.

83. See Mahling, " 'Schweig' und tanze!' " for more on Loïe Fuller's 1895 Salome danced to Gabriel Pierné's music; in 1907 Florent Schmitt (on a

libretto by Robert d'Humières) wrote a ballet for Fuller's troupe called
La Tragédie de Salomé in two acts with seven tableaux; Maud Allan's
Die Vision Salome was performed in Vienna in 1906 – the year before
Strauss's opera first played there.

84. See McCarren, "The 'Symptomatic Act' circa 1900," 752.

85. Dempster, "Women Writing the Body," 27–28.

86. Marc Weiner in "Response" talks of seeing Ken Russell's production
of the opera, which used "tap dance, soft shoe, fornication (simulated,
I presume), and a host of other devices that made the dance far more
shocking, and culturally contemporary, than an archival retrieval of
the original, orientalist production would have been."

87. Cited in Bizot, "The Turn-of-the-Century Salome Era," 73.

88. Conrad, *Romantic Opera and Literary Form*, 156.

89. Of course, a completely different interpretation is offered by Joseph
Kerman in *Opera as Drama*, who finds it a *"gemütlich* bellydance"
at which he doesn't know "whether to laugh or cry" (211). However,
others do see it as a Dionysian prefiguring of the end of the opera,
like a dance before a human sacrifice: "la dance, comme exhibition
déréglée, dislocation du corps, porte en soi le démembrement, et
annonce la décapitation de Jean-Baptiste" (Petitjean, "Symbolisme
et sacrifice," 134). On the role of the dance as exchange, see Koritz,
Gendering Bodies/Performing Art, 81.

90. See Wallen, "Illustrating *Salome*," on how the dramatic action of the
play "aligns the field of vision with the body and with sexual desire,
in contrast with the verbal field, which is aligned with the immaterial
and the supersensual" (124).

91. Petitjean, "Symbolisme et sacrifice," 132. See also Bucknell, "On 'Seeing' Salome," on the "complex interplay between the eye and the object
of vision" (515). For others on the gaze, see Clément, "Désir de sainte,"
125–26, and Godefroid, "Le Regard interdit," 146–49.

92. See especially chapter 1, "The Noblest of the Senses: Vision from
Plato to Descartes," in Jay's *Downcast Eyes*, 21–82, on the history
of visual primacy in the West. For more on this theme, see also
Berger, *Ways of Seeing*, and Bryson, *Vision and Painting*. In *Noise:
The Political Economy of Music*, Jacques Attali makes a related point
in his opening: "For twenty-five centuries, Western knowledge has
tried to look upon the world. It has failed to understand that the

world is not for the beholding. It is for hearing. It is not legible, but audible" (3).

93. Owens, "The Discourse of Others," 58.

94. Garber, *Vested Interests*, 340. That the situation is far from this simple will soon be clear.

95. Mulvey, "Visual Pleasure and Narrative Cinema," 11. See Jay, *Downcast Eyes*, for extended analyses of the twentieth-century postmodern discourses on the negativity of the gaze, including a cogent treatment of Foucault's critique of ocularcentrism (384–416). He also writes on the film theory debate over gender and the gaze of the camera (489–91, 588–89, 591–92). See also Noël Carroll's critique of Mulvey, which notes that males are often the object of the cinematic gaze (in "beefcake" genres, for instance) and that women are frequently not at all passive but "great doers" ("The Image of Women in Film," 353–54).

96. For a Lacanian analysis of offering oneself to the gaze of the other as an attempt at mastery, see Pollock, "The Gaze and the Look," 117. See also Scarry, *On Beauty and Being Just*, on the vulnerability of the one who gazes as one of the book's main theses.

97. Wilde's less innocent Salomé says she knows why, but Strauss cut this line. The importance of the line for Wilde's text has been argued in Pyle, "Extravagance, or Salomé's Kiss."

98. When the unseen Jochanaan first speaks from the cistern, it is in terms of seeing as well as hearing, the two senses crucial to the staged operatic form. He speaks of Christ, who will come and will make the eyes of the blind see the day as he will open the ears of the deaf ("die Augen der Blinden den Tag sehn . . . die Ohren der Tauben geöffnet").

99. Ayrey, "Salome's Final Monologue," 109, 113. Interestingly, Jochanaan's first condemnation of Herodias is because she gave in to the lust of her eyes and looked upon painted images of men ("die sich hingab der Lust ihrer Augen, die gestanden hat vor buntgemalten Männerbildern"). Whether she looked at erotic images or simply at images women should not have seen, the link between the erotic and the visual is reinforced.

100. This power is aural as well as visual, of course. It is not (as Kramer has argued in "Culture and Musical Hermeneutics," 280) at the end when she kisses Jochanaan's mouth that she is permitted a "triumphant incorporation of the male power of speech," for which she must die. She has that power earlier, and she attains it specifically through

being looked at. After the dance Herod loses his verbal power and is reduced to echoing Salome's words and music ("In einer Silberschüssel"; "einen Eid geschworen"); so too does Herodias ("Du hast einen Eid geschworen"). As Salome insists on her reward in the form of Jochanaan's head, Herod repeatedly protests that she isn't listening to him ("Du hörst nicht zu, du hörst nicht zu"), and indeed she isn't, for he has lost the power to command her listening.

101. Riquelme, "Shalom/Solomon/*Salomé*," 596.

102. Respectively, Kramer, "Culture and Musical Hermeneutics," 277–78; Abbate, "Opera; or the Envoicing of Women," 254.

103. While the visual dominates the text and the aural takes over our ears, all the senses contribute to the representation of Salome's staged physicality: "Salome . . . illustrates desire in so far as desire is figured as bodily, sensual, unmediated, and visible, rather than as hidden, veiled, mediated" (Wallen, "Illustrating *Salome*," 129–30). This is a world "where religious order merges into sexual desire and all the senses are synaesthetically exploited and deranged" (Conrad, *Romantic Opera*, 159). Salome is seen before being heard; Jochanaan is heard before being seen (Koritz, *Gendering Bodies/Performing Art*, 79). But other senses are invoked as well: Salome goes from wanting to speak to Jochanaan to wanting to see him to wanting to touch his body and hair and kiss his lips. After getting her lethal wish, she addresses the head in terms that mix the senses: his voice is associated with incense ("Deine Stimme war ein Weihauchgefäss"), his physical image with music. She describes her desire for him in terms of thirst and hunger that neither rivers nor lakes can relieve ("Nicht die Fluten, noch die grossen Wasser können dieses brünstige Begehren löschen").

104. Hirschfelt (in 1907), cited by Gilliam, ed., *Richard Strauss and His World*, 334. Notice the strange conflation of the senses here: the public is said to stare at the music.

105. Schmidgall, "Imp of Perversity," 13. For an early attack on the musical decadence of Strauss's tonal practice, see Klein, "Die Harmonisation in 'Elektra' von Richard Strauss," 512–14.

106. McClary, *Feminine Endings*, 100. She continues: "Thus as satisfying as the final purging of Salome's chromaticism might be on some levels, Herod's (and Strauss's) appeal to social convention for narrative and tonal closure can be seen as an act of extraordinary hypocrisy: after

Salome's lurid excesses have been exploited throughout the piece, the bid suddenly to frame her as diseased and radically Other is a bit disingenuous" (101). But McClary's claim for these "last-minute repudiations of erotic indulgence" (101) are not substantiated by the text, for Salome's "monstrosity" has been gradually unveiled throughout the opera, culminating, in fact, in this scene.

107. The citations are, respectively, from Schmidgall, *Literature as Opera*, 281, and Murray, "Richard (Georg) Strauss," 569.

108. Chamberlin, "From High Decadence to High Modernism," 606.

109. Holloway, "'Salome': Art or Kitsch?" 149.

110. Huysmans, *Against Nature*, 68. In the French: "Tel que le vieux roi, des Esseintes demeurait écrasé, anéanti, pris de vertige, devant cette danseuse" (*A rebours*, 148).

111. Dottin, "Le Développement du 'mythe de Salomé,'" 14. Klimt's 1907 painting called *Judith* was also inspired by Salome. See di Stefano, *Il complesso di Salomè*. Strauss himself said that, in the world of Klimt, he saw much of his own music, "especially *Salome*" (as cited in Schmidgall, *Literature as Opera*, 286).

112. The difference is, however, important: the bacchantes' dances were said to conclude with the tearing apart and consuming of a live animal.

113. Abbate, "Opera; or the Envoicing of Women," 254. See too Richard Leppert's interpretation in *The Sight of Sound*: "Salome's murder, unlike the offstage beheading of Jokanaan, is seen and meant to be savored. It is accomplished by a sonoric closure, *more noise than music*, that defeats our pleasure in the extraordinary embodied music that Salome has just performed over and on the severed male head. This closure is achieved by recourse to the traditional sonoric inscription of male authority, the military sounds of brass and percussion, rhythmically punctuated at the loudest possible volume" (151, his emphasis).

114. For a different, psychoanalytic reading that, in blunt terms, argues that "[t]o decapitate = to castrate," see Sigmund Freud's brief essay "Medusa's Head." Salome's death has been seen as both a "misogynist anxiety dream" and a "patriarchal wish-fulfillment" by Kramer in "Culture and Musical Hermeneutics," 279. See Chamberlin, "From High Decadence to High Modernism": "Decadent art went to the limit . . . and created conditions in which we might enjoy images of

the most harrowing and depraved of human experiences. In going to this limit, it deliberately tested the character and conditions of aesthetic appeal" (604).

⊰ Act 2. Real Bodies

1. Tito Gobbi wrote in *My Life* that Callas's weight loss "made her a world figure overnight. Now she was not only supremely gifted both musically and dramatically – she was a beauty too" (194). A typical later comment is that of Jane Poole in "Viewpoint": "Maria Callas' amazing weight loss during 1954–55 gave her a new expressive control over her body that enabled directors Luchino Visconti, Franco Zeffirelli, Margherita Wallmann, et al., to stage more demanding movements for her, thereby releasing the dramatic genius within her. By losing too much weight too quickly, however, Callas also sacrificed some physical stamina and vocal bloom" (4).

2. See Green, "Baritonapalooza," C1.

3. See Jordan, "Black Female Concert Singers," on the popular black female concert singers in the United States in the nineteenth century who were denied access to the operatic stage (46), except later through the National Negro Opera Company. Just weeks after contralto Marian Anderson made her groundbreaking Met debut, African American baritone Robert McFerrin played Amonastro in *Aida* at the Metropolitan Opera (1955). In 1945 Todd Duncan had become the first black to sing at the New York City Opera; in 1953 Leontyne Price sang in the Broadway revival of *Porgy and Bess*, and her opera career then took off. In the years since there have been many African American divas but fewer male stars, though Simon Estes does come to mind.

4. Some feel that audiences have been taught today to interpret and understand at the expense of responding and evaluating. Bernard Holland writes in the *New York Times*: "When patrons at the Metropolitan Opera boo, let your blood race. Audiences have been browbeaten into a kind of aesthetic terror, and it is splendid to see them take a chance on themselves" ("Listen with the Ear, Not the Mind," 36).

5. Leder, *The Absent Body*, 1.

6. Nietzsche, *The Birth of Tragedy*, 126–31.

7. Nietzsche, *The Birth of Tragedy*, 132. The form of Greek tragedy also, as Nietzsche argued, represents this balancing: it is "the Apollinian [*sic*] embodiment or sensible representation (*Versinnlichung*) of Dionysian

knowledge," as succinctly described by Azade Seyhan in *Representation and Its Discontents*, 145.

✤ 3. The Performing Body

1. Pahlen, *Great Singers*, 93.
2. Turnbull, *Mary Garden*, 79, 84, 151.
3. Leppert, *The Sight of Sound*, xx. He then continues: "the irony [is] that the 'product' of this activity – musical sonority – lacks all concreteness and disappears without a trace once the musician's 'physical labors' cease (acoustic decay). Precisely because musical sound is abstract, intangible, and ethereal . . . the visual experience of its production is crucial to both musicians and audience alike for locating and communicating the place of musical sound within society and culture" (xx–xxi).
4. See Korte, *Body Language in Literature*, 12–14, on the cultural specificity of the meanings of body language.
5. In Gurewitsch, "Thriller," 8.
6. Clément, *Opera, or the Undoing of Women*, 94.
7. Vogt, *Flagstad*, 172.
8. Edwards, *The Prima Donna*, 6.
9. Rosselli, "Castrato," 766. See also Willier, "A Celebrated Eighteenth-Century Castrato," 95. For more on the history of *castrati*, see Heriot, *The Castrati in Opera*. For stories of how women pretended to be *castrati* in order to have a career, see Pahlen, *Great Singers*, 18, on Casanova's discovery that Bellino was really Bellina.
10. See Kehler, *The Victorian Prima Donna in Literature*, chap. 1; Rosselli, "Castrato," 767; Leonardi and Pope, who write in *The Diva's Mouth*: "The undisputed stars of opera from the mid-seventeenth to the mid-eighteenth century ('Long live the knife, the blessed knife,' screamed frenzied fans), castrati were celebrated and abused – as half-men, capons, geldings, and monsters of vanity, extravagance, and bad temper – from Naples to London" (26). Like Kehler, they argue that these qualities were transferred to women as divas later (27).
11. McKee, "Basta, Diva," 86.
12. Scott, *Maria Meneghini Callas*, 177.
13. Legge, "La Divina," 11; on her myopia, see Koestenbaum, "Callas and Her Fans," 1–2; Matz, "We Introduce Maria Meneghini Callas," 8.
14. Koestenbaum, "Callas and Her Fans," 11–12.

15. See her letter to her husband, Meneghini: "The vocal organ is ungrateful, and doesn't do as I wish. You could even say that it's rebellious and doesn't wish to be commanded or, more precisely, dominated" (qtd. in Meneghini, *My Wife Maria Callas*, 61). See also Stassinopoulos, *Maria Callas*, 40. Tom Harris et al. claim in *The Voice Clinic Handbook*: "A professional singer will describe voice loss like losing a limb. They have an ambivalent relationship with their voice (note how singers sometimes refer to 'the' voice, rather than 'my' voice). When they have a voice problem it is as if their familiar instrument takes on a sinister life of its own, rather like a vocal 'alien.' . . . There is an appalling anxiety in having to perform with an instrument that is unreliable" (212).

16. Legge, "La Divina," 11.

17. Respectively, Horne in Hines, *Great Singers on Singing*, 135, and Sutherland in Meryman, "A Tour of Two Great Throats," 65. In the latter, an interview with Sutherland and Horne, the women talk about what physical sensations they experience when they make certain sounds: they feel sounds in the body and even state that they can feel the other singers' vibrations if they are physically close enough (66). Some singers also report feeling phonatory vibrations in different parts of the body when they sing and remark on how useful these are as feedback. See Sundberg, "Phonatory Vibrations in Singers." Singers obviously pass on their physical experience in teaching. Licia Albanese, for instance, advises singers: "You should leave your belly in, expand your chest and back, and you should use your hands and arms in an upward sweep to get a full breath" (qtd. in Hines, *Great Singers on Singing*, 22).

18. See Kesting, *Maria Callas*, 35. See also Koestenbaum's version: "The diva can't separate self from vocation: her body is her art. When she discovers her diva-incipience, she's discovering the nature of her body" (*The Queen's Throat*, 87).

19. See Ulrich, *Concerning the Principles of Voice Training*, 12.

20. See Wright, *The Nose and Throat in Medical History* on Garcia's presentation of his invention for examining the larynx: "Garcia was entirely unaware of the previous attempts to accomplish his purpose with devices, some of which were identical to his own. His invention, great in utility as it was in the hands of medical men, was merely an incidental contrivance in those of the earnest teacher of singing,

who desired to see the apparatus which produced the sounds he was endeavoring to train into harmony, and the remainder of his communication is largely devoted to the conclusions he drew from what he saw in his own throat of the various laryngeal movements during the act of musical phonation" (206).

21. Mackinlay, *Garcia the Centenarian and His Times*, 114.

22. Or so she claimed (Marchesi, *Marchesi and Music*, 25). Among her pieces of advice, she counseled against "strenuous exercise, singing after meals, exposure to excessive heat or cold, loud speech, and too frequent theater parties" (Coffin, *Historical Vocal Pedagogy Classics*, 33); she also argued against corsets because the lungs should be "expanded at the base to give the greatest quantity of air" (34). Interestingly (and typically) contrary advice is given by other teachers: Giovanni Sbriglia (1832–1916) had belts made to assist singers in holding up their abdomens. See Coffin, *Historical Vocal Pedagogy Classics*, 98–99.

23. See Large and Murry, "Studies of the Marchesi Model," 11.

24. However, Ingo Titze in "The Concept of Muscular Isometrics" points out that any list of principles of vocal pedagogy will likely include both today: "elevating the ribcage for respiration, balancing inspiratory and expiratory effort for the so-called breath support, maintaining a level, or slightly lowered, position of the larynx, and maintaining general relaxation of head, neck and shoulder muscles" (15). See also Wilder, "Prephonatory Chest Wall Adjustments," on inspiratory/expiratory movements of the chest in singers.

25. See Osborne, "Up from the Huff n' Hook," 8; see also Boone and McFarlane, *The Voice and Voice Therapy*, 181–84, on the "yawn-sigh" technique to teach singers with problems to produce a relaxed oral feeling and maintain relaxed phonation.

26. Respectively, Hirano et al., "Vocal Fold Polyp"; Large and Patton, "The Effects of Weight Training"; Troup and Luke, "The Epiglottis"; Reid, "The Nature of Natural Singing."

27. See di Carlo and Autesserre, "Movement of the Velum in Singing," who used sound-synchronized xeroradiography and endoscopy to debunk the tradition that led teachers to stress the importance of raising the soft palate when singing in the upper register.

28. Rosen and Thayer write in *Psychology of Voice Disorders* about how body image is intrinsically bound up with singers' "performance

power"; they also note that the loss of voice can be shattering for the singer's identity (81–83). See chapter 18, "Zen in the Art of Studying Singing," in Young's *Singing Professionally* for a look at the use of psychocybernetics or visualizing to help mind and body coordinate.

29. The images are, respectively, those of Miller, *On the Art of Singing*, 78, and Moure and Bouyer, *The Abuse of the Singing and Speaking Voice*, 13–18.

30. Cited in Bunch, *Dynamics of the Singing Voice*, 12.

31. Sears, "Some Neural and Mechanical Aspects of Singing," 79.

32. Sears, "Some Neural and Mechanical Aspects of Singing," 79–82; Khambata, "Anatomy and Physiology of Voice Production," 63.

33. For some, voice is discussed primarily in terms of vibration, since air passes from the lungs to the larynx, where it opens the cords, which resist and vibrate and thus produce sound. In the discourse of others, it is the biological endowment of singers that is emphasized: the symmetrical vocal organ with wide resonance chambers, a flat and mobile tongue, a broad and flat hard palate, vocal cords that are "white, symmetrical, and perfect in movement" (Luchsinger and Arnold, *Voice Speech Language*, 140–42). For still others, voice is presented mostly as a matter of muscle action or the tension and position of the tongue. See Alexander, *Operanatomy*, 92. There are warnings of real dangers in becoming preoccupied with direct muscular control. See Kagan, *On Studying Singing*, 46. On the physiology of the tongue, which is connected to the hyoid bone and thus affects the movement of the larynx, see Timerding, "Taming the Unruly Tongue," esp. 13–15. Each of these theorists may be correct, but each is operating from a different sense of what is most significant in the act of singing.

34. In Meryman, "A Tour of Two Great Throats," 66.

35. In Mitchell, "Medical Problems of Professional Voice Users," 235.

36. Hines, *Great Singers on Singing*, 135.

37. See Hixon, *Respiratory Function in Speech and Song*, 370, and Sears, "Some Neural and Mechanical Aspects of Singing," 88–89.

38. Sears, "Some Neural and Mechanical Aspects of Singing," 91; Hixon, *Respiratory Function in Speech and Song*, 49.

39. Hixon, *Respiratory Function in Speech and Song*, 61.

40. Hixon, *Respiratory Function in Speech and Song*, 356.

41. See Coffin, *Historical Vocal Pedagogy Classics*, 16, 99, respectively.

42. Cather, *The Song of the Lark*, 164. Later in life, when Thea is a famous opera singer, she learns to trust her body, which is strong and attractive, even when she is "careworn" (359). On stage, when all is going perfectly, she knows that "her body was absolutely the instrument of her idea. Not for nothing had she kept it so severely, kept it filled with such energy and fire. . . . All that deep-rooted vitality flowered in her voice, her face, in her very finger-tips" (398).

43. The marathon image is that of Ethan Mordden in *Demented*, 11; the athlete image is used by him and by Sataloff and Spiegel, "Care of the Professional Voice," 1093, and by singers themselves (Marilyn Horne in Meryman, "A Tour of Two Great Throats," 64). Tom Sutcliffe in *Believing in Opera* writes: "The truth is that opera, live, means singers delivering physically – almost like athletes" (422).

44. An MIT doctoral student, Teresa Marrin, created a spandex jacket to be worn by conductors in order to study the physiology of conducting. See *Chronicle of Higher Education* 3 July 1998: A6. The study of von Karajan was reported in Harrer and Harrer, "Music, Emotion and Autonomic Function," 204–5.

45. In van Sant, "Miss Margaret's Way," 28.

46. Respectively, Robert Merrill with Robert Saffron, *Between Acts*, 113, and Luciano Pavarotti and William Wright, *Pavarotti: My World*, 285.

47. Gobbi, *My Life*, 191.

48. The two citations are, respectively, from Alexander, *Operanatomy*, 111, and Leonardi and Pope, *The Diva's Mouth*, 72.

49. Koestenbaum, *The Queen's Throat*, 128, 127, respectively.

50. Burroughs, "Maria Callas," 1.

51. See Callas, "Callas Speaks," 130–31, 136; Meneghini, *My Wife Maria Callas*, 123–32; Scott, *Maria Meneghini Callas*, 200.

52. See Galatopoulos, *Callas*, 218, and Bret, *Maria Callas*, 209.

53. Allegri and Allegri, *Callas by Callas*, 136–37. On the integrity of the abdominal wall and singing, see Sears, "Some Neural and Mechanical Aspects of Singing," 91.

54. Singer and teacher Margaret Harshaw asserts: "Singing today is not as good as it was, or as it needs to be. It's because singers don't sing *technically*, they sing in the throat – it's wrong and cannot work. All the old singers knew you had to place the voice in the mask. Voices

today don't have depth of tone, and they are not given time to mature" (qtd. in van Sant, "Miss Margaret's Way," 28).

55. In Meneghini, *My Wife Maria Callas*, 67.

56. On a related issue, see Pahlen, *Great Singers*, on Egon van Rijn, who wrote just after the war on the "absurd taboo" that "no emotional rôles, let alone tragic ones, may be interpreted by young singers of an age at all corresponding to that conceived by the composer [and, he should have added, the librettist] for the characters in question" because only older singers were supposed to possess both the physical capability and the "spiritual and psychological maturity" to do so (198).

57. Marchesi, *Marchesi and Music*, 96. She later writes: "No singer ever has, and never will have, to strain his or her vocal chords when studying Gounod's compositions, but too many have already done so with the music of Wagner and his disciples" (288).

58. See Pahlen, *Great Singers*, 228.

59. See Blier, "Time after Time," 11.

60. Mackinlay, *Garcia the Centenarian and His Times*, 141.

61. For a denial, see Alexander, *Operanatomy*, 110; the assertion is that of Miller, *On the Art of Singing*, 73.

62. See Moure and Bouyer, *The Abuse of the Singing and Speaking Voice*, 1–10, on this history of abuse and suggestions.

63. See Merrill, *Between Acts*, 115–16.

64. On vocal hygiene as the way to avoid vocal strain, fatigue, and laryngeal damage, see Boone, "Vocal Hygiene," 35–36.

65. The Latin tag (meaning "a healthy voice in a healthy body") is from von Leden and Alessi, "The Aging Voice," 269; see also Boone, "The Three Ages of Voice," and Comins, "Health."

66. Houden and Austin, "The Effects of Estrogen Replacement Therapy," where they cite Franciska Martienssen-Lohman on the tendency to virilization in women singers: "When a professional singer in these years of highest vocal and artistic power [the climacteric years], is not very consciously defending her characteristic female head voice against the trend towards the coarse, virile, chesty, she will see herself ruined in the midst of her best season" (42).

67. The citations are, respectively, from Mordden, *Demented*, 25, and Meryman, "A Tour of Two Great Throats," 65.

68. Sataloff and Spiegel, "Care of the Professional Voice," 1119. They also describe laryngopathia gravidarum to account for the effects of

pregnancy on the vocal cords. See also Wilson and Purvis, "A Study of Selected Vocal Behaviors," and Boone, "Biologic Enemies of the Professional Voice."

69. See Bernstein, "Is the Opera House Hot or Is It Just Me?" D6–7.

70. See Sataloff and Spiegel, "Care of the Professional Voice," 1119; Benninger, "Medical Disorders in the Vocal Artist," 204–6; Houden and Austin, "The Effects of Estrogen Replacement Therapy"; Wilson and Purvis, "A Study of Selected Vocal Behaviors."

71. Professional singers sometimes develop vocal fatigue by pitching their speaking voices too low. Amusingly, this is called the Bogart-Bacall Syndrome. See Koufman and Blalock, "Vocal Fatigue," 493. On large systemic issues, see Benninger, "Medical Disorders in the Vocal Artist," 190–202. Because these problems are broad system problems, Sataloff and Spiegel, in "Care of the Professional Voice," remind physicians that "maladies of almost any body system may result in voice dysfunction and [so they] must remain alert to conditions outside the head and neck" (1106).

72. Harris et al., *The Voice Clinic Handbook*, 210.

73. Mordden, *Demented*, 25–26.

74. Discussed in Campbell, *The Mozart Effect*™, 42–43.

75. See Ulrich, *Concerning the Principles of Voice Training*, 30, for the pre-1640 period.

76. Pavarotti, *Pavarotti: My Own Story*, 195.

77. Merrill, *Between Acts*, 117.

78. In Bret, *Maria Callas*, 228.

79. Respectively, Sir John Tooley, as recounted in Douglas, *More Legendary Voices*, 21, and Gobbi, *My Life*, 198. For Callas's claim, see Callas, "Callas Speaks," 142.

80. Thanks to baritone Roland Fix for this observation. On the adrenaline "edge," see Nicolai Gedda in Douglas, *More Legendary Voices*, 21–22; Sataloff and Spiegel, "Care of the Professional Voice," 1121; Steptoe and Fidler, "Stage Fright in Orchestral Musicians," 242.

81. Respectively, Pavarotti, *Pavarotti: My Own Story*, 199, 200.

82. See Luchsinger and Arnold, *Voice Speech Language*, 327, for a claim of a reduction of 20–25 percent of optimal ability. On Caruso, see Pahlen, *Great Singers*, 64.

83. Dehorn, "Performance Anxiety," 282.

84. Boone, "Biologic Enemies of the Professional Voice," 19.

85. On memory loss, see Dehorn, "Performance Anxiety," 282; on body block, see Skelton, "Vocal Problem or Body Block?" 10–13.
86. Mordden, *Demented*, 247.
87. Gigli, "When Gigli Knew Fear," 177.
88. See Sobel, "For Stage Fright, a Remedy Proposed." On visualizing and relaxation, see Herbert-Caesari, *The Alchemy of Voice*, 190, and Boone, "Biologic Enemies of the Professional Voice," 18.
89. Sataloff and Spiegel, "Care of the Professional Voice," 1121.
90. See Mitchell, "Medical Problems of Professional Voice Users," 234–35; Boone, "Biologic Enemies of the Professional Voice," 19.
91. Santley's 1908 defense of tobacco and smoking (and its voice-clearing abilities) is striking to our ears today. In *The Art of Singing and Vocal Declamation*, he writes that tobacco is not a "filthy herb" but, instead, "grown in good clean earth, it is washed by the gentle rain which drops from heaven, during its growth it is as tenderly nurtured as the costly orchid; when mature it is still tended by watchful eyes and hands until it is ready for use . . . every process being carried on with perfect cleanliness!" (36–37).
92. Boone, "Biologic Enemies of the Professional Voice," 20.
93. On early periods, see Ulrich, *Concerning the Principles of Voice Training*, 26–27, 33; Moure and Bouyer, *The Abuse of the Singing and Speaking Voice*, 1–2. For later periods, see Santley, *The Art of Singing and Vocal Declamation*, 33–34.
94. Caruso, *How to Sing*, 16–17.
95. Santley, *The Art of Singing and Vocal Declamation*, 32.
96. See studies by Sataloff and Spiegel, "Care of the Professional Voice," on the role of milk and ice cream in increasing the amount and viscosity of mucosal secretions. They also warn against nuts, chocolate, spicy foods, and coffee (1105). In his manual *Singing*, Witherspoon suggests fruit and cereals may be harmful, but meat is needed twice a day (39). Singers also give advice: see Patrice Munsell in Hines, *Great Singers on Singing*, 192. On the more general linking of diet and health in voice manuals, see, for instance, Witherspoon, *Singing*: "Overeating has brought many a singer to grief, and especially when indulged in at night before going to bed" (39). No doubt gastrointestinal reflux is the major culprit here, however. More recently, in "The Effects of Nutritional Training on Voice Evaluation," David Starkey, Margaret

Horvath, and George Letchworth argue that nutritional training has an effect on the quality of the voice.

97. "A Smoky Voice, a Fiery Lady," 44.

98. See Rosenthal, "Callas Remembered," 1014–15; he also cites Carlo Maria Giulini: "There was a unity and logic in everything she did" (1016).

99. Respectively, in "A Smoky Voice, a Fiery Lady," 43, and Legge, "La Divina," 50.

100. See Bianciotti, in "Une Voix et son corps": "sa voix est enfin soutenue par son physique" (8); "Il y a enfin unité: nulle distance ne sépare plus la cantatrice de son image intérieure. Son corps est venu *vêtir* la nudité de la voix" (8).

101. Jellinek, *Callas*, 179.

102. Respectively, Callas, "Callas Speaks," 117, and Meneghini, *My Wife Maria Callas*, 16. Her sister Jackie Callas, in *Sisters*, 73, confirms this, unkindly stating that Callas would have risked becoming "the last of the elephantine divas" (124) had she not stopped her early eating habits.

103. In *My Wife Maria Callas*, Meneghini uses the image (121), but so does Callas herself, comparing herself to her more beautiful sister. See too Matz, "We Introduce Maria Meneghini Callas," 7.

104. See Bret, *Maria Callas*, 114.

105. In Ardoin and Fitzgerald, *Callas: The Art and Life* and *The Great Years*, 112.

106. In Bret, *Maria Callas*, 155.

107. Lionel Dunlop, *Opera*, cited in Lowe, ed., *Callas as They Saw Her*, 67–68.

108. Respectively, in Lowe, ed., *Callas as They Saw Her*, 58, 58–59.

109. See Lowe, ed., *Callas as They Saw Her*, 67–68.

110. Koestenbaum, "Callas and Her Fans," 16. In *Callas*, Jellinek confirms this: "The voice had lost a few shades of its erstwhile brilliance and penetrating strength, but it had become more even, was controlled with more assurance, and was particularly appealing in its warm, vibrant lower register" (180).

111. In Lowe, ed., *Callas as They Saw Her*, 46.

112. "The Prima Donna," 58.

113. For details on these qualities, see Lowe, "Diva Assoluta": on agility with trills, staccato notes, chromatic scales, and rapid passagework, see 8–9.

On size: "Here was a veritable foghorn producing effects normally associated only with flutes and piccolos" (9). On adaptability: "What she in fact demonstrated was that a large soprano voice can develop impressive agility in a bold extension in the upper range and as a consequence can adapt itself to virtually any part" (13–14).

114. Crutchfield, "The Story of a Voice," 100; see also Rodolfo Celletti, cited in "The Callas Debate," trans. Madeleine Fagandini, reprinted in Lowe, ed., *Callas as They Saw Her*, 208.

115. Respectively, on the one side, see Ardoin, *The Callas Legacy*, 204; Stancioff, *Maria Callas Remembered*, citing Rossi-Lemeni, 79–80; Legge, "La Divina," 50. And, on the other side, in *Callas*, Jellinek recounts how Madame Louise Caselotti warned her in January 1948 that she was on the wrong track singing Turandot; de Angelis told her the same about singing *I Puritani* in 1949. See also Bret, *Maria Callas*, 45–46, on her vocal burnout from singing certain roles with great ferocity.

116. See Scott, *Maria Meneghini Callas*, 38.

117. Segalini, "Singing Rediscovered," 178; see also Bret, *Maria Callas*, 68.

118. Lowe, "Diva Assoluta," 8; on health, see Ardoin and Fitzgerald, *Callas: The Art and Life* and *The Great Years*, 22–23, and Ardoin, *The Callas Legacy*, 80.

119. Larry Kelly claims that "she wanted to be wealthy, secure, accepted" and so let down the discipline and regime; therefore, the voice went. Cited in Stancioff, *Maria Callas Remembered*, 154.

120. See Ardoin, *The Callas Legacy*, 85–86, and Lowe, "Diva Assoluta," 8. Others add to the description of problems "the rawness and hardness of tone, the unequalized registers, and the overheated chest voice" (Christiansen, "Callas," 617).

121. "The Prima Donna," 54.

122. Tito Gobbi, one of those who had encouraged her to lose the weight, feels that it eventually did have an effect on her "vocal and nervous stamina" (*My Life*, 194). In *Maria Meneghini Callas*, Scott agrees: "inevitably it proved impossible for her new-found figure, with its frailer resources, to sustain her in the wide-ranging repertory she continued to undertake. By this time it was becoming increasingly difficult to determine which came first: her health problems or her vocal problems. . . . But . . . it was not until after she had lost weight that the demands she made of herself came to create vocal problems" (178).

123. Michael Scott's citations in *Maria Meneghini Callas* are, respectively, from 171, 178, 218, 143, 221; Callas, *My Daughter Maria Callas*, 149.

124. Respectively, Harold Rosenthal in *Opera*, in 1963, in Lowe, ed., *Callas as They Saw Her*, 100; a Chicago reviewer in 1958, also in that volume, 73; Scott, *Maria Meneghini Callas*, 151.

125. Quoted in Bret, *Maria Callas*, 223.

126. In "Singing Rediscovered," Segalini even argues that she lost weight to save opera from an inevitable demise (172).

127. Koestenbaum, *The Queen's Throat*, 139.

128. Schwartz, "The Three Body Problem," 451.

129. In Meryman, "A Tour of Two Great Throats," 65.

130. On high sopranos seen as having "a delicate neck and in many cases a smaller mouth cavity" as well as smaller stature, see Reinders, "Teaching the High Female Voice," 43. On mezzos, see Wood, "Sapphonics," 41.

131. Moure and Bouyer, *The Abuse of the Singing and Speaking Voice*: "These are generally big subjects of great corpulence, with a neck raised and made prominent by a projecting Adam's apple, which betrays the length of their cords" (43).

132. Marafioti, *Caruso's Method of Voice Production*, 4–7.

133. The source of this saying is difficult to trace. In *Coming to Terms*, William Safire credits Dick Motta, coach of the Chicago Bulls (102–3). But he notes that other attributions include Dan Cook, sports editor of the *San Antonio Express-News*, who used it to counter the line "The rodeo ain't over till the bull riders ride."

134. Hines, *Great Singers on Singing*, 324.

135. Burroughs, "Da Capo," 3.

136. Burroughs, "Da Capo," 5–6.

137. In Meryman, "A Tour of Two Great Throats," 65.

138. Burroughs, "Da Capo," 3.

139. Klein, *Eat Fat*, xviii, 20, respectively.

140. Stearns, *Fat History*, vii.

141. Koestenbaum, *The Queen's Throat*, 101; see also Leonardi and Pope, *The Diva's Mouth*, 49, on literary representations of divas as counter-discursive: "the exception to feminine silence and powerlessness" (21).

142. Moon and Sedgwick, "Divinity," 216. Stearns, in *Fat History*, traces both the mid-nineteenth-century taste for rotundity in men and

women, especially on the stage (9, 154–56) and the shift to slimness in the 1890s that is still with us today. "Voluptuousness," however, was allowed for some time in "theatrical women" (12).

143. Koestenbaum, *The Queen's Throat*, 101.

144. Respectively, Abel, *Opera in the Flesh*, 12–13, 16.

145. Abel, *Opera in the Flesh*, 20.

146. Our description here is indebted to Ingram, "Open Wide and Sing Ahhh!" 18–19.

147. See Bunch, *Dynamics of the Singing Voice*, 14.

148. Ingram, "Open Wide and Sing Ahhh!" 19.

149. Alexander, *Operanatomy*, 91–92.

150. Alexander, *Operanatomy*, 92.

151. Pahlen, *Great Singers*, citing teacher Egon van Rijn (198).

152. Bernstein, "Is the Opera House Hot or Is It Just Me?" D6.

153. Huneker, *Bedouins*, 16. On fitness, see Witherspoon, *Singing*, 38; Pahlen, *Great Singers*, 201.

154. Marafiotti, *Caruso's Method of Voice Production*, 35.

155. Green, "Baritonapalooza," C1.

156. Locke, "What Are These Women Doing in Opera?" 65.

157. In Marwick, *Beauty in History*, 14.

158. On the health risks of obesity and how large singers should lose weight gradually, see Sataloff and Sataloff, "Obesity and the Professional Voice User," 192. They continue: "For most singers, an extra 10, 20, or 30 pounds is not perceived as much of a problem. However, as 20 becomes 30, and 30 becomes 40, significant adverse effects occur in the body in general and the vocal tract specifically" (194). Soprano Roberta Peters worries about fat singers: "I maintain that these heavy singers cannot sing so long, because their muscle tone, their energy, is not good . . . it's all fat! It's the worse thing for you. If your muscles and your body tone are good, your vocal tone is going to be good" (in Hines, *Great Singers on Singing*, 239).

159. Pavarotti, *Pavarotti: My World*, 50; see also Pavarotti, *Pavarotti: My Own Story*, 183; Lewis, *The Private Lives of the Three Tenors*, 147.

160. In Pahlen, *Great Singers*, 44.

161. Bronfen, " 'Lasciatemi Morir,' " 431.

162. Innaurato, "As Categories Blur, One Diva Rules," 30.

163. In Turnbull, *Mary Garden*, 170. When she saw Callas perform in 1954, she said: "There's not been anything like this since *I* was up there" (198).

164. Pahlen, *Great Singers*, 35.

165. Teachout, "Does Beauty Matter?" 58. He notes that "this points to a larger shift in operatic priorities: though contemporary audiences are still willing to look the other way for the sake of a really big voice, they now seem more inclined than ever before to expect major-house singers to meet at least minimal standards of pulchritude" (58).

166. Margaret Harshaw tells of being called Junoesque in a review of her first Brangäne at the Met in 1946: "I always took that as a compliment. But today – all these huge sopranos! I think they must have a Fat Girls Club. They get together and say, 'Now, dear, don't lose a pound' " (in van Sant, "Miss Margaret's Way," 28).

167. This is the theory of Poole, "Viewpoint," 4.

168. Slover and Dwyer, "Professional Singers with Obesity," 124. This is corroborated by contralto Maureen Forrester in a joking way in the "Introduction" to Barber, *When the Fat Lady Sings*: "These days there are some wonderful and skinny opera singers. But there didn't used to be, especially if they sang Wagner. It comes from eating at too many receptions" (vi).

169. Clément, *Opera, or the Undoing of Women*, 29.

❧ 4. The Perceiving Body

1. Koestenbaum, *The Queen's Throat*, 39. The epigraph is on 182.

2. Carlson, *Theatre Semiotics*, 96. In his *Dictionary of the Theatre*, Patrice Pavis notes that the physical space of the theater itself has a physical impact on perception: "Light or darkness, overcrowding, the comfort of the seating: these factors weave a subtle fabric that influences the quality of the listening and the aesthetic experience" (305).

3. See Jourdain, *Music, the Brain, and Ecstasy*, 293; Campbell, *The Mozart Effect™*, 44.

4. See Henson, "The Language of Music," in which he argues that "the scope of communication is broadened when words and music combine in composition" (245).

5. Willier, "A Celebrated Eighteenth-Century Castrato," 103.

6. Cather, *The Song of the Lark*, 347–55.

7. Even if audience members look passive, they may be anything but, as Robertson Davies describes in his novel *The Lyre of Orpheus*: "There they sit, all those stockbrokers and rich surgeons and insurance men, and they look so solemn and quiet as if nothing would rouse them. But

underneath they are raging with unhappy love, or vengeance, or some point of honour or ambition – all connected with their professional lives. They go to *La Bohème* or *La Traviata* and they remember some early affair that might have been squalid if you weren't living it yourself; or they see *Rigoletto* and think how the chairman humiliated them at the last board meeting; or they see *Macbeth* and think how they would like to murder the chairman and get his job. Only they don't think it; very deep down they feel it, and boil it, and suffer it in the primitive underworld of their souls. You wouldn't get them to admit anything, not if you begged. Opera speaks to the heart as no other art does, because it is essentially simple" (147–48).

8. For an example, see Crofton and Fraser, *A Dictionary of Musical Quotations*, 80.

9. In *Phenomenology of Perception*, Maurice Merleau-Ponty stresses how the world is manifested to the body as sensory apparatus and argues that a theory of the body is already a theory of perception (203). For the possible impact of such a theory on theater, see Fortier, *Theory/Theatre*, 29–31.

10. Nietzsche is cited in Campbell, *The Mozart Effect*™, 67; the Italian story is from Filippo Filippi, "Wagner: Musical Voyage in the Land of the Future" (1876), reproduced in Haskell, ed., *The Attentive Listener*: "Wagnerphobia reaches the level of paroxysm in certain people: they claim not only that his music (which they never understand) is the negation of art, of melody, of common sense, but also that listening to it is a veritable curse; and serious newspapers do not hesitate to proclaim that listening to a Wagner opera can cause jaundice, smallpox, cholera, and heaven knows how many other diseases" (157). A more low-key example of this belief in the power of opera over the body can be seen in the playing of opera arias to discourage youths from loitering in one of Montreal's largest subway stations. See Bernstein, "The Opera-lover's Revenge."

11. The three citations are from the English translation by Paul de Man of *Madame Bovary*, 161, 162, 163; in the French: "Elle se laissait aller au bercement des mélodies et se sentait elle-même vibrer de tout son être comme si les archets des violons se fussent promenés sur ses nerfs" (208); "Emma se penchait pour le voir, égratignant avec ses ongles le velours de sa loge. Elle s'emplissait le coeur de ces lamentations

mélodieuses qui se traînaient à l'accompagnement des contrebasses, comme des cris de naufragés dans le tumulte d'une tempête . . . et, quand ils [les amants de l'opéra] poussèrent l'adieu final, Emma jeta un cri aigu, qui se confondit avec la vibration des derniers accords" (208–9); "L'odeur du gaz se mêlait aux haleines; le vent des éventails rendait l'atmosphère plus étouffante. . . . [E]lle retomba dans son fauteuil avec des palpitations qui la suffoquaient" (211).

12. See the 1897 article by Binet and Courtier, "Influence de la musique," and the earlier one (1889) by Guibaud, "Contribution à l'étude expérimentale."

13. "These autonomic changes represent the vegetative reflections of psychological processes," we are told by Harrer and Harrer in "Music, Emotion and Autonomic Function," 202. For more overviews of this recent scientific literature, see Abran, *L'Influence de la musique*, 83–84, and Porzionato, *Psicobiologia della musica*, 88–95.

14. See Allen and Blascovich, "Effects of Music" and Winter, Paskin, and Baker, "Music Reduces Stress."

15. There is some disagreement about the interaction of intellect and body here. In *Music and the Mind*, Anthony Storr claims: "Recordings of blood pressure, respiration, pulse-rate and other functions controlled by the involuntary, autonomic nervous system taken from the same subject demonstrated that, when he was completely involved with the music, there were marked changes in the tracings recording evidence of physiological arousal; when, however, he adopted an analytic, critical attitude, these changes were not apparent" (39).

16. See Zentner and Kagan, "Perception of Music by Infants," and Schellenberg and Trehub, "Natural Musical Intervals."

17. See Small, *Musicking*, 137–38.

18. Porzionato, *Psicobiologia della musica*, 62.

19. Barthes, "Phantoms," in *The Responsibility of Forms*, 187.

20. Peter Kivy in *Music Alone* argues that two people may hear the same music and experience the same "*sonic* event," but they might not hear the same *musical* event, which he defines as "an intentional object, determined in part by our beliefs, descriptions, perceptions of it" (100). Who is to say whether the intense responses to opera reportedly felt by the prisoners of the Dade Correctional Institute who belong to the Inmate Opera Club are innate or learned? The artistic skills to produce

their own operas may have to be learned, but the pleasure and release provided by experiencing even recordings and videos may not be. See Yearwood, "Florida Prisoners 'Escaping' with Opera."

21. Other claims have been scientifically debunked. The 1995 article on "Listening to Mozart Enhances Spatial-temporal Reasoning" by Rauscher, Shaw, and Ky was tested experimentally, and its findings were found decidedly lacking. See Newman et al., "An Experimental Test of 'The Mozart Effect.'" For more on the general viability of musical therapy, however, see Schipkowensky, "Musical Therapy in the Field of Psychiatry and Neurology."

22. Reproduced in Meneghini, *My Wife Maria Callas*, 205. See also Koestenbaum, *The Queen's Throat*: "Promotional materials promised that the phonograph would be useful to teach and tranquilize in 'blind asylums, hospitals, the sick chamber' " (49).

23. See the liner notes for the CBS recording of *The Man Who Mistook His Wife for a Hat*, 16, 17.

24. See the work that has been built on that of William Fry, especially Dean, "Humor and Laughter in Palliative Care"; on the cardiological effects, see Leiber, "Laughter and Humor in Critical Care," 164; on respiratory effects, see Bloch, Lemeignan, and Aguilera-T., "Specific Respiratory Patterns."

25. On muscle relaxation, see Leiber, "Laughter and Humor in Critical Care," 164–65; on pain reduction, see Norman Cousins's famous extended account in *Anatomy of an Illness as Perceived by the Patient*; on the immune system, see Wooten, "Humor."

26. Cited in Robinson, "Humor and Health," 111. Darwin also considered this as a topic worthy of study.

27. For laughter in palliative care, see Dean, "Humor and Laughter in Palliative Care"; Erdman, "Laughter Therapy for Patients with Cancer"; Showalter and Skobel, "Hospice." On critical care, see Leiber, "Laughter and Humor in Critical Care." On relief of physical pain, see Cousins, *Anatomy of an Illness*; Mallett, "Use of Humour and Laughter in Patient Care"; Cogan et al., "Effects of Laughter and Relaxation on Discomfort Thresholds." On the pain of loss, see Poland, "The Gift of Laughter." On physical and psychological stress, see Leiber, "Laughter and Humor in Critical Care," 162; Wooten, "Humor"; Martin and Lefcourt, "Sense of Humor." On release theories, see Mosak and

Maniacci, "An 'Alderian' Approach to Humor and Psychotherapy," 1–2; Herth, "Contributions of Humor." On brain function, see Robinson, "Humor and Health," 118–19; Holland, *Laughing*, 76.

28. On the sense of group fellowship, see Mosak and Maniacci, "An 'Alderian' Approach to Humor and Psychotherapy," 3; on the contagiousness of laughter and group response to it, see Banning and Nelson, "The Effects of Activity-Elicited Humor," 514, 510; Martin and Gray, "The Effects of Audience Laughter."

29. Cited in Brown, *Tchaikovsky*, 59. On the shared nature of laughter and the privacy of crying, see Erdman, "Laughter Therapy for Patients with Cancer," 1359. On the relation between laughing and weeping physiologically, see Robinson, "Humor and Health," 119. On the cathartic effects of tears, see Holland, *Laughing*, 80.

30. Koestenbaum, *The Queen's Throat*, 42.

31. On kinesthetics, see Pavis, *Dictionary of the Theatre*, 193–94. On the influence of audience members on each other, see Carlson, *Theatre Semiotics*: "the pressure of audience response can coerce individual members to structure and interpret their experience in a way which might not have occurred to them as solitary readers" (12). On audience-stage impact, see Jan Mukařovský, cited in de Toro, *Theatre Semiotics*: "Not only does the stage action influence the audience, but the audience also influences the stage action. . . . The audience is therefore omnipresent in the structure for stage productions" (97).

32. See Bunch, *Dynamics of the Singing Voice*: "A voice that is consistently strident indicates excessive tension in the speaker or singer. Listeners will usually react with a sympathetic throat ache or feeling of discomfort, and, in the case of the singer, this can even happen to an audience" (11).

33. Respectively, the description of Callas's singing is that of Claudia Cassidy in the *Chicago Tribune* about Callas's 1957 *Turandot*, in Lowe, ed., *Callas as They Saw Her*, 64; the battle image is that of Carlo Maria Giulini, cited in Rosenthal, "Callas Remembered," 1016; the Callas citation is from "The Prima Donna," 55.

34. Brecht is cited in Pavis, *Dictionary of the Theatre*, 348–49, Moffo in Winer, "I Can't Go On," 15.

35. Davies, *The Lyre of Orpheus*, 450.

36. Elam, *The Semiotics of Theatre and Drama*, 35.

37. Pavarotti, *Pavarotti: My Own Story*, 201.
38. Stancioff, *Maria Callas Remembered*, 112. Mimi White, in "They All Sing," argues that in the film the diva's position on recording is an attempt to control "her voice, her space, her corporeality" (34) but that it is also presented as a woman's whim in an age of international markets and electronic and digital recording technology, where it can only be a "nostalgic impossibility" (35).
39. See Storr, *Music and the Mind*, 75–78, on this debate.
40. Plato, *Republic*, 411b, 401d–e, respectively.
41. Brett, "Musicality, Essentialism, and the Closet," 11. The subsequent citation is from 13. In *The Pale of Words*, James Anderson Winn argues that there has been a historical suspicion, in fact, of all performance by word-oriented disciplines. The fear of the irrational, he claims, is tied to the response to public spectacle.
42. Segal, *Orpheus*, 14.
43. See Rohde, *Psyche*, esp. 288–91.
44. On the Dionysiac rites, see Dodds, *The Greeks and the Irrational*, 76; on the bacchantes, see Dodds, "Introduction," xx.
45. Arblaster, *Viva la libertà*, 49.
46. See Elam, *Semiotics of Theatre and Drama*, 96–97, on stimulation, confirmation, and integration as the primary effects of spectator-spectator communication.
47. Walcot, *Greek Drama*, 5.
48. Georg Joseph Vogler, "On the State of Music in France" (1781), in Haskell, ed., *The Attentive Listener*, 48.
49. See Jourdain, *Music, the Brain, and Ecstasy*, 240–41.
50. Leppert, *The Sight of Sound*, 25. For another view of the history of what is seen as increasing audience passivity in spoken theater, see Bennett, *Theatre Audiences*, 3, and for passivity in the concert hall, see Small, *Musicking*, 44. The new social contract in the theater even has its commandments, often published in the program: Thou shalt not open cellophane-wrapped candies during a performance, and so on.
51. Jourdain, *Music, the Brain, and Ecstasy*, 325. He continues: "Musical patterns that produce emotion and pleasure are replicated in a second, particularly extensive neural system – the motor system – and so emotion and pleasure arise in this second medium as well as in the direct experience of sound" (326).

52. Cather, "A Wagner Matinée," 494.

53. The citation is from Schwarz, *Listening Subjects*, 3. Of course, as in theater, we interpret more than just what we hear or see on stage. We are influenced by things like the appearance of the theater, the structuring of intermissions, the images, essays or notes in the program, reviews we might have read, publicity we might have seen or heard. See Carlson, *Theatre Semiotics*, xiii, 18–19, 22–24.

54. Small, *Musicking*, 112.

55. Leppert disagrees and, in *The Sight of Sound*, argues: "Music's auditory impact is insufficient to produce these effects [of muscular as well as auditory *jouissance*], which come about through self-performance, *listening-doing*, the activity of music *making* and not the passive act of 'mere' listening. This music's performance is *in and of* the body, but a *whole* body, an *interpreting* body. To make music is a cognitive-physical act, in which the separation of mind from body momentarily disappears" (215, his emphasis). Our position is closer to that of Christopher Small, who coins the verb "to music": "*To music is to take part, in any capacity, in a musical performance, whether by performing, by listening, by rehearsing or practicing, by providing material for performance (what is called composing), or by dancing*" (9, his emphasis).

56. See Langer, *Feeling and Form*, 27.

57. See philosopher Peter Kivy in *Osmin's Rage*, arguing that only music – and not that "messy world" – can really achieve the perfect resolution of conflict and releasing of tension that opera demands (281). Many musicologists would no doubt agree with him; few opera audiences would.

58. McClary, *Feminine Endings*, 20.

59. Paul Hindemith, cited in Storr, *Music and the Mind*, 75–76.

60. The citation is from McClary, "The Undoing of Opera," xv. For more on the high voice theory, see Poizat, *The Angel's Cry*, and Brophy, *Mozart the Dramatist*, 57. Leslie C. Dunn and Nancy A. Jones, in their introduction to *Embodied Voices*, argue that such a model assumes a male listening subject who experiences "a sensation of radical loss" caused by the body's libidinal drives emerging in the diva's sound: "In this scenario of listening, everything seems to be at stake when women open their mouths, for this experience of loss threatens the

stability of the patriarchal order, indeed that of the male subject itself" (9).

61. Henson, "The Language of Music," 252–53.

62. Starobinski, "Opera and Enchantresses," 19.

63. See Rousseau, "Theatre," on catharsis as "a sterile pity which feeds on a few tears and has never produced the slightest act of humanity. . . . [W]hen a man has gone to admire beautiful deeds in stories and cry for imaginary misfortunes, what more can be asked of him? Is he not pleased with himself? Does he not applaud his beautiful soul?" (126).

64. See Pavis, *Dictionary of the Theatre*, 44–46, on the history of catharsis.

65. Pavis, *Dictionary of the Theatre*, 349.

66. Peraino, "I Am an Opera," 127–28.

67. Paglia, *Sexual Personae*, 96, 602. In "Taking Place," Sam Weber argues that audiences no longer identify with represented characters but with "the spectacle as a performance" (113): "If audiences identify with opera today, it is precisely because of its distance, not in spite of it. Such identification is the result of the exotic artificiality built into operatic form and expected from it" (116). Yet people still cry at the end of *Madama Butterfly*. Franco Moretti argues that literature too can make us cry not just because we read of represented sadness or the suffering of a character but because it brings together the character's realization of the futility of desire with the audience's prior awareness of it. The two temporal lines come together with great force, he argues in *Signs Taken for Wonders*, 179.

68. Henson, in "The Language of Music," agrees, arguing against the separation of the two realms on musical and scientific grounds: "The division of thought and experience into the cognitive or intellectual and emotional or affective aspects may be a convenient convention for neurologists and psychologists to adopt, but it has no sound foundation in neurophysiology and neuropsychology. We can all think of situations in which emotion appears to exclude intellect and *vice versa*, but these episodes are generally passing in normal persons and the two elements combine in virtually all experience. There seems no reason to suppose that musical composition is not associated with parallel neural activity in the several parts of the brain which are particularly concerned with the emotional or intellectual aspects of experience, though one may dominate the other" (245).

69. The citations are from Kivy, *Music Alone*, 42; the comment about nerve endings is from 165. The idea of how and what music actually means is the concern of "expressive" theories of music. See Meyer, *Emotion and Meaning in Music*. But opera is "scripted" music, music written to fit words and drama, and so its meanings are more deliberate.

70. See Kivy's discussion of Descartes in *Music Alone*, 32–36.

71. Kivy, *Music Alone*, 147–48. "Causal arousal theory" argues that music expresses an emotion if it causes listeners to experience a feeling that then causes them to believe that the work expresses that feeling. See Matravers, *Art and Emotion*.

72. Leppert, *The Sight of Sound*, 64–69. The citation is from 69. He argues that music is "an activity subject to the gaze, not least because music, both as social practice and sonority, was thought to possess sensual power. It was understood to act with dangerous immediacy on the sensate body. The 'musical' gaze was supercharged with sexuality, producing an 'interest' simultaneously encoded with pleasure and anxiety" (64). Thus music was a threat to "the instrumentalized variety of reason, to power, and to men" (65).

73. Both Susan McClary and Catherine Clément have argued that this physiological and emotional response to music can make us "forget the plot" (Clément, *Opera, or the Undoing of Women*, 10). As McClary puts it in "The Undoing of Opera": "Now to be sure, most audience members have no idea how Bizet [in his opera *Carmen*] causes their pulse to race more quickly or to suspend breathing in anticipation of the final cadence/stabbing. Because they can claim to be paying less attention to the action per se than to the beauty of the music, they can leave the hall feeling edified – not as though they had just witnessed a snuff film" (xiv). This position, however, ignores the complexity of the emotional response, which arguably has as much to do with the final stabbing as with the final musical cadence.

74. See Henson, "Neurological Aspects of Musical Experience," 8–9. For more precision, see Hachinski and Hachinski, "Music and the Brain": "The right hemisphere is clearly dominant in music interpretation and the processing of global harmonics. As well, the right hemisphere better discriminates subtle harmonic differences within complex tones. The left hemisphere dovetails its abilities with the right, processing and interpreting general contours and local variations in melody. The

left hemisphere is also capable of superior sequencing and rhythmic ability. Closer investigation of both hemispheres reveals some localization of processing for each aspect of musical experience" (295). See also studies such as that of Messerli, Pegna, and Sordet on "Hemispheric Dominance," which also complicates somewhat the assertion that the right brain processes melody.

75. This description is indebted to that of Jourdain, *Music, the Brain, and Ecstasy*, 1–29. For a precise and music-focused description of hearing, see also Hood, "Psychological and Physiological Aspects of Hearing."

76. Barthes, "Listening," in *The Responsibility of Forms*, 245.

77. Jourdain, *Music, the Brain, and Ecstasy*, 249.

78. Jourdain, *Music, the Brain, and Ecstasy*, 264. See also 258–68 for more details on this processing.

79. Cather, "A Wagner Matinée," 495.

80. Clément, *Opera, or the Undoing of Women*, 43. She later says: "Reason returns – that stinking reason that has me standing now, walking, and accepting a dinner invitation, when what I need is to run straight for the sea" (175). Her description of her feelings at the end of the opera, however, brings together the Dionysian and the Apollonian: "My mind bristles with strange symptoms like the hysteric's body; I am full of excrescences, I am pimply with ideas and feverish with thoughts" (175).

81. Clément, *Opera, or the Undoing of Women*, 174.

82. Turnbull, *Mary Garden*, 110. It has been suggested that this may be one of the cases where pathology was involved.

83. See Koestenbaum, *The Queen's Throat*, 111; Pahlen, *Great Singers*, for Malibran (21), Lind (26), and Marie Renard (44); Kaufman, "The Grisi-Viardot Controversy, 1848–1852," 10, on Viardot.

84. One of the most amusing descriptions of a claque appears in Robertson Davies' novel *The Lyre of Orpheus*: "[A] claque is a small body of experts; applause, certainly, but not unorganized row; you must have your *bisseurs* who call out loud for encores; your *rieurs* who laugh at the right places – but just appreciative chuckles to encourage the others, not from the belly; your *pleureurs* who sob when sobs are needed; and, of course, the kind of clapping that encourages the uninformed to join in, which is not vulgar hand-smacking that makes the clapper look like a drunk. Good clapping must sound intelligent, and that calls for skill; you must know what part of the palm to smack. And all of

this must be carefully organized – yes, orchestrated – by the *capo di claque*" (390–91).

85. Leonardi and Pope, *The Diva's Mouth*, 43–44.

86. The citations and anecdotes are from, respectively, Ardoin and Fitzgerald, *Callas*, 99, and Bret, *Maria Callas*, 146–49.

87. Storr, *Music and the Mind*, 24–25.

88. Cather, "Paul's Case," 472, 477.

89. See Williams, "Film Bodies," 3–4; Peraino makes the same connection in "I Am an Opera," 127.

90. David Schwarz in *Listening Subjects* has linked this feeling to the "oceanic" fantasies we are said to experience when "the boundary separating the body from the external world seems dissolved or crossed in some way" (7).

91. For more detail, see Rohde, *Psyche*, 255–86.

92. Jourdain, *Music, the Brain, and Ecstasy*, 331. On a related medical point, Harrer and Harrer describe an experiment in which "almost complete suppression of music-induced autonomic responses" was effected through the administration of tranquilizers "without any concomitant reduction or alteration in the emotional musical experiences." This challenges the "view that the physical and autonomic components of affect constitute an inseparable entity" ("Music, Emotion and Autonomic Function," 216).

93. See Critchley, "Ecstatic and Synaesthetic Experiences," 219, and, for the previous point, 218.

94. See Levinthal, *Messengers of Paradise*, 178, on the study using Naloxone, a drug that blocks opiate receptors in the brain. Experimental subjects listening to music who were given the drug reported substantially reduced pleasure.

95. See Panksepp, "The Emotional Sources," 190–95, 173.

96. Respectively, these theories are those of Panksepp, "The Emotional Sources," 171, where it is argued that social neuropeptides are released in the brain both during music listening and when infant animals are separated from their mothers; Schwarz, according to whose Lacanian view in *Listening Subjects*, goose bumps on the skin are a sign of crossing the "sonorous threshold" between our adult bodies and our retrospective fantasies of the child's experience of being in the "sonorous envelope" of the womb (8); Twitchell, in *Dreadful Pleasures*,

who studies this adrenaline rush in horror films; and Goldstein, "Music/Endorphin Link."

97. See Henson, "Neurological Aspects of Musical Experience," 14–15; Critchley, "Ecstatic and Synaesthetic Experiences."

98. Barthes, *S/Z*, 109–10.

99. Respectively, Koestenbaum, *The Queen's Throat*, 4, and Abel, *Opera in the Flesh*, 91.

100. Abel, *Opera in the Flesh*, 92, 86, 28.

101. Levin, "Is There a Text in This Libido?"

102. Related questions would be: Why does Terry Castle use it when talking about diva worship by women in "In Praise of Birgitte Fassbänder"? Why does Elizabeth Wood, in "Sapphonics," feel the need to define a particular voice that thrills her as what she calls Sapphonic? That the answer lies in gay and lesbian criticism's focus on sexuality is obvious but not complete.

103. Davenport, *Of Lena Geyer*, 225, 232.

104. Poizat, *The Angel's Cry*, 36.

105. McClary, *Feminine Endings*, 24–25.

106. Storr, *Music and the Mind*, 94.

107. See, for examples, Small, *Musicking*, 147, and McClary, *Feminine Endings*, 12.

↣ Postlude. A Toast to Opera's Bodies

1. This is Nicholas Hytner's nonliteral but spirited translation of the libretto by Niccolò Minato, revised by Silvio Stampiglia. The Italian reads: "Del mio caro baco amabile / nell'impero suo potabile / amo solo d'abitar" ("L'acqua rende ipocondriaco, / il bon vin sin nel zodiaco, / la mia testa fa inalzar").

2. On the scientific work, see Heath, "An Introduction"; Serjeant, *A Man May Drink*, 109–12, 115, 148–64; Greenberg, "Alcohol in the Body"; Keller, "Other Effects of Alcohol." For the personal experience, consult your own memories.

3. It is not always easy to be convincing because so much physical action is involved. For example, in Johann Strauss's *Die Fledermaus*, when the drunken jailer answers a knock at the door, he returns to tell his superior that there are two women at the door – or maybe there is just one, for he is seeing everything double. Not only vision is affected, of course; balance, dexterity, and coordination are impaired, as the

jailer's superior notes when he tries to walk after drinking too much champagne at the party. In Rimsky-Korsakov's *May Night* (1880), Kalenik tries to dance but finds it impossible to move his feet properly. Speech errors, of course, are also commonly represented in opera. (See the extended study of Chin and Pisoni, *Alcohol and Speech*, 313–14.) While audiences today usually respond with laughter to such visual and aural humor, in North America, for instance, changing attitudes to public displays of drunkenness can alter audience response. Nevertheless, when the inebriation is clearly feigned, the laughter is usually unconditional: in Rossini and Sterbini's *Il Barbiere di Siviglia* (1816), the amorous Count Almaviva masquerades as a drunken soldier to gain entrance into Don Bartolo's house to see his beloved, Rosina. With their repetitions and clumsy rhythms, his music and speech in this scene offer a parody of those of a drunkard. He keeps missinging Bartolo's surname to great comic effect, calling him Balordo (slow-witted), Bertoldo (blockhead), and Barbaro (barbarian). When corrected, he simply asserts that there's little difference between those versions and Bartolo! And opera's many snoozing drunks, of course, also attest to another of alcohol's powers, its ability to produce drowsiness, a side-effect taken to its limits by the Polovtsi in Borodin's *Prince Igor* (1890) who drink and dance themselves into a stupor.

4. It would seem that only North American indigenes and Pacific Islanders did not manufacture their own fermented, brewed, or distilled beverages; Europeans introduced them into those cultures. See Marshall, "Introduction," 2. Alcohol was probably discovered accidentally through naturally fermenting fruit or some such source.

5. See Rohde, *Psyche*, 259.

6. Nahoum-Grappe, "Histoire du vin," 297–300.

7. Heath, "Anthropological Perspectives," 37.

8. See Serjeant, *A Man May Drink*, 20; Younger, *Gods, Men, and Wine*, 323.

9. Baudelaire, *Artificial Paradises*, "Wine," 5. In the French, in *Les Paradis artificiels*, "Le Vin": "Profondes joies du vin, qui ne vous a connues? Quiconque a eu un remords à évoquer, une douleur à noyer, un château en Espagne à bâtir, tous enfin vous ont invoqué, dieu mystérieux caché dans les fibres de la vigne. Qu'ils sont grands les spectacles du vin, illuminés par le soleil intérieur! Qu'elle est vraie et brûlante cette seconde jeunesse que l'homme puise en lui! Mais combien

sont redoutables aussi ses voluptés foudroyantes et ses enchantemens énervans [*sic*]" (28).

10. See, for instance, Gerber, "The Measure of Bacchus," 40 n.; Bratanov, "Le Problème de l'alcoolisme."

11. See O'Brien and Seller, "Attributes of Alcohol," for a detailed account. We can see this theme on the operatic stage in Benjamin Britten's *Noye's Fludde* (1958), his setting of the Chester Miracle Play, which retells the biblical story of Noah. In this version (unlike in Genesis), Noye's rebellious wife refuses to go into the ark, preferring to stay on land and drink "a pottill of Malmsine, good and strong" with her female "gossips." The opera's portrayal of Mrs. Noah as a "grotesque caricature" has been noted by critics: she is "depicted as ill-tempered, stubborn and ungracious, while her gossips (all female) are a bunch of gibbering idiots who can scarcely see further than the ends of their noses. So tedious are they that we are invited to greet their drowning as a blessed relief" (Wilcox, *Benjamin Britten's Operas*, 72). This loss of judgment from drink forces her sons to pick her up and carry her on board to save her life. In Genesis it is not Noah's wife but Noah himself, the first tiller of the soil and planter of vines, who becomes drunk. See Genesis 9: 20–27.

12. In the French, "Entends-tu s'agiter en moi et résonner les puissants refrains des temps anciens, les chants de l'amour et de la gloire? Je suis l'âme de la patrie, je suis moitié galant, moitié militaire. Je suis l'espoir des dimanches. *Le travail fait les jours prospères*, le vin fait les dimanches heureux. Les coudes sur la table de famille et les manches retroussés, tu me glorifieras fièrement, et tu seras vraiment content" ("Le Vin," 29–30, emphasis his).

13. See Jenner, "Medicine and Addiction," 21; Blocker Jr., "Introduction," 36; Porter, "The Drinking Man's Disease," 390–93.

14. See Poznanski, "Our Drinking Heritage," 43; Serjeant, *A Man May Drink*, 126–27; Austin, *Alcohol in Western Society*; Berton Roueché, "Alcohol in Human Culture."

15. Baudelaire, "Wine," 24; "Le Vin": "active la digestion, fortifie les muscles, et enrichit le sang" (53). He goes on to call wine "un support physique" (54).

16. See Warner, "Physiological Theory," 235. The move from seeing disease as the result of overstimulation (and therefore treatable through

purgatives and bloodletting) to seeing it as enfeebling and in need of stimulants such as alcohol is responsible for some of this retention of alcohol for therapeutic purposes.

17. See Kopperman, "The Cheapest Pay," 461–62, on the use of alcohol by medical officers in the eighteenth-century English army.

18. Jackson, *The Medicinal Value of French Brandy*, 244–51.

19. See also Watkins, introduction to *Wine*, discussing two papers in his collection that address wine antioxidants and the inhibition of cancer in animal models (by tempering thrombogenic risk factors) and French wine as inhibiting platelet aggregation and prolonging bleeding time (xi); see also Leake and Silverman, *Alcoholic Beverages in Clinical Medicine.*

20. See Cottino, "Italy," 160.

21. Serjeant, *A Man May Drink*, 127. At about the same time Lippich applied statistical methods to observations of two hundred alcohol users, demonstrating shortened life spans, while Rosch correlated physical degeneration to prior alcohol use from autopsy studies. See Sournia, *A History of Alcoholism*, 26, on F. W. Lippich, *Grundzuge zur Dipsobiostatik* (1834) and Rosch, *De l'abus des boissons spiriteuses* (1838).

Not surprisingly, the conjunction of the moral and the medical raised concerns about the offspring of drinking parents: the morbid tendency to drink might be passed on; the child might have increased congenital abnormalities or reduced vitality, or, if conceived when a parent was intoxicated, might suffer from epilepsy, imbecility, or other abnormalities of degeneracy. See Bynum, "Alcoholism and Degeneration," 59, on Emil Abderhalden's *Bibliographie der gesamten wissenschaftlichen Literatur über den Alkohol und den Alkoholismus*; see also Longmate, *The Waterdrinkers*, and Richardson, *The Temperance Lesson Book*. In fact, alcohol became a major concern in the nineteenth-century discourse of degeneracy deployed by all European (and North American) nations, though in different ways and at different moments. What all showed was a move to medicalize alcoholic excess into a syndrome of constitutional susceptibility called dipsomania and a chronic disease called alcoholism. These were linked to reduced productivity and vitality and thus to racial or national decline. On England, see Johnstone, "From Vice to Disease?" 38–52, and McDonald, "Introduction," 3–6; on France, see Bynum, "Alcoholism and Degeneration,"

60–61, and Huertas, "Madness and Degeneration, II," 2; on Germany, see Bynum, "Alcoholism and Degeneration," 62–64. In France placards urged the population (whose numbers were declining because of a decreasing birth rate) to save the endangered nation and fight alcoholism. Criminality and mental derangement were further linked to alcohol abuse by the Italian criminologist Cesare Lombroso and others, and the risk of progressive deterioration through hereditary decline was taken very seriously all across Western Europe and North America: Max Nordau's 1892 *Degeneration*, which was quickly translated into other European languages, was the most influential of these assertions of decline. This led in time to the questionable but ubiquitous eugenics discourse of the twentieth century. See Salasa, "Emile Zola," 15, and Marrus, "Social Drinking in the *Belle Epoque*," 118.

What these different nations also shared in their attitudes to drinking was a certain class bias: the largely middle-class temperance movements tended to see alcoholism as a problem of the working classes. Social historians have argued that times of widespread social change – such as the Industrial Revolution – were historically marked by increased drinking rates. As Peter C. Mancall notes in *Deadly Medicine*, 8, Friedrich Engels wrote in the 1840s of the widespread drunkenness that characterized the inhabitants of England's industrial areas, leading to declining health and morals, poverty, and broken homes. Unlike the private drinking habits of the middle and upper classes, the workers tended to drink in public houses in England, Germany, and France; therefore, their indulging was visible. Indeed, because it could be seen, this drinking was deemed potentially dangerous. See Schivelbusch, *Tastes of Paradise*, 166; Roberts, *Drink, Temperance and the Working Class*, 18; Logan, "The Age of Intoxication," 87. Excess was considered a threat to the social order, and the temperance movements became the middle-class intervention of choice. Of course, the bourgeois trading and manufacturing classes stood to gain directly from temperance in other ways: the work ethic, discipline, self-control, and sobriety were all means of protecting capitalist investment. Chronic intoxication made for unproductive workers: "The old drinking patterns were incompatible with modern industrial processes – with the precision and regularity required from the factory's work force," as Harrison writes in "The Power of Drink," 205. See Husch, "Leisure, Work, and Drugs,"

402–3; Snow, "Socialism," 244; Adler, "From Symbolic Exchange," 388; Huertas, "Madness and Degeneration, II," 11; Barrows, "After the Commune," 205; Brennan, *Public Drinking*, 78; Haine, *The World of the Paris Café*, 88–97. Emile Zola famously chronicled these lower-class drinking patterns of *belle époque* France in his novel *L'Assommoir*.

22. On temperance literature, see Booth, "The Drunkard's Progress."

23. Hippocrates: "id est cibi, potus, somnii, Venus, omnia moderata sint" [all things in moderation: food, drink, sleep, Venus]; "Luxuriosa res vinum et tumultuosa ebrietas" [Wine is a mocker, strong drink is raging]. St. Benedict's rules include "Vinum apostatare facit enim sapientes" [Wine makes even wise men go astray].

24. Belfiore, "Wine and *Catharsis*," 424.

25. Nahoum-Grappe, "France," 80.

26. See Green, *Shakespeare's* Merry Wives of Windsor, 95.

27. See Schmidgall, *Shakespeare and Opera*, 321–29, on the other operas on this subject.

28. White, *The Merry Wives of Windsor*, 14. In "Drunkenness in Shakespeare," Albert H. Tolman tries to argue (without great success) that Shakespeare was against drunkenness. Of interest is his noting of the diary entry of John Ward, vicar of Stratford: "Shakespeare, Drayton, and Ben Jonson had a merry meeting, and it seems drank too hard, for Shakespeare died of a fever there contracted" (88).

29. Respectively, White, *The Merry Wives of Windsor*, 81, and Roberts, *Shakespeare's English Comedy*, 106.

30. Conrad, *A Song of Love and Death*, 36. Conrad also calls Falstaff "a reverent Dionysian, the heir to both Don Giovanni and Wagner's Tristan" (36).

31. Corse, *Opera and the Uses of Language*, 95.

32. This shift of emphasis continues throughout the opera. When the "merry wives," Alice Ford and Meg Page, choose their terms of abuse for him, the insults are related not simply to his size (as in the play) but specifically to his drinking and excess: "Quell'otre! Quel tino! Quel re delle pancie" [That wineskin! That tub! That king of paunches]. Caius tells the jealous, suspicious husband Ford that Falstaff has voracious appetites ("voglie vorace"), and Bardolph uses elaborate descriptive imagery that draws on Falstaff's bad habits: "Quel paffuto plenilunio che il color del vino imporpora" [That plump full moon that the color

of wine turns purple]. The faithless Pistol too advises Ford to ply Falstaff with wine in order to get him to talk, since the knight inclines toward wine the way the willow tree leans toward the water ("Come all'acqua inclina il salice / così al vin quel Cavaliere").

33. In *"Libiamo, libiamo . . ."* Franco Onorati calls him humanized and interiorized, compared to the play's character (160).

34. Corse, *Opera and the Uses of Language*, 108. See Onorati's account in *"Libiamo, libiamo . . ."* of how the score accepts the challenge of the text: "man mano che il vino riscalda Falstaff, l'orchestra ci invia prima il trillo del flauto, poi quello degli archi e dei fiati, fino al coinvolgimento di tutta l'orchestra sulla battuta finale di Falstaff: 'E il trillo invade il mondo!' " (161).

35. Lindenberger, *Opera: The Extravagant Art*, 78.

36. In Act 2 of Kurt Weill and Bertolt Brecht's *Aufstieg und Fall der Stadt Mahagonny* (1930), at the "Here-You-May-Do-Anything Inn" Jim learns the consequences of the license to "swill your booze as long as you can." Because he cannot pay for his indulgence and his generous hospitality to his friends, he is condemned to death.

37. In the first act of Wagner's *Götterdämmerung*, Gunther and Siegfried mix their own blood together with wine and drink to blood-brother-hood ("Blut-Brüderschaft"). Drinking together – with or without sharing actual blood from arm wounds – has long been a symbolic way of consecrating the artificial blood relationship of friendship. The origins of this way of establishing human bonding appear to be religious, as is the case with the specific linking of blood and wine. The Christian notion of actually partaking of the blood of Christ has its antecedents in Dionysian practices, for we have seen that the gift of this god has consistently been considered a fertility symbol and a life-giving substance. See Faraone, "Introduction," and Obbink, "Dionysus Poured Out," on Dionysian sacramental practices.

The Christian communion consecrates and celebrates the blood and body of Christ through the sacramental wine and bread. In Beethoven's only opera, *Fidelio* (1805, 1814), when the jailer, Rocco, and the prisoner's disguised wife, Leonora, offer her imprisoned husband, Florestan, wine and bread, he blesses them and tells them they will be rewarded in a better world. This symbolic moment of communion is sufficient for Leonora to be able to assure her husband that there is indeed a Providence watching over him. But the Christian communion also includes within it the idea of a fraternal meal, a communal dimension of conviviality, communication, and bonding. Therefore, communicants not only become one with the godhead by the act of physical incorporation of the transubstantiated blood, but they unite with their fellow humans. In the European cultural context, each time this human union is reenacted and celebrated through social drinking, these Christian associations (with their pagan history) are implicitly evoked.

Sometimes the evocation is explicit, however, as it is in Wagner's final work *Parsifal* (1882). The Holy Grail – according to legend, the cup used at the Last Supper that then received the blood from the wound in the side of the crucified Christ – is the focus of a "Liebesmahle," a feast of love, among the Grail Knights. In a barely disguised Eucharistic celebration, the bread and wine are consecrated as youthful voices sing: "Nehmet hin mein Blut, / nehmet hin meinen Leib, / auf dass ihr mein gedenkt!" [Take and drink my blood, / take my body and eat, / as a remembrance of me!]. They sing of the Last Supper and Christ's first transfiguration of bread and wine through the power of love and compassion as the knights partake of and seek transcendence through eating and drinking these symbolic elements. As a result they are at once spiritually refreshed and also united in brotherhood – and courage – with each other. The brotherhood of knights is affirmed and strengthened through this communal activity.

While the southern parts of Europe – Italy, Spain, Greece – show less tolerance for Dionysian excess, drinking is associated with specifically male sociability. Here, excess is seen as incompatible with the elaborate network of social relationships based on drinking that is part of these cultures. See Cottino, "Italy," 158, and Gefou-Madianou, "Introduction," 8–12, for a feminist reading of male bonding through drink. See Driessen, "Drinking on Masculinity," 73, on Spanish, specifically Andalusian, ritualized behavior in taverns. In the Sicilian village of Mascagni's *Cavalleria Rusticana* (1890), Turiddu sings a *brindisi* to sparkling wine, which, like the laugh of a lover, brings joy: "Viva il vino ch'è sincero / e che annega l'umor nero / nell'ebbrezza tenera" [Long live wine, which is unadulterated / and which chases away black moods / in tender inebriation]. He offers a glass to Alfio, the cuckolded husband of his lover, Lola. When Alfio refuses, saying it would be like poison in his breast, he is in fact refusing any relationship of community with Turiddu. The audience recognizes that this breach of the custom of hospitality is the sign of a deliberate and major social infraction: the two men exchange challenges and agree to fight. It is because these strict codes of social bonding are so well known and so widely accepted that infringing upon them can be a powerful dramatic device in an opera.

38. On the physiological studies, see Brain, *Alcohol and Aggression*; for a typical study of violence and drink, see Forrest and Gordon, *Substance Abuse*.

39. On France, see Haine, *The World of the Paris Café*, 102, 115; on English and American legal decisions, see McCord, "The English and American History."

40. Alban Berg's 1925 opera *Wozzeck* features drinking in many diverse but equally revealing situations and contexts, many of which end up involving violence. In the garden of an inn, two journeymen sing about drinking in utterly different ways. One is a morose drunk, lamenting that his immortal soul stinks of brandy ("Meine Seele, meine unsterbliche Seele / stinket nach Branntewein!") and that the world is filled only with sadness. His companion, a happy drunk, sings about the beauty of the world and friendship: "Ich wollt', unsre Nasen wären zwei / Bouteillen, und wir könnten sie uns / einander in den Hals giessen. / Die ganze Welt ist rosenrot! / Branntwein, das is mein Leben!" [I wish our noses were two / bottles and we could pour them / down each other's throats. / The whole world is rosy red! / Brandy, that's my life!]. This scene sets up a later one in which we witness firsthand the aggression associated with alcohol consumption. An impoverished soldier, Wozzeck cannot afford to drink; the Drum Major, however, can. One night, he returns drunk to the barracks to taunt Wozzeck about his sexual dalliance with Marie, Wozzeck's woman: "Da, Kerl, sauf'! / Ich wollt', die Welt wär / Schnaps, Schnaps, der / Mensch muss saufen" [There, you fellow, drink! / I wish the world were / schnapps, schnapps, a / man must drink]. Manliness is clearly tied to drink, and here alcohol leads to violence: beating the hapless Wozzeck, the Drum Major then sings with self-satisfied pleasure of what a man he is ("was bin ich für ein Mann!").

41. See Cottino, "Science and Class Structure," 49–52, on Lombroso's work on this topic.

42. Kerman, *Opera as Drama*, 116.

43. Review by Filippo Filippi in *La Perseveranza*, 15 February 1887, in Hans Busch, ed., *Verdi's* Otello *and* Simon Boccanegra, 2: 683.

44. Budden, *The Operas of Verdi*, 345.

45. In Busch, *Verdi's* Otello *and* Simon Boccanegra, 2: 510. The discussion that follows is from the following page.

46. Hepokoski, *Giuseppe Verdi:* Otello, 5; Budden, *The Operas of Verdi*, 347.

47. Hepokoski, *Giuseppe Verdi:* Otello, 4.

48. Camille Bellaigue, in the *Revue des deux mondes*, 1 March 1887, in Busch, *Verdi's* Otello *and* Simon Boccanegra, 2: 694.

49. In Busch, *Verdi's* Otello *and* Simon Boccanegra, 2: 644.

50. The citations are, respectively, from Kerman, *Opera as Drama*, 116, and Hepokoski, *Giuseppe Verdi:* Otello, 4.

51. In a letter to Verdi (6 September 1886), Boito wrote that women could be added to the chorus in this scene as long as they did not spoil "the masculine boldness of this piece." See Busch, *Verdi's* Otello *and* Simon Boccanegra, 1: 235.

52. Antonioli, "L'Eloge du vin," 135–37.

53. See Bruun, "Drinking Practices," 224, on Donald Horton's work on how drink reduces feelings of anxiety and is therefore experienced as a reward, gets repeated, and then becomes a social custom. But drink also encourages transgression of social norms through expressions of sexual and aggressive impulses. Awkwardly, but accurately, these reactions have been called drink's "control-anesthetizing (disinhibiting) effects" in the *Encyclopedia Britannica*, 15th ed., 13: 198.

54. See Burnham, *Bad Habits*, for an extended study of the role of respectability and countercultural "bad habits."

55. Bledsoe, in "Chastity and Darkness," writes that "the public community aspect of this scene (II,i) celebrates chastity with a smirk, but the musical allusions to *Tristan* prepare us for the possibility of a less farcical attitude to chastity than before – less farcical but much more comic" (128–29). On the function of musical parody in the opera, see Evans, *The Music of Benjamin Britten*, 145–62.

56. Mitchell, "The Serious Comedy": "nowhere is the *inside/outside* nature of Albert's predicament spelled out more clearly in this subtle opera" (47).

57. Kennedy, *Britten*, 174, and Oliver, *Benjamin Britten*, 132. In "Character and Caricature," Philip Brett argues that the threnody is really

about the mourning of the village over its loss of power over Albert (547).

58. White, *Benjamin Britten*, 155.

59. White, *Benjamin Britten*, 155–56; del Mar, "The Chamber Operas II," 149; Evans, *The Music of Benjamin Britten*, 156.

60. Oliver, *Benjamin Britten*, 132. See also Howard, *The Operas of Benjamin Britten*: "nothing in his 'liberated' character in the last scenes leads us to imagine that he could ever achieve it [Sid's idea of love]. The puritan confusion which enabled the inhabitants of Loxford to identify love and drunkenness as being sins of a kind seems also to have confused the composer and librettist" (51). This assumes, however, that neither creator intended the mediated transposition from one "bad habit" to another.

61. There has been considerable debate over Albert's sexual orientation. In *Benjamin Britten's Operas*, Michael Wilcox argues that "the serious core of the drama" is Albert's homosexual initiation and enumerates the coded references in the libretto: it is dedicated to E. M. Forster, known to be attracted to young, lower-class men; Albert notes, "Girls don't care for chaps like me"; the contemporaneous codes of cruising are invoked (the Swan Vesta matches about which Albert sings, the man whistling in the dark) (37–44). Brett reads it as a "parable of liberation" in which Albert becomes himself, sexually as well as psychologically ("Character and Caricature," 545). In *Britten*, Christopher Headington opposes the gay reading, arguing that the opera is not about sex at all but "a serious statement about the whole human condition" (66). Whatever Albert's sexual orientation, the point seems to be that the alcohol liberated him sufficiently that he could break with social restraints and be sexually initiated. The earlier finding of his May King wreath of flowers crushed on the roadway is an obvious and playful symbol of his defloration.

62. Stein, "*Albert Herring*," 132. Arnold Whittall, in *The Music of Britten and Tippett*, notes that the final music suggests that "Albert seems almost smugly content" (122).

63. Law, "Daring to Eat a Peach," 5, 8.

64. On the Bacchus/Venus conjunction, when the chorus sings in celebration of carnival in Franz Schmidt's opera *Notre Dame*, it links together wine and love through their respective deities: "Bacchus lebe hoch!

Frau Venus hoch." This Dionysian connection with the erotic is so frequently made on the operatic stage that it is now a cliché. In Act 3 of *La Bohème* (1896), the voices heard from inside the tavern where Marcello and Musetta work sing the pleasures of love and wine: "Chi nel ber trovò il piacer / nel suo bicchier, nel suo bicchier! Aa! / D'una bocca nell'ardor, / trovò l'amor, trovò l'amor!" [Whoever found pleasure in drinking / from his glass, from his glass! Ah! / In passion, from a mouth / found love, found love!]. There has been a long association of alcohol with the arousal and intensification of erotic desire – at least when consumed in moderation: it seems that, for men, excess leads to impotence, if not simply sleep. But moderate drinking appears to result in social disinhibition and an increase in sexual risk taking. See Schuster, *Alcohol and Sexuality*, 115. Yet recent experiments have shown that women as well can feel that sexual arousal is facilitated by drinking even though the physiological evidence does not exist to support such a view. Perhaps that is why drink is featured so often as an aid to seduction. Think of Richard Strauss and Hugo von Hofmannsthal's *Der Rosenkavalier* (1911), in which the libidinous Baron Ochs tries to seduce the (doubly) cross-dressed maid "Mariandel" with wine that "she" keeps refusing. Mozart and Da Ponte's even more disreputable *Don Giovanni* tells his servant, Leporello, to prepare a great drunken feast for the local peasants: "Fin ch'han dal vino / calda la testa" [Until they have from the wine / a hot head]. His aim? The next morning there should be more women's names to add to his famous list of conquests. The man whom Leporello describes as having a barbarous appetite ("barbaro appetito") – for women, wine, and food – understands well the time-tested relationship between wine and sexual conquest.

The even more frequent dramatic task of alcohol in opera is to act as a more benign kind of facilitator or mediator in love. It is not accidental that love potions (real or fake) are usually wine-based. Auber's *Le Philtre* (1831) and Donizetti's *L'Elisir d'Amore* (1832) both tell the same story of love aided and abetted by wine. In each, the heroine reads aloud the legend of Tristan and Isolde (not the operatic one, for it came later) and tells of the love potion that sealed their passion and their fate. A visiting quack then sells the desperate and gullible hero a bottle of wine that he claims is the love potion of Queen Isolde. As he drinks the claret, Donizetti's Nemorino sings of its pleasant warmth coursing through his veins ("qual di vena in vena / dolce calor mi scorre!"). He begins to believe in the efficacy of the "potion" when all the village girls start to pay attention to him: what he does not yet know is that they are already aware that his rich uncle has died and left him a wealthy and thus exceedingly attractive man.

However, it does not take the pretense of a love potion for wine to have a positive effect on relations between the sexes. In that famous *brindisi* in *La Traviata* (1853), Alfredo's toast is to the joy of drink that, as the libretto puts it, can bring on love and even warmer kisses. Violetta answers him with a *carpe diem* message focused entirely on love – as if the wine were no longer even required. Mead rather than wine serves this same symbolic function in Wagner's *Die Walküre* (1870), when Sieglinde offers a horn of the honey wine to the stranger, Siegmund, initially simply as a sign of hospitality. However, when he asks her to drink from it first, he alters the public, social rule to a more intimate one, and their exchanged looks tell of their strong physical attraction.

Because of this recurrent cultural linking of the realms of Dionysus and Venus, alcohol and passion, the toast specifically to love is commonplace in opera. It is because of the strength and ubiquity of this love-toast convention that transgressions of it stand out for audiences as morally reprehensible. In Puccini's *Madama Butterfly* (1904), just before the American sailor, Pinkerton, is about to "wed" the devoted Cio-Cio-San, he sings a cynical toast to the day when he will get married for real – that is, to an American wife ("E al giorno in cui mi sposerò con vere nozze, a una vera sposa . . . americana"). For Pinkerton to betray the social conventions of the love toast is, in effect, publicly to declare himself to the audience as the cad he is.

65. Préaud, "Le Vin et la mélancolie," 289–90.

66. Baudelaire, "Wine," 27.

67. There is considerable disagreement about whether the historical Hoffmann was actually an alcoholically inspired genius or simply yet another writer who used drink as a minor stimulant to higher artistic production: his autobiographical character, Johannes Kreisler, certainly saw alcohol as "a kind of psychic lubricant favoring the realization of poetic images" (Jennings, "The Role of Alcohol," 182). See also Jeanvoine, "Hoffmann," 340–41; Hewett-Thayer, *Hoffmann*, 161–62.

Some critics are quick to point out that, in Hoffmann's stories, the drink-induced visions merely mirror sober ones: "Hoffmann's alcohol is a mind-enhancing drug. It may be the key to ethereal bliss; it may animate and then befuddle; it may yield glimpses of heaven or hell. It does nothing, however, that the mind may not do alone" (Jennings, "The Role of Alcohol," 190).

68. See Neumann, "Der Erzählakt als Oper," 49, on the debate that involved figures such as Alfred de Musset, Théophile Gautier, Gérard de Nerval, as well as Baudelaire. The Barbier and Carré play of 1851 captures some of the debate, adding the tension between aesthetic inspiration and the erotic. In 1864 Cesare Lombroso attributed Hoffmann's genius to an intoxicated, debilitated mind, calling him a "mad drinker"; see McGlathery, *Mysticism and Sexuality*, 35. This view continued in the representations of Hoffmann as a man of unsound mind, debauched by a life of excess. His knowledge of madness, as manifested in his writings, was therefore seen as autobiographical, though others argue that his trips to the asylum at St. Gereu outside Bamberg were the real source of this knowledge. See Taylor, *Hoffmann*, 70. In "Hoffmann buveur de vin," Pierre Brunel attempts to sort out the French literary myth of Hoffmann from the biographical reality. See also Montandon, "L'Imaginaire du vin," 162, on Hoffmann's desire to cure his ailments by drinking inspired by the Scots doctor, Dr. John Brown, for whom wine was a stimulant used to cure diseases caused by lack of excitation. See also Faris, *Jacques Offenbach*, on the popularity of Hoffmann in France (196–98) and the evidence about his actual drinking (207).

69. Nahoum-Grappe, "France," 79.

70. Barrows, "After the Commune," 208.

71. Baudelaire, "Wine," 13; in "Le Vin": "certaines boissons contiennent la faculté d'augmenter outre mesure la personnalité de l'être pensant, et de créer, pour ainsi dire, une troisième personne, opération mystique, où l'homme naturel et le vin, le dieu animal et le dieu végétal, jouent le rôle du Père et du Fils dans la Trinité; ils engendrent un Saint-Esprit, qui est l'homme supérieur, lequel procède également des deux" (39).

72. Bachelard, *The Psychoanalysis of Fire*, 87, 89.

73. On the possibility of schizophrenia, see Enachescu, "Alcoolisme et création littéraire," 145.

74. Warner, "Editor's Introduction," 182.

75. Younger, *Gods, Men, and Wine,* 69.

76. Goodwin, "Alcohol as Muse," 4; Crowley, *The White Logic.*

77. Conrad, *A Song of Love and Death,* 38.

78. Lindenberger, *Opera in History,* 98.

79. Lindenberger, *Opera in History,* 76, his emphasis, and 271; see also Lindenberger, *Opera: The Extravagant Art.*

80. See Rossi, "A Tale of Two Countries," 96.

Bibliography

Abbate, Carolyn. "Elektra's Voice: Music and Language in Strauss's Opera." In *Richard Strauss: Elektra*. Ed. Derrick Puffett. Cambridge: Cambridge University Press, 1989. 107–27.

———. "Opera; or the Envoicing of Women." In *Musicology and Difference: Gender and Sexuality in Music Scholarship*. Ed. Ruth A. Solie. Berkeley: University of California Press, 1993. 225–58.

———. *Unsung Voices: Opera and Musical Narrative in the Nineteenth Century*. Princeton NJ: Princeton University Press, 1991.

Abel, Sam. *Opera in the Flesh: Sexuality in Operatic Performance*. Boulder CO: Westview Press, 1996.

Abran, Henri. *L'Influence de la musique sur l'apprentissage, le comportement et la santé*. Montreal: Editions Québec/Amérique, 1989.

Adam, Elgna, and Laurent Worms. "Salomé au pays des hommes." *L'Avant-scène opéra* 47–48 (1983): 154–57.

Adams, Karen C. "Neoplatonic Aesthetic Tradition in the Arts." *College Music Symposium* 17.2 (1977): 17–24.

Adams, Nancy Ruth. " 'Elektra' as Opera and Drama." Diss., University of Pennsylvania, 1989.

Adler, Marianna. "From Symbolic Exchange to Commodity Consumption: Anthropological Notes on Drinking as a Symbolic Practice." In *Drinking: Behavior and Belief in Modern History*. Ed. Susanna Barrows and Robin Room. Berkeley: University of California Press, 1991. 376–98.

Adorno, Theodor W. "Bourgeois Opera." In *Opera through Other Eyes*. Ed. David J. Levin. Stanford CA: Stanford University Press, 1994. 25–43.

———. "The Curves of the Needle." Trans. Thomas Y. Levin. *October* 55 (1990): 48–55.

———. "Opera and the Long-Playing Record." Trans. Thomas Y. Levin. *October* 55 (1990): 62–66.

———. "Richard Strauss, Part II." *Perspectives of New Music* 4.2 (1966): 113–25.

Aeschylus. *The Libation Bearers.* In *The Orestes Plays of Aeschylus.* Trans. Paul Roche. New York: New American Library, 1962. 101–53.

Albert, Jean-Pierre. "Le Vin sans l'ivresse: Remarques sur la liturgie eucharistique." In *Le Ferment divin.* Ed. Dominique Fournier and Salvatore D'Onofrio. Paris: Editions de la maison des sciences de l'homme, 1991. 77–92.

Alexander, Alfred. *Operanatomy.* Boston: Crescendo, 1974.

Allegri, Renzo, and Roberto Allegri. *Callas by Callas: The Secret Writings of "la Maria."* New York: Universe Publishing, 1997.

Allemand, Evelyn-Dorothée, and Catherine Camboulives. " 'La Belle Dame sans merci.' " In *Salomé dans les collections françaises.* St.-Denis: Musée d'art et d'histoire, 1988. 25–27.

Allen, K., and J. Blascovich. "Effects of Music on Cardiovascular Reactivity among Surgeons." *Journal of the American Medical Association* 21 September 1994: 882–84.

Alliez, Eric, and Michel Feher. "Reflections of a Soul." Trans. Janet Lloyd. In *Fragments for a History of the Human Body.* Ed. Michel Feher, Ramona Naddaff, and Nadia Tazi. New York: Zone, 1989. 2:46–84.

Andry, Nicolas. *Orthopaedia: Or, the Art of Correcting and Preventing Deformities in Children.* 1742. Birmingham AL: Classics of Medicine Library, 1980.

Antonioli, Roland. "L'Eloge du vin dans l'oeuvre de Rabelais." *L'Imaginaire du vin: Colloque pluridisciplinaire.* Ed. Max Milner and Martine Chatelain. Marseille: Jeanne Laffitte, 1983. 132–38.

Apte, Mahadev L. *Humor and Laughter: An Anthropological Approach.* Ithaca NY: Cornell University Press, 1985.

Arblaster, Anthony. *Viva la libertà: Politics in Opera.* London: Verso, 1992.

Ardoin, John. *The Callas Legacy: The Complete Guide to Her Recordings on Compact Discs.* 4th ed. London: Duckworth, 1995.

Ardoin, John, and Gerald Fitzgerald. *Callas: The Art and Life* and *The Great Years.* New York: Holt, Rinehart and Winston, 1974.

Aschheim, Steven E. *The Nietzsche Legacy in Germany 1890–1990.* Berkeley: University of California Press, 1992.

Attali, Jacques. *Noise: The Political Economy of Music.* Trans. Brian Massumi. Minneapolis: University of Minnesota Press, 1985.

Austin, Gregory A. *Alcohol in Western Society from Antiquity to 1800: A Chronological History.* Santa Barbara CA: ABC-Clio Information Services, 1985.

Ayrey, Craig. "Salome's Final Monologue." In *Richard Strauss: Salome*. Ed. Derrick Puffett. Cambridge: Cambridge University Press, 1989. 109–30.

Babor, Thomas. *Alcohol: Customs and Rituals*. London: Burke, 1986.

Bachelard, Gaston. *The Psychoanalysis of Fire*. Trans. Alan C. M. Ross. Boston: Beacon Press, 1964.

Bade, Patrick. *Femme Fatale: Images of Evil and Fascinating Women*. London: Ash and Grant, 1979.

Bakhtin, Mikhail. *Rabelais and His World*. Trans. Hélène Iswolsky. Cambridge MA: MIT Press, 1968.

Bales, Suzanne E. "*Elektra*: From Hofmannsthal to Strauss." Diss., Stanford University, 1984.

Banes, Sally. *Dancing Women: Female Bodies on Stage*. London and New York: Routledge, 1998.

Banks, Paul. "Richard Strauss and the Unveiling of 'Salome.'" In *Richard Strauss: Salome and* Elektra. ENO Opera Guide 37. London: Calder; New York: Riverrun, 1988. 7–21.

Banning, Mary Rus, and David L. Nelson. "The Effects of Activity-Elicited Humor and Group Structure on Group Cohesion and Affective Responses." *American Journal of Occupational Therapy* 41.8 (1987): 510–14.

Barber, David W. *When the Fat Lady Sings: Opera History as It Ought to Be Taught*. Toronto: Sound and Vision, 1990.

Barr, Andrew. *Drink*. New York: Bantam, 1996.

Barrows, Susanna. "After the Commune: Alcoholism, Temperance, and Literature in the Early Third Republic." In *Consciousness and Class Experience in Nineteenth-Century Europe*. Ed. John M. Merriman. New York: Holmes and Meier, 1979. 205–18.

Barrows, Susanna, and Robin Room, eds. *Drinking: Behavior and Belief in Modern History*. Berkeley: University of California Press, 1991.

Barthes, Roland. *The Responsibility of Forms: Critical Essays on Music, Art, and Representation*. Trans. Richard Howard. New York: Hill and Wang, 1985.

———. *S/Z*. Trans. Richard Miller. New York: Hill and Wang, 1974.

Battersby, Christine. *Gender and Genius*. London: Women's Press, 1989.

Baudelaire, Charles. *Artificial Paradises*. Trans. Stacy Diamond. New York: Citadel Press, 1996.

———. *Les Paradis artificiels*. Ed. Yves Florenne. Paris: Livre de poche, 1972.

Beal, Timothy K., and David M. Gunn, eds. *Reading Bibles, Writing Bodies: Identity and the Book*. London and New York: Routledge, 1997.

Beaudoin, Charles. *Psychanalyse de Victor Hugo*. Geneva: Editions du Mont-Blanc, 1943.

Becker, Heinz. "Richard Strauss als Dramatiker." In *Beiträge zur Geschichte der Oper*. Ed. Heinz Becker. Regensburg: Gustav Bosse Verlag, 1969. 165–81.

Becker-Leckrone, Megan. "Salome© : The Fetishization of a Textual Corpus." *New Literary History* 26 (1995): 239–60.

Bednar, Elisabeth A. "Self-Help for the Facially Disfigured: Commentary on 'The Quasimodo Complex.'" In *The Tyranny of the Normal: An Anthology*. Ed. Carol Donley and Sheryl Buckley. Kent OH: Kent State University Press, 1996. 53–54.

Bekker, Paul. "Elektra." *Neue Musik Zeitung* 30.14 (1909): 293–98.

———. "Elektra." *Neue Musik Zeitung* 30.17 (1909): 387–91.

Belfiore, Elizabeth. "Wine and *Catharsis* of the Emotions in Plato's *Laws*." *Classical Quarterly* 36.2 (1986): 421–37.

Bennett, Susan. *Theatre Audiences: A Theory of Production and Reception*. 2d ed. London and New York: Routledge, 1997.

Benninger, Michael. "Medical Disorders in the Vocal Artist." In *Vocal Arts Medicine: The Care and Prevention of Professional Voice Disorders*. Ed. Michael S. Benninger, Barbara H. Jacobson, and Alex F. Johnson. New York: Theieme Medical Publishers, 1994. 177–268.

Benninger, Michael S., Barbara H. Jacobson, and Alex F. Johnson, eds. *Vocal Arts Medicine: The Care and Prevention of Professional Voice Disorders*. New York: Theieme Medical Publishers, 1994.

Bentley, Eric. *The Playwright as Thinker*. New York: Reynal, 1946.

Berger, John. *Ways of Seeing*. London: BBC; Markham ON: Penguin, 1978.

Bermúdez, José Luis, Anthony Marcel, and Naomi Eilan, eds. *The Body and the Self*. Cambridge MA: MIT Press, 1995.

Bernstein, Tamara. "Is the Opera House Hot or Is It Just Me?" *National Post* 10 May 1999: D6–7.

———. "The Opera-lover's Revenge." *National Post* 21 December 1998: D8.

Bianciotti, Hector. "Une Voix et son corps." *L'Avant-scène opéra* 44 (1982): 8–9.

Binet, A., and J. Courtier. "Influence de la musique sur la respiration, le coeur et la circulation capillaire." *L'Année psychologique* 3 (1897): 104–26.

Bizot, Richard. "The Turn-of-the-Century Salome Era: High and Pop-Culture Variations on the Dance of the Seven Veils." *Choreography and Dance* 2.3 (1992): 71–87.

Bjerén, Gunilla. "Drinking and Masculinity in Everyday Swedish Culture." In *Alcohol, Gender and Culture*. Ed. Dimitra Gefou-Madianou. London and New York: Routledge, 1992. 157–66.

Blackmer, Corinne E., and Patricia Juliana Smith, eds. *En Travesti: Women, Gender Subversion, Opera*. New York: Columbia University Press, 1995.

Blau, Herbert. *Blooded Thought: Occasions of Theatre*. New York: Performing Arts Journal Publications, 1982.

Bledsoe, Robert Terrell. "Chastity and Darkness in *Albert Herring*." *Mosaic* 18.4 (1985): 125–33.

Blier, Steven. "Time after Time." *Opera News* (October 1996): 10–14, 64.

Bloch, Susana, Madeleine Lemeignan, and Nancy Aguilera-T. "Specific Respiratory Patterns Distinguish among Human Basic Emotions." *Internal Journal of Psychophysiology* 11.2 (1991): 141–54.

Blocker, Jack S., Jr. "Introduction." Special issue on the Social History of Alcohol of *Social History* 54 (1994): 225–39.

Bondeson, Jan. *A Cabinet of Medical Curiosities*. Ithaca NY: Cornell University Press, 1998.

Boone, Daniel R. "Biologic Enemies of the Professional Voice." *Journal of Research in Singing and Applied Voice Pedagogy* 16.2 (1993): 15–24.

———. "The Three Ages of Voice: The Singing/Acting Voice in the Mature Adult." *Journal of Voice* 11.2 (1997): 161–64.

———. "Vocal Hygiene: The Optimal Use of the Larynx." *Journal of Research in Singing* 4.1 (1980): 35–43.

Boone, Daniel R., and Stephen C. McFarlane. *The Voice and Voice Therapy*. 4th ed. Englewood Cliffs NJ: Prentice-Hall, 1971.

Booth, Michael R. "The Drunkard's Progress: Nineteenth-Century Temperance Drama." *Dalhousie Review* 44 (1964): 205–12.

Bordo, Susan. "Kvetchy, Vain, Bald Men and Glamorous Women." *Chronicle of Higher Education* 14 August 1998: B9.

———. *Unbearable Weight: Feminism, Western Culture, and the Body*. Berkeley: University of California Press, 1993.

Bottenberg, Joanna. "Richard Strauss's Interpretation of the Recognition Scene in Hofmannsthal's *Elektra*." *Seminar* 30 (1994): 360–77.

Bottomley, F. *Attitudes to the Body in Western Christendom*. London: Lepus Books, 1979.

Brain, Paul F., ed. *Alcohol and Aggression*. London: Croom Helm, 1986.

Bratanov, Dimitre. "Le Problème de l'alcoolisme dans la littérature mondiale." *Revue de l'alcoolisme* 15 (1969): 215–32.

Breed, Warren, and James DeFoe. "The Portrayal of the Drinking Process on Prime-Time Television." *Journal of Communication* 31 (1981): 58–67.

Brennan, Thomas. *Public Drinking and Popular Culture in Eighteenth-Century Paris*. Princeton NJ: Princeton University Press, 1988.

———. "Towards the Cultural History of Alcohol in France." *Journal of Social History* 23 (1989): 71–92.

Brèque, Jean-Michel. "La Salomé d'Oscar Wilde." *L'Avant-scène opéra* 47–48 (1983): 24–35.

Bret, David. *Maria Callas: The Tigress and the Lamb*. London: Robson Books, 1997.

Brett, Philip. "Character and Caricature in 'Albert Herring.'" *Musical Times* 127 (October 1986): 545–47.

———. "Eros and Orientalism in Britten's Operas." In *Queering the Pitch: The New Gay and Lesbian Musicology*. Ed. Philip Brett, Elizabeth Wood, and Gary C. Thomas. New York and London: Routledge, 1994. 235–56.

———. "Musicality, Essentialism, and the Closet." In *Queering the Pitch: The New Gay and Lesbian Musicology*. Ed. Philip Brett, Elizabeth Wood, and Gary C. Thomas. New York and London: Routledge, 1994. 9–26.

Brett, Philip, Elizabeth Wood, and Gary C. Thomas, eds. *Queering the Pitch: The New Gay and Lesbian Musicology*. New York and London: Routledge, 1994.

Breuer, Robert. "*Elektra* in der Bearbeitung von Sophokles und Hofmannsthal-Strauss." *Richard Strauss–Blätter* 30 (December 1993): 22–31.

Bronfen, Elisabeth. "'Lasciatemi Morir': Representations of the Diva's Swan Song." *Modern Language Quarterly* 53 (1992): 427–48.

Brooks, Peter. *Body Work: Objects of Desire in Modern Narrative*. Cambridge MA: Harvard University Press, 1993.

Brophy, Brigid. *Mozart the Dramatist: The Value of His Opera to Him, to His Age, and to Us*. Rev. ed. London: Libris, 1988.

Brouillet, George Antoine. *Voice Manual*. 1936. Boston: Crescendo Publishing, 1974.

Brown, David. *Tchaikovsky: The Crisis Years, 1874–1888*. New York: Norton, 1983.

Brown, Peter. *The Body and Society: Men, Women and Sexual Renunciation in Early Christianity*. New York: Columbia University Press, 1988.

Brunel, Pierre. "Hoffmann buveur de vin: Un mythe du romantisme français?" In *L'Imaginaire du vin: Colloque pluridisciplinaire*. Ed. Max Milner and Martine Chatelain. Marseille: Jeanne Laffitte, 1983. 167–80.

Bruun, Kettil. "Drinking Practices and Their Social Function." In *Alcohol and Civilization*. Ed. Salvatore Pablo Lucia. New York: McGraw-Hill, 1963. 218–28.

Bryson, Norman. *Vision and Painting: The Logic of the Gaze*. New Haven CT: Yale University Press, 1983.

Bucknell, Bradley. "On 'Seeing' Salome." *ELH* 60 (1993): 503–26.

Budden, Julian. *The Operas of Verdi*. 3 vols. Oxford and New York: Clarendon Press, 1992.

Bunch, Meribeth. *Dynamics of the Singing Voice*. 4th ed. Vienna: Springer, 1997.

Burkert, Walter. *Greek Religion*. Trans. John Raffan. Cambridge MA: Harvard University Press, 1985.

Burnham, John C. *Bad Habits: Drinking, Smoking, Taking Drugs, Gambling, Sexual Misbehavior, and Swearing in American History*. New York: New York University Press, 1993.

Burroughs, Bruce. "Da Capo . . ." *Opera Quarterly* 9.3 (1993): 1–9.

———. "Maria Callas: 'Yes, but . . .' " *Opera Quarterly* 6.4 (1989): 1–6.

Busch, Hans, ed. *Verdi's* Otello *and* Simon Boccanegra *(Revised Version) in Letters and Documents*. Trans. Hans Busch. 2 vols. Oxford: Clarendon Press, 1988.

Buss, David M. "The Strategies of Human Mating." *American Scientist* 82 (1994): 238–49.

Bynum, Carolyn. "Why All the Fuss about the Body? A Medievalist's Perspective." *Critical Inquiry* 22 (1995): 1–33.

Bynum, William F. "Alcoholism and Degeneration in Nineteenth-Century European Medicine and Psychiatry." *British Journal of Addiction* 79 (1984): 59–70.

———. "Chronic Alcoholism in the First Half of the Nineteenth Century." *Bulletin of the History of Medicine* 42 (1968): 160–85.

Bynum, W. F., Roy Porter, and Michael Shepherd, eds. *The Anatomy of Madness: Essays in the History of Psychiatry*. Vol. 2. *Institutions and Society*. London: Tavistock, 1985.

Callas, Evangelina. With Lawrence G. Blochman. *My Daughter Maria Callas*. New York: Fleet, 1960.

Callas, Jackie. *Sisters*. London: Macmillan, 1989.

Callas, Maria. "Callas Speaks." Transcribed by Anita Pensotti. In *Callas as They Saw Her*. Ed. David A. Lowe. New York: Ungar, 1986. 112–61.

Camboulives, Catherine. "J'aime les navrantes têtes coupées de décollés et de martyres . . ." In *Salomé dans les collections françaises*. St.-Denis: Musée d'art et d'histoire, 1988. 21–23.

Campbell, Don. *The Mozart Effect™: Tapping the Power of Music to Heal the Body, Strengthen the Mind, and Unlock the Creative Spirit*. New York: Avon, 1997.

Campbell, Harry. *Differences in the Nervous Organization of Man and Woman: Physiological and Pathological*. London: H. K. Lewis, 1891.

Carey, Jonathan Sinclair. "The Quasimodo Complex: Deformity Reconsidered." In *The Tyranny of the Normal: An Anthology*. Ed. Carol Donley and Sheryl Buckley. Kent OH: Kent State University Press, 1996. 27–52.

Carlson, Marvin. *Theatre Semiotics: Signs of Life*. Bloomington: Indiana University Press, 1990.

Carnegy, Patrick. "The Novella Transformed: Thomas Mann as Opera." In *Benjamin Britten: Death in Venice*. Ed. Donald Mitchell. Cambridge: Cambridge University Press, 1987. 168–77.

Carner, Mosco. "Witches Cauldron." *Opera News* 27 February 1971: 24–26.

Carpenter, Humphrey. *Benjamin Britten: A Biography*. London: Faber and Faber, 1992.

Carpenter, Tethys. "The Musical Language of 'Elektra.'" In *Richard Strauss: Elektra*. Ed. Derrick Puffett. Cambridge: Cambridge University Press, 1989. 74–106.

———. "Tonal and Dramatic Structure." In *Richard Strauss: Salome*. Ed. Derrick Puffett. Cambridge: Cambridge University Press, 1989. 88–108.

Carpenter, Thomas H., and Christopher A. Faraone, eds. *Masks of Dionysus*. Ithaca NY: Cornell University Press, 1993.

Carroll, Charles Michael. "Eros on the Operatic Stage: Problems in Manners and Morals." *Opera Quarterly* 1.1 (1983): 38–46.

Carroll, Noël. "The Image of Women in Film: A Defense of a Paradigm." *Journal of Aesthetics and Art Criticism* 48 (1990): 349–60.

Caruso, Enrico. *How to Sing*. 1919. New York: Opera Box, 1973.

Castle, Terry. "In Praise of Brigitte Fassbänder: Reflections on Diva-Worship." In *En Travesti: Women, Gender Subversion, Opera*. Ed. Corinne E. Blackmer and Patricia Juliana Smith. New York: Columbia University Press, 1995. 20–58.

Cather, Willa. "Paul's Case." In *Stories, Poems, and Other Writings*. New York: Viking, 1992. 468–87.

———. *The Song of the Lark*. 1915. Introduction by Sharon O'Brien. New York: Signet, 1991.

———. "A Wagner Matinée." In *Stories, Poems, and Other Writings*. New York: Viking, 1992. 489–96.

Chamberlin, J. Edward. "From High Decadence to High Modernism." *Queen's Quarterly* 87 (1980): 591–610.

———. *"Ripe Was the Drowsy Hour": The Age of Oscar Wilde*. New York: Seabury Press, 1977.

Chin, Steven B., and David B. Pisoni. *Alcohol and Speech*. San Diego: Academic Press, 1997.

Christiansen, Rupert. "Callas: A Polemic." *Opera* 38 (1987): 617–22.

———. *Prima Donna: A History*. 1984. Rev. ed. London: Pimlico, 1995.

Clayton, Alfred. *"Der Zwerg."* In *The New Grove Dictionary of Opera*. Ed. Stanley Sadie. London and New York: Macmillan, 1992. 4:1250–51.

Clément, Catherine. "Désir de sainte." *L'Avant-scène opéra* 47–48 (1983): 123–26.

———. *Opera, or the Undoing of Women*. Trans. Betsy Wing. London: Virago, 1989.

Clements, Andrew. *"The Bassarids."* In *The New Grove Dictionary of Opera*. Ed. Stanley Sadie. London and New York: Macmillan, 1992. 1:343–45.

Clifton, Thomas. *Music as Heard: A Study in Applied Phenomenology*. New Haven CT: Yale University Press, 1983.

Coffin, Berton. *Historical Vocal Pedagogy Classics*. Metuchen NJ: Scarecrow Press, 1989.

Cogan, Rosemary, Dennis Cogan, William Waltz, and Melissa McCue. "Effects of Laughter and Relaxation on Discomfort Thresholds." *Journal of Behavioral Medicine* 10.2 (1987): 139–44.

Cogny, Pierre. "J.-K. Huysmans: Du reginglat au vin de messe." In *L'Imaginaire du vin: Colloque pluridisciplinaire*. Ed. Max Milner and Martine Chatelain. Marseille: Jeanne Laffitte, 1983. 181–89.

Cohen, Jeffrey Jerome, ed. *Monster Theory: Reading Culture*. Minneapolis: University of Minnesota Press, 1996.

Comins, Jayne. "Health: Voice Clinic – Making the Break." *Singer* (August–September 1996): 14–15.

Conati, Marcello. *Rigoletto: Un'analisi drammatico-musicale*. Venice: Marsilia, 1992.

Cone, Edward T. *Music, a View from Delft: Selected Essays*. Chicago: University of Chicago Press, 1989.

Connerton, Paul. *How Societies Remember*. Cambridge: Cambridge University Press, 1989.

Connors, Gerard J., and Victor S. Alpher. "Alcohol Themes within Country-Western Songs." *International Journal of the Addictions* 24 (1989): 445–51.

Conrad, Peter. *Romantic Opera and Literary Form*. Berkeley: University of California Press, 1977.

———. *A Song of Love and Death: The Meaning of Opera*. New York: Poseidon Press, 1987.

Cooke, Mervyn. "Britten and the Gamelan: Balinese Influences in 'Death in Venice.'" In *Benjamin Britten: Death in Venice*. Ed. Donald Mitchell. Cambridge: Cambridge University Press, 1987. 115–28.

Corse, Sandra. *Opera and the Uses of Language: Mozart, Verdi, and Britten*. London: Associated University Presses, 1987.

Corse, S., and L. Corse. "Britten's *Death in Venice*: Literary and Musical Structures." *Musical Quarterly* 73 (1989): 344–63.

Cott, Jonathan. "A Conversation with Philip Glass on *La Belle et la Bête*." Compact disc notes, Nonesuch Recording, 1995. 12–21.

Cottino, Amedeo. "Italy." In *International Handbook on Alcohol and Culture*. Ed. Dwight B. Heath. Westport CT: Greenwood Press, 1995. 156–67.

———. "Science and Class Structure: Notes on the Formation of the Alcohol Question in Italy (1860–1920)." *Contemporary Crises* 9 (1985): 45–53.

Couser, G. Thomas. *Recovering Bodies: Illness, Disability, and Life Writing*. Madison: University of Wisconsin Press, 1997.

Cousins, Norman. *Anatomy of an Illness as Perceived by the Patient*. New York: Norton, 1979.

Coutance, Guy. "A Voice for Reconstructing the Theatre." In *Callas as They Saw Her*. Ed. David A. Lowe. New York: Ungar, 1986. 169–72.

Critchley, Macdonald. "Ecstatic and Synaesthetic Experiences during Musical Perception." In *Music and the Brain: Studies in the Neurology of Music*. Ed. M. Critchley and R. A. Henson. London: Heinemann, 1977. 217–32.

Critchley, M., and R. A. Henson. *Music and the Brain: Studies in the Neurology of Music*. London: Heinemann, 1977.

Crofton, Ian, and Donald Fraser. *A Dictionary of Musical Quotations*. New York: Schirmer, 1985.

Crowley, John W. *The White Logic: Alcoholism and Gender in American Modernist Fiction.* Amherst: University of Massachusetts Press, 1994.

Crozier, Eric, and Nancy Evans. "After Long Pursuit: The English Opera Group and *Albert Herring.*" *Opera Quarterly* 11.3 (1995): 3–16.

Crutchfield, Will. "The Story of a Voice." *New Yorker* 13 November 1995: 94–102.

Cusick, Suzanne G. "On a Lesbian Relationship with Music: A Serious Effort Not to Think Straight." In *Queering the Pitch: The New Gay and Lesbian Musicology.* Ed. Philip Brett, Elizabeth Wood, and Gary C. Thomas. New York and London: Routledge, 1994. 67–83.

Dahlhaus, Carl. *Richard Wagner's Music Dramas.* Trans. Mary Whittall. Cambridge: Cambridge University Press, 1979.

———. "Die Tragödie als Oper: *Elektra* von Hofmannsthal und Strauss." In *Geschichte und Dramaturgie des Operneinakters.* Ed. Winfried Kirsch and Sieghart Döhring. Frankfurt am Main: Laaber-Verlag, 1988. 277–84.

Davenport, Marcia. *Of Lena Geyer.* New York: Scribner's, 1936.

David-Ménard, Monique. *Hysteria from Freud to Lacan: Body and Language in Psychoanalysis.* Ithaca NY: Cornell University Press, 1989.

Davies, Robertson. *The Lyre of Orpheus.* Markham ON: Penguin, 1989.

Davis, Lennard J. *Enforcing Normalcy: Disability, Deafness, and the Body.* New York: Verson, 1995.

de Aguilar, Helene J. F. "Dangerous Faith: Benjamin Britten's Language." *Parnassus* (fall–winter 1982): 135–70.

Dean, Ruth A. "Humor and Laughter in Palliative Care." *Journal of Palliative Care* 13 (1997): 34–39.

Dehorn, Allan B. "Performance Anxiety." In *Vocal Arts Medicine: The Care and Prevention of Professional Voice Disorders.* Ed. Michael S. Benninger, Barbara H. Jacobson, and Alex F. Johnson. New York: Theieme Medical Publishers, 1994. 281–90.

del Mar, Norman. "The Chamber Operas II: Albert Herring." In *Benjamin Britten.* Ed. Donald Mitchell and Hans Keller. London: Rockliff, 1952. 146–62.

Dempster, Elizabeth. "Women Writing the Body: Let's Watch a Little How She Dances." In *Bodies of the Text: Dance as Theory, Literature as Dance.* Ed. Ellen W. Goellner and Jacqueline Shea Murphy. New Brunswick NJ: Rutgers University Press, 1995. 21–38.

de Toro, Fernando. *Theatre Semiotics: Text and Staging in Modern Theatre.* Toronto: University of Toronto Press, 1995.

de Van, Gilles. *Verdi: Un théâtre en musique.* Paris: Fayard, 1992.

Devynck, Danièle. " 'La Saulterelle déshonnête.' " In *Salomé dans les collections françaises.* St.-Denis: Musée d'art et d'histoire, 1988. 17–19.

di Carlo, Nicole Scotto, and Denis Autesserre. "Movement of the Velum in Singing." *Journal of Research in Singing and Applied Vocal Pedagogy* 11.1 (1987): 3–13.

Dijkstra, Bram. *Idols of Perversity: Fantasies of Feminine Evil in Fin-de-Siècle Culture.* New York: Oxford University Press, 1986.

di Stefano, Eva. *Il complesso di Salomè: La donna, l'amore e la morte nella pittura di Klimt.* Palermo: Sellerio, 1985.

Dodds, E. R. *The Greeks and the Irrational.* Berkeley: University of California Press, 1951.

———. "Introduction." Euripides. *Bacchae.* 1944. 2nd ed. Oxford: Clarendon Press, 1960. xi–lix.

Dollimore, Jonathan. *Sexual Dissidence: Augustine to Wilde, Freud to Foucault.* Oxford: Clarendon Press, 1991.

Donington, Robert. *The Rise of Opera.* London: Faber and Faber, 1981.

Donley, Carol, and Sheryl Buckley, eds. *The Tyranny of the Normal: An Anthology.* Kent OH: Kent State University Press, 1996.

Dose, Claus Dieter. "The Reception of E. T. A. Hoffmann in the United States, 1940–1976." Diss., New York University, 1980.

Dottin, Mireille. "Le Développement du 'mythe de Salomé.' " In *Salomé dans les collections françaises.* St.-Denis: Musée d'art et d'histoire, 1988. 13–16.

Douglas, Mary. "A Distinctive Anthropological Perspective." In *Constructive Drinking: Perspectives on Drink from Anthropology.* Ed. Mary Douglas. Cambridge: Cambridge University Press; Paris: Maison des sciences de l'homme, 1987. 3–15.

———. *Purity and Danger: An Analysis of the Concepts of Pollution and Taboo.* London and New York: Ark/Routledge and Kegan Paul, 1966.

Douglas, Nigel. *More Legendary Voices.* London: André Deutsch, 1994.

Driessen, Henk. "Drinking on Masculinity: Alcohol and Gender in Andalusia." In *Alcohol, Gender and Culture.* Ed. Dimitra Gefou-Madianou. London and New York: Routledge, 1992. 71–79.

Dubrow, Heather. *Echoes of Desire: English Petrarchism and Its Counterdiscourses.* Ithaca NY: Cornell University Press, 1995.

Dunn, Leslie C., and Nancy A. Jones, eds. *Embodied Voices: Representing*

Female Vocality in Western Culture. Cambridge: Cambridge University Press, 1994.

Dusek, Peter. "Inszenierungsgeschichte der *Elektra* am Beispiel der Filmversion von Götz Friedrich." In *Antiken Mythen im Musiktheater des 20. Jahrhunderts.* Ed. Peter Csobádi, Gernot Gruber, Jürgen Kühnel, Ulrich Müller, and Oswald Panagl. Salzburg: Verlag Ursula Müller-Speiser, 1990. 135–43.

Eagleton, Terry. *The Illusions of Postmodernism.* Oxford: Blackwell, 1996.

Easterling, P. E. "Electra's Story." In *Richard Strauss:* Elektra. Ed. Derrick Puffett. Cambridge: Cambridge University Press, 1989. 10–16.

Eco, Umberto. *Art and Beauty in the Middle Ages.* Trans. Hugh Bredin. New Haven CT: Yale University Press, 1986.

Edwards, Geoffrey, and Ryan Edwards. *The Verdi Baritone.* Bloomington: Indiana University Press, 1994.

Edwards, H. Sutherland. *The Prima Donna: Her Story and Surroundings from the Seventeenth to the Nineteenth Century.* Vol. 1. London: Remington, 1888.

Eilan, Naomi, Anthony Marcel, and José Luis Bermúdez. "Self- Consciousness and the Body: An Interdisciplinary Introduction." In *The Body and the Self.* Ed. José Luis Bermúdez, Anthony Marcel, and Naomi Eilan. Cambridge MA: MIT Press, 1995. 1–28.

Elam, Keir. *The Semiotics of Theatre and Drama.* London and New York: Routledge, 1980.

Elias, Norbert. *The History of Manners.* Vol. 1 of *The Civilizing Process.* Trans. E. Jephcott. New York: Pantheon, 1978.

———. *Power and Civility.* Vol. 2 of *The Civilizing Process.* Trans. E. Jephcott. New York: Pantheon, 1982.

Ellis, Havelock. *Man and Woman: A Study of Human Secondary Sexual Characters.* London: Walter Scott, 1899.

———. *The Task of Social Hygiene.* London: Constable, 1912.

Ellmann, Richard. *Oscar Wilde.* London: Hamish Hamilton, 1987.

———. "Overtures to Wilde's 'Salomé.' " In *Richard Strauss:* Salome. Ed. Derrick Puffett. Cambridge: Cambridge University Press, 1989. 21–35.

Empson, William. "*The Beggar's Opera*: Mock-Pastoral as the Cult of Independence." In *Twentieth Century Interpretations of* The Beggar's Opera. Ed. Yvonne Noble. Englewood Cliffs NJ: Prentice-Hall, 1975. 15–41.

Bibliography

Enachescu, Constantin. "Alcoolisme et création littéraire (Essai d'analyse psychopathologique d'écrivains alcooliques)." *Revue de l'alcoolisme* 16.2 (1970): 141–50.

Engh, Barbara. "Adorno and the Sirens: Tele-phono-graphic Bodies." In *Embodied Voices: Representing Female Vocality in Western Culture*. Ed. Leslie C. Dunn and Nancy A. Jones. Cambridge: Cambridge University Press, 1994. 120–35.

Erdman, Lynn. "Laughter Therapy for Patients with Cancer." *Oncology Nursing Forum* 18 (1991): 1359–63.

Erzgräber, Willi. "Tanz und Tod bei Oscar Wilde, W. B. Yeats und James Joyce." In *Tanz und Tod in Kunst und Literatur*. Ed. Franz Link. Berlin: Duncker and Humblot [sic], 1993. 317–34.

Etcoff, Nancy. *Survival of the Prettiest: The Science of Beauty*. New York: Doubleday, 1999.

Euripedes. *The Bacchae and Other Plays*. Trans. Philip Vellacott. Rev. ed. London: Penguin, 1973.

Evans, John. "*Death in Venice*: The Apollonian/Dionysian Conflict." *Opera Quarterly* 4.3 (1986): 102–15.

———. "Twelve-Note Structures and Tonal Polarities." In *Benjamin Britten: Death in Venice*. Ed. Donald Mitchell. Cambridge: Cambridge University Press, 1987. 99–114.

Evans, Martha Noel. *Fits and Starts: A Genealogy of Hysteria in Modern France*. Ithaca NY: Cornell University Press, 1991.

Evans, Peter. *The Music of Benjamin Britten*. 1979. Oxford: Oxford University Press, 1996.

———. "Synopsis: The Story, the Music Not Excluded." In *Benjamin Britten: Death in Venice*. Ed. Donald Mitchell. Cambridge: Cambridge University Press, 1987. 76–85.

Faraone, Christopher A. "Introduction." In *Masks of Dionysus*. Ed. Thomas H. Carpenter and Christopher A. Faraone. Ithaca NY: Cornell University Press, 1993. 1–10.

Faris, Alexander. *Jacques Offenbach*. London: Faber and Faber, 1980.

Fee, Elizabeth. "Nineteenth-Century Craniology: The Study of the Female Skull." *Bulletin of the History of Medicine* 53 (1979): 415–33.

Feher, Michel. "Introduction." Trans. Lydia Davis. In *Fragments for a History of the Human Body*. Ed. Michel Feher, Ramona Naddaff, and Nadia Tazi. New York: Zone, 1989. 1:11–17.

Feher, Michel, Ramona Naddaff, and Nadia Tazi, eds. *Fragments for a History of the Human Body*. New York: Zone, 1989.

Fiedler, Leslie A. "The Tyranny of the Normal." In *The Tyranny of the Normal: An Anthology*. Ed. Carol Donley and Sheryl Buckley. Kent OH: Kent State University Press, 1996. 3–10.

Flach, M. "Indisposition und akute Dysphonie beim Berufssänger." *Laryngorhinootologie* 71.5 (1992): 233–35.

Flaubert, Gustave. *Madame Bovary: Moeurs de province*. Paris: Garnier, 1961.

———. *Madame Bovary*. Trans. Paul de Man. New York: Norton, 1965.

———. *Trois contes*. Paris: Gallimard, 1966.

Fludas, John. "Fatal Women: Exploring the Eternal Mystique of the Femmes Fatales." *Opera News* 12 February 1977: 15–18.

Forel, August. *The Sexual Question*. Trans. C. F. Marshall. London: Rebman, 1908.

Forrest, Gary G., and Robert H. Gordon. *Substance Abuse, Homicides and Violent Behavior*. New York: Gardner, 1990.

Forsyth, Karen. "Hofmannsthal's 'Elektra': From Sophocles to Strauss." In *Richard Strauss:* Elektra. Ed. Derrick Puffett. Cambridge: Cambridge University Press, 1989. 17–32.

Fortier, Mark. *Theory/Theatre: An Introduction*. London and New York: Routledge, 1997.

Foucault, Michel. *The Archaeology of Knowledge and the Discourse on Language*. Trans. A. M. Sheridan Smith. New York: Pantheon, 1972.

———. *The Birth of the Clinic: An Archaeology of Medical Perception*. Trans. A. M. Sheridan Smith. New York: Vintage, 1975.

———. *An Introduction*. Vol. 1 of *The History of Sexuality*. Trans. Robert Hurley. New York: Vintage, 1980.

Fournier, Dominique, and Salvatore D'Onofrio, eds. *Le Ferment divin*. Paris: Editions de la maison des sciences de l'homme, 1991.

Freud, Sigmund. "Medusa's Head." In *The Standard Edition of the Complete Psychological Works of Sigmund Freud*. Ed. James Strachey. London: Hogarth Press and Institute of Psycho-Analysis, 1955. 18:273–74.

Friedrich, Rainer. "Everything to Do with Dionysos? Ritualism, the Dionysiac, and the Tragic." In *Tragedy and the Tragic: Greek Theatre and Beyond*. Ed. M. S. Silk. Oxford: Clarendon Press, 1996. 257–83.

Frueh, Joanna. *Erotic Faculties*. Berkeley: University of California Press, 1996.

Galatopoulos, Stelios. *Callas: Prima Donna Assoluta*. London: W. H. Allen, 1974.

Gamella, Juan F. "Spain." In *International Handbook on Alcohol and Culture*. Ed. Dwight B. Heath. Westport CT: Greenwood, 1995. 254–69.

Gangestad, S. W., and R. Thornhill. "The Evolutionary Psychology of Extrapair Sex: The Role of Fluctuating Asymmetry." *Evolution and Human Behavior* 18 (1997): 69–88.

Gangestad, S. W., R. Thornhill, and R. A. Yeo. "Facial Attractiveness, Developmental Stability, and Fluctuating Asymmetry." *Ethology and Sociobiology* 15.2 (1994): 73–85.

Ganz, Arthur. "Transformations of the Child Temptress: Mélisande, Salomé, Lulu." *Opera Quarterly* 5.4 (1987–88): 12–20.

Garber, Marjorie. *Vested Interests: Cross-Dressing and Cultural Anxiety*. 1992. New York: HarperPerennial, 1993.

Garfield, Laeh Maggie. *Sound Medicine: Healing with Music, Voice, and Song*. Berkeley CA: Celestial Arts, 1987.

Gatens, Moira. *Imaginary Bodies: Ethics, Power and Corporeality*. London and New York: Routledge, 1996.

Gay, John. *The Beggar's Opera*. Ed. Edgar V. Roberts. London: Edward Arnold, 1968.

Gefou-Madianou, Dimitra. "Introduction: Alcohol Commensality, Identity Transformations and Transcendence." In *Alcohol, Gender and Culture*. Ed. Dimitra Gefou-Madianou. London and New York: Routledge, 1992. 1–34.

Gefou-Madianou, Dimitra, ed. *Alcohol, Gender and Culture*. London and New York: Routledge, 1992.

Gerber, Douglas E. "The Measure of Bacchus: Evenus Fr.2 West, Gent.-Pr-Anth. Pal. 11,49." *Mnemosyne* 41.1–2 (1988): 39–45.

Gerlach, Reinhard. "Farbklang-Klangfarbe." *Neue Zeitschrift für Musik* 134.1 (1973): 10–18.

———. "Die Tragödie des inneren Menschen: 'Elektra'-Studien." In *Neue Musik und Tradition*. Ed. Josef Kuckertz, Helga de la Motte-Haber, Christian Martin Schmidt, and Wilhelm Seide. Frankfurt am Main: Laaber Verlag, 1990. 389–416.

Gigli, Beniamino. "When Gigli Knew Fear." In *The Alchemy of Voice*. By E. Herbert-Caesari. London: Robert Hale, 1965. 177–79.

Gil, José. *Metamorphoses of the Body*. Trans. Stephen Muecke. Minneapolis: University of Minnesota Press, 1998.

Gillespie, Gerald. "Mann and the Modernist Tradition." In *Approaches to Teaching Mann's "Death in Venice" and Other Short Fiction.* Ed. Jeffrey B. Berlin. New York: Modern Language Association, 1992. 93–104.

Gilliam, Bryan. *Richard Strauss's* Elektra. Oxford: Clarendon Press, 1991.

———. "Strauss's Preliminary Opera Sketches: Thematic Fragments and Symphonic Continuity." *19th-Century Music* 9.3 (1986): 176–88.

Gilliam, Bryan, ed. *Richard Strauss and His World.* Princeton NJ: Princeton University Press, 1992.

Gilman, Sander L. *Disease and Representation: Images of Illness from Madness to AIDS.* Ithaca NY: Cornell University Press, 1988.

———. "The Fat Body." Paper presented at the annual meeting of the Modern Language Association of America, San Francisco CA, December 1998.

———. "The Image of the Hysteric." In *Hysteria beyond Freud.* Ed. Sander L. Gilman, Helen King, Roy Porter, G. S. Rousseau, and Elaine Showalter. Berkeley: University of California Press, 1993. 345–452.

———. "Salome, Syphilis, Sarah Bernhardt and the 'Modern Jewess.'" *German Quarterly* 66.2 (1993): 195–211.

———. "Strauss and the Pervert." In *Reading Opera.* Ed. Arthur Groos and Roger Parker. Princeton NJ: Princeton University Press, 1988. 306–27.

Gilman, Sander L., Helen King, Roy Porter, G. S. Rousseau, and Elaine Showalter, eds. *Hysteria beyond Freud.* Berkeley: University of California Press, 1993.

Girard, René. "Scandal and the Dance: Salome in the Gospel of Mark." *New Literary History* 15 (1984): 311–24.

———. *The Scapegoat.* Trans. Yvonne Freccero. Baltimore MD: Johns Hopkins University Press, 1986.

———. *Violence and the Sacred.* Trans. Patrick Gregory. Baltimore MD: Johns Hopkins University Press, 1977.

Girouard, Mark. *Life in the English Country House.* Harmondsworth: Penguin, 1980.

Giulini, Carlo Maria. "Tributes to Callas." *Opera* 28 (1977): 1015–17.

Gobbi, Tito. From *My Life.* 1980. Reprinted in *Callas as They Saw Her.* Ed. David A. Lowe. New York: Ungar, 1986. 190–99.

Godefroid, Philippe. "Le Regard interdit." *L'Avant-scène opéra* 47–48 (1983): 146–49.

Goellner, Ellen W., and Jacqueline Shea Murphy, eds. *Bodies of the Text:*

Dance as Theory, Literature as Dance. New Brunswick NJ: Rutgers University Press, 1995.

Goffman, Erving. *Stigma: Notes on the Management of Spoiled Identity*. Englewood Cliffs NJ: Prentice-Hall, 1963.

Goldet, Stéphane. "Commentaire littéraire et musicale." *L'Avant-scène opéra* 47–48 (1983): 53–110.

Goldstein, Avram. "Music/Endorphin Link." *Brain/Mind Bulletin* 21 January, 11 February 1985: 1–3.

Gomberg, Edith Lisansky, Helene Raskin White, and John A. Carpenter, eds. *Alcohol, Science and Society Revisited*. Ann Arbor: University of Michigan Press, 1982.

Goodwin, Donald W. "Alcohol as Muse." *Dionysos* 5 (1993): 3–13.

Grant, Marcus. "The Alcoholic as Hero." In *Images of Alcoholism*. Ed. Jim Cook and Mike Lewington. London: British Film Institute, 1974. 30–36.

Gray, Piers. "The Comedy of Suffering." *Critical Quarterly* 33.4 (1991): 41–57.

Green, Rebecca. "Baritonapalooza." *Globe and Mail* 30 November 1998: C1.

Green, William. *Shakespeare's* Merry Wives of Windsor. Princeton NJ: Princeton University Press, 1962.

Greenberg, Leon A. "Alcohol in the Body." In *Drinking and Intoxication: Selected Readings in Social Attitudes and Controls*. Ed. Raymond G. McCarthy. New Haven CT: College and University Press, 1959. 7–12.

Greenblatt, Stephen. "Filthy Rites." *Daedalus* 3.3 (1982): 1–16.

Greene, David B. *Listening to Strauss Operas: The Audience's Multiple Standpoints*. New York: Gordon and Breach, 1991.

Grey, Thomas S. *Wagner's Musical Prose: Texts and Contexts*. Cambridge: Cambridge University Press, 1995.

Grosz, Elizabeth. *Space, Time, and Perversion: Essays on the Politics of Bodies*. New York and London: Routledge, 1995.

———. *Volatile Bodies: Toward a Corporeal Feminism*. Bloomington: Indiana University Press, 1994.

Grosz, Elizabeth, and Elspeth Probyn, eds. *Sexy Bodies: The Strange Carnalities of Feminism*. London and New York: Routledge, 1995.

Guibaud, M. "Contribution à l'étude expérimentale de l'influence de la musique sur la circulation et la respiration." *L'Année psychologique* 5 (1889): 645–49.

Guillet, Jacques. "Le Vin de la bible et de l'eucariste." In *L'Imaginaire du vin: Colloque pluridisciplinaire*. Ed. Max Milner and Martine Chatelain. Marseille: Jeanne Laffitte, 1983. 65–69.

Gurewitsch, Matthew. "Thriller: Powerhouse Mezzo Dolora Zajick Always Delivers." *Opera News* (December 1996): 8–11.

Hachinski, K. Vlad, and Vladimir Hachinski. "Music and the Brain." *Canadian Medical Association Journal* 151 (1995): 293–96.

Hadlock, Heather Leigh. "Romantic Visions of Women and Music: Jacques Offenbach's 'Les Contes d'Hoffmann.'" Diss., Princeton University, 1996.

Haine, W. Scott. *The World of the Paris Café: Sociability among the French Working Class, 1789–1914*. Baltimore MD: Johns Hopkins University Press, 1996.

Hamard, Marie-Claire. "La Femme fatale: *Salome* et le *Yellow Book*." *Cahiers victoriens et édouardiens* 36 (1992): 29–49.

Harpham, Geoffrey Galt. *On the Grotesque: Strategies of Contradiction in Art and Literature*. Princeton NJ: Princeton University Press, 1982.

Harrer, G., and H. Harrer. "Music, Emotion and Autonomic Function." In *Music and the Brain: Studies in the Neurology of Music*. Ed. M. Critchley and R. A. Henson. London: Heinemann, 1977. 202–16.

Harris, Ruth. "Melodrama, Hysteria and Feminine Crimes of Passion in the Fin-de-Siècle." *History Workshop* 25 (1988): 31–63.

Harris, Tom, Sarah Harris, John S. Rubin, and David M. Howard. *The Voice Clinic Handbook*. London: Whurr Publishers, 1998.

Harrison, Brian. "The Power of Drink." *Listener* 13 February 1969: 204–6.

Haskell, Harry, ed. *The Attentive Listener: Three Centuries of Music Criticism*. London: Faber and Faber, 1995.

Hausamann, Torsten. *Die tanzende Salome in der Kunst vor der christlichen Frühzeit bis um 1500*. Zürich: Juris Druck, 1980.

Haydon, Peter. *The English Pub: A History*. London: Robert Hale, 1994.

Hayles, N. Katherine. *How We Became Posthuman: Virtual Bodies in Cybernetics, Literature, and Informatics*. Chicago: University of Chicago Press, 1999.

———. "The Seductions of Cyberspace." In *Rethinking Technologies*. Ed. Verena Andermatt Conley. Minneapolis: University of Minnesota Press, 1993. 173–90.

Headington, Christopher. *Britten*. London: Omnibus Press, 1996.

Heath, Dwight B. "Anthropological Perspectives on the Social Biology of Alcohol: An Introduction to the Literature." In *Social Aspects of Alcoholism*. Ed. Benjamin Kissin and Henri Begleiter. New York: Plenum Press, 1976. 37–76.

———. "An Introduction to Alcohol and Culture in International Perspective." In *International Handbook on Alcohol and Culture*. Ed. Dwight B. Heath. Westport CT: Greenwood Press, 1995. 1–6.

———. "Some Generalizations about Alcohol and Culture." In *International Handbook on Alcohol and Culture*. Ed. Dwight B. Heath. Westport CT: Greenwood Press, 1995. 348–62.

Heath, Dwight B., ed. *International Handbook on Alcohol and Culture*. Westport CT: Greenwood Press, 1995.

Henrichs, Albert. "Loss of Self, Suffering, Violence: The Modern View of Dionysus from Nietzsche to Girard." *Harvard Studies in Classical Philology* 88 (1984): 205–40.

Henson, R. A. "The Language of Music." In *Music and the Brain: Studies in the Neurology of Music*. Ed. M. Critchley and R. A. Henson. London: Heinemann, 1977. 233–54.

———. "Neurological Aspects of Musical Experience." In *Music and the Brain: Studies in the Neurology of Music*. Ed. M. Critchley and R. A. Henson. London: Heinemann, 1977. 3–21.

Hepburn, Alan. "Icons: History as Personality in Contemporary American Opera." Paper presented at the annual convention of the Modern Language Association of America, San Francisco CA, December 1998.

Hepokoski, James. *Giuseppe Verdi: Otello*. Cambridge: Cambridge University Press, 1987.

Herbert-Caesari, E. *The Alchemy of Voice*. London: Robert Hale, 1965.

Herd, Denise. "Ideology, Melodrama, and the Changing Role of Alcohol Problems in American Films." *Contemporary Drug Problems* 13 (1986): 213–47.

Heriot, Angus. *The Castrati in Opera*. 1956. New York: Da Capo Press, 1974.

Herth, Kaye. "Contributions of Humor as Perceived by the Terminally Ill." *American Journal of Hospice Care* 7.1 (1990): 30–40.

Hewett-Thayer, Harvey W. *Hoffmann: Author of the Tales*. Princeton NJ: Princeton University Press, 1948.

Hindley, C. "Contemplation and Reality: A Study in Britten's 'Death in Venice.'" *Music and Letters* 71 (1990): 511–23.

Hines, Jerome. *Great Singers on Singing*. New York: Doubleday, 1982.

Hirano, Minoru, Shegejiro Kurita, Koichi Matsuo, and Kazuto Nagata. "Vocal Fold Polyp and Polypoid Vocal Fold (Reinke's Edema)." *Journal of Research in Singing* 4.2 (1981): 33–44.

Hixon, Thomas J., et al. *Respiratory Function in Speech and Song*. Boston: Little, Brown, 1987.

Holland, Bernard. "Listen with the Ear, Not the Mind." *New York Times* 20 December 1998: sec. 2: 1, 36.

Holland, Norman N. *Laughing: A Psychology of Humor*. Ithaca NY: Cornell University Press, 1982.

Holloway, Robin. "The Orchestration of 'Elektra': A Critical Interpretation." In *Richard Strauss:* Elektra. Ed. Derrick Puffett. Cambridge: Cambridge University Press, 1989. 128–47.

———. " 'Salome': Art or Kitsch?" In *Richard Strauss:* Salome. Ed. Derrick Puffett. Cambridge: Cambridge University Press, 1989. 145–60.

Honigman, John J. "Alcohol in Its Cultural Contexts." In *Beliefs, Behaviors, and Alcoholic Beverages: A Cross-Cultural Study*. Ed. Mac Marshall. Ann Arbor: University of Michigan Press, 1979. 30–35.

Hood, J. D. "Psychological and Physiological Aspects of Hearing." In *Music and the Brain: Studies in the Neurology of Music*. Ed. M. Critchley and R. A. Henson. London: Heinemann, 1977. 32–47.

Höslinger, Clemens. " 'Salome' und ihr österreichische Schicksal 1905 bis 1918." *Österreichische Musik Zeitschrift* 32 (1977): 300–309.

Hötzl, Ernst. "Richard Strauss–Hugo von Hofmannsthal, Die *Elektra* – Ein Psychogramm der Atriden-Trilogie." In *Antiken Mythen im Musiktheater des 20. Jahrhunderts*. Ed. Peter Csobádi, Gernot Gruber, Jürgen Kühnel, Ulrich Müller, and Oswald Panagl. Salzburg: Verlag Ursula Müller, 1990. 123–33.

Houden, Helen, and Steve Austin. "The Effects of Estrogen Replacement Therapy on the Menopausal Singing Voice." *Journal of Research in Singing and Applied Vocal Pedagogy* 14.2 (1992): 41–50.

Howard, Patricia. *The Operas of Benjamin Britten: An Introduction*. London: Cresset Press, 1969.

Huertas, Raphael. "Madness and Degeneration, II: Alcohol and Degeneration." *History of Psychiatry* 4 (1993): 1–21.

Huffman, Richard S. "*Les Contes d'Hoffmann*: Unity of Dramatic Form in the Libretto." *Studies in Romanticism* 15 (1976): 97–117.

Hugo, Victor. *Cromwell*. Paris: Garnier-Flammarion, 1968.

———. *Le Livre de Lucrèce Borgia*. Chaillot: Actes Sud, Herbert Hyssen, 1985.

———. *Notre-Dame de Paris*. Trans. Alban Krailsheimer. Oxford: Oxford University Press, 1993.

————. *Notre-Dame de Paris, 1482*. Ed. Jacques Seebacher and Yves Gohin. Paris: Gallimard, 1975.

————. *Le Roi s'amuse*. Paris: Hetzel/Maison Quantin, 1882.

Huneker, James. *Bedouins*. New York: Charles Scribner's Sons, 1920.

Hunt, Lynn, ed. *Eroticism and the Body Politic*. Baltimore MD: Johns Hopkins University Press, 1991.

Hurley, Ken. *The Gothic Body: Sexuality, Materialism, and Degeneration at the Fin-de-Siècle*. Cambridge: Cambridge University Press, 1996.

Husch, Jerri A. "Leisure, Work, and Drugs: A Perspective of Use." *Loisir et société/Society and Leisure* 14 (1991): 399–409.

Hutcheon, Linda, and Michael Hutcheon. *Opera: Desire, Disease, Death*. Lincoln: University of Nebraska Press, 1996.

Huysmans, J.-K. *Against Nature*. Trans. Robert Baldick. London: Penguin, 1959.

————. *A rebours*. 2nd ed. Paris: Gallimard, 1977.

Huyssen, Andreas. *Twilight Memories: Marking Time in a Culture of Amnesia*. New York: Routledge, 1995.

Ingram, Jay. "Open Wide and Sing Ahhh!" *Opera Canada* (winter 1992): 18–19.

Innaurato, Albert. "As Categories Blur, One Diva Rules." *New York Times* 24 May 1998: sec. 2: 1, 30.

Iser, Wolfgang. *The Implied Reader*. Baltimore MD: Johns Hopkins University Press, 1974.

Jackson, George H. *The Medicinal Value of French Brandy, with Many Illustrations*. Montreal: Thérien Frères, 1928.

James, Nick. "I for Intoxication." *Sight and Sound* 7 (1997): 26–28.

Janet, Pierre. *The Major Symptoms of Hysteria*. 1907. 2nd ed. New York: Macmillan, 1929.

Jay, Martin. *Downcast Eyes: The Denigration of Vision in Twentieth-Century French Thought*. Berkeley: University of California Press, 1993.

Jeanvoine, Michèle. "Hoffmann dans les *Contes d'Hoffmann* d'Offenbach: Trahison ou fidélité." In *E. T. A. Hoffmann et la musique*. Ed. Alain Montandon. Bern: Peter Lang, 1987. 337–47.

Jefferson, Alan. *The Operas of Richard Strauss in Britain 1910–1963*. London: Putnam, 1963.

Jellinek, George. *Callas: Portrait of a Prima Donna*. New York: Ziff-Davis, 1960.

Jenner, F. A. "Medicine and Addiction." In *Beyond the Pleasure Dome: Writing and Addiction from the Romantics*. Ed. Sue Vice, Matthew Campbell, and Tim Armstrong. Sheffield: Sheffield Academic, 1994. 18–22.

Jennings, Lee B. "The Role of Alcohol in Hoffman's Mythic Tales." In *Fairy Tales as Ways of Knowing*. Ed. Michael M. Metzger and Katharina Mommsen. Bern: Peter Lang, 1981. 182–94.

Joe, Jeongwon. "Opera on Film, Film in Opera: Postmodern Implications of the Cinematic Influence on Opera." Diss., Northwestern University, 1998.

Johnson, Mark. *The Body in the Mind: The Bodily Basis of Meaning, Imagination, and Reason*. Chicago: University of Chicago Press, 1987.

Johnstone, Gerry. "From Vice to Disease? The Concepts of Dipsomania and Inebriety, 1860–1908." *Social and Legal Studies* 5 (1996): 37–59.

Jordan, Carolyn Lamar. "Black Female Concert Singers of the Nineteenth Century: Nellie Brown Mitchell and Marie Selika Williams." In *Feel the Spirit: Studies in Nineteenth-Century Afro-American Music*. Ed. George R. Keck and Sherril V. Martin. Westport CT: Greenwood Press, 1988. 36–48.

Jourdain, Robert. *Music, the Brain, and Ecstasy: How Music Captures Our Imagination*. New York: William Morrow, 1997.

Kagan, Sergius. *On Studying Singing*. Toronto: Rinehard and Co., 1950.

Kamuf, Peggy. "The Replay's the Thing." In *Opera through Other Eyes*. Ed. David J. Levin. Stanford CA: Stanford University Press, 1994. 79–105.

Kaplan, Julius. *The Art of Gustave Moreau: Theory, Style and Content*. Ann Arbor: UMI, 1982.

Katz, Ruth. *Divining the Powers of Music: Aesthetic Theory and the Origins of Opera*. New York: Pendragon Press, 1986.

Kaufman, Tom. "The Grisi-Viardot Controversy, 1848–1852." *Opera Quarterly* 14.2 (1997–98): 7–22.

Kay, Sarah, and Miri Rubin, eds. *Framing Medieval Bodies*. Manchester: Manchester University Press, 1996.

Keates, Jonathan. "Introduction." In *Rigoletto*, by Giuseppe Verdi. Opera Guide 15. London: John Calder; New York: Riverrun Press, 1982. 7–13.

Kehler, Grace. "Questionable Embodiment: The Castrato in Corbiau's *Farinelli*." *Tessera* 21 (1996): 13–25.

———. *The Victorian Prima Donna in Literature and the Ghosts of Opera Past*. Forthcoming.

Keller, Mark. "Other Effects of Alcohol." In *Drinking and Intoxication: Selected Readings in Social Attitudes and Controls*. Ed. Raymond G. McCarthy. New Haven CT: College and University Press, 1959. 13–17.

Kellogg-Dennis, Patricia. "Oscar Wilde's *Salomé*: Symbolist Princess." In *Rediscovering Wilde*. Ed. C. George Sandulescu. Gerrards Cross, U.K.: Colin Smythe, 1994. 224–31.

Kennedy, Michael. *Britten*. 1981. London: J. M. Dent, 1993.

———. *Richard Strauss*. Oxford: Oxford University Press, 1995.

Kerényi, Carl. *Dionysos: Archetypal Image of Indestructible Life*. Trans. Ralph Manheim. Princeton NJ: Princeton University Press, 1976.

Kerman, Joseph. *Opera as Drama*. 1956. Rev. ed. Berkeley: University of California Press, 1988.

Kesting, Jürgen. *Maria Callas*. Trans. John Hunt. London: Quartet, 1992.

Khambata, A. S. "Anatomy and Physiology of Voice Production: The Phenomenal Voice." In *Music and the Brain: Studies in the Neurology of Music*. Ed. M. Critchley and R. A. Henson. London: Heinemann, 1977. 59–77.

Kittler, Friedrich. "World-Breath: On Wagner's Media Technology." In *Opera through Other Eyes*. Ed. David J. Levin. Stanford CA: Stanford University Press, 1994. 215–35.

Kivy, Peter. *Music Alone: Philosophical Reflections on the Purely Musical Experience*. Ithaca NY: Cornell University Press, 1990.

———. *Osmin's Rage: Philosophical Reflections on Opera, Drama, and Text*. Princeton NJ: Princeton University Press, 1988.

Klausner, Samuel Z. "Sacred and Profane Meanings of Blood and Alcohol." *Journal of Social Psychology* 64 (1964): 27–43.

Klein, Richard. *Eat Fat*. New York: Vintage, 1996.

Klein, Walter. "Die Harmonisation in 'Elektra' von Richard Strauss." *Der Merker* 2 (1911): 512–14.

Kluckhohn, Paul. *Die Auffassung der Liebe in der Literatur des 18. Jahrhunderts und in der deutschen Romantik*. Tübingen: Niemeyer, 1966.

Koestenbaum, Wayne. "Callas and Her Fans." *Yale Review* 79 (1989): 1–20.

———. "A Fan's Apostasy." *University of Toronto Quarterly* 67 (1998): 828–40.

———. *The Queen's Throat: Opera, Homosexuality, and the Mystery of Desire*. New York: Poseidon Press, 1993.

Köhler, Joachim. *Nietzsche and Wagner: A Lesson in Subjugation*. Trans. Ronald Taylor. New Haven CT: Yale University Press, 1998.

Kopperman, Paul E. "The Cheapest Pay: Alcohol Abuse in the Eighteenth-Century British Army." *Journal of Military History* 60 (1996): 445–70.

Koritz, Amy. *Gendering Bodies/Performing Art: Dance and Literature in Early Twentieth-Century British Culture*. Ann Arbor: University of Michigan Press, 1995.

Korte, Barbara. *Body Language in Literature*. Toronto: University of Toronto Press, 1997.

Koufman, James A., and P. David Blalock. "Vocal Fatigue and Dysphonia in the Professional Voice Use: Bogart-Bacall Syndrome." *Laryngoscope* 98 (1988): 493–98.

Kracauer, S. *Orpheus in Paris: Offenbach and the Paris of His Time*. Trans. Gwenda Davis and Eric Mosbacher. New York: Knopf, 1938.

Krafft-Ebing, Richard von. *Psychopathia Sexualis with Especial Reference to the Antipathetic Sexual Instinct*. Trans. F. J. Rebman. London: William Heinemann, 1931.

Kramer, Lawrence. "Culture and Musical Hermeneutics: The Salome Complex." *Cambridge Opera Journal* 2 (1990): 269–94.

———. "The Musicology of the Future." *repercussions* 1 (1992): 5–18.

Krause, Ernst. *Richard Strauss: The Man and His Work*. London: Collet's, 1964.

Krebs, Wolfgang. *Der Wille zum Rausch: Aspecte der musikalischen Dramaturgie von Richard Strauss' Salome*. Munich: Fink Verlag, 1991.

———. "Zur musikalischen Dramaturgie von Richard Strauss' *Salome*." In *Geschichte und Dramaturgie des Operneinakters*. Ed. Winfried Kirsch and Sieghart Döhring. Frankfurt am Main: Laaber-Verlag, 1988. 251–71.

Kristeva, Julia. *Powers of Horror: An Essay on Abjection*. Trans. Léon Rudiez. New York: Columbia University Press, 1982.

Kuryluk, Ewa. *Salome and Judas in the Cave of Sex: The Grotesque – Origins, Iconography, Technique*. Evanston IL: Northwestern University Press, 1987.

Lacambre, Geneviève. *Gustave Moreau: Maître sorcier*. Paris: Gallimard, 1997.

Lacoue-Labarthe, Philippe. *Musica Ficta (Figures of Wagner)*. Trans. Felicia McCarren. Stanford CA: Stanford University Press, 1994.

Langer, Suzanne K. *Feeling and Form*. New York: Scribner's, 1953.

Large, John, and Robert Patton. "The Effects of Weight Training and Aerobic Exercise on Singers." *Journal of Research in Singing* 4.2 (1981): 23–31.

Large, John, and Thomas Murry. "Studies of the Marchesi Model for Female Registration." *Journal of Research in Singing* 1.2 (1978): 1–13.

Law, Joe K. "Daring to Eat a Peach: Literary Allusion in *Albert Herring.*" *Opera Quarterly* 5.1 (1987): 1–10.

Lawrence, Christopher, and Steven Shapin, eds. *Science Incarnate: Historical Embodiments of Natural Knowledge.* Chicago: University of Chicago Press, 1998.

Lea, K. M. *Italian Popular Comedy.* Oxford: Clarendon Press, 1934.

Leake, Chauncey D. "Good-Willed Judgment on Alcohol." In *Alcohol and Civilization.* Ed. Salvatore Pablo Lucia. New York: McGraw-Hill, 1963. 3–22.

Leake, Chauncey D., and Milton Silverman. *Alcoholic Beverages in Clinical Medicine.* Cleveland: World Publishing, 1966.

Lebeck, Anne. *The Oresteia: A Study in Language and Structure.* Washington DC: Center for Hellenic Studies, 1971.

Lebrecht, Norman, ed. *The Book of Musical Anecdotes.* London: André Deutsch, 1985.

Leder, Drew. *The Absent Body.* Chicago: University of Chicago Press, 1990.

Lee, M. Owen. *First Intermissions.* New York: Oxford University Press, 1995.

Lee, William. *Brandy and Salt: Being an Effectual Remedy for Most of the Diseases which Afflict Humanity.* Quebec: W. Neilson, 1836.

Legge, Walter. "La Divina: Callas Remembered." *Opera News* (November 1977): 9–11, 50.

Legrand du Saulle, Henri. *Les Hystériques: Etat physique et état mental – Actes insolites, délictueux, et criminels.* Paris: Ballière, 1891.

Lehnert, H. "Thomas Mann's Early Interest in Myth and Erwin Rohde's *Psyche.*" *PMLA* 79 (1964): 297–304.

Leiber, Deborah Burton. "Laughter and Humor in Critical Care." *Dimensions of Critical Care Nursing* 5.3 (1980): 162–70.

Leonardi, Susan J., and Rebecca A. Pope. *The Diva's Mouth: Body, Voice, Prima Donna Politics.* New Brunswick NJ: Rutgers University Press, 1996.

Leppert, Richard. *The Sight of Sound: Music, Representation, and the History of the Body.* Berkeley: University of California Press, 1993.

Levin, David J. "Is There a Text in This Libido? *Diva* and the Rhetoric of Contemporary Opera Criticism." Paper presented at the annual convention of the Modern Language Association, San Francisco CA, December 1998.

————. "Introduction." In *Opera through Other Eyes.* Stanford CA: Stanford University Press, 1994. 1–18.

————, ed. *Opera through Other Eyes.* Stanford CA: Stanford University Press, 1994.

Levin, Thomas Y. "For the Record: Adorno on Music in the Age of Its Technological Reproducibility." *October* 55 (1990): 21–47.

Levinthal, Charles F. *Messengers of Paradise: Opiates and the Brain.* New York: Doubleday, 1988.

Lewington, Mike. "Alcoholism in the Movies: An Overview." In *Images of Alcoholism.* Ed. Jim Cook and Mike Lewington. London: British Film Institute, 1974. 22–29.

Lewis, Hanna B. "Salome and Elektra: Sisters or Strangers." *Orbis Litterarum* 31 (1976): 125–33.

Lewis, Marcia. *The Private Lives of the Three Tenors: Behind the Scenes with Placido Domingo, Luciano Pavarotti, and José Carreras.* Secaucus NJ: Birch Lane Press, 1996.

Lindenberger, Herbert. *Opera: The Extravagant Art.* Ithaca NY: Cornell University Press, 1984.

————. *Opera in History.* Stanford CA: Stanford University Press, 1998.

Lisansky, Edith S. "Psychological Effects." In *Drinking and Intoxication: Selected Readings in Social Attitudes and Controls.* New Haven CT: College and University Press, 1959. 18–25.

Littlejohn, David. "The Odd Couple: Offenbach and Hoffmann." In *The Ultimate Art: Essays around and about Opera.* Ed. David Littlejohn. Berkeley: University of California Press, 1992. 224–34.

Locke, Ralph P. "What Are These Women Doing in Opera?" In *En Travesti: Women, Gender Subversion, Opera.* Ed. Corinne E. Blackmer and Patricia Juliana Smith. New York: Columbia University Press, 1995. 59–98.

Logan, John Frederick. "The Age of Intoxication." *Yale French Studies* 50 (1974): 81–95.

Lombroso, Caesar, and William Ferrero. *The Female Offender.* New York: Philosophical Library, 1958.

Longmate, Norman. *The Waterdrinkers: A History of Temperance.* London: Hamish Hamilton, 1968.

Loraux, Nicole. "Therefore, Socrates Is Immortal." Trans. Janet Lloyd. In *Fragments for a History of the Human Body.* Ed. Michel Feher, Ramona Naddaff, and Nadia Tazi. New York: Zone, 1989. 2: 12–45.

Bibliography

Lowe, David A. "Diva Assoluta: Life, Art, Legacy." In *Callas as They Saw Her*. Ed. David A. Lowe. New York: Ungar, 1986. 1–14.

———, ed. *Callas as They Saw Her*. New York: Ungar, 1986.

Luchsinger, Richard, and Godfrey E. Arnold. *Voice Speech Language: Clinical Communicology: Its Physiology and Pathology*. Trans. Godfrey E. Arnold and Evelyn Robe Finkbeiner. Belmont CA: Wadsworth, 1965.

Lucia, Salvatore Pablo. "The Antiquity of Alcohol in Diet and Medicine." In *Alcohol and Civilization*. Ed. Salvatore Pablo Lucia. New York: McGraw-Hill, 1963. 151–66.

———, ed. *Alcohol and Civilization*. New York: McGraw-Hill, 1963.

MacIntyre, A. *After Virtue: A Study in Moral Theory*. 2d ed. Notre Dame: University of Notre Dame Press, 1984.

Mackinlay, M. Sterling. *Garcia the Centenarian and His Times*. New York: Appleton, 1908.

Madden, J. S. "Some Cultural Aspects of Drinking." *British Journal on Alcohol and Alcoholism* 17.1 (1982): 1–4.

Magli, Patrizia. "The Face and the Soul." In *Fragments for a History of the Human Body*. Ed. Michel Feher, Ramona Naddaff, and Nadia Tazi. New York: Zone, 1989. 2: 86–127.

Mahling, Christoph-Hellmut. " 'Schweig' und tanze!' Zum 'tönenden Schweigen' bei Richard Strauss." In *Die Sprache der Musik: Festschrift Klaus Wolfgang Niemöller*. Ed. Jobst Peter Fricke. Regensburg: Gustav Bosse, 1989. 371–79.

Mallett, Jane. "Use of Humour and Laughter in Patient Care." *British Journal of Nursing* 2.3 (1993): 172–75.

Mancall, Peter C. *Deadly Medicine: Indians and Alcohol in Early America*. Ithaca NY: Cornell University Press, 1995.

Mandelbaum, David G. "Alcohol and Culture." In *Beliefs, Behaviors, and Alcoholic Beverages: A Cross-Cultural Study*. Ed. Mac Marshall. Ann Arbor: University of Michigan Press, 1979. 14–30.

Mann, Thomas. "Death in Venice." In *Death in Venice and Seven Other Stories*. Trans. H. T. Lowe-Porter. New York: Vintage, 1989.

———. *Der Tod in Venedig*. Ed. T. J. Reed. London: Oxford University Press, 1971.

Mann, William. *Richard Strauss: A Critical Study of the Operas*. London: Cassell, 1964.

Marafioti, P. Mario. *Caruso's Method of Voice Production: The Scientific Culture of the Voice*. New York: Appleton, 1922.

Marchesi, Mathilde. *Marchesi and Music.* New York: Harper and Brothers, 1898.

Marek, George R. "Cry of Anguish." *Opera News* 8 December 1984: 16–18.

Marin, Louis. *Food for Thought.* Trans. Mette Hjort. Baltimore MD: Johns Hopkins University Press, 1989.

Marinus of Samaria. *The Life of Proclus or Concerning Happiness.* Trans. Kenneth S. Guthrie. Grand Rapids MI: Phanes Press, 1986.

Marrus, Michael R. "Social Drinking in the *Belle Epoque.*" *Journal of Social History* 7.2 (1974): 115–41.

Marshall, Mac, ed. *Beliefs, Behaviors, and Alcoholic Beverages: A Cross-Cultural Study.* Ann Arbor: University of Michigan Press, 1979.

———. "Conclusions." In *Beliefs, Behaviors, and Alcoholic Beverages: A Cross-Cultural Study.* Ed. Mac Marshall. Ann Arbor: University of Michigan Press, 1979. 451–57.

———. "Introduction." In *Beliefs, Behaviors, and Alcoholic Beverages: A Cross-Cultural Study.* Ed. Mac Marshall. Ann Arbor: University of Michigan Press, 1979. 1–11.

Martin, G. N., and C. D. Gray. "The Effects of Audience Laughter on Men's and Women's Responses to Humor." *Journal of Social Psychology* 136 (1996): 221–31.

Martin, Rod A., and Herbert M. Lefcourt. "Sense of Humor as a Moderator of the Relation between Stressors and Moods." *Journal of Personality and Social Psychology* 45 (1983): 1313–24.

Marwick, Arthur. *Beauty in History: Society, Politics and Personal Appearance c. 1500 to the Present.* London: Thames and Hudson, 1988.

Mathieu, Pierre-Louis. *Gustave Moreau: Sa vie, son oeuvre.* Paris: Bibliothèque des arts, 1976.

———. "La Religion dans la vie et l'oeuvre de Gustave Moreau." In *Gustave Moreau et la Bible.* Nice: Musée national message biblique Marc Chagall, 1991. 15–24.

Mathison, Richard R. *The Eternal Search: The Story of Man and His Drugs.* New York: G. P. Putnam's Sons, 1958.

Matravers, Derek. *Art and Emotion.* Oxford: Clarendon Press, 1998.

Matz, Mary Jane. "We Introduce Maria Meneghini Callas." *Opera News* 3 December 1956: 6–8.

Maudsley, Henry. *The Physiology and Pathology of Mind.* 2d ed. London: Macmillan, 1868.

Maupassant, Guy de. "Le Rosier de Madame Husson." *Contes et nouvelles.* Ed. Albert-Marie Schmidt. Paris: Albin Michel, 1957. 2: 680–97.

McCarren, Felicia. "The 'Symptomatic Act' circa 1900: Hysteria, Hypnosis, Electricity, Dance." *Critical Inquiry* 21 (1995): 748–74.

McCarthy, Raymond G., ed. *Drinking and Intoxication: Selected Readings in Social Attitudes and Controls.* New Haven CT: College and University Press, 1959.

McClary, Susan. *Feminine Endings: Music, Gender, and Sexuality.* Minneapolis: University of Minnesota Press, 1991.

———. "The Undoing of Opera: Toward a Feminist Criticism of Music." In *Opera, or the Undoing of Women* by Catherine Clement. Trans. Betsy Wing. London: Virago, 1989. ix–xviii.

McCord, David. "The English and American History of Voluntary Intoxication to Negate *Mens Rea*." *Journal of Legal History* 11 (1990): 372–95.

McCracken, Tim. "Redeeming Salome: The Face in the Figure." Unpublished ms.

McDonald, Maryon. "Introduction: A Social-Anthropological View of Gender, Drink and Drugs." In *Gender, Drink and Drugs.* Ed. Maryon McDonald. Oxford: Berg, 1994. 1–31.

McGlathery, James M. *E. T. A. Hoffmann.* New York: Twayne, 1997.

———. *Mysticism and Sexuality: E. T. A. Hoffmann; Part One: Hoffmann and His Sources.* Las Vegas: Peter Lang, 1981.

McKee, David. "Basta, Diva." *Opera News* 6 December 1997: 86.

Meltzer, Françoise. "A Response to René Girard's Reading of Salome." *New Literary History* 15 (1984): 325–32.

———. *Salome and the Dance of Writing: Portraits of Mimesis in Literature.* Chicago: University of Chicago Press, 1987.

Meneghini, Giovanni Battista, with Renzo Allegri. *My Wife Maria Callas.* Trans. Henry Wisneski. New York: Farrar, Straus and Giroux, 1982.

Merkel, Kerstin. *Salome: Ikonographie im Wandel.* Frankfurt am Main: Peter Lang, 1990.

Merleau-Ponty, Maurice. *Phenomenology of Perception.* Trans. Colin Smith. 1962. London: Routledge, 1994.

Merrill, Robert, with Robert Saffron. *Between Acts: An Irreverent Look at Opera and Other Madness.* New York: McGraw-Hill, 1976.

Meryman, Richard. "A Tour of Two Great Throats." *Life Magazine* 26 June 1970: 64–71.

Bibliography

Messerli, P., P. Pegna, and N. Sordet. "Hemispheric Dominance for Melody Recognition in Musicians and Non-Musicians." *Neuropsychologia* 33.4 (1995): 395–405.

Messmer, Franzpeter, ed. *Kritiken zu den Uraufführungen der Bühnenwerke von Richard Strauss*. Pfaffenhofen: W. Ludwig Verlag, 1989.

Meyer, Leonard. *Emotion and Meaning in Music*. Chicago: University of Chicago Press, 1956.

Meyer-Baer, K. *Music of the Spheres and the Dance of Death: Studies in Musical Iconology*. Princeton NJ: Princeton University Press, 1970.

Micale, Mark S. "Hysteria Male/Hysteria Female: Reflections on Comparative Gender Construction in Nineteenth-Century France and Britain." In *Science and Sensibility: Gender and Scientific Inquiry*. Ed. Marina Benjamin. Oxford: Blackwell, 1991. 200–239.

Miller, Richard. *On the Art of Singing*. New York: Oxford University Press, 1996.

Milner, Max, and Martine Chatelain, eds. *L'Imaginaire du vin: Colloque pluridisciplinaire*. Marseille: Jeanne Laffitte, 1983.

Mirzoeff, Nicholas. *Bodyscape: Art, Modernity and the Ideal Figure*. London and New York: Routledge, 1995.

Mitchell, David T., and Sharon L. Snyder, eds. *The Body and Physical Difference: Discourses of Disability*. Ann Arbor: University of Michigan Press, 1997.

Mitchell, Donald, ed. *Benjamin Britten: Death in Venice*. Cambridge: Cambridge University Press, 1987.

———. "*Death in Venice*: The Dark Side of Perfection." In *The Britten Companion*. Ed. Christopher Palmer. Cambridge: Cambridge University Press, 1984. 238–49.

———. "An Introduction in the Shape of a Memoir." In *Benjamin Britten: Death in Venice*. Ed. Donald Mitchell. Cambridge: Cambridge University Press, 1987. 1–25.

———. "The Serious Comedy of *Albert Herring*." *Opera Quarterly* 4.3 (1986): 45–59.

Mitchell, Ronald E. *Opera Dead or Alive: Production, Performance, and Enjoyment of Musical Theatre*. Madison: University of Wisconsin Press, 1970.

Mitchell, Stephen A. "Medical Problems of Professional Voice Users." *Comprehensive Therapy* 22 (1996): 231–38.

Bibliography

Montandon, Alain. "L'Imaginaire du vin dans le romantisme allemand." In *L'Imaginaire du vin: Colloque pluridisciplinaire*. Ed. Max Milner and Martine Chatelain. Marseille: Jeanne Laffitte, 1983. 159–66.

Moon, Michael, and Eve Kosofsky Sedgwick. "Divinity: A Dossier/A Performance Piece/A Little-Understood Emotion." In *Tendencies*. By Eve Kosofsky Sedgwick. Durham: Duke University Press, 1993. 215–52.

Mordden, Ethan. *Demented: The World of the Opera Diva*. New York: Franklin Watts, 1984.

Moreau, Gustave. *L'Assembleur de rêves: Ecrits complets de Gustave Moreau*. Fontfroide: Bibliothèque artistique et littéraire, Fata Morgana, 1984.

Moretti, Franco. *Signs Taken for Wonders*. London: Verso, 1983.

Morgan, Robert P. "*The Tempest*." In *The New Grove Dictionary of Opera*. Ed. Stanley Sadie. London: Macmillan, 1992. 4: 685.

Mosak, Harold, and Michael Maniacci. "An 'Alderian' Approach to Humor and Psychotherapy." In *Advances in Humor and Psychotherapy*. Ed. William F. Fry, Jr., and Waleed A. Salamel. Sarasota FL: Professional Resource Exchange, 1993. 1–18.

Mosher, Clelia D. *The Mosher Survey: Sexual Attitudes of 45 Victorian Women*. Ed. James MaHood and Kristine Wenburg. New York: Arno Press, 1980.

Moss, Harold Gene. "*The Beggar's Opera* as Christian Satire." In *Twentieth Century Interpretations of* The Beggar's Opera. Ed. Yvonne Nobel. Englewood Cliffs NJ: Prentice-Hall, 1975. 55–64.

Moure, E. J., and A. Bouyer. *The Abuse of the Singing and Speaking Voice*. Trans. Macleod Yearsley. London: Kegan Paul, Trench, Trübner, 1910.

Mueller, Martin. "Hofmannsthal's *Elektra* and Its Dramatic Models." *Modern Drama* 29.1 (1986): 71–91.

Müller, J. "Die Figur des Trinkers in der deutschen Literatur seit dem Naturalismus." *Psychiatrie, Neurologie und medizinische Psychologie: Zeitschrift für Forschung und Praxis* 21.6 (1969): 201–11.

Mulvey, Laura. "Visual Pleasure and Narrative Cinema." *Screen* 16.3 (1975): 6–18.

Murray, David. "*Ariadne auf Naxos*." In *The New Grove Dictionary of Opera*. Ed. Stanley Sadie. London: Macmillan, 1992. 1: 178–82.

———. "*Elektra*." In *The New Grove Dictionary of Opera*. Ed. Stanley Sadie. London: Macmillan, 1992. 2: 32–35.

———. "Richard (Georg) Strauss." In *The New Grove Dictionary of Opera*. Ed. Stanley Sadie. London: Macmillan, 1992. 4: 565–75.

————. "*Salome*." In *The New Grove Dictionary of Opera*. Ed. Stanley Sadie. London: Macmillan, 1992. 4: 146–49.

Nahoum-Grappe, Véronique. *La Culture de l'ivresse: Essai de phénoménologie historique*. Paris: Quai Voltaire, 1991.

————. "France." In *International Handbook on Alcohol and Culture*. Ed. Dwight B. Heath. Westport CT: Greenwood Press, 1995. 75–87.

————. "Histoire du vin: Un Choix socioculturel et technique dans la France d'ancien régime." In *L'Imaginaire du vin: Colloque pluridisciplinaire*. Ed. Max Milner and Martine Chatelain. Marseille: Jeanne Laffitte, 1983. 297–305.

Negus, Kenneth. *E. T. A. Hoffmann's Other World: The Romantic Author and His "New Mythology."* Philadelphia: University of Pennsylvania Press, 1965.

Neitzel, Otto. " 'Salome' von Oskar Wilde und Richard Strauss." *Neue Musik Zeitung* 28.17 (1907): 365–71, 390–92.

Neumann, Gerhard. "Der Erzählakt als Oper Jules Barbier–Michel Carré: Drama und Libretto 'Les Contes d'Hoffmann.' " In *Jacques Offenbachs Hoffmanns Erzählungen*. Ed. Gabriele Brandstetter. Laaber: Laaber Verlag, 1988. 39–114.

Newman, Ernest. *More Opera Nights*. London: Putnam, 1954.

Newman, J., J. H. Rosenbach, K. L. Burns, B. C. Latimer, H. R. Matocha, and E. R. Vogt. "An Experimental Test of 'The Mozart Effect': Does Listening to His Music Improve Spatial Ability?" *Perceptual and Motor Skills* 81.3, pt. 2 (1995): 1379–87.

Nietzsche, Friedrich. *The Birth of Tragedy* and *The Case of Wagner*. Trans. Walter Kaufmann. New York: Vintage, 1967.

————. *Thus Spoke Zarathustra*. Trans. Walter Kaufmann. Harmondsworth: Penguin, 1985.

————. *Werke*. Vol. 1. *Die Geburt der Tragödie*. Ed. Karl Schlechta. Frankfurt am Main: Ullstein, 1972.

Noble, Yvonne, ed. *Twentieth Century Interpretations of* The Beggar's Opera. Englewood Cliffs NJ: Prentice-Hall, 1975.

Nordau, Max. *Degeneration*. 2nd ed. 1892. Intro. by George L. Mosse. New York: Howard Fertig, 1968.

Obbink, Dirk. "Dionysus Poured Out: Ancient and Modern Theories of Sacrifice and Cultural Formation." In *Masks of Dionysus*. Ed. Thomas A. Carpenter and Christopher A. Faraone. Ithaca NY: Cornell University Press, 1993. 65–88.

O'Brien, John Maxwell, and Sheldon C. Seller. "Attributes of Alcohol in the Old Testament." *Drinking and Drug Practices Surveyor* 18 (1982): 18–24.

Oliver, Michael. *Benjamin Britten*. London: Phaedon, 1996.

Olivesi, Jean-Marc. " 'La Lune s'attristait . . .' " In *Salomé dans les collections françaises*. St.-Denis: Musée d'art et d'histoire, 1988. 29–31.

Onorati, Franco. *"Libiamo, libiamo . . .": Trasgressioni conviviali nell'opera lirica e dintorni*. Rome: Il Ventaglio, 1987.

Osborne, Charles. *Rigoletto*. London: Barrie and Jenkins, 1979.

Osborne, Conrad L. "Up from the Huff n' Hook: New Books on Voice." *Musical Newsletter* 7.1 (1977): 8–20.

Otto, Walter F. *Dionysus: Myth and Cult*. Trans. Robert B. Palmer. Bloomington: Indiana University Press, 1965.

Owens, Craig. "The Discourse of Others: Feminism and Postmodernism." In *The Anti-Aesthetic: Essays on Postmodern Culture*. Ed. Hal Foster. Seattle: Bay Press, 1983. 57–82.

Pacteau, Francette. *The Symptom of Beauty*. Cambridge MA: Harvard University Press, 1994.

Padel, Ruth. *Whom Gods Destroy: Elements of Greek and Tragic Madness*. Princeton NJ: Princeton University Press, 1995.

Paglia, Camille. *Sex, Art, and American Culture*. New York: Vintage, 1992.

———. *Sexual Personae: Art and Decadence from Nefertiti to Emily Dickinson*. New York: Vintage, 1990.

Pahlen, Kurt. *Great Singers: From the Seventeenth Century to the Present Day*. Trans. Oliver Colburn. London: W. H. Allen, 1973.

Palmer, Christopher. "Britten's Venice Orchestra." In *Benjamin Britten: Death in Venice*. Ed. Donald Mitchell. Cambridge: Cambridge University Press, 1987. 129–53.

———, ed. *The Britten Companion*. London: Faber and Faber, 1984.

Panksepp, Jaak. "The Emotional Sources of 'Chills' Induced by Music." *Music Perception* 13.2 (1995): 171–207.

Papagaroufali, Eleni. "Uses of Alcohol among Women: Games of Resistance, Power and Pleasure." In *Alcohol, Gender and Culture*. Ed. Dimitra Gefou-Madianou. London and New York: Routledge, 1992. 48–67.

Paquin, Rev. L. P. *Lecture on the Hurtful Qualities of Spiritous Liquors*. Quebec: C. Darveau, 1880.

Parker, Roger. "The Music of 'Rigoletto.' " In *Rigoletto*. By Giuseppe Verdi. ENO Opera Guide Series. London: John Calder; New York: Riverrun Press, 1982. 15–24.

————. "*Rigoletto.*" In *The New Grove Dictionary of Opera.* Ed. Stanley Sadie. London: Macmillan, 1992. 3: 1327–30.

Partanen, Juha. *Sociability and Intoxication: Alcohol and Drinking in Kenya, Africa, and the Modern World.* Finnish Foundation for Alcohol Studies. Vol. 39. 1991.

Pater, Walter. "A Study of Dionysus: The Spiritual Form of Fire and Dew." *Fortnightly Review* 20 (1876): 752–72.

Pavarotti, Luciano, with William Wright. *Pavarotti: My Own Story.* Garden City NY: Doubleday, 1981.

Pavarotti, Luciano, and William Wright. *Pavarotti: My World.* New York: Crown, 1995.

Pavis, Patrice. *Dictionary of the Theatre: Terms, Concepts, and Analysis.* Trans. Christine Shantz. Toronto: University of Toronto Press, 1998.

Pearce, Charles E. *Polly Peachum: The Story of Lavinia Fenton and* The Beggar's Opera. New York: Benjamin Blom, 1968.

Pearsall, Ronald. *The Worm in the Bud.* London: Pimlico, 1969.

Peraino, Judith A. "I Am an Opera: Identifying with Henry Purcell's *Dido and Aeneas.*" In *En Travesti: Women, Gender Subversion, Opera.* Ed. Corinne E. Blackmer and Patricia Juliana Smith. New York: Columbia University Press, 1995. 99–131.

Perniola, Mario. "Between Clothing and Nudity." Trans. Roger Friedman. In *Fragments for a History of the Human Body.* Ed. Michel Feher, Ramona Naddaff, and Nadia Tazi. New York: Zone, 1989. 2: 236–65.

Petitjean, Martial. "Symbolisme et sacrifice." *L'Avant-scène opéra* 47–48 (1983): 132–37.

Phelan, Peggy. *Mourning Sex: Performing Public Memories.* London and New York: Routledge, 1997.

Phillips-Matz, Mary Jane. *Verdi: A Biography.* Oxford: Oxford University Press, 1993.

Piper, Myfanwy. "The Libretto." In *Benjamin Britten:* Death in Venice. Ed. Donald Mitchell. Cambridge: Cambridge University Press, 1987. 45–54.

Pirie, Peter J. *The English Musical Renaissance.* London: Victor Gollancz, 1979.

Plant, Martin A. "The United Kingdom." In *International Handbook on Alcohol and Culture.* Ed. Dwight B. Heath. Westport CT: Greenwood Press, 1995. 289–99.

Plato. *The Collected Dialogues.* Ed. Edith Hamilton and Huntington Cairns. Princeton NJ: Bollingen Series LXXI, n.d.

———. *Phaedrus.* Trans. R. Hackforth. In *The Collected Dialogues.* Ed. Edith Hamilton and Huntington Cairns. Princeton NJ: Bollingen Series LXXI, n.d. 476–525.

———. *Republic.* Trans. Paul Shorey. In *The Collected Dialogues.* Ed. Edith Hamilton and Huntington Cairns. Princeton NJ: Bollingen Series LXXI, n.d. 575–844.

———. *Symposium.* Trans. Michael Joyce. In *The Collected Dialogues.* Ed. Edith Hamilton and Huntington Cairns. Princeton NJ: Bollingen Series LXXI, n.d. 527–74.

———. *Timaeus.* Trans. Benjamin Jowett. In *The Collected Dialogues.* Ed. Edith Hamilton and Huntington Cairns. Princeton NJ: Bollingen Series LXXI, n.d. 1151–1211.

Plaut, Eric A. "Offenbach's *The Tales of Hoffmann*: The Impoverished German Jew and the Celebrated French Catholic." In *Grand Opera: Mirror of the Western Mind.* Chicago: Ivan R. Dee, 1993. 199–216.

Poizat, Michel. *The Angel's Cry: Beyond the Pleasure Principle in Opera.* Trans. Arthur Denner. Ithaca NY: Cornell University Press, 1992.

Poland, Warren S. "The Gift of Laughter: On the Development of a Sense of Humor in Clinical Analysis." *Psychoanalytic Quarterly* 59.2 (1990): 197–225.

Pollock, Griselda. "The Gaze and the Look: Women with Binoculars – A Question of Difference." In *Dealing with Degas: Representations of Women and the Politics of Vision.* Ed. Richard Kendall and Griselda Pollock. New York: Universe, 1992. 106–30.

Poole, Jane L. "Viewpoint." *Opera News* (February 1989): 4.

Porter, Roy. "The Body and the Mind, the Doctor and the Patient: Negotiating Hysteria." In *Hysteria beyond Freud.* Ed. Sander L. Gilman, Helen King, Roy Porter, G. S. Rousseau, and Elaine Showalter. Berkeley: University of California Press, 1993. 225–85.

———. "The Drinking Man's Disease: The 'Pre-History' of Alcoholism in Georgian Britain." *British Journal of Addiction* 80 (1985): 385–96.

Porzionato, Giuseppe. *Psicobiologia della musica.* Bologna: Pàtron, 1980.

Poznanski, Andrew. "Our Drinking Heritage." In *Drinking and Intoxication: Selected Readings in Social Attitudes and Controls.* Ed. Raymond G. McCarthy. New Haven CT: College and University Press, 1959. 42–43.

Praz, Mario. "Salome in Literary Tradition." In *Richard Strauss: Salome.* Ed. Derrick Puffett. Cambridge: Cambridge University Press, 1989. 11–20.

Bibliography

Préaud, Maxime. "Le Vin et la mélancolie." In *L'Imaginaire du vin: Colloque pluridisciplinaire*. Ed. Max Milner and Martine Chatelain. Marseille: Jeanne Laffitte, 1983. 289–93.

"The Prima Donna." *Time* 29 October 1956: 54–58.

Psomiades, Kathy Alexis. *Beauty's Body: Femininity and Representation in British Aestheticism*. Stanford CA: Stanford University Press, 1997.

Puffett, Derrick. "Introduction." In *Richard Strauss: Elektra*. Ed. Derrick Puffett. Cambridge: Cambridge University Press, 1989. 1–9.

———. "Introduction." In *Richard Strauss: Salome*. Ed. Derrick Puffett. Cambridge: Cambridge University Press, 1989. 1–10.

———. "The Music of 'Elektra': Some Preliminary Thoughts." In *Richard Strauss: Elektra*. Ed. Derrick Puffett. Cambridge: Cambridge University Press, 1989. 33–43.

———. "Postlude: Images of Salome." In *Richard Strauss: Salome*. Ed. Derrick Puffett. Cambridge: Cambridge University Press, 1989. 161–64.

———. " 'Salome' as Music Drama." In *Richard Strauss: Salome*. Ed. Derrick Puffett. Cambridge: Cambridge University Press, 1989. 58–87.

———, ed. *Richard Strauss: Elektra*. Cambridge: Cambridge University Press, 1989.

———, ed. *Richard Strauss: Salome*. Cambridge: Cambridge University Press, 1989.

Pyle, Tres. "Extravagance, or Salome's Kiss." Lecture presented at the University of Toronto, 22 October 1997.

Pym, Anthony. "The Importance of Salomé: Approaches to a *Fin de siècle* Theme." *French Forum* 14 (1989): 311–22.

Rauscher, R. H., G. L. Shaw, and K. N. Ky. "Listening to Mozart Enhances Spatial-Temporal Reasoning: Towards a Neurophysiological Basis." *Neuroscience Letter* 185.1 (1995): 44–47.

Reed, T. J. "Mann and His Novella: 'Death in Venice.' " In *Benjamin Britten: Death in Venice*. Ed. Donald Mitchell. Cambridge: Cambridge University Press, 1987. 163–77.

Reid, Cornelius L. "The Nature of Natural Singing." *Journal of Research in Singing and Applied Vocal Pedagogy* 11.2 (1988): 3–21.

Reinders, Ank. "Teaching the High Female Voice." *Journal of Research in Singing and Applied Vocal Pedagogy* 12.1 (1988): 43–46.

Richardson, Benjamin Ward. *The Temperance Lesson Book: A Series of Short Lessons on Alcohol and Its Action on the Body*. London: National Temperance Publication Depot, n.d.

Riquelme, J. P. "Shalom/Solomon/*Salomé*: Modernism and Wilde's Aesthetic Politics." *Centennial Review* 39 (1995): 575–610.

Roach, Joseph R. *The Player's Passion.* Cranbury NJ: Associated University Presses, 1985.

———. "Power's Body: The Inscription of Morality as Style." In *Interpreting the Theatrical Past.* Ed. Thomas Postlewait and Bruce A. McConachie. Iowa City: University of Iowa Press, 1989. 99–118.

Roach, Mary K. "The Biochemical and Physiological Effects of Alcohol." In *Alcohol, Science and Society Revisited.* Ed. Edith Lisansky Gomberg, Helene Rasking White, and John A. Carpenter. Ann Arbor: University of Michigan Press, 1982. 17–37.

Robb, Graham. *Victor Hugo.* London: Picador, 1997.

Roberts, James. *Drink, Temperance and the Working Class in Nineteenth-Century Germany.* Boston: Allen and Unwin, 1984.

Roberts, Jeanne Addison. *Shakespeare's English Comedy:* The Merry Wives of Windsor *in Context.* Lincoln: University of Nebraska Press, 1979.

Robinson, Vera B. "Humor and Health." In *Handbook of Humor Research.* Ed. Paul E. McGhee and Jeffrey H. Goldstein. New York: Springer-Verlag, 1983. 2: 109–28.

Roch, J. B. "Le Phoniatre et le comédien." *Revue de laryngologie* 111.4 (1990): 379–80.

Rohde, Erwin. *Psyche: The Cult of Souls and the Belief in Immortality among the Greeks.* 1890. 8th ed. London: Kegan Paul, Trench, Trubner; New York: Harcourt, Brace, 1925.

Rohrer, James R. "The Origins of the Temperance Movement: A Reinterpretation." *Journal of American Studies* 24 (1990): 228–35.

Rorem, Ned. "Critical Reception: Britten's Venice." In *Benjamin Britten:* Death in Venice. Ed. Donald Mitchell. Cambridge: Cambridge University Press, 1987. 186–91.

Roseberry, Eric. "Tonal Ambiguity in 'Death in Venice': A Symphonic View." In *Benjamin Britten:* Death in Venice. Ed. Donald Mitchell. Cambridge: Cambridge University Press, 1987. 86–98.

Rosen, Deborah Caputo, and Robert Thayer. *Psychology of Voice Disorders.* San Diego: Singular Publishing Group, 1997.

Rosenthal, Harold. "Callas Remembered." *Opera* 28 (1977): 1012–15.

Rosselli, John. "Castrato." In *The New Grove Dictionary of Opera.* Ed. Stanley Sadie. London: Macmillan, 1992. 1: 766–68.

Bibliography

Rossi, Nick. "A Tale of Two Countries: The Operas of Mario Castelnuovo-Tedesco." *Opera Quarterly* 7.3 (1990): 89–121.

Roueché, Berton. "Alcohol in Human Culture." In *Alcohol and Civilization.* Ed. Salvatore Pablo Lucia. New York: McGraw-Hill, 1963. 167–82.

Rouse, John. "Comment." *Theatre Journal* 49 (1997): 394–95.

Rousseau, Jean-Jacques. "Theatre." In *The Indispensible Rousseau.* Ed. John Hope Mason. London: Quartet, 1979. 120–33.

Ruthrof, Horst. *Semantics and the Body: Meaning from Frege to the Postmodern.* Toronto: University of Toronto Press, 1997.

Rycenga, Jennifer. "Lesbian Compositional Process: One Lover-Composer's Perspective." In *Queering the Pitch: The New Gay and Lesbian Musicology.* Ed. Philip Brett, Elizabeth Wood, and Gary C. Thomas. New York and London: Routledge, 1994. 275–96.

Sadie, Stanley, ed. *The New Grove Dictionary of Opera.* 4 vols. London: Macmillan, 1992.

Sadler, Graham. "*Platée.*" In *The New Grove Dictionary of Opera.* Ed. Stanley Sadie. London: Macmillan, 1992. 3: 1030–32.

Safire, William. *Coming to Terms.* New York: Doubleday, 1991.

Said, Edward. *Orientalism.* 1978. New York: Vintage, 1979.

Salasa, M. H. "Emile Zola and the Concept of Alcoholism in Nineteenth-Century France." *British Journal on Alcohol and Alcoholism* 12.1 (1977): 14–22.

Santley, Sir Charles. *The Art of Singing and Vocal Declamation.* London: Macmillan, 1908.

Sataloff, Dahlia M., and Robert R. Sataloff. "Obesity and the Professional Voice User." In *Professional Voice: The Science and Art of Clinical Care.* By Robert Thayer Sataloff. New York: Raven Press, 1991.

Sataloff, Robert T., and Joseph R. Spiegel. "Care of the Professional Voice." *Otolaryngologic Clinics of North America* 24 (1991): 1093–1124.

Satriani, Luigi Lombardi. "Un Itinéraire du vin: Via-verità-vite." In *Le Ferment divin.* Ed. Dominique Fournier and Salvatore D'Onofrio. Paris: Editions de la maison des sciences de l'homme, 1991. 93–100.

Satzinger, Christa. *The French Influence on Oscar Wilde's* The Picture of Dorian Gray *and* Salome. Lewiston and Salzburg: Edwin Mellen Press, Salzburg University Studies, 1994.

Scarry, Elaine. *On Beauty and Being Just.* Princeton NJ: Princeton University Press, 1999.

Schafer, R. Murray. *E. T. A. Hoffmann and Music*. Toronto: University of Toronto Press, 1975.

Schatt, Peter W. *Exotik in der Musik des 20. Jahrhunderts: Historisch-systematische Untersuchungen zur Metamorphose einer ästhetischen Fiktion*. Munich and Salzburg: Musikverlag Emil Katzbichler, 1986.

Scheier, Helmut. "Old Testament Materials for Ballet and Modern Dance." *Choreography and Dance* 2.3 (1992): 19–26.

Schellenberg, E. Glenn, and Sandra E. Trehub. "Natural Musical Intervals: Evidence from Infant Listeners." *Psychological Science* 7.5 (1996): 272–77.

Schipkowensky, N. "Musical Therapy in the Field of Psychiatry and Neurology." In *Music and the Brain: Studies in the Neurology of Music*. Ed. M. Critchley and R. A. Henson. London: Heinemann, 1977. 433–45.

Schivelbusch, Wolfgang. *Tastes of Paradise: A Social History of Spices, Stimulants, and Intoxicants*. Trans. David Jacobson. New York: Pantheon, 1992.

Schlötterer, Reinhold. "Elektras Tanz in der Tragödie Hugo von Hofmannsthals." *Hofmannsthal Blätter* 33 (1986): 47–49.

Schmidgall, Gary. "Imp of Perversity." *Opera News* 12 February 1977: 11–13.

———. *Literature as Opera*. New York: Oxford University Press, 1977.

———. *Shakespeare and Opera*. New York: Oxford University Press, 1990.

Schmidt, Carl B. "Dance: 1, 2." In *The New Grove Dictionary of Opera*. Ed. Stanley Sadie. London: Macmillan, 1992. 1: 1058–62.

Schmidt-Garre, Helmut. "Der Teufel in der Musik." *Melos* 1.3 (1975): 174–83.

Schmitt, Jean-Claude. "The Ethics of Gesture." Trans. Ian Patterson. In *Fragments for a History of the Human Body*. Ed. Michel Feher, Ramona Naddaff, and Nadia Tazi. New York: Zone, 1989. 2: 128–47.

Schopenhauer, Arthur. *Schopenhauer: Essays and Aphorisms*. Trans. R. G. Mollingdale. Harmondsworth: Penguin, 1970.

———. *The World as Will and Representation*. 2 vols. Trans. E. F. J. Payne. New York: Dover, 1969.

Schultz, William Eben. *Gay's Beggar's Opera: Its Content, History and Influence*. New Haven CT: Yale University Press, 1923.

Schuster, Carlotta. *Alcohol and Sexuality*. New York: Praeger, 1988.

Schwartz, Hillel. "The Three Body Problem and the End of the World." In *Fragments for a History of the Human Body*. Ed. Michel Feher, Ramona Naddaff, and Nadia Tazi. New York: Zone, 1989. 2: 406–65.

Schwarz, David. *Listening Subjects: Music, Psychoanalysis, Culture*. Durham NC: Duke University Press, 1997.

Scott, Jill. "Electra after Freud: Death, Hysteria and Mourning." Diss., University of Toronto, 1998.

Scott, Michael. *Maria Meneghini Callas.* London: Simon and Schuster, 1991.

Sears, T. A. "Some Neural and Mechanical Aspects of Singing." In *Music and the Brain: Studies in the Neurology of Music.* Ed. M. Critchley and R. A. Henson. London: Heinemann, 1977. 78–94.

Segal, Charles. "The Gorgon and the Nightingale: The Voice of Female Lament and Pindar's Twelfth *Pythian Ode.*" In *Embodied Voices: Representing Female Vocality in Western Culture.* Ed. Leslie C. Dunn and Nancy A. Jones. Cambridge: Cambridge University Press, 1994. 17–34.

———. *Orpheus: The Myth of the Poet.* Baltimore MD: Johns Hopkins University Press, 1989.

Segalini, Sergio. "Singing Rediscovered." In *Callas as They Saw Her.* Ed. David A. Lowe. New York: Ungar, 1986. 172–79.

Segar, Kenneth. "Hofmannsthal's 'Elektra': From Drama to Libretto." In *Richard Strauss:* Salome *and* Elektra. ENO Opera Guide 37. London: Calder; New York: Riverrun Press, 1988. 55–62.

Serjeant, Richard. *A Man May Drink: Aspects of a Pleasure.* London: Putnam, 1964.

Serrou, Bruno. "Mille et un regards sur Salomé." In program for Opéra de Paris 1994 production of *Salome.* 14–20.

Seyhan, Azade. *Representation and Its Discontents: The Critical Legacy of German Romanticism.* Berkeley: University of California Press, 1992.

Showalter, Elaine. *The Female Malady: Women, Madness, and English Culture, 1830–1980.* New York: Pantheon, 1985.

———. "Hysteria, Feminism, and Gender." In *Hysteria beyond Freud.* Ed. Sander L. Gilman, Helen King, Roy Porter, G. S. Rousseau, and Elaine Showalter. Berkeley: University of California Press, 1993.

Showalter, Sherry E., and Steven Skobel. "Hospice: Humor, Heartache and Healing." *American Journal of Hospice and Palliative Care* 13.4 (1996): 8–9.

Sidorov, Pavel I. "Russia." In *International Handbook on Alcohol and Culture.* Ed. Dwight B. Heath. Westport CT: Greenwood Press, 1995. 237–53.

Simon, John. "Daughter of Death." *Opera News* 11 April 1992: 15–18.

Simpson, R. R. *Shakespeare and Medicine.* Edinburgh: E. and S. Livingstone, 1959.

Skelton, Laurie S. "Vocal Problem or Body Block? A Look at the Psyche of the Singer." *Journal of Singing* 53.5 (1997): 9–18.

Slover, Angela N., and Johanna T. Dwyer. "Professional Singers with Obesity or Eating-Related Problems." *Nutrition Today* 30.3 (1995): 123–27.

Small, Christopher. *Musicking: The Meanings of Performing and Listening.* Hanover NH: Wesleyan University Press, 1998.

Smith, Christopher. "Victor Hugo." In *The New Grove Dictionary of Opera.* Ed. Stanley Sadie. London: Macmillan, 1992. 2: 764–65.

Smith-Rosenberg, Carroll, and Charles Rosenberg. "The Female Animal: Medical and Biological Views of Woman and Her Role in Nineteenth-Century America." In *Concepts of Health and Disease: Interdisciplinary Perspectives.* Ed. Arthur L. Caplan, H. Tristram Englehard, Jr., and James J. McCartney. Reading MA: Addison-Wesley, 1981.

"A Smoky Voice, a Fiery Lady: Maria Callas: 1923–1977." *Time* 26 September 1977: 43–44.

Snodgrass, Chris. *Aubrey Beardsley, Dandy of the Grotesque.* New York: Oxford University Press, 1995.

Snow, George E. "Socialism, Alcoholism, and the Russian Working Classes before 1917." In *Drinking: Behavior and Belief in Modern History.* Ed. Susanna Barrows and Robin Room. Berkeley: University of California Press, 1991. 243–64.

Sobel, Dava. "For Stage Fright, a Remedy Proposed." *New York Times* 20 November 1979: C 1–2.

Sophocles. *Electra.* In *Electra and Other Plays.* Trans. E. F. Watling. Harmondsworth: Penguin, 1953. 68–117.

Sournia, Jean-Charles. *A History of Alcoholism.* Trans. Nick Hindley and Gareth Stanton. Oxford: Blackwell, 1990.

Specht, Richard. *Richard Strauss und sein Werk II: Der Vokalkomponist, der Dramatiker.* Leipzig: E. P. Tal, 1921.

Stafford, Barbara Maria. *Body Criticism: Imaging the Unseen in Enlightenment Art and Medicine.* Cambridge MA: MIT Press, 1991.

Stallybrass, Peter, and Allon White. *The Politics and Poetics of Transgression.* Ithaca NY: Cornell University Press, 1986.

Stancioff, Nadia. *Maria Callas Remembered.* New York: Dutton, 1987.

Starkey, David, Margaret Horvath, and George Letchworth. "The Effects of Nutritional Training on Voice Evaluation." *Journal of Research in Singing* 6.2 (1983): 22–29.

Starobinski, Jean. "The Natural and Literary History of Bodily Sensation: A Short History of Bodily Sensation." Trans. Sarah Matthews. In *Fragments for a History of the Human Body*. Ed. Michel Feher, Ramona Naddaff, and Nadia Tazi. New York: Zone, 1989. 2: 350–70.

———. "Opera and Enchantresses." Trans. Adam Bresnick. In *Opera through Other Eyes*. Ed. David J. Levin. Stanford CA: Stanford University Press, 1994. 19–23.

Stassinopoulos, Arianna. *Maria Callas: The Woman behind the Legend*. New York: Simon and Schuster, 1981.

Stearns, Peter N. *Fat History: Bodies and Beauty in the Modern West*. New York: New York University Press, 1997.

Stein, Erwin. "*Albert Herring*." In *The Britten Companion*. Ed. Christoher Palmer. London: Faber and Faber, 1984. 127–32.

Steiner, George. "Two Suppers." *Salmagundi* 108 (1995): 33–62.

Steinitzer, Max. *Richard Strauss*. Berlin: Schuster and Loeffler, 1911.

Steptoe, Andrew, and Helen Fidler. "Stage Fright in Orchestral Musicians: A Study of Cognitive and Behavioural Strategies in Performance Anxiety." *British Journal of Psychology* 78 (1987): 241–49.

Storm, William. *After Dionysus: A Theory of the Tragic*. Ithaca NY: Cornell University Press, 1998.

Storr, Anthony. *Music and the Mind*. New York: Ballantine, 1993.

Stott, Rebecca. *The Fabrication of the Late-Victorian Femme Fatale: The Kiss of Death*. London: Macmillan, 1992.

Stratton, Jon. *The Desirable Body: Cultural Fetishism and the Erotics of Consumption*. Manchester: Manchester University Press, 1996.

Strauss, Richard. "Reminiscences of the First Performance of My Operas." In *Recollections and Reflections*. Ed. Willi Schuh. Trans. L. J. Laurence. London: Boosey and Hawkes, 1953. 146–67.

Strauss, Richard, and Hugo von Hofmannsthal. *The Correspondence between Richard Strauss and Hugo von Hofmannsthal*. Trans. Hanns Hammelmann and Ewald Osers. London: St. James's Place, 1961.

Strauss, Richard, and Romain Rolland. *Correspondence*. Berkeley: University of California Press, 1968.

Suleiman, Susan Rubin, ed. *The Female Body in Western Culture: Contemporary Perspectives*. Cambridge MA: Harvard University Press, 1986.

Sundberg, Johan. "Phonatory Vibrations in Singers: A Critical Review." *Music Perception* 9.3 (1992): 361–82.

Sutcliffe, Tom. *Believing in Opera*. Princeton NJ: Princeton University Press, 1996.

Szasz, Thomas. *The Myth of Mental Illness: Foundation of a Theory of Personal Conduct.* New York: Harper and Row, 1961.

———. *Sex: Facts, Frauds and Follies.* Oxford: Basil Blackwell, 1980.

Taddie, Daniel. "The Devil, You Say: Reflections of Verdi's and Boito's Iago." *Opera Quarterly* 7.1 (1990): 52–71.

Taruskin, Richard. "*Khovanshchina.*" In *The New Grove Dictionary of Opera.* Ed. Stanley Sadie. London: Macmillan, 1992. 2: 982–87.

Taylor, Ronald. *Hoffmann.* London: Bowes and Bowes, 1963.

Teachout, Terry. "Does Beauty Matter?" *Opera News* 14 March 1998: 58.

Temperance Tracts Issued by the National Temperance Society and Publication House. New York: National Temperance Society and Publication House, 1881.

Tenschert, Roland. "Strauss as Librettist." In *Richard Strauss:* Salome. Ed. Derrick Puffett. Cambridge: Cambridge University Press, 1989. 36–50.

———. *3 x 7 Variationen über das Thema Richard Strauss.* Vienna: Wilhelm Frick Verlag, 1944.

Thacker, Eugene. "The Voice's Body." *American Book Review* (March–April 1998): 1, 29.

Thesander, Marianne. *The Feminine Ideal.* London: Reaktion Books, 1997.

Thomas, Martine. "Oscar Wilde's *Salome*: A Few 'Fin de Siècle' Aspects." *Cahiers victoriens et édouardiens* 36 (1992): 153–69.

Thomson, Rosemarie Garland. *Extraordinary Bodies: Figuring Physical Disability in American Culture and Literature.* New York: Columbia University Press, 1997.

Thorne, Guy. "Inebriety in Fiction." *British Journal of Inebriety* 10.1 (1912): 35–39.

Timerding, Eric Francis. "Taming the Unruly Tongue: Problems and Remedies Associated with the Singer's Tongue." *Journal of Singing* 54.2 (1997): 13–20.

Titze, Ingo. "The Concept of Muscular Isometrics for Optimizing Vocal Intensity and Efficiency." *Journal of Research in Singing* 1.3 (1978): 15–25.

Tolman, Albert H. "Drunkenness in Shakespeare." *Shakespeare Studies* 34 (1919): 82–88.

Tranchefort, François-René. "Le Mythe subverti." *L'Avant-scène opéra* 47–48 (1983): 127–31.

Treves, Sir Frederick. *The Elephant Man and Other Reminiscences.* 1923. New York: Gryphon Editions, Classics of Medicine Library, 1993.

Troup, Gordon. "The Physics of the Singing Voice." *Journal of Research in Singing* 6.1 (1982): 1–26.

Troup, Gordon, and H. A. Luke. "The Epiglottis as an Articulator in Singing." *Journal of Research in Singing and Applied Voice Pedagogy* 12.1 (1988): 3–11.

Trudgill, Eric. *Madonnas and Magdalens: The Origins and Development of Victorian Sexual Attitudes.* London: Heinemann, 1976.

Turnbull, Michael T. R. B. *Mary Garden.* Hants, England: Scolar Press, 1997.

Turocy, Catherine. "The Dance Was at the Root of Baroque Opera." *Opera News* 1 July 1994: 30–33.

Twitchell, James. *Dreadful Pleasures: An Anatomy of Modern Horror.* New York: Oxford University Press, 1985.

Übersfeld, Anne. *Le Roi et le bouffon.* Paris: José Corti, 1974.

Ulrich, Bernard. *Concerning the Principles of Voice Training During the A Cappella Period and until the Beginning of Opera (1474–1640).* Trans. John W. Seale. 1910. Minneapolis: Pro Musica Press, 1973.

Vaget, Hans Rudolf. "The Spell of Salome: Thomas Mann and Richard Strauss." In *German Literature and Music: An Aesthetic Fusion, 1890–1989.* Ed. Claus Reschke and Howard Pollack. Munich: Wilhelm Fink Verlag, 1992. 39–60.

van Sant, James A. "Miss Margaret's Way." *Opera News* (March 1996): 26–29.

Vellacott, Philip. "Introduction." In *The Bacchae and Other Plays.* By Euripides. 1954. Rev. ed. London: Penguin, 1973. 9–38.

Verdi, Giuseppe. *Letters of Giuseppe Verdi.* Trans. and ed. Charles Osborne. London: Victor Gollancz, 1971.

Vieuille, Marie-Françoise. "La Voix de Salomé ou la danseuse." *L'Avant-scène opéra* 47–48 (1983): 139–45.

Vlad, Roman. "Alcune osservazioni sulla struttura delle opere di Verdi." In *Atti del III Congresso internazionale di studi verdiani.* Parma: Istituto de studi verdiani, 1972. 495–522.

Vogt, Howard. *Flagstad: Singer of the Century.* London: Secker and Warburg, 1987.

Vogt, Irmgard. "Germany." In *International Handbook on Alcohol and Culture.* Ed. Dwight B. Heath. Westport CT: Greenwood Press, 1995. 88–98.

von Buchau, Stephanie. "Pitch Problems." *Opera News* 28 March 1998: 54.

von Leden, Hans, and David M. Alessi. "The Aging Voice." In *Vocal Arts*

Medicine: The Care and Prevention of Professional Voice Disorders. Ed. Michael S. Benninger, Barbara H. Jacobson, and Alex F. Johnson. New York: Theieme Medical Publishers, 1994. 269–80.

von Nor, Günther. "Das Leitmotiv bei Richard Strauss dargestellt am Beispiel der 'Elektra.'" *Neue Zeitschrift für Musik* 130.1, pt. 8 (1971): 418–22.

Wagner, Richard. "Art and Revolution." In *The Art-Work of the Future and Other Works*. Trans. Willaim Ashton Ellis. Lincoln: University of Nebraska Press, 1993.

————. *Frühe Prosa und Revolutionstraktate*. Vol. 5 of *Dichtungen und Schriften: Jubiläumsausgabe in zehn Bänden*. Ed. Dieter Borchmeyer. Frankfurt am Main: Insel Verlag, 1983.

Walcot, Peter. *Greek Drama in Its Theatrical and Social Context*. Cardiff: University of Wales Press, 1976.

Wallen, Jeffrey. "Illustrating *Salome*: Perverting the Text?" *Word and Image* 8.2 (1992): 124–32.

Waller, Marguerite R. "If 'Reality Is the Best Metaphor,' It Must Be Virtual." *Diacritics* 27.3 (1997): 90–104.

Warner, John Harley. "Physiological Theory and Therapeutic Explanation in the 1860s: The British Debate on the Medical Use of Alcohol." *Bulletin of the History of Medicine* 54 (1980): 235–57.

Warner, Nicholas O. "Editor's Introduction: Alcohol in Literature: Studies in Five Cultures." *Contemporary Drug Problems* 13 (1986): 179–85.

Watkins, Tom R., ed. *Wine: Nutritional and Therapeutic Benefits*. Washington DC: American Chemical Society, 1997.

Weber, Samuel. "Taking Place: Toward a Theater of Dislocation." In *Opera through Other Eyes*. Ed. David J. Levin. Stanford CA: Stanford University Press, 1994. 107–46.

Weiner, Marc. "Response." Paper presented at the annual convention of the Modern Language Association, San Francisco, December 1998.

————. *Richard Wagner and the Anti-Semitic Imagination*. Lincoln: University of Nebraska Press, 1995.

White, Eric Walter. *Benjamin Britten: His Life and Operas*. 2d ed. London: Faber and Faber, 1983.

White, John-Paul, and Edith Diggory. "Assessment of the Singing Voice." In *Vocal Arts Medicine: The Care and Prevention of Professional Voice Disorders*. Ed. Michael S. Benninger, Barbara H. Jacobson, and Alex F. Johnson. New York: Theieme Medical Publishers, 1994. 112–76.

White, Mimi. "They All Sing . . . : Voice, Body, and Representation in *Diva*." *Literature and Psychology* 34.4 (1988): 33–43.

White, R. S. *The Merry Wives of Windsor*. Harvester New Critical Introductions to Shakespeare. New York: Harvester Wheatsheaf, 1991.

Whittall, Arnold. "*Death in Venice*." In *The New Grove Dictionary of Opera*. Ed. Stanley Sadie. London: Macmillan, 1992. 1: 1095–96.

———. "Dramatic Structure and Tonal Organization." In *Richard Strauss: Elektra*. Ed. Derrick Puffett. Cambridge: Cambridge University Press, 1989. 55–73.

———. *The Music of Britten and Tippett: Studies in Themes and Techniques*. Cambridge: Cambridge University Press, 1982.

Wilcox, Michael. *Benjamin Britten's Operas*. Bath: Absolute Press, 1997.

Wilde, Oscar. *The Picture of Dorian Gray*. London: Penguin, 1992.

———. *Salome: A Tragedy in One Act*. Trans. Alfred Douglas. New York: Dover, 1967.

Wilder, Carol. "Prephonatory Chest Wall Adjustments in Trained Singers." *Journal of Research in Singing* 3.1 (1980): 1–17.

Wiley, Roland J. "Dance: 3, 4." In *The New Grove Dictionary of Opera*. Ed. Stanley Sadie. London: Macmillan, 1992. 1: 1062–67.

Wilhelm, Kurt. *Richard Strauss: An Intimate Portrait*. Trans. Mary Whittall. New York: Rizzoli, 1989.

Williams, Linda. "Film Bodies: Gender, Genre, and Excess." *Film Quarterly* 44.4 (1991): 2–13.

Williamson, John. "Critical Reception." In *Richard Strauss: Salome*. Ed. Derrick Puffett. Cambridge: Cambridge University Press, 1989. 131–44.

Willier, Stephen A. "A Celebrated Eighteenth-Century Castrato: Gasparo Pacchierotti's Life and Career." *Opera Quarterly* 11.3 (1995): 95–110.

Wilson, Deborah S., and Christine Moneera Laennec, eds. *Bodily Discursions: Genders, Representations, Technologies*. Albany: State University of New York Press, 1997.

Wilson, Frank, and Jennifer Purvis. "A Study of Selected Vocal Behaviors during the Menstrual Cycle of Trained Singers." *Journal of Research in Singing* 3.2 (1980): 15–19.

Winckelmann, Johann Joachim. *Gedanken über die Nachahmung der griechischen Werke in der Malerei und Bildhauerkunst*. Ed. B. Seuffert. Heilbronn: Gebr. Henninger, 1885.

———. *Geschichte der Kunst des Altertums*. Ed. Marianne Gros. 1764. Mainz am Rhein: P. Von Zabern, 1993.

Winer, Deborah Grace. "I Can't Go On." *Opera News* (June 1989): 14–16.

Winn, James Anderson. *The Pale of Words: Reflections on the Humanities and Performance.* New Haven CT: Yale University Press, 1998.

Winter, M. J., S. Paskin, and T. Baker. "Music Reduces Stress and Anxiety of Patients in the Surgical Holding Area." *Journal of Post Anesthesia Nursing* 9.6 (1994): 340–43.

Wintle, Christopher. "Elektra and the 'Elektra Complex.'" In *Richard Strauss: Salome and Elektra.* ENO Opera Guide 37. London: Calder; New York: Riverrun, 1988. 63–79.

Wise, Jennifer. *Dionysus Writes: The Invention of Theatre in Ancient Greece.* Ithaca NY: Cornell University Press, 1998.

Witherspoon, Herbert. *Singing: A Treatise for Teachers and Students.* 1925. New York: Da Capo Press, 1980.

Wolf, Naomi. *The Beauty Myth.* London: Chatto and Windus, 1990.

Wood, Elizabeth. "Sapphonics." In *Queering the Pitch: The New Gay and Lesbian Musicology.* Ed. Philip Brett, Elizabeth Wood, and Gary C. Thomas. New York and London: Routledge, 1994. 27–66.

Woods, Gregory. *A History of Gay Literature: The Male Tradition.* New Haven CT: Yale University Press, 1998.

Wooten, Patty. "Humor: An Antidote for Stress." *Holistic Nursing Practice* 10.2 (1996): 49–56.

Wright, Jonathan. *The Nose and Throat in Medical History.* St. Louis: Lewis S. Matthews, 1860.

Yearwood, Lori. "Florida Prisoners 'Escaping' with Opera." *Toronto Star* 5 December 1998: K11.

Young, Arabella Hong. *Singing Professionally: Studying Singing for Actors and Singers.* Portsmouth NH: Heinemann, 1995.

Younger, William. *Gods, Men, and Wine.* London: Wine and Food Society, Ltd., 1966.

Zagona, Helen Grace. *The Legend of Salome and the Principle of Art for Art's Sake.* Geneva: Droz; Paris: Minard, 1960.

Zentner, Marcel R., and Jerome Kagan. "Perception of Music by Infants." *Nature* 5 September 1996: 29.

Žižek, Slavoj. "'The Wound Is Healed Only by the Spear That Smote You': The Operatic Subject and Its Vicissitudes." In *Opera through Other Eyes.* Ed. David J. Levin. Stanford CA: Stanford University Press, 1994. 177–214.

Index

Index

85, 86–87, 90, 100, 104, 105–6, 110, 117, 156–64, 169–70, 221 n.71, 222 n.76, 240 n.6; as instigator of communal emotions, 10, 16, 24, 115, 160, 165–67, 174–75, 212 n.17; paradoxes of, 6, 7–8, 212 n.15, 212–13 n.18; and wine, 1, 5, 6, 136, 183–205, 211–12 n.13, 212–13 n.18
dionysian. *See* Dionysus
disability studies, 54, 56–57, 69–70, 79, 83. *See also* body: deformed, disabled, or unbeautiful in opera
Diva (film by Jean-Jacques Beneix), 163, 272 n.38
Dodds, E. R., 5, 31, 169, 211 n.11, 211–12 n.13, 212–13 n.18, 221 n.71, 226 n.105, 272 n.44
Don Carlos. See Verdi, Giuseppe
Don Giovanni. See Mozart, Wolfgang Amadeus
Donizetti, Gaetano: *L'Elisir d'amore*, 288–90 n.64; *Lucrezia Borgia*, 80–82
Douglas, Mary, 42–43, 79

Eagleton, Terry, xv, 88
Eaton, John: *The Tempest*, 54
Eco, Umberto, 47, 229 n.10, 230 n.13 n.18, 239 n.93
ecstasy. *See* body: and the physiology and psychology of perceiving opera
Egoyan, Atom, 11, 103, 107
Elam, Kier, 162–63, 222–23 n.77, 272 n.46
Elektra. See Strauss, Richard
Elephant Man (John Merrick), 63
L'Elisir d'amore. See Donizetti, Gaetano
Ellis, Havelock, 97, 99, 246 n.48 n.49
Die Entführung aus dem Serail. See Mozart, Wolfgang Amadeus
Euripides, 5–6, 17, 20, 31, 33, 165, 177, 219–20 n.60, 221 n.71, 226 n.103

Falstaff. See Verdi, Giuseppe
Farinelli (film by Gérard Corbiau), 15, 120
feminist theory, xvii, xviii, 47, 54, 70, 86, 88–89, 180–81, 209 n.23, 240 n.4
femme fatale: description of, 80, 91, 94,

101, 109, 244 n.37, 245 n.38 n.40 n.41; pathologizing of, 93–102, 246 n.49 n.50 n.52 n.54, 246–47 n.55, 247 n.57 n.58, 247–48 n.59, 248 n.61
Fidelio. See Beethoven, Ludwig van
Flaubert, Gustave, 90, 106, 156, 241 n.23, 242 n.25, 268–69 n.11
Die Fledermaus. See Strauss, Johann
Fleming, Renée, 150, 151
Foucault, Michel, xi, 25, 223 n.84, 247 n.58, 251 n.95
Francesca da Rimini. See Zandonai, Riccardo
Die Frau ohne Schatten. See Strauss, Richard
Freud, Sigmund, 17, 21, 99, 159, 181, 214 n.24, 246–47 n.55, 253–54 n.114

García, Manuel, 123–24, 126–27, 149, 256–57 n.20
Garden, Mary, 118, 150, 175, 266 n.163
gay and lesbian: themes, 6, 30–35, 47, 48–52, 180, 200, 225 n.100, 226 n.106, 232 n.29; theory, xiv, xviii, 145–46, 278 n.102
gaze: ocularcentrism and, 28, 106, 250–51 n.92, 251 n.95; theory of, 38, 98, 106–9, 111–12, 250 n.91, 251 n.95 n.96
Gershwin, George: *Porgy and Bess*, 65–66, 194
Giasone. See Cavalli, Francesco
Gigli, Beniamino, 135–36
Gilman, Sander, 27, 224 n.92, 233 n.40, 248 n.63, 249 n.80
Girard, René, 73, 211 n.12, 212 n.17, 212–13 n.18, 213 n.20, 233–34 n.50
Glass, Philip: *La Belle et la bête*, 11, 61–62, 235–36 n.62; *Monsters of Grace*, 219 n.57; *Orphée*, 11
Gluck, Christoph Willibald: *Orfeo ed Euridice*, 85
Gobbi, Tito, 128, 254 n.1, 264 n.122
Goffman, Erving, 56–57, 63, 233 n.48, 236 n.67

Index

347